S . FAIRCLOUGH .

VISION IN VEHICLES – IV

VISION IN VEHICLES – IV

Edited by

A. G. GALE
Queen's Medical Centre
Nottingham, U.K.

Co-edited by

I. D. BROWN
MRC Applied Psychology Unit
Cambridge, U.K.

C. M. HASLEGRAVE
University of Nottingham
Nottingham, U.K.

H. W. KRUYSSE
Leiden University
Leiden, The Netherlands

S. P. TAYLOR
Melson Wingate
Bournemouth, U.K.

N·H

1993

NORTH-HOLLAND
AMSTERDAM ● LONDON ● NEW YORK ● TOKYO

ELSEVIER SCIENCE PUBLISHERS B.V.
Sara Burgerhartstraat 25
P.O. Box 211, 1000 AE Amsterdam, The Netherlands

ISBN: 0 444 89362 8

This book is printed on acid-free paper.

Printed in The Netherlands

PREFACE

The Fourth International Conference on Vision in Vehicles (VIV4) was held at the University of Leiden, The Netherlands, 27-29 August, 1991. Like its predecessors the meeting was organised by the Applied Vision Association in conjunction with the Ergonomics Society and the Association of Optometrists. The aim of the conference series, which started in 1985, is to provide an international forum for the exchange of information on current research encompassing all aspects of vision and its relationship to vehicle design. This includes both the internal and external design of the vehicle as well as the perceptual and cognitive limitations of the vehicle controller. As in previous years the concept of a vehicle is almost exclusively translated by speakers as an automobile which is somewhat unfortunate as it is important to consider research advances employing other vehicles and differing transportation systems. The great strength of the conference is that it attracts such a diverse range of disciplines, including; optometrists, psychologists, physiologists, human factors specialists and engineers, who otherwise would be unlikely to meet in such an informal gathering as provided by VIV4.

The papers are arranged here to provide the reader with a coherent view of the conference. Issues specifically related to the vision of the driver are initially addressed. The problems of vehicle glazing and light transmission are next considered. Then the major topic of 'visual perception and vehicle control' are covered in three related chapters encompassing; collision avoidance, vehicle signalling systems and the acquisition of visual information. Moving on to the external environment and its relationship to vision, traffic signs are discussed. Approaches to the measurement and modelling of driver behaviour are dealt with and then the area of telerobotic control of vehicles is considered. 'In-vehicle displays' are covered in two related chapters addressing issues of visual workload and effects of display type. Finally some of the posters are presented, together with a short report which gives an overview of the workshop on Visual standards.

The Conference organising committee included I.D. Brown, C.M. Haslegrave, P.A. Smith, S.P. Taylor and H.W. Kruysse. Additionally at the conference E. Tenkink, L.L. Avant, W.W. Wierwille and O. Haase acted as chairpersons. We are indebted to Mr. M.J. Koornstra for his Keynote Address which set the scene for the rest of the conference. We would also like to thank Ir. P.M.W. Elsenaar, Head of the Department of Transportation and Traffic Research in the Netherlands who welcomed the Conference to Leiden. His talk demonstrated how one country is approaching some of the problems dealt with by research papers at the meeting and his speech is presented next in this volume.

Anyone interested in future Vision in Vehicle conferences should contact the Applied Vision Association , 10 knaresborough Place, London SW5 0TG, UK.

The conference organisation was very ably handled by Bell Howe Conferences, represented at the meeting by Liz Howe. The final production of this volume owes much to the unstinting work of Sarah Rivington and Evelyn Pawley.

Alastair Gale

WELCOME

Although mobility has been increasing a reduction can be seen in the number of fatal accidents as compared to the kilometres travelled . This exponential drop has been observed since 1950, in both Germany and the Netherlands. In absolute figures, the traffic in The Netherlands has resulted annually, in 1400 fatalities and 50,000 casualties; 20,000 of the latter requiring hospitalisation. In comparison with other countries the Dutch traffic could be regarded as safe, but the figures of 1400 fatalities and 20,000 hospital cases is far too high. As a response the Dutch government has set itself the difficult task of reducing the number of fatalities and casualties by a figure of 25% in the year 2000 as compared to 1985.

The above mentioned reduction in the accident rate compared to the rise in mobility is due to the measures already taken to increase road safety. But in order to achieve this goal which the government has set itself it has proven necessary to search for new measures, to look at new technical developments and not only to rely on well tried methods. The fact that the Dutch government has been willing in the past to implement new measures can be exemplified, for instance, in the introduction of the so called 'woonerven' residential areas in which the speed of traffic is limited to walking speed and the rules of the road are adjusted. A second example is the introduction 10 years ago of the Motorway Control and Signalling System. While still being quite advanced, it integrates three functions ie perturbation warning, warnings of changes in the road situation and data collection, and has been implemented far more in The Netherlands than any comparable system in another country.

The role that visual perception plays in road safety is obvious as a road user receives most of the information visually. Studies of road accidents show that human perception errors and perception related misjudgements form a main causal factor in road accidents. The importance that visual perception plays in road safety has been readily recognised by the Dutch government which has taken various measures to enhance visual perception in traffic, ie.

1.   The rear and side retro-reflectors of bicycles.
2.   Ergonomic traffic signs which give clear and precise information when required by the road user.
3.   The plans to introduce Daytime Running Lights in October 1992 as part of an experiment in cooperation with other Benelux countries. This was a topic of the last "Vision in Vehicles" congress in Aachen.

In the future the role of visual perception will be very important with the introduction of new technical developments such as in-car electronics and self-explaining roads.

In-car electronics is the theme of the last two sessions of the present congress. In the near future the motorist will be presented with an ever-increasing amount of information.

In the European research programme 'DRIVE' the topic of Road Transport Informatics has been studied. Research projects within the DRIVE framework, such as route-guidance and warning systems, will result in a large increase in the information that will be accessible to the driver of the future. Here the concern will be with the reduction in the motorist's performance as a result of overloading them with information. Therefore the research into giving the motorist the right information at the right time and in the right way will have to be stimulated.

The lay-out of **Self-explaining roads** induce the road user automatically to behave in a correct fashion. The lay out of the road is designed in such a way that the road user knows what type of road it is and for example what the safe speed limit is. Self-explaining roads can be seen as part of a future inherently safe traffic and transport system.

At this moment the policy of road safety is aiming at solving the problems of UNSAFE traffic situations afterwards. In an inherently safe traffic and transport system the system is designed to avoid unsafe situations.

While there remains a lot of blank spaces to be filled by a vast amount of future research, I am happy to see when looking at the programme of this congress, the number of different aspects of visual perception research that is already going on involving both technical and cognitive aspects as well as attempts to measure and model facets of this perception. It is essential that in order to fill these blank spaces the research efforts of international institutes is finely tuned and therefore hopefully over the coming three days you will play your part in the tuning process. I wish you the best of success with your deliberations.

P.M.W. Elsenaar, M. Pol & J.J.W. Huijbers
Ministry of Transportation
Rotterdam
The Netherlands

CONTENTS

12: POSTERS AND WORKSHOP REPORT

1

KEYNOTE ADDRESS

VISION IN VEHICLES – IV
A.G. Gale et al. (Editors)
3

SAFETY RELEVANCE OF VISION RESEARCH AND THEORY

Matthijs J. KOORNSTRA

Institute for Road Safety Research SWOV, P.O. Box 170, 2260 AD Leidschendam, The Netherlands.

Abstract
Visual perception is vital for road safety: visual perception error forms the majority of reported causes of road accidents. It is argued that visual perception in traffic asks for a kind of dynamic foreseeing. Vision research can be relevant for road safety if it concerns moving perceivers of moving objects in a 3-D field and more so if this dynamic visual perception is studied under non-optimal visual field and perceiver conditions. Its potential relevance for safety increases from static to dynamic perceivers (1) as well as objects (2) and from normal to worsened visual field conditions (3) as well as optimal to multiple impairments of perceivers (4). The three past VIV-conferences are scored on these four dimensions. The more potential safety relevance there is, the less frequent the papers are. The number of papers on vision of moving objects and perceivers is increasing, but there are hardly any studies which relate to multiple (in contrast to single) non-optimal field or impaired perceiver conditions. Studies on combinations of impairments and worsened field conditions as well as on their interaction with dynamic 3-D vision are absent.

A comparable structuring of the general literature on visual perception theory also shows that dynamical theories, apart from optical flow theory, are very recent and still incomplete. Some suggestions for a dynamic foreseeing theory of visual perception are made. In absence of such a coherent foreseeing theory one only can hint at some road safety strategies from fragmentary evidence in vision research. This is tentatively tried in conclusion.

1. VISUAL PERCEPTION AND ROAD SAFETY

1.1. Evidence of relevance
There is no doubt that visual perception is vital to traffic safety. Visual perception in traffic is not only determined by visibility, nor is it independent from cognition. Perception is closely related to the attention level, the selection and the activation of memory elements and also to the central information processing that leads to judgements and motor performances. Perception in driving generally takes place in dynamic conditions. Visual perception in traffic is active cognitive perception and may be better described as foreseeing. Seeing elicits in the experienced road user a selection of learned optic-motoric sequences relevant to the dynamics of the road user. He has to foresee the next coming conditions by a routinely prediction of the road situation and the behaviour of other road users, in order to adjust his own behaviour. In traffic incorrect seeing or foreseeing can be

fatal. Studies of accidents by in-depth analysis and by interviewing involved road users have revealed that human visual perception errors play a dominant role in the causation of accidents.

MAIN CAUSE	PERCENTAGE
DID NOT NOTICE/OCCUPIED WITH OTHER THINGS	21.6
OBSTRUCTED VISIBILITY	8.1
BELIEVED ENOUGH ATTENTION WAS PAID	16.3
DELAYED PERCEPTION FOR OTHER REASONS	7.8
SUBTOTAL VISUAL PERCEPTION ERRORS	53.7
BELIEVED OTHER PARTY WOULD AVOID ACCIDENT	4.9
OTHER JUDGEMENT ERRORS (road, signals, etc)	32.3
SUBTOTAL JUDGEMENT ERRORS	37.2
NON-HUMAN FAILURES AND UNKNOWN FACTORS	9.1

Table 1. MAIN ACCIDENT CAUSES BY TYPE OF ERROR
    (Nagayama, 1978)

This detailed study from Japan (Nagayama, 1978) is given in Table 1 as one example. It specifies the percentages of factors in the main causes of 38,625 accidents. These findings are sustained by Australian and German in-depth studies (Cairney & Catchpole, 1991; Otte et al., 1982), but it is not always well understood why this is the case. There is, however, not much theory needed to understand its plausibility.

Although the traffic infrastructure can be regarded as rather safe under optimal conditions for visual perception without any vision impairment of road users, its safety markedly changes if field conditions for visual perception worsen and especially if some impaired visual perception is involved. The following example serves to illustrate this:

- hypothesize that visual perception in darkness under wet
  road conditions is worsened such that visual perception of
  accident danger decreases by 20% ;
- assume that some perceptual acuity deficiency and bad night
  vision contributes to a decrease of the detection of
  accident danger by 10%.

Under these non-optimal circumstances and visual impairments the accident probability for two road users to become involved in an accident between the two is nearly doubled. This follows from some simple probability calculus. Denoting the probability of causing an accident under optimal conditions for unimpaired road users as p, the accident avoidance chance of two unimpaired road users for accidents under optimal conditions caused by either independently is $(1-p)^2$. For a single road user the accident avoidance probability becomes under the mentioned non-optimal visual conditions and impairments 0.80 x 0.90 x (1-p) and for both road users doing so independently this becomes $[0.72 \times (1-p)]^2 = 0.5184 \times (1-p)^2$.

In North-Western Europe it rains or snows more than 15% of the time and in more than 25% of the daytime the perception conditions are non-optimal and clearly more than 50% of the time it is dark or twilight. Moreover, some type of mild vision impairment applies to a majority of road users. So even if safety is more or less guaranteed under optimal vision and perceptual field conditions, it is quite understandable that it is not in daily traffic, where so called visual perception errors are indeed very likely the majority of causes contributing to road accidents.

The lesson to be learned is that the traffic system should be relatively safe under multiple non-optimal visual perception conditions and under mild impairments of vision. The human evolution of visual perception capabilities was not guided by selection principles based on self-movement with high speed. Apparently visual perception under high speed, however, is not too difficult for unimpaired perceivers in optimal circumstances. But the records of road accidents show that the visual perception of static and moving objects under high speed self-movement and of fast moving objects for the slowly moving perceiver are seriously hampered by worsened visual field conditions and vision impairments. Therefore, in order to be able to construct a safe traffic system of roads, vehicles, traffic equipment and rules, one needs more than knowledge of visual perception of static contours by unimpaired perceivers under ideal circumstances.

1.2. Structure of relevance

Visual perception research will be more potentially relevant for traffic safety the more the research is directed to moving perceivers and to moving objects in a three dimensional space, as is illustrated by diagram 1.

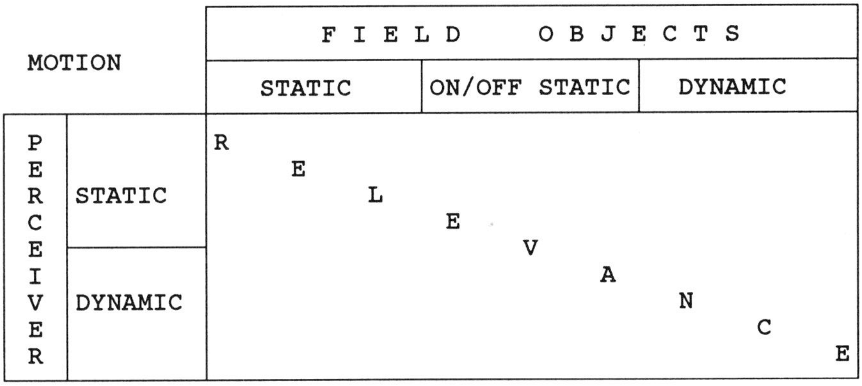

MOTION		F I E L D O B J E C T S		
		STATIC	ON/OFF STATIC	DYNAMIC
P E R C E I V E R	STATIC	R E L	E V	
	DYNAMIC		A	N C E

Diagram 1.   SAFETY RELEVANCE OF MOTION IN VISION

Moreover, the potential road safety relevance increases if the research concerns the influence of worsened visual field conditions and vision impairments. Human beings are quite capable of compensatory strategies for single handicaps, but multiple impairments or multiple worsened conditions can deteriorate human performance seriously. The potential safety relevance, therefore, is enhanced the more the research is directed to the effects of multiple worsened conditions and impairments, as is illustrated in diagram 2.

The four dimensions of diagrams 1 and 2 constitute the reference frame for my evaluation of the safety relevance of vision research and theory.

CONDITION		FIELD CONDITIONS		
		NORMAL	ONE COND. BAD	MULTIPLE BAD
I M P A I R M .	NONE	R E L	E	
	ONE		V A	N C
	MULTIPLE			E

Diagram 2.   SAFETY RELEVANCE OF CONDITIONS IN VISION

2. RESEARCH EVALUATION OF VISION IN VEHICLES

	FIELD OBJ.	STATIC	ON/OFF	DYNAMIC	TOTAL
	YEAR	85 87 89	85 87 89	85 87 89	
P E R C	STAT.	85 5	7	9	21
		87 4	4	7	15
		89 4	5	12	21
E I		TOT. 13	16	28	57
V E R	DYN.	85 3	1	11	15
		87 4	0	10	14
		89 4	0	20	24
		TOT. 11	1	41	53
T O T A L		8 8 8	8 4 5	20 17 32	110

Table 2.   VIV-STUDIES ON MOTION DIMENSIONS

2.1. Motion dimensions in VIV-conferences

All contributions to the past three "Vision in Vehicles"-conferences (Gale et al., 1986;

1988; 1991), with exclusion of general key note papers and introduction to sessions, are placed in the categories of the two motion dimensions of diagram 1. The results are displayed in Table 2. Although, there was sometimes uncertainty and subjective judgement involved the pattern of frequencies, as given in Table 2, is clear. With time the number of studies on moving objects by static as well as by moving observers increases. So there is a growing potential safety relevance of the work in the more recent conferences. In fact most of the 41 double dynamic studies concern an aspect of visual perception in real traffic. It is remarkable that detection studies (on/off) for moving perceivers are nearly absent, while detection for the static observer mainly concerns vision tests. What the movement of the observer does to the quality of detection is apparently not researched, but from a safety point of view variable traffic signs must not remain unnoticed by drivers. Anyhow, the absolute level in dynamic visual perception studies is high and is increasing in time.

2.2. Condition dimensions in VIV-conferences

Table 3 presents a comparable scoring for the condition dimensions of diagram 2.

FIELD COND.	YEAR	NORMAL 85	87	89	ONE BAD 85	87	89	MULT.BAD 85	87	89	TOTAL
P NONE	85	16			3			3			22
E	87		13			8			1		22
R	89			25			11			1	37
C **.**	TOT.	54			22			5			81
I ONE	85	11			3			0			14
M	87		6			0			0		6
P	89			6			0			0	6
A **I** **R**	TOT.	23			3			0			26
M MULT	85	0			0			0			0
E	87		1			0			0		1
N	89			2			0			0	2
T **S**	TOT.	3			0			0			3
T O T A L		27	20	33	6	8	11	3	1	1	110

Table 3.   VIV-STUDIES ON CONDITION DIMENSIONS

Here the relevance evaluation is less positive. Half the studies investigate visual perception under normal field conditions without any vision impairment. Twenty percent is concerned with one worsened field condition without vision impairment (like driving at night) and another twenty percent with a single vision impairment under normal field conditions. Very few papers studied multiple worsened field or vision impairments. Only three papers combine one worsened visual field condition with a single visual handicap. Studies on multiple vision impairments as well as multiple worsened field conditions are never combined with a single factor or multiple factors of the other.

It can be concluded that research reported in the VIV- conferences on these two dimensions of vision impairments and worsened visual field conditions is less relevant for safety, while studies on the interaction of visual field conditions with visual impairments are rare or absent. There seems to be no clear time pattern or it must be the increase of studies on one worsened field condition and maybe a small change from in single to multiple impairments.

2.3 Conditions and motion in VIV-conferences

The combination of the four dimensions is not easy to display. Their condensation is achieved by a relevance rating of each two dimensional table, as shown in Table 4.

	OBJECTS	STATIC	ON/OFF	DYNAMIC
P E R	STATIC	1	2	3
	DYNAMIC	2	3	4
	FIELD CON	NORMAL	ONE BAD	MULT. BAD
I M P .	NONE	1	2	3
	ONE	2	3	4
	MULTIPLE	3	4	4

Table 4.   SAFETY RELEVANCE RATINGS

These rank order ratings allow the inspection of safety relevance on one combined motion and one combined condition dimension in a two-way layout, as is presented in Table 5.

On the VIV-conferences there is no research on perception of static fields by static observers without any impairment (the zero in left upper corner of Table 5). This, indeed, is rather irrelevant for vision of drivers in vehicles. Two streams of research seem to explain the pattern of Table 5. The researchers with a medical-optometric background study mainly static perception with mostly one vision impairment under rather optimal field conditions, while the visual perception psychologists mainly study detection or dynamic perception without vision impairments under normal or a single worsened (like driving in darkness) field condition. The latter causes the increase from left to right in the first row of Table 5, while the orientation of both groups result in a U-shaped distribution in the second row of that table. From Table 3 and the scoring of Table 4 it is clear that the fourth row must be empty, since no combinations of multiple factors of one dimension with single or multiple factors of the other dimension are studied. As can be seen from the third row of Table 5 perception of moving objects and observers is also hardly investigated under combined single or multiple factors.

In conclusion, it seems to me that the two mentioned streams of researchers have so much in common that an intensified cooperation should produce fruitful research more often than has been the case up to now. Surely road safety would benefit from such joint forces.

RELEVANCE			MOTION RATINGS				
			1	2	3	4	TOT.
C O N + I M P	R A T I N G S	1	0	15	17	22	54
		2	11	7	9	18	45
		3	2	5	3	1	11
		4	0	0	0	0	0
TOT.			13	27	29	41	110

Table 5. VIV-STUDIES ON RELEVANCE RATINGS

3. THEORETICAL KNOWLEDGE

3.1. The state of the art
In section 1 the importance of knowledge of dynamic visual perception under worsened field conditions and or under mild vision impairments was stressed. I distinguish three types of knowledge which are needed for progress.

- Type I knowledge is knowledge of dynamic visual perception
  based on studies under ideal circumstances.

Type I knowledge is necessary, but not sufficient for safety relevant knowledge.

- Type II knowledge concerns questions of how dynamical
  visual perception is affected by
    a) worsened field conditions,
    b) mild vision impairments,
    c) interactive effects within and between a) and b).

We need Type II knowledge since ideal circumstances only may exist in laboratories, but most times not in real life.

- Type III knowledge concerns the questions of how dynamic
  visual perception can be enhanced under non-optimal field
  conditions and vision impairments.
  Type III knowledge serves the application to road safety.

It can be concluded from our analysis of VIV-conferences and other literature on visual perception that Type I knowledge is partially available and growing. Type IIa knowledge is only fragmentary available and even for single worsened field conditions very incomplete. Type IIb knowledge is available for static perception, but its generalization to dynamic perception and possible new and vital aspects of dynamic perception deficiencies are completely unknown. Type IIc knowledge is most relevant but nearly of a speculative nature at the moment, because its empirical research with respect to dynamic perception is absent. Type III knowledge is only based on evaluative research of specific traffic problems for one worsened condition or a single impairment. Sometimes we know from evaluations that particular visual perception measures may improve

OBJECTS		STATIC	ON/OFF	DYNAMIC
P E R	S T A T I C	CLASSICAL PSYCHOPHYSICS GESTALT PSYCH. PRIM. SKETCH PARALLEL DISTR. PROCESS.	PSYCHOPHYSICS DISCR./RECOG. SIMILARITY SCALING SIGNAL DETECTION	CORRELATION MODELS GRADIENT MODELS COMPONENTS INTEGRATION
C	D Y N .	OPTICAL FLOW	FEATURE DETECTION ZERO-CROSSING OF EDGES	MAPPING OF COORDINATE SYSTEMS

E
 	
I
 	
V
	S
	T
	A
	T
	I
	C
		Fechner 1860
		
		Wertheimer 1912
		Marr 1982
		
		Steinbuch 1959
		Rumelhart-
		McCelland 1986
			Stevens 1957
			Luce et al.
			            1963-65
			Coombs 1964
			Shepard et al.
			            1972
			Swets et al1961
			Broadbent 1972
				Reichardt 1969
				Adelson-Berger
				            1985
				Marr-Ullman1981
				Hildreth 1984
				Johansson 1973
				Nakayama-Loomis
				/1979 Koch 1987

E
 	
R
	D
	Y
	N
	.
		Gibson 1950
		Lee-Lishman1977
		Reed-Jones 1982
			Marr-Hildreth
			            1980
			Watt 1988
				Turvey et. al.
				            1978
				Feldman 1985
				Koenderik 1986

Table 6. SAFETY RELEVANCE ORDERING OF VISION THEORIES

safety, but we can not theoretically explain the magnitude of the effect; for example: daytime running lights (Koornstra, 1989). The state of the art is a small blame to the application oriented researchers. Lack of theory which has meaning for the rather complex problems of vision tasks in traffic is also a major obstacle for progress. In order to illustrate this statement the main developments in (visual) perception theory are placed in the structure of diagram 1.

Table 6 gives in the upper part short titles for the type of theory in the categories of the framework and subsequently lists in the lower part the corresponding authors of the main contributions with its year of publication. As can be seen from the lower part of the table the more relevant the theory is the more recent the development. The more recent the theory development the less stabilized and more incomplete the theoretical work tends to be.

I shall not elaborate on this, may be far too crude and simplified, summary in table 6. An outstanding and complete reference to theory development can be found in Bruce and Green (1990), where the references to authors not mentioned at the end of this paper can be found. The earliest experimentation based theoretical work on motion perception is perhaps from gestalt psychology, but I placed it in the double static corner because its theory is mainly based on induced motion. A milestone is Gibson's optical flow theory which proved to be very fruitful for excellent work on vision in vehicles (Lee, 1976; Stewart, 1991). A recent promising theoretical integration is Feldman's mapping of several frames, but the theory has too many loose ends to posses predictive power. Most open theoretical issues in dynamic visual perception center around the connections between visual processes, cognition and optomotor responses.

3.2. Dynamic foreseeing theory of visual perception

In my opinion, however, there is something fundamental missing with respect to the dynamics of visual perception theory. The foreseeing dynamics are not only to be explained by the momentary sequences of the external flow and the perceived trajectories of moving objects in that external flow, although it fully causes these dynamics. There are also internal dynamics created by focal vision deviations from vision and context-conditioned expectations. It seems to me that Helson's adaptation-level theory (Helson, 1964), which has been so well tested and has been proven to be effective in many fields of behavioural studies (Appley, 1971), is too often overlooked in visual perception theories. According to adaptation level theory the effective magnitude of sensations are not related to absolute levels of stimulation, but relate to an adapted level induced by previous focal sensations and context. Here, my opinion that a dynamic perception theory must be a theory of foreseeing fits in. If adaptation-level theory would be integrated into visual perception theory, then visual contexts and previous visual sensations determine the "adaptation level", or, as modern cognitive psychologists would say, "expectations". Focal visual sensations only are effective in so far as they deviate from that level. The internal dynamics arise if it is noticed that deviating sensations also changes the adaptation level for the next sensations. This is what I mean by internal dynamics of visual perception or in the words of Helson: "adaptation-level theory explains how perceptions changes the perception of perceptions".

Here it is not the place to go into this matter more deeply. Moreover, I am not the qualified person to do so. However, I can not resist the temptation of presenting a short sketch of what in my opinion a foreseeing theory of dynamic perception should look like. Such a theory should integrate:

-1) multicomponent mapping (Feldman's retinotopic frames) in
     which the motion frame is represented by
          a) common and relative motion cues,
          b) (de)composite vectorial direction features,
          c) optical flow cues for velocities and distances;
-2) deviations from perceptual expectancies (Helson's

adaptation-level theory);
-3) a hierarchy of information processing time frames
(Broadbent's focal filtering, temporary pigeon holing
    and long term categorizing);
-4) optomotor back-propagation (Rumelhart-McClelland's
    parallel distributed processing).

Although this is probably much too fragmentary, it stresses the real point I wanted to make and that is the role of internal process dynamics with regard to visual expectations in a dynamic foreseeing theory of visual perception.

4. VISION BASED SAFETY STRATEGIES

In the absence of a coherent dynamic foreseeing theory of visual perception one only can hint at some strategies for vision based road safety improvement from fragmentary evidence in vision and road safety research. A tentative list of principles for such a vision based strategy follows:

INTRODUCE REDUNDANCY OF CUES FOR
        'LEE'-FEATURES IN THE OPTICAL FLOW,
        'HINTON'-FEATURES IN IMAGE MOVEMENTS,
        'JOHANSSON'-FEATURES IN VECTORIAL DIRECTIONS.
DELETE OR REPLACE VISUAL CUES WHICH CAN BE
        MISLEADING 'LEE'- OR 'HINTON' FEATURES,
        AMBIGUOUS FOR RECOGNITION.
INCREASE CUES FOR
        RECOGNITION AND EXTRAPOLATION,
        TIMELY CHANGES IN EXTRAPOLATION.
INTRODUCE GRADUALLY CUES FOR CHANGES IN
        EXPECTATIONS IN FOCAL SENSATION,
        EXPECTATIONS OF CONTEXT SENSATIONS.
REDUCE VISUAL VARIABILITY UNLESS FOR
        THE NEED OF ATTENTION ATTRACTION,
        RELEVANCE OF MOTION AND RECOGNITION.

Modern in-car and road electronics can also sustain or unload by other perception modes the visual task of the road user. Vision research has much relevance in this matter, but it is not a topic to expand on here.
I realize that this last section is too compact, but I did not want to conclude without showing that the situation is not so disappointing as might be inferred from my critical evaluation. We do not know enough, but still vision research has revealed very much more than what is already applied.

5. REFERENCES

Appley, M.H. (Ed.). (1971). Adaptation-level theory. Academic Press, New York.

Broadbent, D.E. (1971). Decision and stress. Academic Press, London.

Bruce, V. & Green, P.R. (1990). Visual Perception (2nd ed.). Erlbaum Ass., Hilsdale (USA).

Cairney, P.T. & Catchpole, J.E. (1990). Road user behaviours which contribute to accidents at urban arterial/local intersections. ARRB Research Report 197, Victoria(Aus.)

Coombs, C.H. (1964). A theory of data. Wiley, New York.

Gale, A.G. et al. (Eds.) (1986). Vision In Vehicles. North Holland, Amsterdam.

Gale, A.G. et al. (Eds.) (1988). Vision in Vehicles II. North-Holland. Amsterdam.

Gale, A.G. et al. (Eds.) (1991). Vision in Vehicles III. North-Holland. Amsterdam.

Helson, H. (1964). Adaptation-level theory. Harper & Row, New York.

Koornstra, M.J. (1989). Road safety and day time running lights. R-89-4, SWOV, Leidschendam.

Lee, D.N. (1976). A theory of visual control of braking based on information about time-to-collision. Perception, 5:437-459.

Luce, D.R. et al. (Eds.).(1975). Handbook of mathematical psychology, Vol. I. Wiley, New York.

Nagayama, Y. (1978). Role of visual perception in driving. IATSS Research 2 (1978): 66-73.

Otte, D. et al. (1982). Erhebungen an Unfallort. Unfall-und Sicherheitsforschung Strassenverkehr Heft 37. BAST, Köln.

Shepard, R.N. et al. (1972). Multidimensional scaling. Seminar Press, New York.

Steinbuch, K. Mensch und Automat. Stuttgart.

Stewart, D. (1989). Driver perceptual error and child pedestrian safety. In Gale et.al. (1988) p. 143-152

Swets, J.A. et al. (1961). Decision processes in perception. Psych. Rev. 89 752-765

Stevens, S.S. (1957). On the psychophysical law. Psych. Rev. 64: 153-181.

2

DRIVER'S VISION

VISION IN VEHICLES – IV
A.G. Gale et al. (Editors)

THE DEVELOPMENT OF VISUAL STANDARDS IN THE UK

C.G.F. MUNTON

Kent County Ophthalmic & Aural Hospital, Maidstone, ME14 1DT.
Chairman, Visual Standards Committee, The College of Ophthalmologists, London.

Abstract

Currently United Kingdom (UK) law requires potential drivers to be able to read a standard number plate in good daylight. The test has some merit as a square wave contrast sensitivity test in the real outdoor environment. The law puts the burden of self testing on the driver during the validity of his licence. Drivers are also required to report relevant (actual) and prospective disabilities. Relevant disabilities discussed are, inability to meet the number plate test, an inadequate field of vision, double vision, night blindness, and recurrent obscurations of vision. Prospective disabilities are, cataract, glaucoma, macular disease, high myopia, uveitis, keratitis, diabetic retinopathy and retinitis pigmentosa.

The development of a standard for minimal field of vision consistent with safe driving is outlined and redefined on a scientific basis using the III4e settings of the Goldmann perimeter. Equivalent perimetry programs for use with second and third generation auto perimeters have been developed so that the standard can be easily applied in a way that is not equipment specific. These standards are currently in use in the UK by the Medical Advisers at the Driver Vehicle Licencing Agency (DVLA).

1. INTRODUCTION

1.1 The right to drive

Driving is a Civil Liberty and not a fundamental human right: as such it may be licenced by the state and equally the state may legitimately withdraw a driving licence if there is indication of danger to other road users, or to the driver or his passengers. Thus <u>to restrict the driving licence of a citizen is to withdraw an important civil liberty</u>. These precepts underlie the current work of the Visual Standards Committee of the College of Ophthalmologists and the advice it offers to the U.K. Minister of Transport. In consequence while we must have standards for drivers visual performance, these standards must not be so stringent as to disbar a large proportion of the population, or those older drivers whom we know from previous evidence at this conference, to have somewhat reduced visual function (Buyk, 1988). These older drivers in most cases drive with less verve than very young drivers, the latter having been shown to have greater risk of accident (de Velde, 1991).

1.2 Development of standards

Driving is a largely automatic process often subconscious, for which vision is clearly necessary to perceive and respond to changing conditions in our complex traffic. We must therefore look at what is needed for visual fitness to drive actually, and in law.

The origins of a visual standard for driving in the UK are largely empirical and date from 1934 when the simple number plate test was made and self-administered (Gilkes, 1988). We do not know on what basis the distance requirement for this test was decided (ie A standard number plate 3 1/2 inches high at 75 feet or 3 1/8" at 67ft in good daylight). It was probably based on a common sense approach, allowing for vehicle speed at that time. The test has not long been regulated as part of the initial licence test. Empirically this test has been found to correspond approximately to 0.6 (6/10 Snellen). Not withstanding its simplicity the test has served quite well and is in broad agreement with the driving tests of several European states and the EC, though some states in the USA have lower standards (ie 0.3 or 6/18). Few states prescribe a higher standard. There is indeed little evidence in the several large surveys that could link visual acuity and road accidents (Burg, 1977, Davidson, 1985). For instance the Ministry of Transport recently used a computer projection using their own accident statistics of testing vision of all drivers over 54 years of age using the EC rules, it was found that 2% would fail so that of 6.6 million tests 6.5 million would prove unnecessary. Of the fails 147,000 would be accident free and 3,800 accident involved. Of the passes 196,000 would be accident involved. The conclusion was that this would not be cost effective.

2. PRESENT STANDARD

A more coherent standard for the UK was laid down in 1968 by the Medical Commission on accident prevention in conjunction with the Faculty of Ophthalmologists with the publication of "Medical Aspects of Fitness to Drive" and revised 1985. The important chapter on 'Vision' (Cross, 1985) includes the concept of relevant (actual) and prospective disabilities as well as the special case of Vocational Licences. Any disability which might cause driving to be a danger to the public is required to be reported at application for a licence and at any time during its tenure (at present till 70). This requirement is written into the UK licence. The obligation to notify DVLA is clearly placed on the licence holder. A doctor must <u>advise</u> his patient of any failure to meet the standard, and should record this advice on the case notes. He should advise his patient (the driver) that not only is the licence invalid but also any insurance may be invalid by failing to meet the licence conditions. Only in the most serious of danger to the public should the doctor feel the obligation to break his medical confidence in this respect. I do not believe that we should seek to change this balance of responsibility. All the visual parameters can change rapidly in the event of disease, even during short term licence periods such as 1 year so that the value of frequent sight tests is much more limited than generally recognised. Self test has much to offer in this respect though one may properly ask how often it is done.

2.1 Other visual parameters

EC Law (1980[1], amended 1989[2]) requires attention to visual acuity, field of vision, night vision, and progressive disease, as well as recording the need for corrective lenses on the licence. UK is signatory to this but like other states derogates from parts of it. Where a prospective disability (roughly equivalent to 'progressive disease') for instance diabetes, frequent medical reports are associated with a short term licence (ie 2 or 3 years). These reports are reviewed by the medical advisers to the DVLA. They apply particular attention to those conditions likely to cause defective visual fields ie glaucoma, diabetic retinopathy and its treatment by laser, (both progressive diseases) and cerebrovascular accidents (strokes). Specific ophthalmic reports and disclosure of the visual field records are usually requested in these cases. Reports may also be requested for the diseases of ocular motility involving double vision, whether congenital or following neurological disease.

2.2 Relevant disabilities

These are actual disabilities and lead to licence witholding. For example: failure to meet the number plate test, inadequate visual fields, frequent obscurations of vision, intractable diplopia, oculogric crises, the rare ophthalmoplegic migraine, and ocular muscle pareses causing transient diplopia due to vertebrobasillar artery insufficiency and other neuropathology. These latter carry special risks for driving and may occur while reversing; syncope attacks are even possible.

2.3 Prospective disabilities

Cataract, glaucoma, macular disease, high myopia, uveitis, keratitis, diabetic retinopathy, and retinitis pigmentosa are all prospective disabilities. This list is not exclusive. In the event of any of these being notified, the DVLA advisers often call for ophthalmic or medical reports and may require retests at 1 to 3 year intervals, with supporting reports. It is apparent from demographic statistics that at least 18% of insulin dependent diabetes is not disclosed, possibly on account of the insurance premium penalties that might well occur. It is instructive to look at these prospective groups to see how our current standards work.

2.4 Cataract

Cataract is invariably accompanied by bright light blur. In this context the present number plate test may actually be superior to 'in office' tests of visual acuity using standard optotypes. Some 40% of the population over 70 years of age may have some degree of cortical lens opacification. Optical flare around headlights is well known to such drivers and many self restrict their night driving on this account. Experiments in bright daylight, and using various bright light glare acuity testers such as the Miller Nadler device (Neumann, 1988) have shown that while 71% of drivers with early cataract can achieve 0.5 (6/12) in office, only 30% can achieve the same outdoors or under bright glare conditions. 70% were 2 Snellen lines worse; 20% were 5 lines worse. These tests may have some validity for the future, but our number plate test is simple to self test and has all this built in. Failure to achieve a satisfactory driving acuity may be good indication for early cataract surgery. Glare also affects those who have had the newer techniques of radial keratotomy for myopia, and epikeratophakia. Both these can be considered similarly in the light of the foregoing.

2.5 Aphakia/Pseudophakia

There are still a significant number of aphakic, (that is without natural lens) drivers following their cataract surgery. This applies especially to developing countries. Glasses to correct aphakia have chromatic and spherical aberation as well as more than 25% magnification. The optics of the lens edge gives rise to a roving ring scotoma. To some extent these can be overcome by aspheric lenses of the 'Hi drop' type. Even where the visual acuity standard can be met the visual field may be spatially incorrect and only just wide enough (vide infra). Even then the combination of the roving ring scotoma, and the magnification combine in the "Jack in the box phenomenon". Beyond the lens edge the images are blurred; within the edge there is the gap of the roving ring scotoma of 10-20° width; traversing objects ie traffic, then suddenly loom into the central magnified area of the lens to disappear equally suddenly in reverse order. This is not a scenario for safe driving. It has been said "Aphakic glasses are a disease". Though contact lenses overcome most of this, older patients do not all cope well with them.

An increasing percentage of cataract surgery is now done with intraocular lens, (pseudophakia) which offers better spatial co-ordination and better adaptation to driving after surgery. There may be some variation of visual space due to altered astigmatism and initially some photophobia. So how soon after surgery should cataract be permitted? Generally if the acuity is adequate, patients may drive one week after pseudophakic surgery for cataract.

2.6 Strabismus and diplopia

Strabismus (squint) does not disbar from driving if the acuity standard is met and there is no diplopia. Prism controlled diplopia is usually accepted. Diplopia in only a small part of the field may be acceptable and in general a field of binocular single vision of 120° width is accepted, on cases referred to the Visual Standards Committee by DVLA. Stereopsis is mostly related to near vision tasks. There is little evidence that lack of stereopsis is of great relevance to accidents in driving.

2.7 Field of Vision

Some field restriction occurs by outside factors such as car cabin and windscreen design and the prominence of the A posts of the car (Porter, 1986). Helmets and goggles worn by motorcyclists can also significantly restrict the field in driving, (Hayward and Marsh, 1988) and similarly spectacle frame design is important.

An adequate field of vision is necessary for safe driving, though published data shows equivocal and in some cases conflicting evidence of the correlation between field of vision defects and accidents (Burg, 1977, Davison, 1985, Johnson, 1983, Council, 1974, North, 1985). There is a slight preponderance in the literature of a correlation between restricted fields and side swipe accidents. It has been widely accepted by ophthalmologists, neurologists and medical advisers to the DVLA that significant homonymous defects, and bitemporal defects may be hazardous for driving, and that the total field of vision should be at least 120° wide using one or both eyes together. 120° is specified as representing the equivalent of the minimum acceptable field of one eye alone. While this has been largely advisory in the UK, it is statutory under European Community Law, though the parameters of the 120° field are not defined by the EC instrument (EC Commission[2]). This requirement is in line with several other non EC states; in particular the United States (Esterman, 1982).

Some critics of this requirement say that "the eyes constantly scan during driving, and that field defects, including hemianopias are compensated."

While it is true that scanning occurs in driving there is experimental evidence that any scanning or saccades during driving are of a vertical sawtooth character with slight angulation or tilt according to the curves of the road ahead (Kayser, 1991, Jurgeson, 1991). The benefits of this scanning are not at present quantifiable whereas the field defect is quantifiable evidence of a potentially hazardous defect. Strong evidence was aduced by Hedin and Lovsund (1991), in their driving simulator experiments, that there was little evidence of adaptation to serious field defects. The peripheral field also contributes significantly to visual flow rates, and thereby estimation of speed and traffic manoeuvring (Osaka, 1988).

In 1986 a meeting was convened by the Senior Medical Officer to the Minister of Transport, between the Neurologists Advisory Panel and the Visual Standards Committee of the Faculty of Ophthalmologists in order to discuss these matters and the question of the quadrantopias. There was a divergence of opinion between the neurologists, who felt from their knowledge of gait that inferior defects are of greater importance, and the ophthalmologists who felt (with one dissenter) that all the severe quadrantopic defects are of importance to driving. Examination of the case indicates that this is well founded in relation to traffic delays, motorway gantry displays, and truck rear end overhangs.

As a result of these discussions the Council of the Faculty of Ophthalmologists in 1986 defined the requirement in the statement: "The minimal field for safe driving could suitably be defined as a field of vision of at least 120° width above and below the horizontal measured by perimetry using a 3mm white test object at 1/3 of a meter (or equivalent perimetry). By these means homonymous defects which come close to fixation whether hemianopic or quadrantopic would not be accepted as safe for driving" (Faculty of Ophthalmologists, 1986).

This 'non stringent' standard has not yet been incorporated in the booklet "Medical Aspects of Fitness to Drive" but the standard is applied by the medical advisers at the DVLA. The perimeter was chosen as the simplest effective apparatus available capable of giving a full perimetric test under 'controlled' conditions. Unfortunately this excellent first attempt at a defined minimal field does not define luminance or contrast of the target/background though it does in effect define the angle subtended by the target to the eye. It is therefore inexact and incompletely scientifically based.

The parameters of the average 'basic' perimeter prove this standard to have been an inspired intelligent guess in relation to a truly scientific standard and also to the American Medical Association (AMA) standard (AMA[3], 1984; Esterman, 1968). The <u>Goldmann Perimeter</u> provides facilities which define all the necessary parameters of the field; ie target and bowl luminance, and hence contrast, angle subtended by the target to the eye, width of the field, and monitoring of fixation, all under exact controlled conditions.

The settings closest to the previous standard are III4e with a subtended angle 0.7°, target luminance 1000 Asb, bowl luminance 31.5 Asb, and therefore a contrast (target/bowl luminance) of 15dB (1.5 log units).

Defining the field as before, but using these parameters and the III4e settings gives an exact standard under controlled and repeatable conditions and has been adopted by the College of Ophthalmologists[4]. The standard does not define the use of one eye or both eyes together since either condition is allowed. Adoption of this standard fortuitously brings the recommendations into line with the AMA standard and that of other national states, and the Concillum Ophthalmologicum, 1982 (AMA[3,5]).

2.8 The standard of the minimum field of vision for safe driving

"The minimal visual field for safe driving is a field of vision of at least 120° on the horizontal and of at least 20° width above and below the horizontal measured by the Goldmann perimeter using the III4e settings (or equivalent perimetry). By these means homonymous defects which come close to fixation whether hemianopic or quadrantopic would not be accepted as safe for driving. Significant isolated scotomata represented in the binocular field near to the central fixation area may also be inconsistent with safe driving".

It is essential that the application of the standard should not be equipment specific and 'equivalent perimetry' allows the development of equivalent programs using other perimeters such as the first and second generation autoperimeters. It is also important that these equivalents should give simple easily specified programs that are not time consuming. Thus we can derive the following list of equivalents which will satisfy the standard:-

a.   The older manual perimeters (Priestly Smith etc) using 3mm targets at 1/3m continue to satisfy the standard.

b.   The Tubinger TAP2000ct (Program No 6). Target 1000cd/m sq, bowl 10cd/m sq.

c.   The Humphrey Perimeter. 3 zone 61 or more points program[6].

d.   The Dicon Perimeter. AP2000 with Esterman software. Target 2500Asb. Bowl 31.5 Asb (Mills, 1985).

e.   The Octopus Perimeter 500EZ. Uses a special algorithm comparing the current test to the standard 'Hill of Vision' Program No 07[7] (1983).

f.   The Gultron Biotronics Autofield I and Fieldmaster I Perimeters, using their basic programs.

g.   The Esterman Test (Esterman, 1982; 1968). The Visual Standards Committee examined the merits of the Esterman test which can be programmed into perimeters such as the Humphrey and the Dicon. This test which may be binocular or monocular provides a print out field and a 'score' output. The program can test 130° of field with some enhancement of binocular field (as naturally occurs). The literature and personal experience suggests that while there is a + and - 6% variation of performance, the binocular test which allows fixation by the dominant eye, is the least stringent test which will satisfy the standard using the autoperimeters. This test can be exactly related to the Goldmann 1114e settings and is also accepted by the AMA[3].

2.9 Migraine

Teichopsae: bright scintillations in fortification and rainbow patterns may occur in migraine as well as dark obscurations of much of the field of vision. The driver should stop during the teichopsic attack. These are at least a prospective disability and licence restriction may be advised if frequent or associated with homonymous migraine defects.

2.10 Dark adaptation

Principally this occurs in retinal dysplasias such as retinitis pigmentosa. The fields of vision are restricted and severely restricted in reduced luminance and dark adaptation. While a few states allow driving under good daylight conditions there is difficulty in defining this and the luminance cut off point. UK law designates the driving licence for all conditions, by day or night and there are no plans to alter this. A polled opinion taken at the Oxford Ophthalmological Congress 1988 showed unanimous opposition to any change in the law to enable day time driving only. All these patients should report a prospective disability; few are able to retain their driving licence far into adult life because of progression of the disease.

The laser treatment of proliferative diabetic retinopathy by ablating mid peripheral retina may also cause peripheral field defects particularly under scotopic (dark) conditions, sufficient to jeopardise the right to drive (Williamson, 1991). Warning of this possibility properly forms part of informed consent. At the same time physicians should point out that failure to treat will almost certainly result in imminent blindness.

2.11 Night myopia

While this undoubtedly exists, we do not drive in the dark. The law properly requires us to drive by headlights, which at least allow mesopic vision.

3. Vocational Drivers

The Visual Standards Committee recognise that professional drivers are a special case. While speed is often (though not invariably) less, and cab visibility is better (by height and area), these drivers have greater annual mileages, larger and often articulated vehicles, more difficult to control both on the open road and when backing or manoeuvring to deliver in urban environments. Their gross weight is greater and the brake efficiency is lower. Many passengers may also be carried. Accident statistics per kilometre reflect these parameters.

EC and UK law recognises these constraints and applies a higher standard. Thus, 0.8 (6/7.5) and 0.5 (6/12) are required corrected and with 0.05 (3/60) unaided in respective eyes. No one-eyed drivers are permitted. Any optical correction must be tolerated; for instance the kind of refractive discrepancy that might occur in unilateral aphakia. Bilateral aphakia disbars though satisfactory pseudophakia with its near normal spatial orientation is permitted. Insulin dependent diabetics are not permitted without satisfactory medical report of good control. Diplopia and any pathological field defect also disbars. There is good supportive evidence for this more stringent overview of vocational drivers[8].

4. Conclusion

Perhaps driving automation will eventually make good sight unnecessary except to programme the vehicle. Until then we must have fair standards that incorporate tests not so stringent that too many are denied the important civil liberty of being available, affordable, cost effective, or proven (Danielson, 1957). We should remember 'It is the liberties and habits of driving permitted by good vision that kill us on the road.'

5. FOOTNOTES

1   "Minimum standards of physical and mental fitness" 31.12.80. Official Journal of the European Community 1375/11.7.2.
2   Proposals for council directive on the driving licence 13/1/89. Commission of the European Communities COM (88) 705 Final.
3   Guidelines; Evaluation of permanent impairment" (1984). Chicago AMA, 141-151.
4   Drivers fields agreed (1991). College News 6. Quarterly Bulletin of the College of Ophthalmologists, London, Spring, 1991.
5   AMA Committee: Rating mental, physical impairment (1971). AMA, Chicago, 93-101.
6   The field analyser primer. Allergan Humphrey. ISBN 0-939-425-01-7.
7   Perimeter Digest (1983), 41,44. Interzeag, Zurich.
8   The monocular driver (1974). US Department of Transportation, April 1974.

6. REFERENCES

Burg A, Hills B L (1977). Analysis of California drivers vision data. TRRL Report 768.

Buyk A, Missotten L, Maes M J, Van de Voorde H (1988). Assessment of driving behaviour in visual handicapped persons. In A G Gale et al. (Eds) Vision in Vehicles - II , North Holland, Amsterdam.

Council F M, Allen J A (1974). A study of the fields of North Carolina drivers and their relationship to accidents. Chapel Hill. University of North Carolina, Highway Safety Centre.

Dainielson R W (1957). The relationship of field of vision to safety in driving. AJO, 44:657-680.

Davison P A (1985). Inter-relationships between British drivers' visual disabilities, age and road accident histories. Oph. Physiol. Optics, 5:195-204.

Esterman B (1968). Grid for scoring visual fields by perimeter. Arch Ophthal, 79:400-406.

Esterman B (1982). Functional scoring of the binocular field. Ophthalmology, 89:1226-1234.

Faculty of Ophthalmologists (1986-87). 42nd Annual Report, 14-15.

Gilkes M J (1988). The basis of the medical recommendations for drivers' visual standards in the United Kingdom. , 143, 147. In A G Gale et al. (Eds) Vision in Vehicles II, North Holland, Amsterdam.

Hayward J M, Marsh R J (1988). Visual field restriction by motorcycle helmets. In A G Gale et al. (Eds) Vision in Vehicles II, North Holland, Amsterdam.

Hedin A, Lovsund P (1986). Effects on driving performance of visual field defects. In A G Gale et al. (Eds) Vision in Vehicles II, North Holland, Amsterdam.

Johnson C A, Keltner J L (1983). Incidence of field loss in 20,000 eyes and its relationship to driving performance. Arch Ophthal, 101:371-375.

Jurgeson T, Neculau M, Willumeit H P (1991). Visual scanning pattern in curve negotiation. In A G Gale et al. (Eds) Vision in Vehicles III, North Holland, Amsterdam.

Kayser M J, Heggs M (1991). The dependence of drivers viewing behaviour on speed and street environment structure. In A G Gale et al. (Eds) Vision in Vehicles III, North Holland, Amsterdam.

Medical aspects of fitness to drive (1985). The Medical Commission on Accident Prevention. HMSO, 56-7.

Mills R P, Drance S M (1985). Esterman disability ratingin severe glaucoma. Ophthalmology, 83(3):371-376.

Neumann A C, McCarty S R, Steedle T O, Sanders D R, Raanan M G (1988). The relationship between indoor and outdoor Snellen visual acuity in cataract patients. J Cataract & Implant Surgery, 14:35-39.

North R V (1985). Relationship between extent of field and driving performance. Oph Physiol Opt, 5:205-210.

Osaka N (1988). Speed estimation through restricted visual field. In A G Gale et al (Eds) Vision in Vehicles II, North Holland, Amsterdam.

Porter J M, Stearn M C (1986). Assessment of external visible requirements. In A G Gale et al. (Eds) Vision in Vehicles, North Holland, Amsterdam.

de Velde Harnsenhorst J J, Lourens P F (1991). Aspects of driving behaviour in learner and inexperienced drivers. In A G Gale et al (Eds) Vision in Vehicles III, North Holland.

Williamson T H, George N, Flannagan D W, Norris V, Blamires T (1991). Driving standards visual fields in diabetic patients after pan retinal laser photocoagulation. In A G Gale et al. (Eds) Vision in Vehicles III, North Holland, Amsterdam.

VISION IN VEHICLES – IV
A.G. Gale et al. (Editors)
1993 Elsevier Science Publishers B.V.

TRAFFIC ACCIDENT ANALYSES AND PERCEPTUAL ISSUES

R. SCHANDERSSON

Swedish Road and Traffic Research Institute, S-581 01 Linköping, Sweden

Abstract

The purpose of quantitative accident analyses is often to show relationships between accidents or accident risk (rate) and different road or external factors. These are often difficult to explain at the macro level, but might serve as a basis for hypotheses about different aspects of driver behaviour.

Two examples are investigations of accident rate variation with pavement surface wear and with amount of rainfall. One shows that traffic safety is higher on roads with worn surfaces. The other indicates that although heavy rainfall increases the accident risk, small amounts of rain might actually decrease the accident rate compared to dry conditions.

These results are not satisfactorily explained by differences in speed. Most likely there are also other aspects of driver behaviour that are important - aspects related to driver vision and behaviour.

1. INTRODUCTION

Accident analyses at the macro level sometimes lead to results that are difficult to explain satisfactorily - at least within this research approach.

The two investigations discussed below are of that category. They treat accident rate (i.e. number of accidents divided by vehicle mileage) variation with pavement surface conditions and rainfall. These variations are difficult to explain fully with macro level models. Therefore questions are raised related to perception, stimuli processing, cognition, car driver behaviour, risk compensation etc. From the results hypotheses can be formed related to these issues.

2. THE TWO INVESTIGATIONS

Both investigations (Schandersson 1989, 1991a; 1991b) used similar approaches. Road and traffic data for homogenous road sections were matched with data on casualty accidents reported by the police and with meteorological data. The analyses were based on day-by-day data on traffic flows, accidents, temperature and precipitation for each road section.

Junctions were excluded in both investigations and the road sections were predominately (85%) rural. With few exceptions the accidents involved only cars.

2.1   Accident rates on roads with different road surface wear

A common opinion is that resurfacing increases traffic safety. Such results have been reported (Sabo and Hauer, 1987), but also opposite results (Kallberg and Beilinsson, 1983) and varying ones (Craus, et al. 1990) are known. Lately it has been more widely accepted that resurfacing actually leads to more accidents (TRB, 1987).

In a joint Nordic research project (Hemdorf et al., 1989) traffic safety was investigated for roads with different pavement surfaces. One part of the project dealt with the accident rate for different surface wear (Schandersson 1989, 1991a).

The purpose was to show accident rate variation in different weather conditions on rural roads with different pavement wear (ruts, unevenness). Data from four Nordic countries were used (Denmark, Finland, Norway and Sweden).

Figure 1 shows the main result (based on 10,914 road sections, 18,567 kilometers, 2,886 casualty accidents in 1982-1986, junctions excluded).

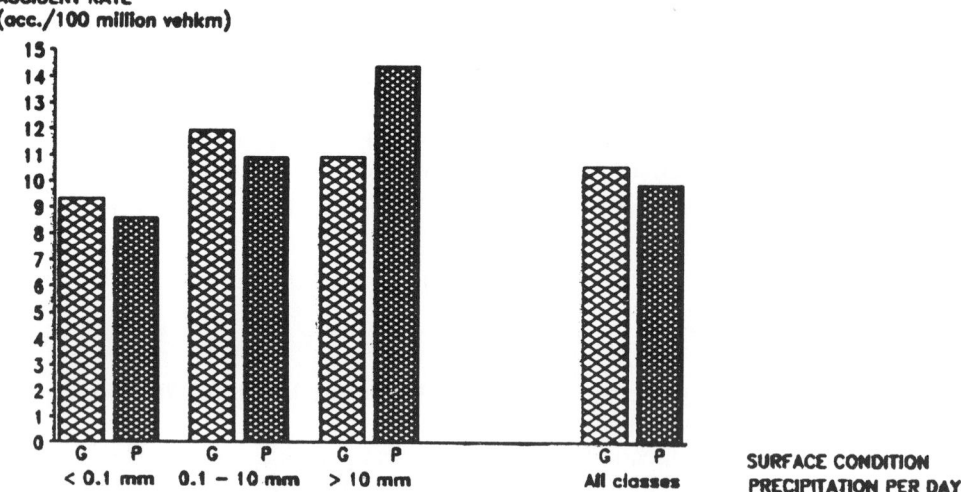

Figure 1.   Accident rate (accidents per 100 million vehicle kilometers) for good(G) and poorer(P) pavement surface conditions. Based on 2,886 casualty accidents.

The year in which a section was resurfaced could not be included in the data. Thus, both new and very worn pavement surfaces were excluded from analysis. Therefore "good" and "poorer" - in figure 1 and below - should be interpreted as respectively slightly worn surfaces and surfaces with considerable wear.

The figure shows that

    * The average accident rate - the group with two bars to the right - is lower for roads with poorer pavement surfaces than for those with good surfaces (9.9±0.5 vs. 10.6±0.6 accidents/100 million vehicle kilometers with 95% confidence intervals).

    * This difference is explained by the lower accident rate during days without

precipitation (accident rates 8.6±0.6 vs. 9.3±0.7) or with small or medium amounts (accident rates 10.9±0.8 vs. 11.9±0.9).

* However, during days with more precipitation than 10 millimeters the accident rate is highest on the poorer pavement surfaces (14.4±2.9 compared to 10.9±2.8).

This pattern for the accident rate was consistent. With minor variations it was found for the different countries, for different types of road, road widths, speed limits, average daily traffic, pavement types etc. It was concluded that the accident rate variation shown above was independent of any of the available road and traffic parameters.
By grouping the data into summer and winter, as well as into different temperature classes, it was possible to show that almost all the positive traffic safety effect for the poorer pavement surfaces was due to differences during summer and days during winter with temperatures above +2o centigrade. The conclusion was drawn that the accident rate pattern found is only relevant for bare road surfaces - i.e. periods without snow. Figure 2 shows the results for such periods.

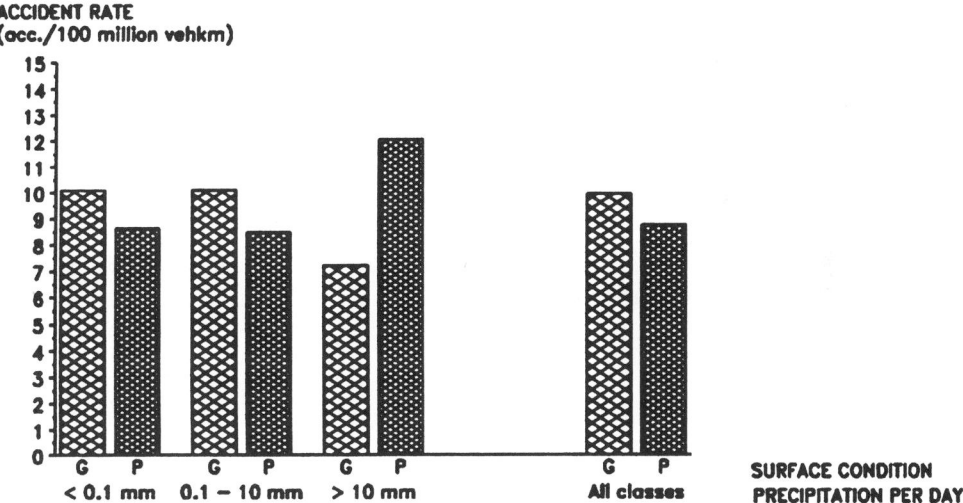

Figure 2.   Accident rate (accidents per 100 million vehicle kilometers) for good(G) and poorer(P) pavement surface conditions. Summer and winter periods with temperatures above +2o centigrade. Based on 1,792 casualty accidents.

In figure 2 the highest precipitation class (> 10 mm) is based on few data - only 33 accidents on good surfaces and 66 on poorer ones leading to accident rates with large 95% confidence intervals: 7.2±2.5 and 12.1±2.9. The 95% confidence intervals for all other bars in the figure are much smaller - between 0.5 and 0.9.

A few additional results from the investigation ought to be mentioned:

* On poorer pavement surfaces a lower proportion of the accidents occurred in darkness or dusk. This could only be found for summer data.

* The injury consequences (number of injured or killed per accident) were less severe for roads with poorer pavement surfaces. This too could only be shown for summer data. Winter data showed the opposite.

Perhaps the most interesting result of the whole investigation is that the accident rate in "normal" conditions (during days with very little or no precipitation) is 6-8% lower on the poorer pavement surfaces for the whole year and as much as 12% during summer.

To some extent this can be explained by lower speed levels on poorer surfaces, which is indicated by the lower accident severity. However, many studies (e.g. Sakshaug, 1988; Linderoth, 1981; Kolsrud and Nilsson, 1981) indicate that this difference in speed level is less than 1-2 km/h. The accepted formula that the quotient between speed levels squared equals the quotient between accident rates[1] can only explain at the most half the difference found - at least at speed levels of 90-100 km/h. Even tripling the speed level quotient would not be quite sufficient. There have to be other contributing factors as well.

Three such factors or mechanisms were proposed in the report:

* Pavement ruts "channel" the traffic and leads to less lateral variation both for individual vehicles and between vehicles.

* A worn pavement surface makes the driver more observant on the road surface. Perhaps headways increase to allow this.

* A worn pavement surface might increase driver attention in general leading to fewer accidents.

2.2 Accident rate during days with different rainfall

It is well documented that the accident rate is higher on wet roads than on dry ones (OECD, 1976). It is also often assumed that the accident rate increases with increasing rainfall. However, the shape of this relationship is not known.

A current investigation (Schandersson, 1991b) shows how the accident rate varies with the amount of rainfall. A unique, very large data material has been used. Originally it was compiled for other purposes. It comprises road data for almost all paved, rural roads in Sweden during 1977-1980, supplemented with data on accidents during this period and detailed day-by-day data on traffic flows and weather conditions.

Figure 3 shows the main result. It is based on 7,983 accidents in which persons were injured during summer (May 1 to September 30) in 1977-80. Accidents at junctions were excluded. The vehicle mileage for these periods on the studied road sections was 60 billion vehicle kilometers.

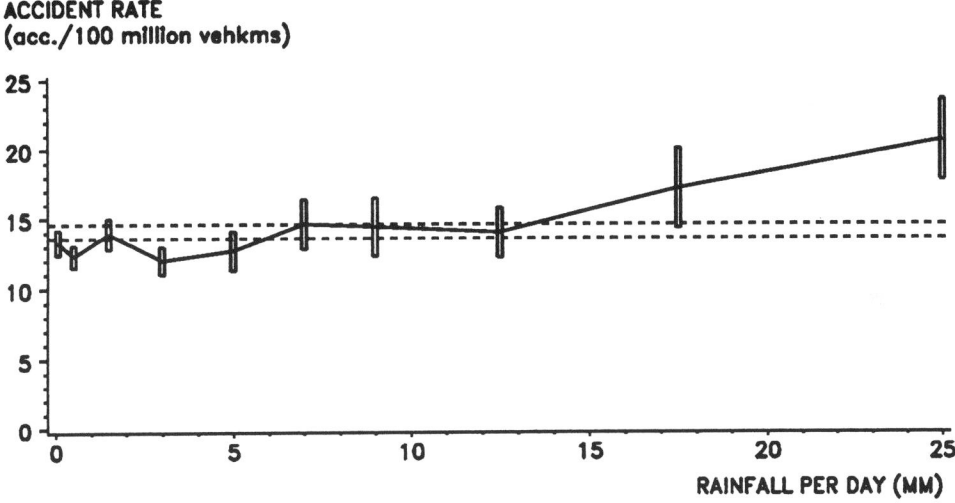

ACCIDENT RATE
(acc./100 million vehkms)

Figure 3.   The accident rate for days with different rainfall. 95% confidence limits are indicated with bars. The two dashed lines indicate the confidence limits for the accident rate during days without rain. Based on 7,983 casualty accidents.

As can be seen in the figure data were grouped into classes depending on rainfall per day: no rain at all, < 0.1 mm, 0.1-0.9 mm, 1.0-1.9 mm, 2.0-2.9 mm etc. This aggregation was made for the original investigations.

The figure shows that during days with heavy rainfall the accident rate is high - up to 40-50% higher than during dry days. For comparison the 95% confidence interval for the accident rate during dry days (the two dashed lines) has been drawn across the figure.

The low accident rate during days with very light or medium rainfall should be noted. This rate is about 10% lower than during dry days.

The same pattern emerged when different subgroups were studied - eg. different road types, speed limits, pavement types etc, even though the accident rate level of course varied.

Other results showed that the proportion of single vehicle accidents increased with increasing rainfall and that there were proportionally more accidents in darkness during days with rainfall. The data also showed a weak tendency towards lesser accident severity during days with rain. The exceptions were days with heavy rainfall. On such days the average severity was about the same as for dry days.

There are investigations of speed levels on wet roads. Swedish results (Nilsson, 1984) show a reduction of 3-6 km/h on wet compared to dry road surfaces. It is likely that the difference is less between completely dry days and days with small rainfall. Few investigations exist of speeds in different rain intensities (mm per hour). A Swedish one shows that the speed reduction is of the order of 5-6 km/h per millimeter rain per hour.

Although speed differences might have caused the lower accident rate for days with little rain, it is unlikely that they explain all of the difference. Influence from other factors can be suspected also for these results.

Speeds cannot of course explain the high accident rate during days with heavy rainfall. The most likely causes are aqua planing and reduced visibility.

3. CONCLUDING REMARKS

One important comment about the two investigations is that the results are not directly comparable. This is indicated by the different accident rate levels. In the first investigation (the one which focused on pavement surface conditions) there were more major roads with, presumably, better road geometry. The second investigation also covered minor paved roads - hence the higher accident rate levels.

Besides the results themselves, a couple of general points can be made. One is that aggregated data can conceal differences that may differ from the overall picture. In the first investigation the overall result was a lower accident rate for worn pavement surfaces than for less worn. However, when data were differentiated by amount of rainfall per day it could be shown that the influence of increasing rain was somewhat different. A point to keep in mind, though, is that the differentiated data still are aggregates - although at a lower level.

A second point is the difficulty to understand, or explain - at the macro level - the phenomena showed by the two investigations. In the first case it was shown that a certain type of relationship exists between surface condition, rainfall and accident rate; in the second the relationship was between rainfall and accident rate only. In both cases a common explanation was tried - that differences in speed levels explain the differences in accident rate.

There is sufficient knowledge about speed levels on roads with different surface conditions to state that speed levels alone do not explain the difference in accident rate in dry weather. Probably not more than half the difference found can be explained this way.

There is less knowledge about speeds on days with rain and without rain. On days with rain the road surface is also often dry some period(s). Therefore it is likely that speed differences are smaller than between wet and dry surfaces. If so, it is unlikely, although possible, that speed differences alone explain that the accident rate is lower on days with some rain compared to completely dry days.

One conclusion from the investigations is that other explanatory factors must be sought. Naturally the interest turns both to how drivers see and experience the road and its surface in different weather and to driver behaviour.

Drivers adjust their speed slightly when driving on worn surfaces, in rain and on wet surfaces. The question is if (and which) other adjustments are made. Do drivers increase their distance to the vehicle ahead? Do they drive more straight (i.e. with less and/or smaller lateral variation)? The latter might possibly be the case both when visibility is reduced and when it is (possibly) enhanced by the longitudinal ruts on worn pavement surfaces. Of course it is also possible that the ruts act purely mechanically on the vehicle making it travel more straight.

The investigations indicate that driver compensation may result in maintaining the risk level (expressed as accident rate) or even lowering it somewhat during days with a little rain. During days with heavy rainfall, though, reduced driving speed and possible other adjustments do not suffice to compensate for qualitatively different driving conditions (much reduced visibilty, risk for aqua planing etc).

There is need for better knowledge about driver behaviour in different driving conditions, if we want to understand results such as those presented here. Measurements of traffic stream characteristics is one possibility, but in such studies it is often necessary to aggregate data to a level where explanatory power is lost. Studies of individual driving in different weather conditions and on different types of road and road surfaces are probably more useful contributions.

Hopefully the results of how the accident rate varies with pavement surface condition and rainfall can serve as "food for thought" for researchers specializing in human factors and the vehicle driving process.

4. FOOTNOTE

[1] $r_1 = r_0^* (v_1/v_0)^2$, r=accident rate, v=speed level.

5. REFERENCES

Craus J., Livneh M. and Ishai I.: (1990) Effect of Pavement and Shoulder Condition on Highway Accidents. Preprint of paper No. 890243 to 69th Annual Meeting of Transportation Research Board in 1990.

Hemdorf, S. et al.:(1989) Trafiksäkerhet och vägytans egenskaper (TOVE). Slutrapport. VTT Research Notes 1075, Esbo.

Kallberg V-P. and Beilinson L.: (1983) Kestopäällysten kuluneisuden vaikutus liikenneonnettomuuksin. VTT Internal Report 391, Esbo.

Kolsrud B. and Nilsson G. K.: (1981) Samband mellan vägyta och reshastighet. Etapp 2. Jämförelse mellan ytbehandling och massabeläggning. VTI Meddelande nr 277,Linköping.

Linderoth U.: (1981) Samband mellan vägyta och hastighet. Etapp 1. Beläggningsunderhåll på hårt slitna vägar. VTI Meddelande nr 273, Linköping.

Nilsson, G.K.: (1984) "Undersökning av personbilars hastighet dels vid halt och dels vid torrt väglag på vägar med hastighetsgränserna 90 och 110 km/h", VTI Meddelande 389, Linköping

OECD Road Research Report: (1976) Adverse Weather, Reduced Visibility and Road Safety, Paris.

Sabo P. A. and Hauer E.: (1987) The Safety Effect of Resurfacing Rural Highways. Institute of Transportation Engineers. 12th Annual Meeting. Proceedings.

Sakshaug K.: (1988) Trafikksikkerheten og vegdekkets egenskaper (TOVE). Dekketilstandens innvirkning på hastigheten. Notat nr 617/88, SINTEF, Trondheim.

Schandersson, R.: (1989) Trafiksäkerhet och vägytans egenskaper (TOVE). VTI Meddelande 594, Linköping.

Schandersson, R.: (1991) Road Surface and Safety in Proceedings. In Third European
        Workshop on Recent Developments in Road Safety Research, April 26-27,
        1990.VTI   Report 366A, Linköping.
Schandersson, R.: Accident rate during days with different rainfall. (to be published in the
        VTI Meddelande series).
Tang, Shumei: (1985) "Models of Speed vs. Rainfall Density in Rural Condition",
        unpublished Memo at VTI, dated April 11.
TRB: (1987) Designing Safer Roads. Practices for Resurfacing, Restoration and
        Rehabilitation. Transportation Research Board, Special Report 214.

VISION IN VEHICLES – IV
A.G. Gale et al. (Editors)

CHANGES IN REFRACTIVE ERROR UNDER NIGHT-TIME DRIVING CONDITIONS

K. CHAUHAN and W. N. CHARMAN

Department of Optometry and Vision Sciences, U.M.I.S.T., P.O. Box 88,
Manchester. M60 1QD., U.K.

Abstract

It is well known that under very low levels of illumination most young eyes tend to become myopic. As a result there has long been controversy as to whether night-time road accidents would be reduced if drivers wore a specific complete or partial correction for their individual night myopia. Much of the disagreement stems from argument as to the extent to which the full night myopia is manifest under the typically mesopic levels of illumination that are found during night driving.

Using an objective, infra-red optometer which allows subjects a free view of the environment (Canon R-1) we have measured the refractive errors of a group of young subjects (19-22 years, N=20) under both binocular and monocular conditions of fixation. Refraction was determined under normal, photopic consulting room conditions (150 cdm-2), when viewing a well-lit street at night (~ 0.5 cdm-2), and under complete darkness.

Mean myopic refractive changes in complete darkness were found to be ~ 1.0 D. However, under the relatively high mesopic levels of street lighting the mean change was < 0.1 D. It was also found that the myopic shifts in an otherwise completely dark environment were reduced to < 0.1 D if a small (6 min. arc, luminance 40 cdm-2) fixation target was present, simulating such features as reflecting road markers. Thus our results are consistent with the view that night myopia is not normally manifest under the environmental lighting conditions applying during night driving and that specific night driving corrections are unlikely to offer significant advantages.

1. INTRODUCTION

Night myopia is the phenomenon in which the ocular refraction becomes more myopic when measured under dim, scotopic conditions than under the normal relatively bright, photopic conditions of the consulting room. Following recognition of these refractive changes, it was soon suggested that they may be of significance in the context of night-driving. It was reasoned that the occurrence of any myopic refractive change would lead to a blurring of the retinal image and a reduction in the ability to detect significant detail in the driving environment. This in turn might lead to a safety hazard. Thus there have been recurrent suggestions that drivers might benefit from wearing specific night-driving glasses with a correction tailored to their night myopia (see, e.g. Richards, 1967, 1978; Hope and

Rubin, 1984; Taylor, 1990 for reviews). In this paper we briefly review the salient features of night myopia in relation to current road lighting conditions and describe an experimental study which supports the view that specific night-driving corrections are of doubtful value.

1.1. Night Myopia.

Although Maskelyne (1789) and Rayleigh (1883) both reported that their eyes became effectively more myopic by night than by day, it was not until the Second World War, when detection of ships and aircraft by night was of crucial importance, that systematic study of the phenomenon began. This work soon established that the young adult eye may become around 0.5 to 2 dioptres more myopic under dim lighting conditions (e.g. Otero and Duran, 1943; Wald and Griffin, 1947). We note that the term *night myopia* is often employed rather loosely. We shall use the term *twilight myopia* to refer to any anomalous myopic changes manifested under mesopic conditions in which both rods and cones are active (about 10-3 to 3 cdm-2), *night myopia* for scotopic conditions under which only rods are functional (about 10-6 to 10-3 cdm-2) and dark focus for complete darkness.

Several explanations for night myopia were put forward:

i)   It is due to the existence of under-corrected or positive ocular spherical aberration, combined with the pupil dilation that occurs in dim light (Rayleigh, 1883).

ii)   That the Purkinje shift from cone to rod vision associated with scotopic conditions makes the eye relatively more sensitive to blue light and this, combined with the longitudinal chromatic aberration of the eye, gives a shift towards relative myopia (Ronchi, 1948; Wald and Griffin, 1947).

iii)   Since under scotopic conditions peak acuity is achieved not at the central fovea but at about 10° of the visual axis, oblique astigmatism may make the eye more myopic (Biessels, 1954).

iv)   The eye accommodates slightly at low light levels, making it effectively more myopic (Otero 1951, 1953; Campbell 1953, 1954; Chin and Horn, 1956).

With the advent of laser optometers, infra-red autorefractors and other devices which are well suited to the rapid determination of refractive error under dim lighting conditions, a much clearer picture of the nature of night myopia emerged. Early results with laser optometers soon suggested that there was, in fact, a considerable spread in both dark focus and night myopia between different individuals (Fig. 1a, Leibowitz and Owens, 1978) although the mean value (about 1.5 D) was in reasonable accord with earlier findings for much smaller groups of subjects. Confirmation that accommodation was a major factor involved came with the demonstration that there was a high degree of correlation between the myopic shifts found in dim lighting or darkness for any observer and those occurring when an empty field was observed or with the accommodation exercised when focussing visual instruments such as telescopes or microscopes (Leibowitz and Owens 1975a, b; Smith, 1983). The three *anomalous myopias* (night or dark, empty-field and instrument) all appear to be manifestations of the tonic accommodation of the individual, i.e. the equilibrium or resting state of the individual's accommodation system, to which the system

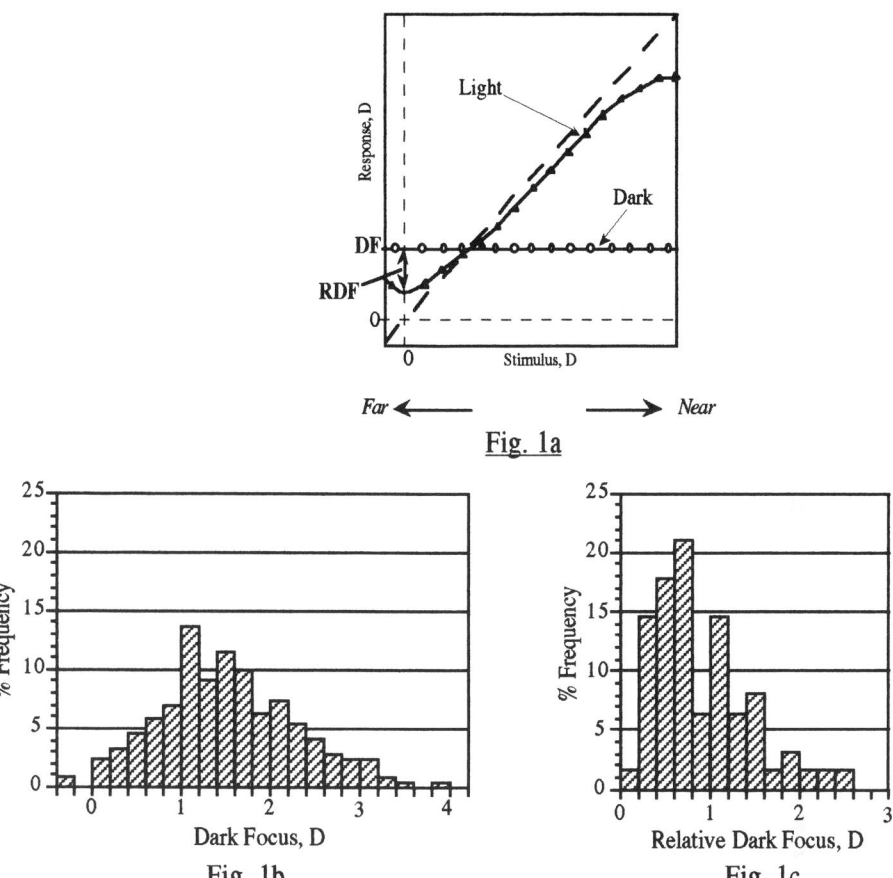

Fig. 1a

Fig. 1b

Fig. 1c

Figure 1.(a).Schematic relation between the dioptric accommodation stimulus (reciprocal of target distance) and the corresponding accommodation response, under light (photopic) and completely dark conditions. The dashed line at 45° represents the 'ideal' situation in which the response and stimulus are numerically equal. Under photopic conditions there is normally some over-accommodation for distance objects and under-accommodation at near.In the absence of any visible stimulus the response collapses to the dark focus level DF (tonic accommodation). Because clinical refractive techniques normally leave the refractive state of the eye slightly myopic for a distant target, the relative dark focus, RDF (i.e. the change in response to a zero vergence stimulus between light and darkness) is less than the dark focus. (b). Frequency distribution of dark focus values in a sample of 200 college-age subjects. Dark focus was measured by a laser speckle optometer in relation to a nominal base value of emmetropia as determined by conventional refractive procedures. The mean and standard deviation are after Leibowitz and Owens, 1978). (c) Frequency distribution for relative dark focus in 62 college-age subjects as determined by the difference between the refractions as measured by infrared autorefractor at photopic light levels and in complete darkness. The mean value of 0.91 D +/- SD is smaller than the mean dark focus in (a). (After McBrien and Millodot, 1987).

returns in the absence of an adequate accommodation stimulus (Fig. 1b, e.g. Owens, 1984; Ciuffreda, 1991).

However, this picture needs some refinement if potential problems in night-driving are to be properly understood. We note first that laser optometer studies which yield distributions of the type shown in Fig. 1a may tend to over-estimate the refractive change occurring in complete darkness. This is because the subjects are first rendered emmetropic by corrections determined by conventional refractive techniques under photopic lighting levels and then the vergence of the plane which is conjugate with the retina under conditions of darkness is measured (i.e. the dark focus) by the laser technique. Conventional refractive procedures, however, almost always leave the eye slightly myopic (least minus, most plus correction, see Fig. 1b), relying on ocular-depth-of-focus to give clear vision at distance. Thus the true refractive change between light and darkness is smaller in magnitude than the vergence of the conjugate plane in darkness. If the same refractive technique (e.g. an infra-red autorefractor) is used for both the light and dark refractive measurements, and the difference between the two is taken (sometimes called the relative dark focus, Simonelli, 1980), significantly smaller myopic mean shifts are found (e.g. McBrien and Millodot, 1987, Fig. 1c).

It is obvious, too, that any accommodative shift will only affect pre-presbyopic drivers below the age of about 55 whose accommodation system is still active. Above this age only aberration can contribute and, in practice, night myopia is found to diminish to almost zero as this age is reached (e.g. Simonelli, 1980; Epstein, 1984; Ramsdale and Charman, 1989; Ciuffreda, 1991). Any specific night-driving correction will, then, only benefit the younger driver.

Even for younger individuals it must be remembered that the accommodation system normally receives input from the disparity information provided by both eyes as well as blur information associated with defocus. Thus during normal binocular observations at any luminance level, this additional convergence input can help to maintain the accuracy of the accommodation response to a higher level than would occur under monocular conditions (Miller, 1980; Leibowitz et al., 1988).

Lastly, it is clear that when driving at night the road and its immediate environment are lit by both the vehicle ϝs headlights and, frequently, streetlamps and other light sources. This raises the question as to how the refraction of the young eye changes from its photopic value to the dark focus state as the illumination gradually reduced. Following exploratory work by early authors (Wald and Griffin, 1947; Carreras, 1951; Campbell, 1954; Nadell and Knoll, 1956), Johnson (1976) was able to demonstrate that, rather than an abrupt shift in refraction occurring at a particular luminance level, the accommodation response to a zero vergence target gradually increased toward its dark focus value as the luminance level was reduced from photopic levels to zero (Fig. 2). Thus the change in effective ocular refraction will be much smaller if the relevant environmental illumination levels are mesopic (twilight myopia) rather than scotopic (night myopia). It was these considerations that led Owens and Leibowitz (1976) to suggest, somewhat arbitrarily, that a correction equal to half the dark focus value might be appropriate for night-driving corrections.

1.2. Luminance Levels During Night Driving.

Following CIE recommendations (CIE, 1977), the British Standards Institutions specify that good contemporary street lighting should give average luminance levels ranging from

Fig. 2

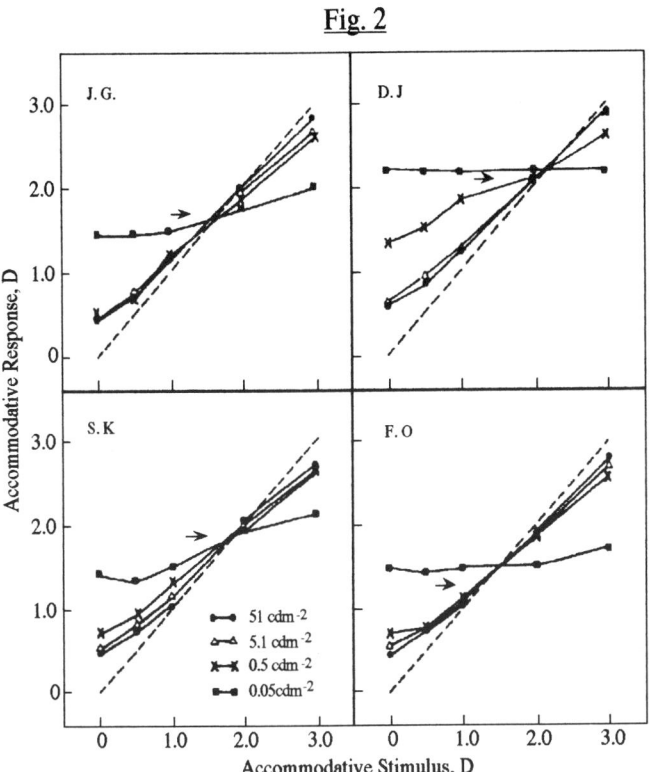

Figure 2. Examples of the effect of luminance level on the steady-state accommodation responses to targets at different vergences (ie the reciprocal of the target at distance in metres) for 4 young subjects. If the eye remained in perfect focus its responses would follow the dashed line at 45°. In fact the response to distance stimuli (zero vergence) becomes progressively less accurate as the luminance level is lowered, until it eventually stabilises at the dark focus level whatever the vergence of the target. Note that for 3 of the 4 subjects the response to a 0 D stimulus shows little change until the luminance falls below 0.5 cdm^{-2}. The arrows represent the dark focus values of the individual subjects (after Johnson, 1976).

0.5 cdm^{-2} for local distributor roads to 2 cdm^{-2} for the main carriageways of motorways (BSI, 1987), with overall uniformity ratios of 0.4. In practice the level of road surface luminance achieved depends upon the nature of the road surface, the presence of surface water, shading by trees, and other factors (Bodman and Schmidt, 1989) but Hargroves (1981) found that measured values of the order of 1 cdm^{-2} were typical of a wide variety of British roads under dry conditions.

Vehicle lighting contributes further to the illuminance of the road surface. Unlike the quasi-uniform illumination of the road surface provided by street lighting, against which objects appear dark, vehicle headlamps are most effective at illuminating obstacles so that they appear bright against the darker background of the road. We would expect, then, that

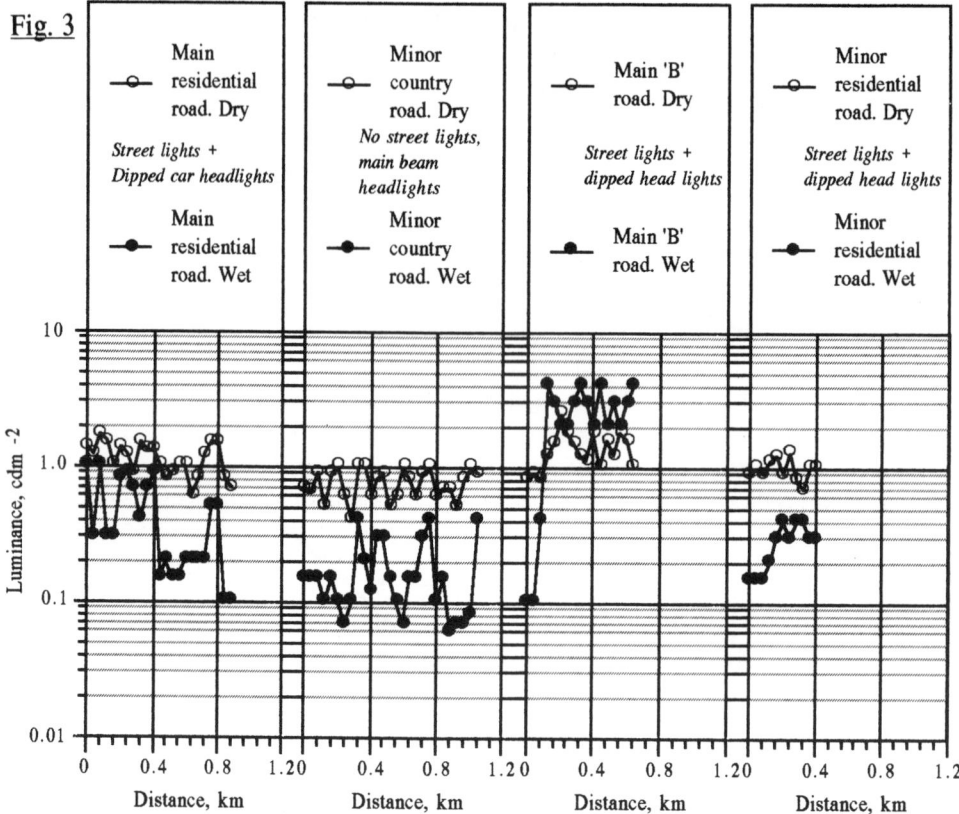

Figure 3. Example of measured road luminances under the lighting conditions indicated. Two runs over the same lengths of road are shown, one under wet (full circles) and one dry conditions (open circles). Readings refer to the road surface approximately 30 m in front of the vehicle.

the ocular adaptation would be much more variable when only vehicle lighting was available,depending on the nature, position and orientation of the surfaces lit by the headlamp beams. With typical observed beam intensities of the order of 3×10^4 cd (Alferdinck and Padmos, 1988), road surface luminances of around 0.1 to 1 cdm^{-2} might be expected at a distance of 30 m. If, however, roadside objects such as walls or hedges were caught in the headlight beams, the adaptation luminance might rise to many tens of cdm^{-2}. The presence of other light sources, particularly the headlights of opposing vehicles, would also raise the adaptation level.

Inevitably, then, the driver on a typical mixed urban and rural journey may encounter a variety of field luminances around his area of fixation. As an example of such variations, Fig. 3 shows some representative measurements of the road luminance at a distance of approximately 30 m in front of a vehicle under various road conditions. Measurements were made on the same sequence of roads at ~ 40 m intervals under both wet and dry conditions. The highest levels occur on well-lit urban main roads.

The key point is that under typical night driving conditions the state of the driver's adaptation is normally such that vision is towards the upper end of the mesopic range rather than scotopic (around 0.1 to 1 cdm^{-2}). As a result, only very modest refractive changes would be expected in the light of Johnson's (1976) data (Fig. 2).

2. AN EXPERIMENTAL STUDY OF REFRACTIVE SHIFTS UNDER ROAD LIGHTING

We have explored the typical refractive shift that might occur with young drivers by measuring the refraction of a group of 20 young, normal subjects using an objective infrared autorefractor (Canon Autoref R-1, see Matsumura et al., 1983; Berman et al., 1984; McBrien and Millodot, 1985). The advantage of this device is that it is an open-view instrument in which the subject can be refracted when looking through an infrared reflecting / visible transmitting beamsplitter at any desired object (this simulates reasonably well the effect of a driver looking through a windscreen). The refraction of each eye was determined both under monocular (with the other eye occluded) and binocular conditions (with both eyes observing the target) for the following laboratory and street illumination levels:

i)   When viewing a test chart at 6 m under normal consulting room conditions (ambient luminance ~ 150 cdm^{-2}). This checked that the subjects were effectively emmetropic or had been made so by correcting contact lenses.

ii)   In total darkness. This gave the dark focus value.

iii)   When in darkness apart from a small green fixation light (subtense 6 min arc, luminance 40 cdm^{-2}). The intention here was to determine whether vergence input under binocular conditions affected the dark focus values. The intention here was to determine whether the presence of such a stimulus (provided on the road , e.g. the lights of other vehicles or reflecting road markings) and the associated vergence input under binocular conditions affected the dark focus values.

iv)   When viewing a distant illuminated sign when sitting in a street illuminated with streetlamps to an illuminance of approximately 5 lux. This condition simulated closely that encountered when driving on minor urban roads with typical levels of street lighting.

The results (Fig.4) showed that the average relative dark focus, i.e. the myopic changes in refraction in complete darkness, took the typical value of about 1.0 D (one individual value was as high as 4.5 D). However, under the mesopic conditions of street lighting the refractive shifts were negligible. The mesopic nature of vision under these conditions was supported by the finding that the corresponding pupil size averaged 5 +/- 0.5 mm, in comparison with the value of about 7.5 +/- 0.5 mm recorded in complete darkness.

It is interesting to note the significant difference, ($p < 0.01$, ANOVA, using a post hoc Scheffe F-test), between the relative dark focus value and the condition in similar ambient lighting, but fixating the small target. Furthermore, there is also a significant difference ($p < 0.05$, ANOVA, using a post hoc Scheffe F-test) between monocular and binocular

K. Chauhan and W.N. Charman

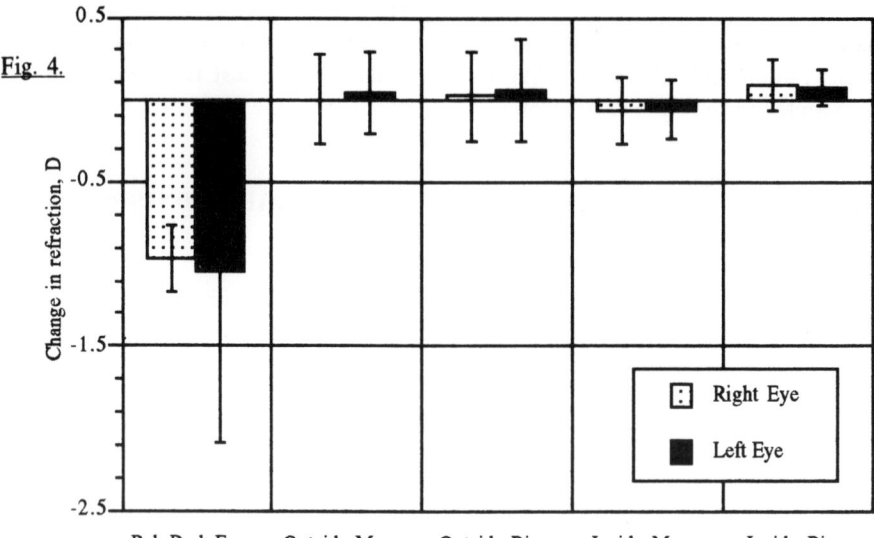

Figure 4. Means and standard deviations of the differences between the ocular refractions in photopic conditions for a group of 20 college-age observers and their refractions under the following conditions:

(a)   In the laboratory in complete darkness ie the relative dark focus ("Rel. Dark Focus").

(b)   Under outside street lighting when viewing a distant sign over a road surface with a luminance of approximately 0.5 cdm^{-2} under monocular conditions, the other eye being occluded ("Outside Mono").

(c)   As for (b) but with binocular observation of the fixation target ("Outside Bino").

(d)   In the laboratory which was in complete darkness except for a distant, small green fixation target which was viewed monocularly ("Inside Mono").

(e)   As for (d) but with binocular observation ("Inside Bino").

fixation of the target in the same lighting conditions. Hence, the vergence input to the system when viewing the target binocularly appears to have a significant controlling effect. It should be noted, also, that the relative dark focus value was significantly different from all the other conditions (p<0.01, ANOVA).

3. DISCUSSION

There is no doubt that night myopia exists in pre-presbyopes. However, it would appear that, with contemporary standards of street and vehicle lighting, adaptation under night-time driving conditions is such that vision is normally in the high mesopic range, so that this night myopia is not manifest. We recognise, however, that simple simulations of the type we have carried out may not fully represent the true driving situation, and we hope to extend the present study to the direct measurement of refraction and pupil diameter in a moving vehicle at night.

Glare rather than night myopia is a more probable cause of visual difficulties at night.

Additionally many uncorrected low myopes who maintain reasonable acuity by day, when their pupils are small and the ocular depth-of-focus is large, experience blur at night as the diameters of both the pupils and the retinal blur circles increase in size. The most fruitful steps to improving night-time road vision may therefore involve a careful correction of *"conventional"* refractive errors, anti-reflection coating of lenses and, probably careful cleaning of the windscreen to minimise scattered light, rather than subtle corrections for night myopia (Taylor, 1990).

4. REFERENCES

Alferdinck, J. W. A. M. and Padmos, P. (1988). Car headlamps: influence of dirt, age and poor aim on glare and illumination intensities. Lighting Res. Technol. 20, 195-198.

Berman, M., Nelson, P. and Caden, B. (1984). Objective refraction: a comparison of retinoscopy and automated techniques. Am. J. Optom. Physiol. Opt. 61, 204-209.

Biessels, W. J. (1954). An explanation of twilight myopia ?. Brit. J. Physiol. Opt. 11, 176-180.

Bodman, H. W. and Schmidt, H. J. (1989). Road surface reflection and road lighting: field investigations. Lighting Res. Technol. 21, 159-170.

BSI (1987) BS 5489. Road lighting. Part 2. Code of practice for lighting traffic routes, p. 24. British Standards Institution, London.

Campbell, F. W. (1953). Twilight myopia. J. Opt. Soc. Am. 43, 925-926.

Campbell, F. W. (1954). The minimum quantity of light required to elicit the accommodation reflex in man. J. Physiol. (London) 123, 357-366.

Carreras, M. M. (1951). La myopia nocturna e influencia sobre la miasma de la amplitude de accomodacion. Arch. Soc. Oftalm. Hispano-Americana .11, 1443-1489.

Chin, N. B. and Horn, R. E. (1956). Infrared skiascopic measurements of refractive changes in dim illumination and in darkness. J. Opt. Soc. Am. 46, 60-66.

CIE (1977). Publication No. 12.2 (TC-4.6) Recommendations for the lighting of roads for motorized traffic.

Ciuffreda, K. J. (1991). Accommodation and its anomalies. In Vision and Visual Dysfunction: Vol.1 Visual Optics and Instrumentation. Edited by Charman, W. N., Chapter 11, pp. 231-279. Macmillans, London.

Epstein, D. (1984). The correlation between amplitude of accommodation and low-luminance myopia. Acta Ophthalmologica 62, 955-960.

Epstein, D., Ingelstam, E., Jansson, K. and Tengroth, B. (1981). Low luminance myopia as measured with a laser optometer. Acta Ophthalmologica 59, 928-943.

Hargroves, R. A. (1981)). Road lighting - as calculated and as in service. Lighting Res. Technol. 13, 130-136.

Hope, G. M. and Rubin, M. L. (1984). Night myopia. Surv. Ophthalmol. 29, 129-136.

Johnson, C. A. (1976). Effects of luminance and stimulus distance on accommodation and visual resolution. J. Opt. Soc. Am. 66, 138-142.

Leibowitz, H. W. and Owens, D. A. (1975a). Anomalous myopias and the intermediate dark focus of accommodation. Science 189, 646-648.

Leibowitz, H. W. and Owens, D. A. (1975b). Night myopia and the intermediate dark focus of accommodation. J. Opt. Soc. Am. 65, 1121-1128.

Leibowitz, H. W. and Owens, D. A. (1978). New evidence for the intermediate position of relaxed accommodation. Doc. Ophthalmol. 46, 133-147.

Leibowitz, H. W., Gish, K. W. and Sheehy, J. B. (1988). Role of vergence accommodation in correcting night myopia. Am. J. Optom. Physiol. Opt. 65, 383-386.

Maskelyne, N. (1789). An attempt to explain a difficulty in the theory of vision, depending on the different refrangibility of light. Phil. Trans. Royal Soc. London 79, 256-264.

Matsumura, I., Maruyama, S., Ishikawa, Y., Hirano, R., Kobayashi, K. and Kohayakawa, Y. (1983). The design of an open view autorefractometer. In Advances in Diagnostic Visual Optics, Proc. 2nd Int. Symp., Tuscon, Ariz. Edited by G. M. Breinin and I. M.   Spiegel. Springer-Verlag, New York, 99. 36-42.

McBrien, N. and Millodot, M. (1985). Clinical evaluation of the Canon Autoref. R-1. Am. J. Optom. Physiol. Opt. 62, 786-792.

McBrien, N. A. and Millodot, M. (1987). The relationship between tonic accommodation and refractive error. Invest. Ophthalmol. Vis. Sci. 28. 997-1004.

Miller R. J. (1980). Ocular vergence-induced accommodation and its relation to dark focus. Perc. Psychophys. 28, 125-132.

Nadell, M. C. and Knoll, H. A. (1956). The effect of luminance, target configuration, and lenses upon the refractive state of the eye. Parts I and II. Am. J. Optom. Arch. Am. Acad. Optom. 33, 22-42 and 86-95.

Otero, J. M. (1951). Influence of the state of accommodation on the visual performance of the eye. J. Opt. Soc. Am. 41, 942-948.

Otero J. M. (1953). Measurement of accommodation in dim light and in darkness by means of the Purkinje images. J. Opt. Soc. Am. 43, 925.

Otero, J. M. and Duran, A. (1943). Influencia del efecto de Purkinje combinado con aberracion cromatic del ojo en la miopia nocturna. Anales Fis. y Quim. 39, 597.

Owens, D. A. (1984). The resting state of the eye. Am. Scientist. 72, 378-387.

Owens, D. A. and Leibowitz, H. W. (1976). Night myopia: causes and a possible basis for amelioration. Am. J. Optom. Physiol. Opt. 53, 709-717.

Ramsdale, C. and Charman, W. N. (1989). A longitudinal study of the changes in the static accommodation response. Ophthal. Physiol. Opt. 9, 255-263.

Rayleigh, Lord. (1883). On the invisibility of small objects in a bad light. Proc. Camb. Phil. Soc. 4, 4.

Richards, O. W. (1967). Night myopia at night automobile driving luminances. Am. J. Optom. Arch. Acad. Optom. 44, 517-523.

Richards, O. W. (1978). Night myopia at night automobile luminances: final report. Am. J. Optom. Physiol. Opt. 55, 469-470.

Simonelli, N. M. (1980). The effects of age and ametropia on the dark focus of accommodation. Human Factors 25, 85-92.

Smith, G. (1983). The accommodative resting states, instrument accommodation and their measurement. Optica Acta 30, 347-359.

Taylor, S. (1990). Night myopia and driving. Optician, Aug. 3rd, 12-14.

Wald, G. and Griffin, D. R. (1947). The change in the refractive power of the human eye in dim and bright light. J. Opt. Soc. Am. 37, 321-336.

VISION IN VEHICLES – IV
A.G. Gale et al. (Editors)

SURVEY OF PROBLEMS EXPERIENCED BY DRIVERS AT NIGHT : PILOT STUDY

M. C. M. DUNNE, E. K. WHITE[1] and G. GRIFFITHS[2]

Department of Vision Sciences, Aston University, Birmingham B4 7ET, U.K.[1]
Lancaster and Thorpe Opticians, 23, Churchgate, Leicester LE1 3AL, U.K.[2]

Abstract

In view of the present resurgence of interest in night myopia a pilot survey was conducted in order to investigate the problems experienced by drivers at night. A total of 88 (55 male; 33 female) randomly selected drivers were questioned from those attending sight tests at various practices of the Lancaster and Thorpe group. Ages ranged from 19 to 87 years (mean age 42.5 ± 16.3 years). Details regarding refractive error, ocular abnormalities and spectacle wear habits were noted. The level of driving experience attained during night time conditions was assessed. Patients were then asked to describe any visual problems they experienced during driving.

Seven drivers did not drive at night. Four of these drivers intentionally avoided visual discomfort from glare or otherwise felt unsure of their night time vision. Of those that did drive at night, 29 drivers reported visual problems. In most cases (23 drivers) the problem was visual discomfort (including glare, flare and reflections) whereas only 6 drivers complained of visual difficulties (including reduced vision and judgment) which could possibly be attributed to night myopia. The majority (61%) of those questioned stated, when asked, that they would like their night vision tested.

1. INTRODUCTION

A recent study involving 4463 patients attending routine eye tests revealed that 2.5% complained specifically of difficulties whilst driving at night and that 0.25% demonstrated a change in refractive balance on the duochrome with reduction in light level (Taylor, 1990). Although the incidence of night driving difficulties due to myopia was only small it was felt that more work was needed to assess what part night myopia plays in night driving. To this end, this pilot survey attempts to gain some initial insight into the range of problems experienced by drivers at night and to assess the influence of such factors as the amount of time spent driving at night, the type of night time conditions encountered as well as the effects of gender, age, refractive error, spectacle wearing habits and the presence of ocular abnormalities.

2. METHOD

This study was conducted from November 9 1990 to December 31 1991 to maximise the amount of night driving likely to have been carried out by those drivers questioned. A total of 88 (55 male; 33 female) randomly selected drivers were questioned from those attending sight tests at 8 Lancaster and Thorpe practices. Ages ranged from 19 to 87 years (mean age 42.5 ± 16.3 years). For this purpose a questionnaire was designed a version of which is shown in Figure 1.

SURVEY

Date :
A. Personal details :
D.O.B. :   Sex :
Occupation :
Prescription   :
R   V.   Rx.   V.A.   Add.   N.V.A.
L   V.   Rx.   V.A.   Add.   N.V.A.
Other relevant details (ocular abnormalities):

B. Questions relating to general driving :
How long have you been driving?

How often do you drive?

Do you wear any glasses/contact lenses for driving?
                Yes   No
Do you have any problems with your vision while you are driving?
                Yes   No   Don't Know
if yes, please describe any problems you have :

C. Questions relating to night driving :
Do you drive at night?
                Yes   No
if no, please say why not :

(if applicable) how often do you drive at night?

(if applicable) which of the following best describe the conditions in which you
most often drive in at night?
lighting :   well lit [ ]   poorly lit [ ]   unlit [ ]
area :   city [ ]   residential [ ]   country [ ]
(if applicable) do you have any problems with your vision while you are driving
at night?
                Yes   No   Don't Know
if yes, please describe any problems you have :

Would you like your optometrist to provide a night vision testing service?
                Yes   No   Don't Know

Figure 1. Questionnaire used in present study

Each patient was questioned by an optometrist. Part A of the questionnaire records biographical data including details regarding refractive status. From this section, the only factors considered in the present study were age, gender, mean spherical equivalent refractive error and any information regarding ocular abnormalities. Part B assessed overall driving experience. Aspects of this section used in the present study were spectacle or contact lens wear habits and details of any visual problems experienced with general driving. Finally, section C concentrated on night time driving experience. All aspects of this section were used in the present study which included the amount of time spent driving at night, the type of night time conditions encountered and degree and nature of problems suffered during night driving. Some indication was also sought as to public interest with regards to night vision testing.

Completed questionnaires were compiled and the results expressed in percentage terms. Statistical analysis of relevant findings was carried out employing the Chi-square test.

3. RESULTS

	NUMBER OF DRIVERS		
FACTOR	DISCOMFORT	DIFFICULTY	STATISTICS
Frequency of night driving :			
over 3.5 days/week	11 (69%)	5 (31%)	
3.5 days/week or less	12 (92.5%)	1 (7.5%)	NS
Night time lighting conditions (average grade: 1=unlit; 2=poorly lit; 3=well lit) :			
over 1.5	18 (78%)	5 (22%)	
1.5 or less	5 (83%)	1 (17%)	NS
Area most frequently driven in at night (average grade: 1=rural; 2=residential; 3=city) :			
over 1.5	16 (76%)	5 (24%)	
1.5 or less	7 (87.5%)	1 (12.5%)	NS
Gender :			
male	16 (76%)	5 (24%)	
female	7 (87.5%)	1 (12.5%)	NS
Age :			
19 - 29 years	6 (67%)	3 (33%)	
30 - 49 years	12 (80%)	3 (20%)	
50 years +	5 (100%)	0 (0%)	NS
Refractive error (mean spherical equivalent) :			
Emmetropes (±0.50D)	3 (75%)	1 (25%)	
Hyperopes (>+0.50D)	4 (80%)	1 (20%)	
Myopes (>-0.50D)	12 (80%)	3 (20%)	
Anisometropes (>1.00D)	4 (80%)	1 (20%)	NS
Correction wear habits :			
none	6 (86%)	1 (14%)	
spectacles	14 (74%)	5 (26%)	
contact lenses	3 (100%)	0 (0%)	NS
Ocular abnormalities :			
Present	7 (78%)	2 (22%)	
Absent	16 (80%)	4 (20%)	NS

Table 1. Factors influencing the incidence of night driving problems

Of all 88 drivers questioned, 7 (8%) did not drive at night. Of these 7 individuals, 4 (57%) intentionally avoided visual discomfort from glare or otherwise felt unsure of their night time vision whilst the remainder (43%) simply had no need to drive at night.

Table 1 investigates the effect of the factors tested in this study upon the incidence of night driving problems in the 81 drivers who did drive at night. Certain general trends were observed. Slightly more visual problems were experienced by those drivers who did more night driving compared to those who did less; who tended to drive on better lit roads compared to unlit roads; and who drove most often in rural areas compared to city areas. None of the differences observed, however, achieved statistical significance.

More notable differences in the incidence of visual problems were observed for the other factors tested. Here, more problems were experienced by males compared to females; younger drivers compared to older drivers; myopes and anisometropes compared to emmetropes and hyperopes; those wearing spectacles or contact lenses compared to those wearing no optical correction; and those exhibiting ocular abnormalities compared to those with none.

Only the effects of refractive error were found to be statistically significant. Here, no significant differences occurred between the number of drivers reporting visual problems either in the emmetropic group compared to the hyperopic group or in the myopic group compared to the anisometropic group. However, significantly (Chi-square = 7.841; df = 1; $P < 0.01$) more problems were reported by the pooled myopic and anisometropic group compared to the pooled emmetropic and hyperopic group.

It is of interest that of the 18 drivers exhibiting ocular abnormalities, 11 included "media disturbances" such as cataract, keratoconus, corneal scarring or ulceration. The remaining 7 included "other defects" such as amblyopia, strabismus, glaucoma and retinal changes. Problems occurred slightly more often for drivers with "media disturbances" (54.5%) compared to those with "other defects" (43%) but this difference was not statistically significant.

The problem with table 1 is that it assumes that all factors act independently. It is most likely, however, that some of the trends described above were influenced by the range of refractive errors, ages, etc., falling within each factor group. In a controlled experiment these variables would have been matched. However, the drivers questioned in this study were randomly selected so that no control of variables was possible. Table 2 was therefore constructed in order to take a closer look at the composition of each factor group.

In table 2, each row represents a factor group. Each column indicates how balanced a particular factor is within a given factor group. For example, taking the first factor (night driving frequency) of the first factor group (gender), we see that males report an average night driving frequency of 5 days/week whilst the frequency for females is only 3.5 days/week. Clearly, this particular factor is not balanced in the factor group for gender. The question now arises as to whether this imbalance could account for the observation (table 1) that males more often experience visual problems at night compared to females. Inspection of table 1 reveals that the factor for night driving frequency has little effect upon the number of times problems are reported by drivers and therefore the imbalance in this factor is unlikely to have influenced the trends observed for gender.

		NUMBER OF DRIVERS	
FACTOR	CATEGORY	PROBLEMS	STATISTICS
Frequency of night driving :			
over 3.5 days/week	43	16 (37%)	
3.5 days/week or less	38	13 (34%)	NS
Night time lighting conditions (average grade: 1 =unlit; 2=poorly lit; 3=well lit) :			
over 1.5	64	23 (36%)	
1.5 or less	17	6 (35%)	NS
Area most frequently driven in at night (average grade: 1 =rural; 2=residential; 3=city) :			
over 1.5	63	21 (33%)	
1.5 or less	18	8 (44%)	NS
Gender :			
male	52	21 (40%)	
female	29	8 (28%)	NS
Age :			
19 - 29 years	19	9 (47%)	
30 - 49 years	41	15 (37%)	
50 years +	21	5 (24%)	NS
Refractive error (mean spherical equivalent) :			
Emmetropes (±0.50D)	21	4 (19%)	
Hyperopes (>+0.50D)	21	5 (24%)	Chi-square = 7.954
Myopes (>-0.50D)	29	15 (52%)	df = 3
Anisometropes (>1.00D)	10	5 (50%)	P < 0.05
Correction wear habits :			
none	26	7 (27%)	
spectacles	47	19 (40%)	
contact lenses	8	3 (38.5%)	NS
Ocular abnormalities :			
Present	18	9 (50%)	
Absent	63	20 (32%)	NS

Table 2. Interactions between factors

The treatment just described was repeated in table 2 for all tested factors within all factor groups. Should imbalances found for a given factor appear to have been partially responsible for trends observed for a certain factor group, that factor was underlined in table 2. An interaction score of +1 was also added. Conversely, should this imbalance have appeared to conflict with the observed trend then that factor was shown in italics and an interaction score of -1 added. If little or no imbalance occurred or the factor was shown (table 1) to have little influence upon the number of times problems were reported, then that factor was written in plain text in table 2 and assigned an interaction score of 0. Finally, the interaction scores were added up in order to rank each factor. It must be emphasised that this approach was only approximate.

Interaction scores were not applied to factors for frequency of night driving, night time lighting conditions and area most often driven in at night. These were considered to have little influence upon the incidence of visual problems during night driving (table 1).

Factors for refractive error (score 2) and spectacle/contact lens wear habits (score 2) achieved the highest interaction score ranking. That refractive error was found to significantly effect the frequency of visual problems reported during night driving (table 1) at least adds some credence to the unconventional approach adopted in this study. Next in order were factors for ocular abnormalities (score 1) and gender (score 1). The factor for age (score -3) achieved the lowest rank.

FACTOR GROUP	Frequency mean±sd	Lighting (grade) mean±sd	Area (grade) mean±sd	Gender (ratio) M:F	Age mean±sd	Refraction (R+L/2) mean±sd	Correction (%) N:Spex:CL	Abnormalities (%) Y:N
Gender :								
male	5.0±2.3	2.3±0.7	2.1±0.6		45±17	-1.0±2.6	27:63:10	31:69
female	3.5±2.0	2.2±0.7	1.9±0.6		37±13	-1.0±2.6	41:48:11	7:93
SCORE					-1	0	+1	+1
Age :								
19-29	4.3±2.3	2.2±0.8	2.0±0.7	1.4:1		-1.7±3.2	42:48:10	11:89
30-49	5.3±2.0	2.3±0.7	2.1±0.7	1.6:1		-1.1±3.5	34:51:15	20:80
50+	3.1±2.2	2.2±0.6	2.0±0.4	3.2:1		-0.7±4.4	28:72:0	38:62
SCORE				-1		+1	-1	-1
Refractive error :								
Myo/Aniso	4.6±2.2	2.3±0.8	2.0±0.7	1.8:1	41±17		5:74:21	31:69
Emm/Hyp	4.4±2.4	2.3±0.7	2.1±0.6	1.8:1	43±15		55:45:0	14:86
SCORE				0	0		+1	+1
Correction wear habits :								
none	4.7±2.4	2.1±0.7	2.0±0.5	1.2:1	38±14	+0.2±0.8		4:96
spectacles	4.3±2.3	2.4±0.7	2.1±0.7	2.4:1	45±17	-1.0±4.1		30:70
contact lenses	4.9±2.0	2.3±0.7	2.0±0.8	1.7:1	34±8	-5.9±3.0		37:63
SCORE				+1	-1	0		0
Ocular abnormalities :								
Present	4.2±2.4	2.4±0.6	2.1±0.6	8.0:1	53±19	-2.0±6.7	6:78:16	
Absent	4.6±2.3	2.2±0.7	2.0±0.7	1.3:1	39±14	-0.9±2.3	40:52:8	
SCORE				+1	-1	+1	+1	
TOTAL				+1	-3	+2	+2	+1

Table 3. Factors influencing the nature of night driving problems

Of the 29 drivers who reported visual problems, most (23 drivers or 79%) suffered from visual discomfort (including glare, flare and reflections) whereas only 6 drivers (21%) complained of visual difficulties (including reduced vision and judgment). Table 3 gives a summary of the factors influencing the number of drivers experiencing either type of visual problem.

Drivers complaining of visual discomfort remained in the majority for all factors investigated. A further increase in this majority was only evident for those who drove less frequently at night and for successively older drivers. It was also found that more drivers exhibiting media disturbances (5 out of 6 i.e. 83%) suffered from visual discomfort than those suffering other ocular abnormalities (2 out of 3 i.e. 67%). None of these differences achieved statistical significance. It must, however, be pointed out that sample sizes were small and therefore prone to random variation.

At the end of the questionnaire, all participants were asked whether they would like a night vision testing service provided by their optometrist. Fifty four (61%) people said that yes, 13 (15%) said no and 21 (24%) did not know.

4. DISCUSSION AND CONCLUSION

Seven drivers did not drive at night. Four of these drivers intentionally avoided visual discomfort from glare or otherwise felt unsure of their night time vision. Of those that did drive at night, 33% reported visual problems. This is considerably more than the value of 2.5% found by Taylor (1990). One reason could be that the questionnaire used in the present study draws particular attention to night driving problems and may therefore have prompted drivers to report even the slightest difficulties encountered. Gerstle et al. (1971) also used a questionnaire to assess perceived night driving ability. Out of 400 drivers, 6% felt that their night vision was poor which is closer to the value given by Taylor (1990). However, when comparing drivers estimates of night vision with measurements made on a nyctometer, Gerstle et al. (1971) added that a significant proportion of drivers tended to overestimate their night vision ability.

Most (79%) of the visual problems reported in the present study relate to visual discomfort (including glare, flare and reflections). The remainder (21%) complained of visual difficulties (including reduced vision and judgment) which could possibly be attributed to night myopia. This supports the observation made by Taylor (1990) that glare appears to be more of a problem than night myopia.

Factors such as the amount of driving carried out at night, night time lighting conditions and the area most frequently driven in did not appear to strongly influence either the incidence or nature of the problems reported. More notable effects did, however, occur as a result of the other factors which are now briefly summarised.

Refractive error exerted a statistically significant influence upon the incidence of problems reported. Here myopes and anisometropes more frequently complained of problems compared to emmetropes and hyperopes. This is consistent with the study of Marmolin and Rendahl (1975) who found that myopia was strongly related to poor night time vision as measured on a mesoptometer. In the present study, strong interactions occurred between refractive error, spectacle/contact lens wear habits and the presence of ocular abnormalities. As for the type of visual problems reported, neither of the refractive groups exhibited differences between the relative frequencies of problems due to visual discomfort or difficulty.

Spectacle/contact lens wear habits were the next notable factor. Here, those wearing spectacles or contact lenses complained more frequently of problems than drivers with no optical correction. This is again consistent with the study of Marmolin and Rendahl (1975) who found that drivers without spectacles had better night vision ability, as measured with a mesoptometer, than those wearing spectacles. In the present study, there was interaction between the factors for spectacle/contact lens wear and gender. No consistent differences were observed with regard to the nature of visual problems suffered by those wearing contact lenses, spectacle lenses or no correction at all.

Presence of ocular abnormalities was the next ranked factor. Here, as might be expected, drivers with ocular abnormalities suffered more visual problems than those with none. Interactive factors were refractive error, spectacle/contact lens wear habits and gender. The majority of ocular abnormalities could be described as media disturbances which, predictably, gave rise to more glare related visual discomfort than was reported by those with other ocular defects.

With regard to the factor for gender, males complained more often of visual problems compared to females. This is not consistent with the study of Gerstle et al. (1971) for which no difference was found in nyctometer night vision scores between males and females. In the present study interaction occurred between factors for gender, spectacle/contact lens wear habits and the presence of ocular abnormalities. Gender had no major influence upon the type of visual problems reported.

The remaining factor is that of age. Here, younger drivers experienced more problems than older drivers. This is inconsistent with previous studies employing either a nyctometer (Gerstle et al., 1971) or a mesoptometer (Marmolin and Rendahl, 1975) in which better night vision scores were recorded for younger drivers compared to older drivers. In the present study interaction occurred between age and refractive error. Older drivers tended to suffer more glare related visual discomfort than younger drivers.

Clearly, the findings of this pilot study would be better validated with larger patient numbers and supporting tests such as those provided by mesoptometers and nyctometers. Nevertheless, the present findings support the statement that glare is more of a problem than night myopia for those driving at night (Taylor, 1990) and that myopes may be more susceptible (Marmolin and Rendahl, 1975). Here, anti-reflective coatings would be beneficial. However, a larger study is still required before the true effects of the various factors investigated in this study can be elucidated.

5. ACKNOWLEDGEMENT

Data used in this study was collected by staff of Lancaster and Thorpe Opticians. The authors gratefully acknowledge their assistance.

6. REFERENCES

Gerstle, W.J., Kuziomko, L. & Bostik, C.W., (1971) Nightvision and accident involvement, 15th Conference of the American Association of Automotive Medicine, 361-375.
Marmolin, H. & Rendahl, I., (1975) Interindividual differences in mesopic night vision ability measured by the mesoptometer, Report 177, Department of Psychology, University of Uppsala, Sweden.
Taylor, S., (1990) Night myopia and driving, Optician, August 3, 12-14.

53

STUDY OF VISUAL DISCOMFORT CAUSED BY THE USE OF FLASHING LIGHTS

Guy GRATIA[1], Jean-Luc PAUMIER[2], Michèle COLOMB[3] and Jocelyne DORE[4]

[1]Laboratoire Régional des Ponts et Chaussées, 109 avenue Salvador Allende, CSE no 1, 69674 Bron Cedex

[2]Laboratoire Régional des Ponts et Chaussées, 8-10 rue Bernard Palissy, BP 11, 63014 Clermont-Ferrand Cedex

[3]Laboratoire Central des Ponts et Chaussées, 58 Boulevard Lefebvre, 75732 Paris Cedex 15

[4]Institut National de Recherche pour les Transports et leur Securite (INRETS), 2 avenue du Général Malleret-de-Joinville - 94110 Arcueil

Abstract

Discharge type flashing lights are increasingly used in road signalling, to mark work sites and to enhance the effectiveness of signs. In the case of this second application, in which the lights are placed near or on a sign, the question arises wether they might not, in some cases, interfere with reading the sign. Two successive studies have been carried out in an attempt to answer this question. In the first, two types of equipment, discharge lights and conventional incandescent flashing lights, were compared by measuring the reading distances of signs equipped with these two types of light. The results of the study did not reveal significant differences among the reading distances obtained with the various configurations. A second experiment was carried out using only discharge lights of different powers. The same experimental procedure was repeated. In addition to measuring the reading distance, we attempted to assess the discomfort experienced by the observers on a subjective scale of discomfort index with five levels from "no discomfort" to "extreme discomfort". The main result is that the discomfort index varies significantly with the number and the power of the discharge lights, when the reading distance only varies with the number of lights. This corroborates the hypothesis of discomfort glare.

1. INTRODUCTION

To improve the perception of messages to be transmitted to the user, flashing lights of the discharge or incandescent type are used in the field, in fixed installations or work sites. Applications may be placed in three categories: localized warning, marking, reinforcement of signing.

The probability of detecting a luminous stimulus increases with its intensity. This intensity, which enhances the probability of detection can lead to discomfort in reading a signal, and even to glaring. In the case of discomfort, it would be desirable to establish a distinction between dangerous inhibiting glare and psychological annoyance involving the notion of discomfort.

Two experiments were undertaken by the French Road Research Laboratories (LPC) jointly with the INRETS in order to investigate the conditions under which lights used at night for the reinforcement of signing could, according to their luminous power, constitute an annoyance to users.

The first (Paumier et al 1989) sought to compare the discomfort caused to the user by discharge-type flashing lights or incandescent flashing lights. This comparison is made by presenting one, two or three lights of each type having effective intensities of the same order of magnitude.

The purpose of the second experiment (Colomb, Gratia, 1990) was to try to evaluate discomfort on both the physiological (objective) and psychological (subjective) levels caused by reading a road message illuminated by one or three discharge-type flashing lights with varying power levels (the high levels exceed considerably the usual values of signing in order to produce glaring if desired).

2. COMPARISON OF DISCHARGE AND INCANDESCENT FLASHING LIGHTS

2.1. Method and tools

For the first experiment, the measured variable was the distance at which each subject read dynamically (at 60 km/h) a message on a panel, this message being associated with one, two or three discharge or incandescent flashing lights.

The independent variables were related :
-       to the characteristics of the light sources (number from 0 to 3, incandescent or discharge type, distance between the signal and the sources varying with one light at 0.5 m and then 2 m and then 5 m),
-       to the subjects, both male and female, placed in four age groups (20/30; 30/40 ; 40/50 ; 50/60). Three subjects were selected per modality, thus corresponding to 24 subjects in all.

For safety reasons, the tests were conducted on a road circuit in a protected area (INRETS track at Satolas). The panel displaying the message consisted of a 40 cm intermittently illuminated sign with a luminance of about 1 cd/m2. In this panel was placed a Landolt ring (outer diameter of about 20 cm) whose opening was oriented randomly in the experimentation plan; bottom, top, left and right.

The characteristics of the lights used are given in Table 1. The effective intensity was calculated with the Blondel-Rey-Douglas formula (Blondel, Rey., 1911). When there was only one light it was placed in the same plane as the message but at a distance of 0.5, 2 and 5 m from the message. When there were two flashing lights, they were placed laterally at 0,50 m from the sign with the Landolt Ring. When there were three flashing lights, they were placed on top of an equilateral triangle of 1 meter size. The subject was installed as a front passenger in a vehicle driven by a driver and moving at a uniform speed of about 60 km/h. The vehicle was equipped with a distance counter showing the distance between the panel and the subject when he read the sign. The subject communicated his or her answer (orientation of ring) to the experimenter sitting in the back seat of the vehicle. The vision of the observers was checked by means of the visiotest (visual acuity) and the nyctometer (sensitivity to contrast with and without glaring).

	Discharge lights	Incandescent lights
Power supply	220 V	220 V
Optical dimension	18 cm	18 cm
Frequency	1.15 Hz	1.10 Hz
Duration of flash	102 μs	490 ms
Maximum intensity	384 000 cd	54 cd
Effective intensity	58 cd	28 cd

Table 1 Characteristics of flashing lights used in the first experiment.

Based upon the characteristics of light sources, ten different combinations were obtained. Three runs without lights (beginning, middle, end of experimentation) were provided so as to offer a control on possible changes in the subjects response. By adding a reconnaissance tour to familiarize the subject with the work requested, 14 circuit trips were obtained with a different ring position for each trip.

2.2. Results and discussion

2.2.1. General remark

All tests	Minimum distance (m)	Maximum distance (m)	Average distance (m)	Standard deviation (m)
WITHOUT STIMULUS	14	124	62	38
WITH STIMULUS Incandescent lights	6	108	63	21
WITH STIMULUS Discharge lights	13	130	63	27

Table 2. Minimum, maximum and average values and standard deviation of reading distances of subjects for the test conditions.

Table 2 shows the significant scattering of results for the different reading distances of the subjects. During the dynamic tests, this scattering between individuals combines scattering of the vision of individuals and their reaction times.

2.2.2. Various comparisons
A variance analysis has been made to check the significant differences at threshold of 95 % of the mean reading distances obtained for the various conditions :
-        3 presentations without stimulus,
-        presentations for incandescent light and discharge light stimuli ;

With   1 light at 5 m from the sign; 1 light at 2 m; 1 light at 0,5 m; 2 lights at 0,5 m,
         and 3 lights at 0,5 m from the sign.

The results may be summarized as follows:

LIGHT PARAMETERS	INFLUENCE ON READING DISTANCE (at threshold of 95 %)
Technology of lights (incandescent - discharge)	No
Number of lights (1 - 2 - 3)	No
Position of lights in relation to message (0.5 - 2 - 5 m)	No
Presence or absence of light	No

It may be concluded that the objective discomfort translated in terms of a reduction in reading distance does not exist under the conditions of these experiments, since there is no difference between the presentations without lights and those with lights.

A second experiment was thus undertaken, using only discharge lights and increasing the power levels significantly in order to try to reach the objective glaring threshold. It was also considered desirable to estimate at which power the subjects felt a certain discomfort.

3. COMPARISON OF DISCHARGE-TYPE FLASHING LIGHTS OF DIFFERENT POWERS

3.1. Method and tools

The purpose of the second experiment was to evaluate discomfort on both the physiological (objective) and psychological (subjective) levels caused by reading a road message with one or three discharge-type flashing lights with a varying power level.

The adopted dependent variables are :
-       the distance at which each subject reads dynamically (60 km/h) a panel equipped with one or three discharge-type flashing lights with power levels varying with each passage (quantification of disability glare).
-       the discomfort that may be caused by the different powers of the light sources. This discomfort (estimation of psychological glare) will be evaluated subjectively in relation to a scale with five modalities: no discomfort - slight discomfort - moderate discomfort - considerable discomfort - extreme discomfort.

The independent variables are :
-       the characteristics of the light source (one and three lights with five energy levels: 3 - 6 - 9 - 12 - 15 joules),
-       For the subjects, their age (20/35 ; 35/50 ; > 50 years) and the average annual distance travelled (less than 7000 km; about 15000 km; over 30000 km annually).

Two subjects were chosen for each modality, giving a participation of 36 subjects.

Moreover, the number of years that the subject had been driving and the frequency of his night driving was noted. The experimental procedure was the same as previously.The lights used were of the discharge type.

In the single-light configuration, the light had a diameter of 220 mm and was placed at the top of the panel. In the three-light configuration, the lights were arranged in a triangle in the usual arrangement (one on top and two at the bottom). Diameters were then 180 mm. The photometric characteristics are given in Table 3 relating the energy (amount specified by light manufacturers) and the effective intensity (notion related to the sensation of the subject).

Energy (j)	Max. Intensity (10^{6}Cd)		Effective intensity (Cd)		Duration (µs)		Frequency (Hz)	
	Light 1	Light 2	Light 1	Light 2	Light 1	Light 2	Light 1	Light 2
3	1.25	2.40	275	630	430	415	0.63	0.63
6	1.90	3.90	745	1 770	720	735	0.63	0.63
9	2.50	5.05	1 290	3 050	930	1 025	0.63	0.63
12	2.80	5.85	1 850	4 350	1 310	1 935	0.63	0.63
15	3.10	6.60	2 380	5 585	1 610	2 210	0.63	0.63

Table 3 Photometric characteristics of lights (Light 1: 180-mm diameter; Light 2: 220-mm diameter)

The two configurations (one and three lights) and the five power levels lead to ten passages of the subject under different conditions. Three passages involving a neutral control signal (without light) as well as a reconnaissance trip in order to get an idea as to the location of the panel and the lights and to experiment with the operating mode, are added.For each subject, the reading distance and discomfort felt are noted by the researcher in the back seat of the vehicle.

3.2. Results and discussion

Average reading distance (m)					
Without lights		One light		Three lights	
M	s	M	s	M	s
73.3	23.6	72.8	22.6	67.2	21.3

Table 4 Average reading distances (M) and standard deviations (s)

3.2.1. Influence of number of lights and energy levels on reading distance

Table 4 gives average values (M) for reading distances, in meters and standard deviation (s) for three panel configurations: without lights, with one light, with three lights.

Analyses show that:

- there is a significant difference between the averages of the distances for the three configurations.
- there is no significant difference between 0 and 1 light but there is a difference between 0 and 3 lights as well as between 1 and 3 lights.
- the average reading distance decreases when the panel is lit with three lights and that there seems to be an objective annoyance (disability).
- the energy level does not have a significant effect on the reading distance.

3.2.2. Influence of number of lights and energy levels on discomfort felt

This impression of discomfort is felt significantly with an increase in the number of lights as well as an increase in the power levels. The graph (Figure 1) illustrates this tendency by showing the variation of the average discomfort index with the effective intensity.

It is noted that the average appreciation of the subjects is practically proportional to the effective intensity and hence to the sensation felt. The discomfort curve with three lights is always greater or roughly parallel to that with one light. In this experiment, the lowest energy level has an effective intensity of about 700 cd. For this value the analysis of the results shows that 75 % of observers experienced no or slight discomfort and over 90 % experienced no, slight or moderate discomfort. This effective intensity value is much higher than the current French proposals and slightly higher than the international specifications of the IRF. A French draft standard (AFNOR - P 98475 - 1991) proposes an effective intensity of $25 < Ie < 100$ cd, whatever the type of lights, their use or their power supply.

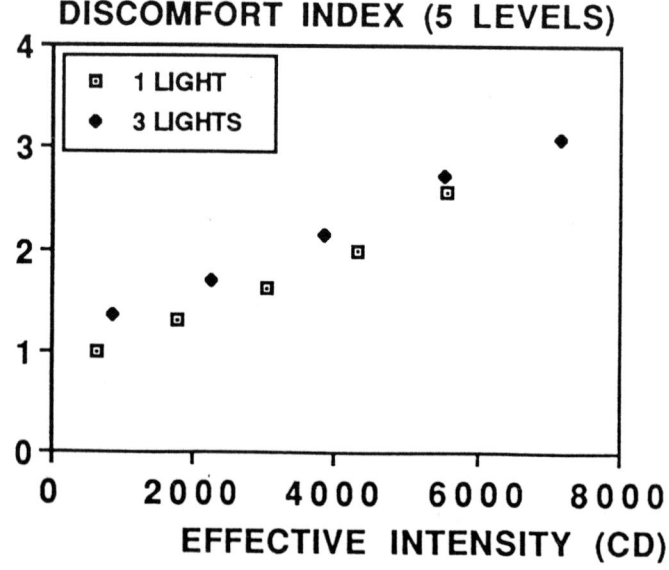

Fig. 1 - Variation of average discomfort index with effective intensity

A draft specification of the International Road Federation (I.R.F 1991) defines various classes of lights according to their use. As regards discharge-type flashing lights used for night-time sign reinforcement, the specific effective intensity Ie values are:-

$$250 < Ie < 500 \text{ cd.}$$

From the results presented above, it would appear possible to raise beyond 100 cd the recommended maximum in the French draft standard for the application considered. This increase in the maximum level of the effective intensity would allow more uniformity with the recommendations of the IRF.

3.2.3. Influence of various factors
The results may be summarized as in Table 5 :

Variables	Significant influence at threshold of 95 %	
	Reading distance	Discomfort felt
Number of lights	yes	yes
Energy level	no	yes
Visual acuity	yes	no
Contrast **without** glare	yes	no
Contrast **with** glare	yes	yes
Age	yes	yes
Sex	no	no
Used to driving at night	yes	yes
km/yr travelled	no	yes

Table 5 Summary of influence of different variables of the survey at the significance threshold of 95%

4. CONCLUSION

For the first experiment, the aim was to establish a comparison between the two technologies, namely incandescent flashing lights and discharge-type flashing lights, used as reinforced warning lights from the viewpoint of the visual discomfort possibly experienced by the motorist. The results show that, for the two types of flashing lights often being used, there is no significant influence on reading distance by the type of flashing lights (incandescent or discharge), their number (0, 1, 2, 3), their position in relation to the message (0.5 - 2 - 5 m). This means that no objective discomfort by flashing lights was measured for the effective intensities studied.

For the second experiment, the aim was to evaluate discomfort on both the physiological (objective) and psychological (subjective) levels caused by the reading of a message reinforced by one or three discharge-type flashing lights with energies varying from 3 to 15 joules (Effective intensity: 630 to 7150 cd). These high values are used in order to approach the dangerous glare threshold. It is observed in particular that the energy level (or effective intensity) has no significant influence on the reading distance (objective discomfort), whereas it has a very clear influence on the amount of discomfort experienced. These two studies can provide basic information for the European group in charge of drawing up recommendations on the powers of lighting used in highway traffic situations.

5. ACKNOWLEDGEMENTS

These studies were performed with the help of Mss Billau, Mr Richard, Arnal and Paviet for the experiment and of Mr Peybernard for the data analysis.

6. REFERENCES

Blondel A., Rey J., (1911). Perception des lumières brèves à la limite de leur portée, Journal de physique, Vol. CL III, p. 54.

Colomb M., Gratia G., (1990). Distance de lisibilité d'un message routier signalé par des feux clignotants à décharge, Lyon, Laboratoire de l'Equipement, 107 p.

Paumier et al, (1989). Etude de localisation et de gêne à la lecture de feux clignotants, Clermont-Ferrand, Laboratoire de l'Äquipement, 39 p.

Requirements for warning and safety devices, (1990). International Road Federation, March 1990.

Equipements de la route, Feux de balisage et d'alerte pour la signalisation routière, spécifications (1991). Normes AFNOR NF P 98-475.

3

VEHICLE GLAZING
AND LIGHT TRANSMISSION

VISION IN VEHICLES – IV
A.G. Gale et al. (Editors)
© 1993 Elsevier Science Publishers B.V. All rights reserved.

EFFECTS OF VARIOUS TRANSMISSION LEVELS IN WINDSHIELDS ON PERCEPTION

Harald DERKUM

Forschungsgemeinschaft Auto-Sicht-Sicherheit e.V., Universitätsstraße 5,
D-5000 Köln (Cologne) 41, Germany

1. INTRODUCTION

As announced at Vision in Vehicles - III, a dynamic perception experiment in the laboratory was carried out in order to investigate the effect of various transmission levels on recognition distances and to answer the following question: Below what transmission in windshields does the perception of the driver during nighttime driving becomes so bad, that vehicles should not be equipped with such windshields?

In order to find a suitable test object for later field experiments, we worked with two objects whose optical characteristics can be mathematically defined: a stripe-pattern and a Landolt-Circle (Fig.1).

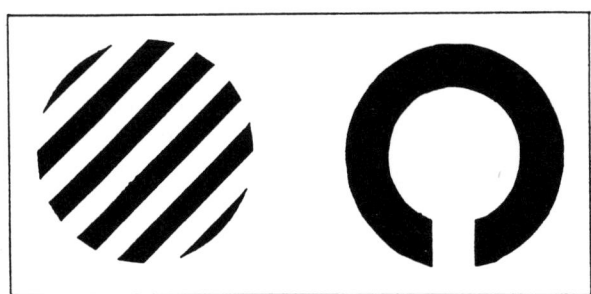

Figure 1.   The two test objects used in the experiment (left: stripe-pattern, right: Landolt-Circle)

The experiment took place in a dark tunnel with black walls located in the Staatliches Materialprüfungsamt (Federal Materials Testing Agency) in Dortmund, Germany. Light conditions were similar to nighttime driving conditions including oncoming car lights. The distances were scaled down by a factor of 10.

2. EXPERIMENTAL CONDITIONS

Range of transmission values:
From 35% to 89%, in steps of 5, measured in mounted position; and one task without windshield (100%) Since we could not get enough windshields (size: 0.70cm x 0.70cm) with our needed transmission values, we constructed an inclinable holder, so that we created our needed transmission scale by inclining the windshields (between 0° and 60°). Doing so, one windshield served us for several transmission values so that the number of windshields used in the experiment could be reduced to 5.

Visual distance:
5.80m to 18m (from test person)

Approaching speed:
0.25 m/s <=> 0.91 km/h

Illumination:
0.052 cd/m² (constant along the entire visual distance)

Contrast $K=(Lo-Lb)/Lb$ between object and surrounding:
0.6 (constant along the whole visual distance)
This contrast was chosen following measurements at locations of vehicle/pedestrian crashes.

Glare:
0.02 lux at 4° at a distance of 11.60m from the subjects

Width of gap in Landolt-Circle resp. width of stripe:
1.6 cm, which is equivalent to a visual angle of 10' in the middle of the visual distance (12m from the subjects) and thus to a mesopic visual acuity of 0.1 Choosing an angle of 10' in the middle of the visual distance, we constructed a scale by which all performances of the subjects could be reflected.

3. TEST PERSONS

22 subjects with a minimum age of 40 years were selected for the experiment. Precondition to be accepted for the experiment was a medical eye examination without negative results (on eye ground, motility, stereoscopy, visual field, astigmatism) and a minimum day light acuity of 1.0 (with correction).
The subjects were not allowed to wear tinted glasses during the experiment.

4. EXPERIMENTAL DESIGN

For every transmission level the subject had to respond to 4 recognition tasks. In pretests we found that more than 4 tasks did not affect the results' significantly.

Each time the object started from its initial position (18m from the test person) its orientation was changed at random (with the restriction that no orientation was presented twice during a block of 4 tasks).

As soon as they recognized its orientation, the test persons stopped the oncoming object by using a foot-pedal. In the same moment, the light on the object went out and a weak red lamp on the response block on their knees was switched on. With this procedure the test persons had no chance to look at the object's orientation after having once stopped it. Then they had 10 seconds time to push the corresponding response button. Not having responded after 10 seconds, the light went on again and the experiment continued with the object returning to its initial position and the computer storing a "no response" message. Otherwise, the computer stored a "right resp. wrong" message and the experiment continued immediately.

"Wrong" and "no response" messages were defined as missing values, so that per transmission level the average of recognition distances followed by a correct response served as raw data.

5. RESULTS

As may be seen in Figure 2, with and without glare, the stripe pattern is recognized much earlier than the Landolt-Circle.

Figure 3 shows the two glare conditions together in one graph for each object. It is evident that the "glare" and "no glare" values from the Landolt-Circle are not as clearly separated from each other as is the case with the stripe pattern. So, taking into consideration that under glare an object should be recognized later, the stripe pattern's values make more sense.

6. DISCUSSION

In spite of equal values as regards contrast and width of gap resp. stripes, the stripe pattern is the better suited object to measure mesopic acuity.

The reason for this result is to be seen in the fact, that the stripe pattern is an object whose spatial frequencies are mathematically defined by the homogenous repetition of the stripes inside the pattern. Due to this circumstance, its optical amplitudes are considerably higher than the background of optical noise. In opposition to this, the distribution of the spatial frequencies of the Landolt-Circle is not homogenous and its gap is a singularity with an amplitude not very much higher than the background of optical noise.

Following this finding, we now focus on the results from the stripe pattern test. Figure 4 summarizes the results of a multiple range test during an analysis of variance and the results from a regression analysis. Computing a regression analysis, we learned that a logarithmic function is the best fitting model to the data of both tests (with and without glare).

The striped area marks the transmission values and their average recognition distances which have been found not to differ significantly from the 90% transmission, which is equivalent to clear (untinted) windshields. When we think about a cut-off point for transmission in windshields, we should refer to clear windshields and not compare vision through tinted windshields with vision without glass at all. Thus, we see that without glare

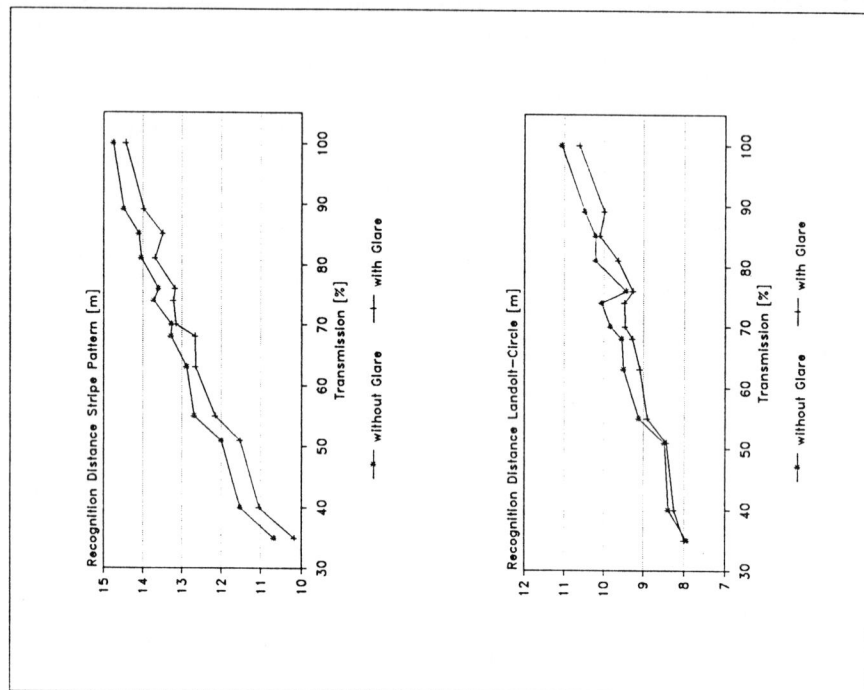

Figure3.   Recognition Distances, Separated by Test Objects (upper part stripe-pattern, lower part Landolt-Circle)

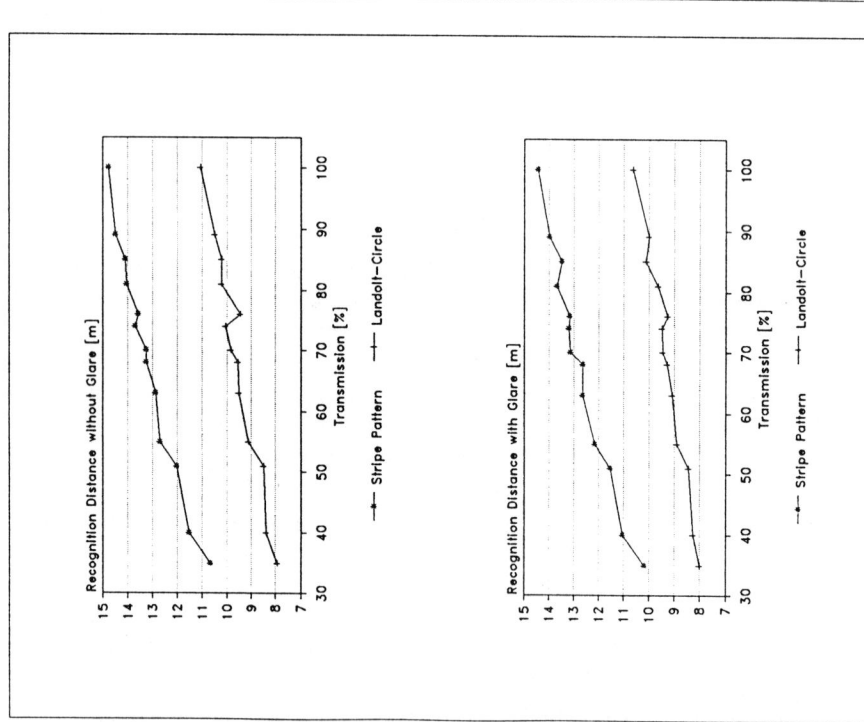

Figure 2.   Recognition Distances, Separated by Glare Condition (upper part without glare, lower part with glare)

the values of the transmission levels down to 68% and with glare down to 63% are not significantly different from the 90% transmission values.

Looking at the regression, we see that for both glare conditions the curve is to be found at 62%. This is the point, seen from left to right, at which the gradients of the regression start declining.

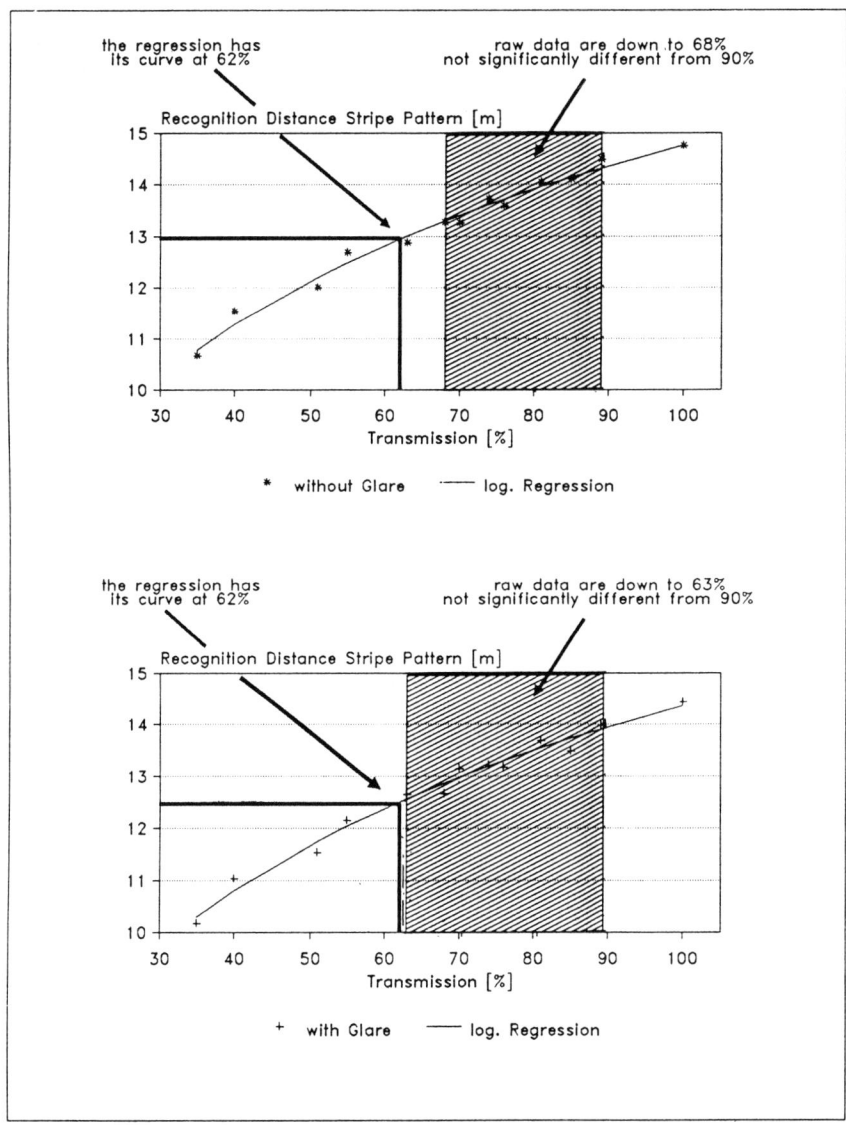

Figure 4: Results from a Multiple Range Test and from a Regression Analysis (upper part without glare, lower part with glare)

7. CONCLUSION AND PROSPECT

As for the question about a cut-off point for transmission in mounted windshields, the results are not homogenous. Looking for the lowest value with no significant difference from clear windshields, we found 68% without glare, but 63% with glare. Analyzing the best fitting mathematical model, we could suggest 62% as well. So what we can say from our experiment's point of view is that the exact transmission value, from which drivers' vision becomes significantly worse, lies between 60% and 70%, a result, which corresponds with results from a static perception experiment in the same tunnel carried out by the Staatliches Materialprüfungsamt (Federal Materials Testing Agency) in 1990.

We will repeat our experiment during this year, using subjects with an acuity which is on the borderline of exclusion from driving.

Field experiments will follow which will also give an answer to the question as regards a cut-off point for stray light in windshields.

LIGHT DIFFUSION CHARACTERISTIC AND VISIBILITY INTERFERENCES IN AUTOMOBILE WINDSHIELDS

Franz Rudolf KEßLER

Techn. Univ. Braunschweig, Institut für Halbleiterphysik und Optik, Pockelsstraße 4, D-3300 Braunschweig

Abstract

Soiling and/or deterioration of automobile glazing causes stray light by transmission or reflection. Stray light impairs the driver's environmental perception. The art and degree of perception interference depend strongly on the stray light characteristic. Wide-angle diffusion (angle of deflection over 2 degrees) is especially discussed.

Following some practical remarks, the possiblility of characterizing the stray object by means of characteristic parameters is discussed. Some quantitative relations based on a theoretical treatment of the problem are given.

The principles of two systems for measurement and analysis of diffusion characteristic are presented together with some typical results. One system uses stationary equipment which is based on the scanning principle. The other instrument involved is a mobile probe for stray light which is used directly on the vehicle.

1. INTRODUCTION

In most cases optical information for the driver of a vehicle passes through the windshield or side and rear windows of the driver's cabin. The optical transformation properties of the windshield and windows therefore play an important role in the conservation of correct information. Moreover, the windows should not be the source of additional irregular information which leads to a misunderstanding of the surroundings and, as a result, to dangerous reactions of the driver.There are several publications concerning this problem, but most of them are empirical (Kunert, 1988; Lundkvist et al., 1988; Helmers et al., 1988; Reiner, 1989; Tinnermann, 1985;Willumeit, 1980;Chmielarz et al., 1989).

This paper is concerned with the problems of the influence of stray light generated by soiling of glass surfaces and surface defects, respectively. Stray light is generated also by microstructural defects in the glass itself or in the components of laminated glass.

The negative influences of stray light affect all components of the image information. The irritations may be classified into 7 groups: i) reduction of contrast, ii) distortion of the contour of the visible object through deformation, iii) misjudgements about the surroundings due to appearance of "ghost images", iv) disturbance of the accommodation, v) disturbance of the adaptation, vi) blinding through glare, vii) disturbance through color modification. In all these cases we have dynamic phenomena, with respect to the reaction of the driver, as traffic is a procedure in motion.

This is not the place to discuss the details of relevant physiological optics (Schober, 1964) or to verify the negative effects on the driver by these phenomena (Lundkvist et al, 1988, Helmers & Lundkvist, 1988, Reiner, 1989, Willumeit, 1980).

Following some remarks about the realistic situation in traffic, a more theoretical treatment will illustrate the physics of stray light and its description by means of modelling. This leads to expected scattering characteristics which we shall compare with the empirical characteristics.

In the last part of the paper, the principles of two instruments for measurement and analysis of diffusion charactertistics are presented together with some typical results (Keßler, 1990).

2. ALIENATION OF IMAGE INFORMATION BY STRAY LIGHT

Soiling, wear and damage of the windshield cause stray light which leads to an intensity splitting from the beam direction of regular transmission (or reflection) into the whole solid angle. The scattered intensities are so high that the eye is affected in a different manner. This is especially true in the case of mesoscopic sight, i.e. if the sensitivity of the eye is adapted to a range of luminance which is comparable with the luminance of the stray light. Particularly in the case of suddenly appearing light sources outside the driver's field of view it is possible that light beams fall on the windshield and are then deflected into the driver's eye by means of the wide-angle light scattering. In this case, due to the backward extrapolation of the beams, a ghost image appears in the field of view.

Figure 1 gives a sketch of a typical situation. In this case, the deflected light beam is itself caused by light scattering, for instance by a soiled headlight. The intensity of such double scattered light is relatively high if the outlet area of the headlight, corresponding to modern styling of cars, is small.

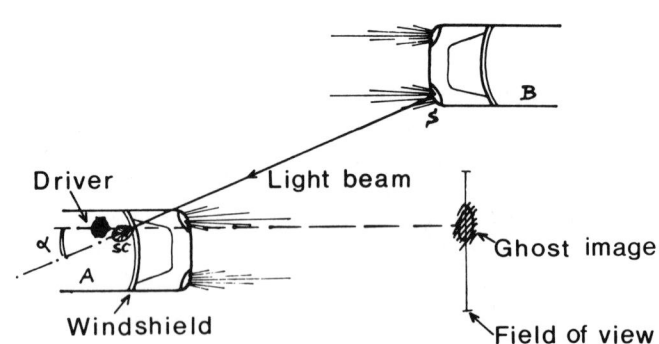

Figure 1   Sketch of the genesis of a ghost image by wide angle light scattering in a soiled windshield

The analogous effects are caused by illumination from road and advertisement lighting. Of course, we have the most significant irritations if the disturbing light sources are the headlights of oncoming traffic corresponding to the normal divergence of the light beam.

3. THE PHYSICS OF LIGHT SCATTERING

The scattering of light depends on the relation between the light wavelength and the characteristic parameter of lateral dimension of the scattering object. In all cases, we have an irregularity of surface roughness and particle structure, respectively, which causes the light scattering so that the integral phenomenon of light scattering is to describe the use of statistical distribution functions. The physical model which is suitable for modelling the light scattering, including the scattering characteristics, is always an approximation to describe the real situation, but offers the possibility to characterize the given irregularity by means of only a few parameters. The model parameters can be used to classify the quality or usefulness of the scattering windshield or other optical means of the vehicle.

If the microstructural dimensions of the scattering object are large, in comparison with the wavelength of light, i.e. greater than about 1 μm, then the scattering of light can be described by means of regular refraction and reflection at the given local function of the position of a small plane surface area as a function of three coordinates. The multireflected parts as well as the local Fresnel coefficients for reflection and transmission, respectively, are to be taken into account. The computer assisted modelling procedure is the analysis of a given surface roughness by means of a superposition of sinusoidal modulations of different local wavelengths. This procedure corresponds to the description of an arbitrary function within the Fourier theorem. In this case, a given roughness is represented by a suitable distribution function f (S) of the value S which is the modulation amplitude H divided by the local wavelength L:

$$S=H/L.$$

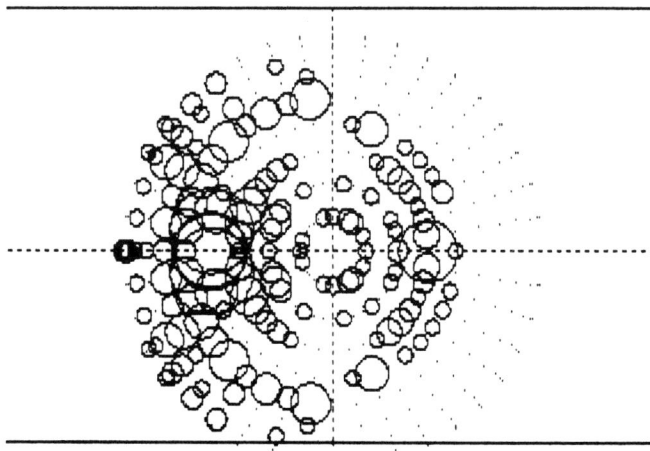

Figure 2 Scattering characteristics of a rough surface in transmission (model calculation; orthographic projection; circle radius prop. intensity; for parameters see text)

Figure 2 gives a rough impression of the result by presenting the scattering characteristics of a surface having different values in superposition: S = 0.125, 0.25, 0.5, and 1.0. The stray light characteristics were computed for the transmission case assuming a windshield having the complex refractive index n = (1.5,0). The angle of incidence is -35 degrees and the azimuth angle with respect to the coordinate axes is zero. One sees that we have a wide-angle scattering up to about 60 degrees.

We expect such coarse structures of destruction of a windshield only in the case of sand impact under special circumstances. In the normal case of soiling or deterioration of a windshield, the lateral dimensions of the contaminating particles or defects are smaller than the light wavelength. Then, the effect of light scattering is predominately given by diffraction. The theoretical treatment of this problem is based on superposition of field amplitude and interference (see Beckmann and Spizzichino, 1987). Also in this case, the statistical roughness of the surface is described by suitable local functions. It was shown that in many cases of statistically rough surfaces the fluctuations of the altitude of the surface parallel to the normal of the undisturbed surface can be described by a Gaussian distribution function in a good approximation having the mean value zero. Then, in this distribution function, the standard deviation δ is the sole parameter. For characterisation, the degree of flatness of the surface a lateral correlation function is used. In most cases this function is an exponential function characterized also by one parameter; that is the correlation length.

Figure 3 shows the result of a computer-aided modelling in this direction: The part of regular transmitted (or reflected) light is given versus the standard deviation of the distribution function of the altitude. It can be seen that at δ = 0.1 μm and δ = 0.3 μm the intensity of the regular transmitted (or reflected) light is reduced by the factor of approx. 2 and 10, respectively. This apparent defect in intensity is caused by light scattering in the whole solid angle. By this means,the diagram leads to insight into the quantities of reduction of transmission of light by scattering and the transformation of the beam intensity into stray light.

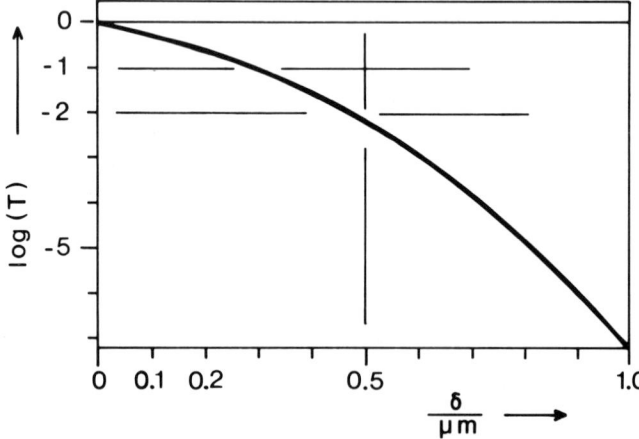

Figure 3   Regular transmission T of a scattering target showing its dependence on the standard deviation δ of the roughness (model calculation; double logarithmic scale; for parameters see text)

Fig. 4 shows the results of the model calculation with respect to the part of scattered light. In a logarithmic scale, the normalized luminance of the stray light is plotted versus the scattering angle. The diagram is computed with respect to a direction of scattered light within the plane of incidence of the beam. The angle of incidence of the beam is -10 degrees with respect to the normal of the undisturbed surface. The different standard deviation is 0.1 and .05. In both cases the correlation length is 1 μm and the light wavelength is assumed to be 0.5 μm (approx. yellow) in both cases. The luminance of the stray light is reduced to 1% only at angle distances of approximately 50 and 30 degrees, respectively. This corresponds to the observable reality.

4. MEASURING METHODS FOR STRAY LIGHT CHARACTERISTICS

Because light scattering is a statistical phenomenon, the measurement of the angle dependence of scattered light has to take into account that the area of the light probe covers a sufficiently large area of the sample. On the other hand, the cross section should be as small as possible to simplify the evaluation of the stray light characteristic with respect to the quantification of the true angle function. Moreover, the incident light beam should be a parallel one. In the modern solid state LASERs we have very comfortable and strong parallel light sources. In general, we can use this monochromatic radiation to acquire the desired information about the stray object.

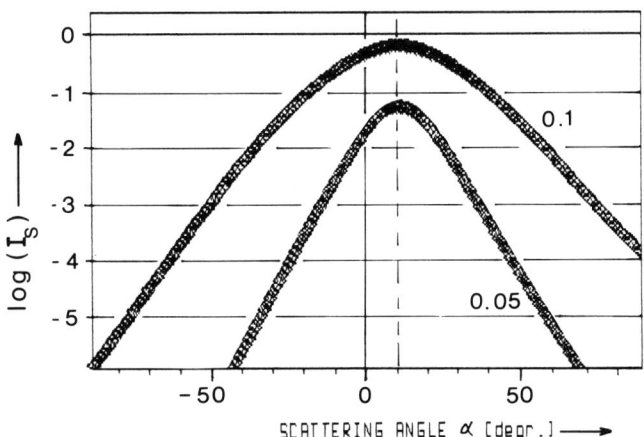

Figure 4 Characteristics of the scattered light part IS (log-scale) due to diffraction by a statistical rough surface (model calculation) curve parameter is standard deviation (see text)

For characterization of optical stray objects, we have developed two different sustem. The first one (see Fig. 5) is a stationary measuring machine. The light beam, which can be chosen, from different light sources passes through a hole in the wall and falls onto the sample. The sample can be oriented in an arbitrary configuration with respect to the angles of incidence. The photodetector is moved by a stepping motor around a circle of approximately 60 cm in diameter to detect the stray light with an angle solution of about 1E-6 sterad. The shielding of the whole apparatus is so perfect that we can detect stray light in this angle resolution down to an intensity ratio of 1:1E-9. The amplifier works

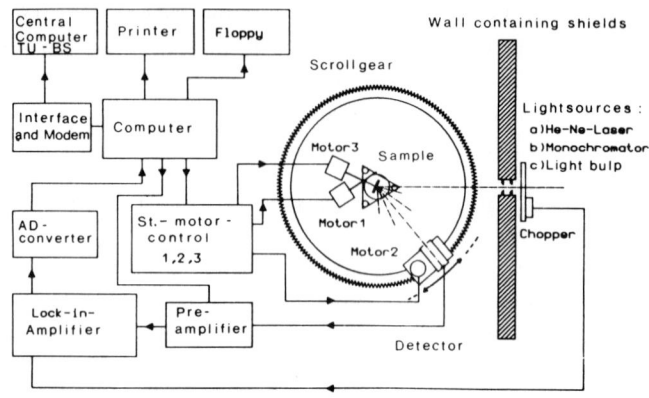

Figure 5   Schematic diagram of the arrangement for measuring the characteristics of stray light

with a number of corresponding steps of sensitivity in lock-in technique. The apparatus allows the measurement of the stray light characteristic in the whole solid angle and works fully computer-assisted.

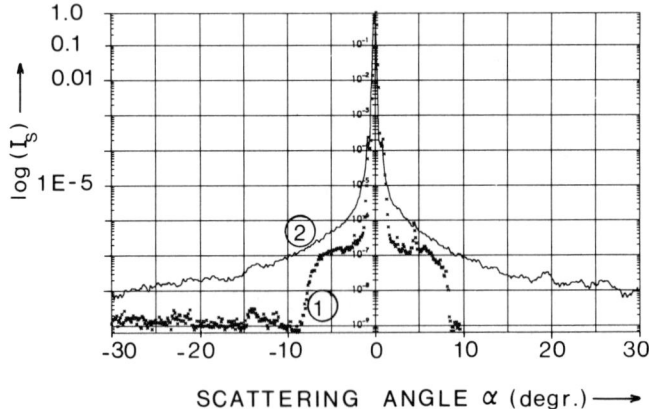

Figure 6 Measured stray characteristics of samples: "1" quite new windshield and "2" real windshield after use for 95,000 km .

Figure 6 shows a typical result. Curve "1" is the intensity disturbance using a quite new windshield for defining the zero point with respect to scattered light. Curve "2" is the angle function of stray light in the plane of incidence for a sample which is a piece of a windshield. This windshield shows normal wear due to use for a longer time. The characteristics show clearly a wide-angle scattering corresponding to the model theory for small scattering particles (see Fig. 4). The relevant result gives a value of the standard deviation $\delta = 0.01$ μm for characterization of the surface roughness and L=0.5 μm for the correlation length.

The second apparatus which we have developed is for more mobile and quicker measurements of stray light in practical cases with a reduced demand for accuracy (see Fig. 7). A hand-held apparatus consisting of a LASER light source is used. The shielding box has an entrance hole and a rear plate supporting a quarter circle of different photovoltaic elements. The elements of one radius are in a separated parallel circuit and lead to a separate measuring value. By this means, we have a suitable resolution of the angle distribution of the scattered light and a sufficient sensitivity.

The rear plate supporting the photo elements can be turned around 360 degrees to detect a possible azimuthal asymmetry in the stray characteristic of the object indicating a "texture" of the surface disturbance, for instance by the wiper blade element. This stray light probe also works in lock-in technique to reduce the sensitivity against strange light incidence. The amplifier and the evaluation of the measured values as well as a printer for data output are also fully computerized.

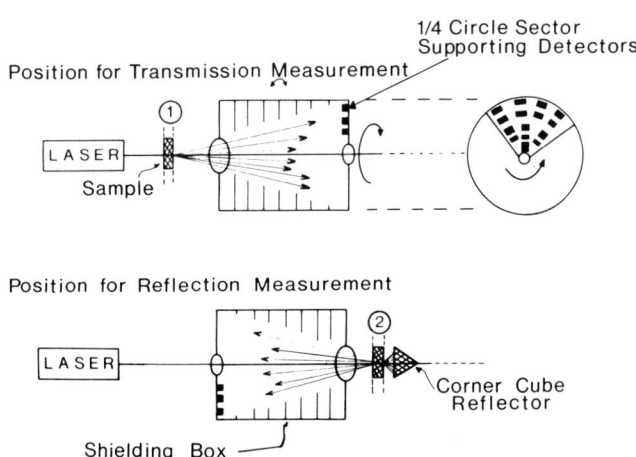

Figure 7 Schematic diagram of the "mobile stray light probe": arrangement for measuring "1" in transmission and "2" in "reflection"

The lower part of Fig. 7 shows the arrangement of the apparatus when the measurements have to be made "in reflection" position. In this case, the shielding box is turned about-face and a corner cube reflector reflects the scattered light which is transmitted without any adjustment.

Figure 8 shows an example of the computer print. The data print contains a "bar diagram" as pseudo graphic presentation of the results. Fig. 8 a) indicates the zero effect using a clean slide of glass as a sample. The sensitivity of the probe is estimated by using the lowest intensity as a fraction of the intensity of stray light, when a nearly perfect Lambert diffuser is used for calibration.

```
a) Test measurement                                    b) Sample measurement
-------------------                                    ---------------------
Sample: "clean slide of glass" ; Azimuth:  0 degree    Sample:  "Audi 100 (1975); 95000 km" ; Azimuth:  0 degree
-------------------------------------------------      -----------------------------------------------------------
Stray angle    Intensity          Scale                Stray angle   Intensity              Scale
 in degr.        in %      One "*" corresponds to 0,02 %  in degr.      in %      One "*" corresponds to 0,2 %
                          I----I----I----I----I----I-                            I----I----I----I----I----I-
    3,3        0,2132    !***********                      3,3        5,3304    !***************************
    4,4        0,1054    !*****                            4,4        5,4936    !****************************
    5,5        0,0982    !*****                            5,5        1,5881    !********
    6,6        0,0855    !****                             6,6        1,8838    !*********
    7,7        0,0858    !****                             7,7        2,2279    !***********
    8,8        0,0638    !***                              8,8        1,6568    !********
    9,8        0,0502    !***                              9,8        0,7260    !****
   10,9        0,0466    !**                              10,9        0,8167    !****
   12,0        0,0348    !**                              12,0        0,6330    !***
   13,0        0,0422    !**                              13,0        0,3758    !**
   14,0        0,0374    !**                              14,0        0,3697    !**
   15,0        0,0342    !**                              15,0        0,3928    !**
```

Figure 8   Data prints obtained with the "mobile stray light probe": samples a) clean slide of glass and b) deteriorated windshield.

Figure 8 b) shows the measured result for the real windshield which was in use over several years. First, one sees that the scattered intensities are in the order of several percentage points higher than the ideal Lambert diffuser and secondly that corresponding intensities are present up to scattering angles of 15 degrees which is the limit of measurement. We found differences up to a factor of approximately 20 indicating a significant state of wear.

5. CONCLUSION

Security and safety in using vehicles depends on undisturbed optical information as regards the surroundings of the driver. This information is transported by light passing through windshields, windows and mirrors. In this manner the information is highly affected if light scattering is present. The light scattering leads to a degradation of the images and/or can add ghost images. In both cases the wide-angle scattering in particular has to be taken into account in this direction.

It was shown that i) the genesis of stray light can be understood by means of physical models, ii) the model parameters are suitable for characterizing the stray object and iii) two systems were developed to analyze the object: a) in a complete and more scientific way and b) in the form of a mobile probe.

In conclusion, it is only left to say that light scattering is an important aspect with respect to the problem of "vision in vehicles". The negative influences of stray light must be studied to reduce the risk in traffic. Obviously this field has to cover more practical investigations together with scientific analysis to detect the interdependences between the behavior of the driver and the physical properties of relevant optical devices of a vehicle.

6. ACKNOWLEDGEMENT

The apparatus for the measurement of scattered light were developed during different periods of examination theses following other scientific aims and in cooperation with students. It is a pleasure for the author to extend to all of them most sincere thanks for support, also for the preceding work. Special thanks go to Ms. Dr. Annette Beckmann, Dipl. Phys., who organized and realized the measurements on windshields as scattering objects. Some parts of the text, figures and tables have already been published (Kessler, 1990). The reproduction is kindly permitted by the Verlag TUV Rheineland, Cologne, Germany.

7. REFERENCES

Beckmann, P., and Spizzichino A. (1987). The Scattering of Electromagnetic Waves from Rough Surfaces, Artech House Inc., Norwood/Mass..

Chmielarz, M., and Schneider, W. (1989). Streulichtatlas, Pilotausgabe der Forschungsgemeinschaft Auto-Sicht-Sicherheit e.V., Köln, Verlag TÜV Rheinland GmbH, Köln.

Helmers, G., and Lundkvist, S.-O. (1988). Detection distances to obstacles on the road seen through windscreen in different states of wear, VTI-rapport 339A, /Linköping/Sweden.

Inst. f. Sicherheitsforschung im Straßenverkehr im TÜV Rheinland e.V.[1] (1980) (ed.), Sicht aus Kraftfahrzeugen, Köln.

Keßler, F.R. (1990). Streucharakteristik und Sichtstörung von Autowindschutzscheiben, in: Derkum, H., (ed.), Sicht und Sicherheit im Straßenverkehr, TÜV Rheinland, Köln.

Kunert, H. (ed.) (1988). Die Orientierung im Straßenverkehr bei Nachtfahrten, Verlag TÜV Rheinland GmbH, Köln.

Lundkvist, S.-O., Helmers, G., and Löfving S. (1988). Kontrastminderung durch Windschutzscheiben, Verlag TÜV Rheinland GmbH, Köln.

Reiner, J. (1989). Irritationen des binokularen Sehens durch Wischerspuren an Windschutzscheiben, Klin. Monatsblätter f. Augenheilkunde, 194, 62-64.

Schober, H., Das Sehen, vol. I and II, (VEB Fachbuchverlag, Leipzig; vol. I: 4. Auflage 1970, vol II: 3. Auflage 1964).

Timmermann, A. (1985). An instrument to measure scattered light due to windshields wear, Tenth Int. Techn. Conf. on Experimental Safety Vehicles, Oxford/England.

Willumeit, H.P., Sichtbeeinträchtigung durch Windschutzscheiben mit hohem
    Streulichtanteil, see 1 above, 147-164.

VISION IN VEHICLES – IV
A.G. Gale et al. (Editors)
© 1993 Elsevier Science Publishers B.V. All rights reserved.

AFTER-MARKET-FILM ON PASSENGER CAR WINDOWS AND LIGHT TRANSMISSION

George-Roman CUNNINGHAM

Forschungsgemeinschaft AUTO-SICHT-SICHERHEIT, Universitätsstr. 5, D-5000 Köln 41

Abstract

In August 1988, producers of an after-market-film, which through application on passenger car windows causes a further reduction of light transmission, submitted a petition to the National Highway Traffic Safety Administration (=NHTSA) in Washington, D.C. for a change of the current regulation as regards light transmission. Application of after-market-film on all side and rear windows of passenger cars, as propagated by the petitioners, would result in a light transmission of 35% and less, a contradiction to the current regulation in the United States which stipulates a light transmission of 70% on all passenger car windows. NHTSA accepted the petition for discussion without changing the regulation. At the same time, the Safety Administration called on various private and state agencies, organizations, businesses as well as persons active in traffic safety research and related areas to offer their answers and opinions to a series of 85 questions and proposals deriving from the petition. In a study of 78 responses (submitted to NHTSA before September 1989) conducted at the Research Institute A.S.S.e.V. in Cologne, Germany, it was found that two-thirds of these responses are strictly against a change of the current transmission regulation. This report gives an analysis of the major pro and con reasons submitted in the responses to the NHTSA inquiry.

1. INTRODUCTION

Should After-Market-Films be allowed on side and rear windows of passenger cars? This is the question which was posed by the National Highway Traffic Safety Admimimistration (NHTSA) in Washington, D.C. A word of clarification as regards the term after-market-film: this is a polyester film with a metal oxide layer, which may be applied to the glazing of a vehicle after it has left the producer, i.e. after purchase.

On August 10, 1988 the following four manufacturers of this easily applied after-market-film submitted a petition to NHTSA for a change of the Federal Motor Vehicle Safety Standards 205 (=FMVSS 205) which regulates glazing materials:

Gila River Products Inc.	Martin Processing, Inc.
Madico Inc.	3M Energy Control Products.

This petition was supported by the report of a scientific study on Safety Benefits and Costs of Tinted Vehicle Glazing conducted by the Illinois Institute of Technology Research Institute (IITRI) in Chicago, Illinois which was submitted as "Exhibit 1".

2. PETITION ACCEPTED AND REQUEST FOR COMMENT ON SPECIFIC ISSUES RAISED IN THE PETITION

The manufacturers of this petitioned a change of the FMVSS 205 to the extent that the tinting of all side and rear windows of passenger cars by means of this after-market-film be allowed. Thus, according to the petitioners, the standard light transmission for these windows would be 35%. In a letter to the lawyer of the petitioners dated January 1989, NHTSA accepted the petition as such and at the same time requested in the form of an extended questionaire that state and local traffic law enforcement agencies, businesses, academic instances, professional and private organisations, insurance institutes etc. submit comments "to specific issues raised in the petition". NB: Light transmission for vehicle windshields is not in question here.

3. NO REVISION OF FMVSS 205

The fact that NHTSA granted this petition is not to be construed as a revision of the current regulations. This was made clear to the petitioners by NHTSA: ". . . the granting of this petition signifies that the agency believes that a review of the issues raised in the petition appears to have merit."

Since the petitioners "seek permission for applying tinting film with 35 percent light transmittance to side and rear windows of passenger cars", this report is concerned exclusively with conditions resulting from lowered light transmission of side and rear windows in passenger cars. Specifically, it reports the results of the questionaire from NHTSA as they relate thereto.

4. AFTER-MARKET-FILM AND LIGHT TRANSMISSION

Under current regulations in the USA a light transmission of 70% is required for all passenger car glazing.

NB: Although this NHTSA regulation is currently valid in the USA, numerous violations of the same may be seen from coast to coast. In addition, various states have their own regulations which, it seems, do not always concur with those of NHTSA. To put it mildly, the situation in the USA is, as far as may be surmised, at the moment not very clear.

The actual consequences of this petition on the light transmission may be seen by the following example: When after-market-film with a 35% light transmission is applied to side and rear windows which, as we have seen, under current regulations already have a light transmission of 70%, these windows will then have an actual light transmission of 24.5%. The petitioners are of course aware of this fact: "Since the film will reduce transmittance through the glass on which the film is installed, IITRI's findings . . . discussed in this Petition focus on absolute transmittance levels. We would expect that an ammended FMVSS 205 would regulate absolute transmittance levels, taking into account the installation of 35% minimum luminous transmittance film."

5. COMMENTS DIVIDED INTO FIVE MAIN AREAS

In the request for comments NHTSA divided specific problems into four main areas which include:

I.	Effect of window transmittance levels on driver visibility and safety
II.	Amelioration of injuries from laceration and/or ejection
III.	Health effects, protection of interior parts and driver comfort
IV.	Law enforcement issues
V.	Addendum Research

The questionaire from NHTSA contained a total of 85 detailed questions all within the five named main areas. As this report deals exclusively with the results of this questionaire, the same five main areas have been used to specify the table which show the most frequently stated arguments with the number of advocates.

A random selection of 78 from the over 100 responses to the NHTSA questionaire was used. A breakdown shows that the vast majority of the responses (56 or ca 75%) originate from state agencies and departments dealing with transport safety and from state and local law enforcement agencies (Table 1). Ca two thirds of all responses (50) are against any change of FMVSS 205 (Table 2). As for the remainder, fifteen reject the change, but support quite clearly the "dark tail"; thirteen responses are for a change but not in all cases as advocated by the petitioners.

6. REJECTION OF ANY CHANGE OF FMVSS 205

6.1 Safety and law enforcement
From the two thirds of those who reject any change of the current regulation 60% give as the main reason for their rejection the opinion that such a change would gravely effect safety and law enforcement through the resulting lower light transmission. Whether this result is due to the fact that the greater part of the responses to the NHTSA inquiry originate from state and local agencies dealing with traffic safety and law enforcement or whether opinions from these types of agencies were more frequently requested cannot be clarified here. Opinions of others who do not deal with traffic safety or law enforcement were, however, similar. Whatever, this is an indication that those of this opinion regard tinted passenger car windows beyond the current stipulation as a pretext for criminal activity - a

TABLE 1: Agencies, organizations, professional persons, businesses etc. who responded
          to NHTSA's call for comments to Docket No. 89-15 Notice 1: Grant Petition for
          rulemaking; and requests for comments.

Total responses	= 78
**	
Federal agencies	= 1
Governor	= 1
State agencies for safety, transport and motor vehicles	= 28
State and city police departments	= 28
State representatives	= 3
Individual police officer	= 1
Business	= 7
Professional organizations	= 3
Universities	= 2
Other private organizations	= 2
Insurance Institute	= 1
Optometrist	= 1
Business association	= 1

TABLE 2: No change in the FMVSS 205; the most frequently stated reasons together with the number of advocates.

I. Visibility Conditions and Traffic Safety

1.	Necessity of eye contact between drivers themselves and between driver and pedestrrians, motorcyclists, bicyclists etc	= 24

2.	Reduction of peripheral,inward and outward visibility through the transient effect and in general	= 22

3.	Reduction of visibility during night time driving at twilight and in adverse weather	= 24

4.	Reduction of visibility for senior citizens and/or drivers with eye ailments	= 9

5.	Ability to observe forward traffic - essential to defensive driving - through the rear window of the forward vehicle as well as the mounted brake light diminshed	= 11

6.	Tinting guarantees no reduction of glare, haze double images etc. At best speculative	= 5

II. Amelioration of Injuries from Laceration and/or Ejection

7.	After-market-film gives no guarantee against laceration or ejection in the event of an accident. At best speculative. Use of seat belt, air bags etc. recommended	= 6

III. Health Effects and Driver Comfort

8.	No proof that after-market tinting offers any significant protection against UV and infrared radiation or reduction of temperature inside the vehicle (resulting in reduced use of air conditioning system)	= 8

9.	Current technology affords sufficient protection against health hazards (e.g. glass absorbs radiation)	= 17

Table 2 (continued)

IV. Law Enforcement Issues

_____

10. After-market tinting endangers the safety and effectiveness
     of law enforcement persons enormously   = 32

_____

11. After-market tinting promotes criminality   = 14

_____

12. Necessity of regulations which are equally valid for all
     states - with a procedure for enforcement; effective use of
     film cards, photometric sensing devices etc. questionable
     - and costly   = 18

_____

V. Addendum; Research

_____

13. As after-market tinting is a matter of fashion which
     exploited by businesses, there is no need for any change
     in the FMVSS 205, as regards light transmission   = 3

_____

14. Research data presented by the petitioners is questionable,
     contradictory and/or not up-to-date; further research necessary   = 18

_____

criminal activity connected with violence: "It is not possible for an officer to discern movements of the hands and movements of weapons inside these vehicles, either during daylight or hours of darkness." - Superintendent of the Idaho State Police. Or "...law enforcement officers feel a definite threat when approaching vehicles with tinted...windows. This threat is more pronounced at night when there is a total inability to see inside the vehicle." - Director of the Division of Motor Vehicles, Delaware Department of Public Safety. Examples from law enforcement officers who fear that the real beneficiary of after-market-film is criminality.

6.2 Eye contact essential; visibility diminished
   In second place with 50% of the responses against a change of the regulation was the opinion that the most essential eye contact between drivers themselves and between drivers and pedestrians, motorcyclists, bicyclists etc. will be diminished. It is believed that a decline in the quality of defensive driving in general will be the result of a lowered light transmission. Even in cases where it is conceded that no negative effects from tinted windows for outward visibility will result, the danger for a driver when he or she cannot see inside a vehicle or through a vehicle to the forward traffic is emphasized: "The ability of

a driver to see out of a car so equipped [with tinting film] is not severely affected, however, the ability for other drivers to see into and through a car so equipped is severely affected." - a safety officer, Department of State Police, Virginia.

Approximately one third of those opposed to a change point out in particular the generally diminished visibility at twilight, during nighttime driving and in adverse weather - already existing problem situations which would only be worsened by a lower light transmission, and this due to an after-market tinting film.

6.3 Diminished Visibility for Senior citizens and drivers with eye deficiencies and ailments

Approximately 10% of those opposed to a change of the regulation were concerned that such a change would bring a general visibility reduction for senior citizens, a growing category of drivers - and for persons with eye deficiencies and ailments - particularly during nighttime driving. NB: The 17 test subjects used in the experiment conducted by the IITRI, whose results are used as a support of the petition, ranged in age from 18 to 45 years. In its response to the NHTSA inquiry the Insurance Institute for Highway Safety in Arlington, Virginia based its opposition to a change, among other things, on the opinion that a "reduced light transmission has potentially hazardous implications for all drivers, in particular for older drivers and those with ocular pathology...at night, especially on unlighted roadways, and during rain or other adverse visibility conditions...."

6.4 Health, comfort and reduction of injuries

In their written request for a change in the transmission regulation as formulated in FMVSS 205 the petitioners listed several advantages for health (i.e. protection against "excessive exposure to UV radiation which may cause skin and eye damage") and comfort (i.e. reduction of glare and of heat inside the vehicle) as well as a reduction of injuries from laceration and/or ejection in the event of an accident. Opponents to a change in the regulation refer to current technology used in the production of glass and vehicle equipment as a safeguard against damage to eyes and skin by radiation as well as protection against ejection (seat belt and air bag) and lacerations (use of tempered glass). The application of after-market-film as a safeguard here is at best speculative. A respondent from the American Optometric Association states in his response that "there is no evidence that additional tinting will have any significant effect on preventing eye damage due to infrared or UV exposure" and the Los Angeles Police Department points out in its response that "medical authorities advise that clear window glass eliminates virtually all of the sun's harmful rays...."

Some of those opposed to a change of the regulation admit that after-market-film without a doubt does give some additional protection against radiation during daylight hours. This advantage does not, however, compensate for the danger which the resulting lowered transmission causes during nighttime driving. A safety officer at the Virginia State Police Department quoted above also points out that there is an existing "technology for producing auto window tinting that provides protection from the five most common dermatological photosensitivity diseases and some of the ophthalmic problems while maintaining a 70 % luminous transmittance."

6.5 Fashion and good business

There were some opponents to a change of the transmission rule who clearly articulated that which many others probably were thinking or which were merely implied. A superintendent of Motor Vehicles in British Columbia, Canada is an example: "It appears by the numerous studies done that window tinting serves more as a stylish item than as a safety related item. We cannot accept the argument that the use of tinting helps with visibility when sunglasses will serve the purpose with much greater flexibility, i.e. [one can] remove sunglasses in less than ideal conditions." Then there is the Iowa state trooper from the heart of the US who spoke certainly not in the accustomed scientific language but for that matter indeed even more clearly: "The Petitioners are in the business to make money by making and selling film. Their request to allow a 35 percent film ties in nicely with it being widely used by alot [sic] of installers already, who ...are in violation...When a car owner goes to a business who installs film and charges that owner up to 250.00 dollars, its [sic] the business who comes out way ahead. A product that costs the installer under 10.00 dollars and in the area of 2 to 3 hours labor, I can see why there is such a push to get the standard lowered. The Petitioners came in the back door on this and I feel this is their attempt to make it right." Since, these opponents argue, this is something fashionable - and therefore not lasting - something which clever business people are exploiting, there is no need to change the rule in this matter at all.

6.6 Research data as submitted by the petitioners questioned

More than 30% of the opponents to a change questioned the scientific report from the IITRI which was attached to the petition as "Exhibit 1". The data were described as questionable, contradictory and not up-to-date. In many cases the demand was for further and/or more thorough research. For instance a respondent from the Insurance Institute for Highway Safety in Arlington, Virginia is of the opinion that "the IITRI report fails to show a reasonable understanding of principal visual functions related to roadway visibility" and furthermore a superintendent of the Maryland State Police observes that "...the petitioners refer to old studies and tests. There is no new evidence cited to indicate window tinting is any safer now than it was 15 years ago." A Professor Emeritus from one University School of Optometry gives the most devastating opinion: "The IITRI experiment probably gains the honor as the worst I've seen." Once again it is the Iowa state trooper from above who inquires of a delicate situation in a not so delicate manner: "How can the IITRI be unbiased in their report when the Petitioners paid IITRI to make the report."

These are some of the most often stated reasons for not making a change in the current regulation. Needless to say, there were others: tinting of rear windows hampers visibility through the rear window when driving reverse; visibility conditions are diminshed through the quick change from one transmission factor to another, the transient effect; diminished visibility of the mounted brake light in the rear window; no clarification of guarantee for quality, standards and durability of the tinted film. The assertion of the manufacturers that this film can serve as an aid against haze, glare, double images, etc. was also strongly doubted by opponents to a change of the rules.

7. NO CHANGE FOR FMVSS 205; APPROVAL OF "DARK TAIL"

Fifteen from the 78 studied responses to the NHTSA inquiry were opposed to a change in the current rules as proposed by the petitioners - in part based on the same arguments presented by those categorically opposed to any change -, however, they do support the so-called "dark tail" system, i.e. a light transmission of 70% for windshields and those windows to the immediate left and right of the driver; tinting of rear windows allowed with various degrees from 35% and less. This, in essence, corresponds with the resolution from the American Association of Motor Vehicle Administrators on this matter.

8. SUPPORT OF A RULE CHANGE, BUT NOT ALWAYS IN ACCORDANCE WITH THE PETITIONERS

Thirteen of the studied responses to the inquiry were clearly in support of a change of the FMVSS 205, but not always in accord with the arguments of the petitioners. These responses originate exclusively from government agencies in states where a law similar to that suggested by the petitioners already exists. Deviation from the suggestions of the petitioners include, on the one hand, various degrees for the allowed light transmission which range from 50% downward to 20%. As in some states vehicle windows are very heavily darkened, a rule change is recommended out of concern for the effectiveness of law enforcement and the safety of those involved as well as traffic safety. Here, arguments for a change of the FMVSS 205 are identical with those presented above as against such a change. It is primarily for this reason that, on the other hand, these responses emphasize the need for uniform regulations as regards tinting of vehicle glazing - regulations equally valid for all states and with a procedure for enforcement, without specialized equipment as is recommended by some.

Other arguments in support of a change of the regulation include an affirmation of the arguments presented by the petitioners as regards comfort and well-being, i.e. protection against radiation, lacerations and ejection in the event of an accident, etc. as well as a reduction of driver fatigue through an optically more friendly environment.

9. ENVIRONMENT AND ECOLOGY

Arguments in support of a regulation change also included one concerning the environment and ecology. Through the reduction of high temperatures inside vehicles (particularly in southern California or Texas where such temperatures are predominant) there will be at the same time a reduction of the use of the air conditioning system which means a reduction in the use of CFC which causes a reduction in the use of energy, all in the interest of the environment and the ecological system.

10. CONCLUSION AND PROSPECTS

During the review of this matter, NHTSA's enforcement department conducted its own investigations of firms which were in the business of applying this after-market-film to passenger car windows. This resulted in injunctions and civil penalties for six firms in the state of Florida - an indication of the illegality of this practice. These legal actions are pending. They did, however, prompt the petitioners to submit a supplemental petition dated May 22, 1990 in which they requested an expedited decision based on the following arguments: a) a consensus standard for after-market-film exists among the states as reflected in their laws; b) should the recommendations of the petitioners be followed, no negative effects on safety and law enforcement would incur; c) failure to approve their recommendation would result in serious economic hardship for those firms engaged in this business.

In view of this petition with its supplementary request, the inquiry and its results as well as other studies made by NHTSA - including studies of European regulations - one may indeed expect some changes in the FMVSS 205. These changes may include: a) a change in the method of measuring light transmission which, until now has been conducted with the light being projected perpendicular to the glass; a system which allows the transmission measurement from the mounted angle of the glass onto the vehicle is certainly more up-to-date; b) uniform requirements for all vehicles which, until now, has not been the case; c) perhaps a change of transmission requirements for particular windows, but, in view of the general opinion that benefits from further tinting of vehicle glazing are, at best, modest but certainly not to the extent of allowing any extreme tinting, the request for a change as petitioned by the manufacturers of the after-market-film will probably not follow. Besides a continually developing technology already has means of producing the benefits for traffic safety and driving comfort without further tinting as proposed by the petitioners.

In this connection, the results of a recent study conducted by the federal Ministry for Transport in Germany show that during twilight hours by indirect visibility, the degree of light transmission through side and rear windows could be considerably lower than the specified 70% before a decline in the performance of test persons, which was calculated from the reaction time and the percentage of correct recognition of objects, could be observed. This too is perhaps a sign of future developments.

4

VISUAL PERCEPTION
AND VEHICLE CONTROL:
COLLISION AVOIDANCE

generally consistent distance headway by alternating between approaching and receding while following the car ahead. Figure 1 shows one driver's distance headway pattern as observed in consecutive 5 second segments during a period of 8 minutes. It can be understood that this subject drove his car at an average distance of 21m from the leading car, with a range of 4 to 34m.

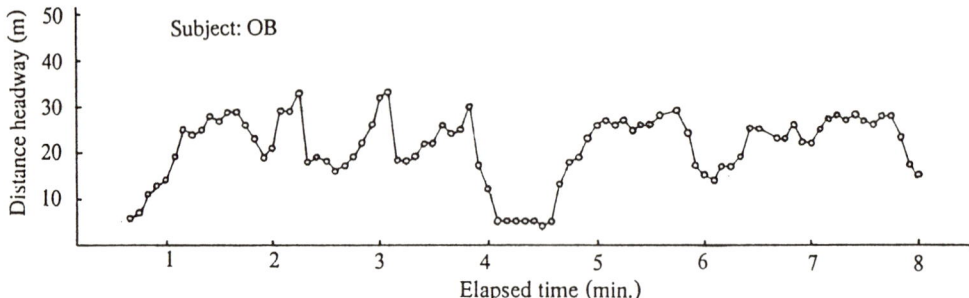

Figure 1 Distance headway shown by one driver

Each driver displays a different wave shape as regards level, amplitude and frequency. The main variables which influence the shape of the wave are three: vehicle factors, traffic environmental factors and drivers' subjective factors. It is important to understand the dynamic relationship between these factors, because the task performance of drivers is considered to be an adjustment-behavior to various traffic environments.

The author examined drivers' car-following behavior using the wave-pattern model and attempted to clarify individual drivers' characteristics by analysing the various wave-shapes they displayed.

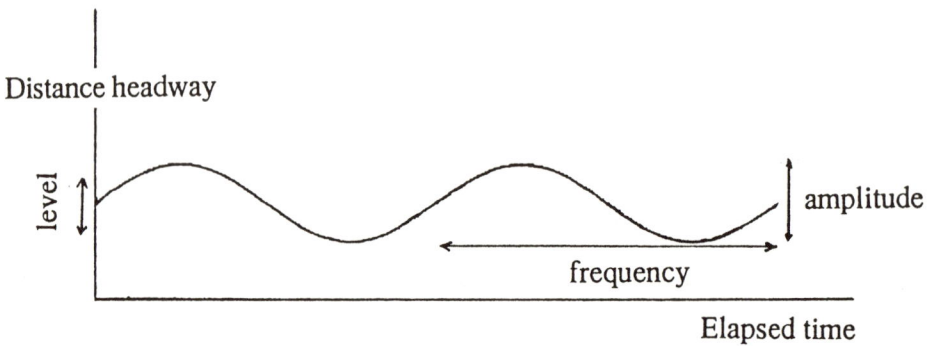

Figure 2 Car following behaviour seen as a wave pattern

1.3 Drivers' Spatial Perception

For the purpose of understanding the characteristics of drivers' spatial perception, a field experiment was conducted using two cars. A portion of the results was presented at the International Conference of Applied Psychology, held in Kyoto in 1990, where the following findings and discussion were reported.

In the experiment, subjects were instructed by 2-way radio to follow the researcher-driven leading car according to four commands involving drivers' subjective feelings or perceptions. Subjects were instructed as follows:

    (1) "Follow the car ahead at the distance at which you feel most comfortable."

    (2) "Approach until you begin to feel the distance is dangerous."

    (3) "Follow the car ahead at the minimum safe distance."

    (4) "Follow the car ahead at a distance which you feel to be neither too far nor too near."

Subjects could definitely differentiate these four kinds of tasks. Referring to the concept of proxemics developed by Hall (1966), there appear to be several kinds of zones observable in drivers' spacing behaviour. Subjects appear to recognize at least four kinds of psychologically distinct zones in the area between themselves and the car ahead, as they clearly differentiated between the four types of distance which they were asked to maintain by the researcher (Figure 3).

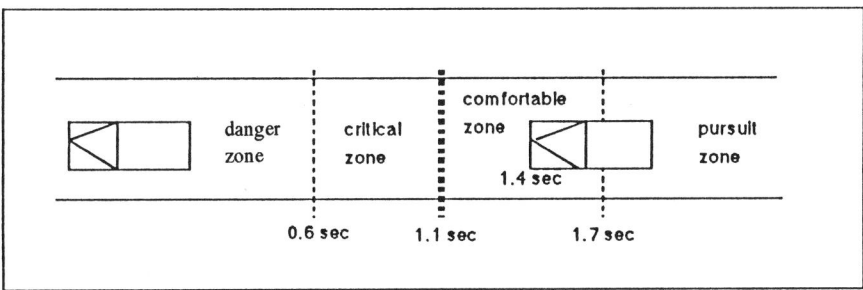

Figure 3 Spacing behavior in driving

The nearest zone might be called a "danger zone". When drivers go into this zone (within 0.6 sec with regard to time headway), they experience a dangerous feeling of potential collision with the car ahead. The range of 0.6 sec to 1.1 sec can be called a "critical zone". This zone lies between the danger zone and the normal driving zone. When drivers enter this zone for some reason, they should then return to the safe zone. The normal driving zone can be considered to exist between the minimum subjective safe distance and the distance which drivers feel to be neither too far nor too near, ie the zero point in terms of subjective risk. Subjects in this experiment appear to feel obliged to drive their cars within this zone under normal driving conditions, although the distance is smaller than they would want to maintain.

Figure 4 shows the distribution of time headway which was observed on the same road (Route 286). It can be observed that just over half of the drivers followed the leading car closer than "zero risk" time headway. It can be concluded that most drivers feel obliged to drive their cars with a smaller headway than they would like. This behavioral tendency appears to be related to the J-curve hypothesis of social norm behavior described by Allport (1934). Rockwell (1972) recommended that drivers maintain at least 2 seconds between themselves and the car ahead for safe driving. However, it seems difficult for drivers, on the average, to maintain this time headway. It is felt to feel uncomfortable because it differs from the social norm. The driving zone with a time headway of greater than 1.7 sec might be perceived as the pursuit zone, which is outside the normal driving zone. Drivers are also uncomfortable here because this zone too is perceived as being outside the social norm.

H. Ohta

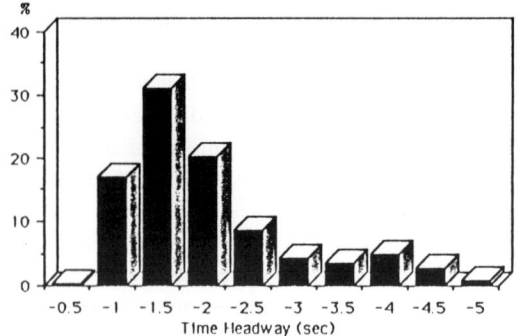

Figure 4 Distribution of time headway

2. EXPERIMENT

2.1 Purpose

One of the three components of the "wave" in distance headway (Figure 2) is amplitude. Analysis was carried out to clarify psychological variables which influence this component. One of the main variables which causes a change in distance headway is driving speed. Generally speaking, the faster the driving speed, the greater the distance maintained from the car ahead. The extent of this change in distance with speed, however, is different from driver to driver. Some drivers seem to be very sensitive to changes in headway, while some drivers seem not to be. Each driver displays a personal pattern of driving, eg, an individual pattern of adjusting the distance headway according to changes in speed of the car ahead. The amplitude of the wave is greater for drivers who sensitively change the distance headway according to speed, in comparison with drivers who try to maintain a constant distance headway even if driving speed is changed.

The author has attempted to clarify the individual characteristics of driver strategy as regards the response to other drivers' behavior or to the traffic environment. For the purpose of studying this theme, the present experiment was conducted to clarify the individual differences in the relationship between speed of the car ahead and the distance headway.

2.2 Method

2.2.1 Subjects

Thirty-one students served as subjects on a voluntary basis. Their age ranged from 19 to 26. Former driving experience ranged from 4 months to 6 years. All subjects drove on a daily basis.

2.2.2 Apparatus and Materials

The experiment was conducted in Sendai on Route 286, which has three lanes and a 50 km/hr speed limit, and on Tohoku Expressway, which has two lanes and an 80 km/h speed limit. Two automobiles were used. One was a station wagon equipped with laser radar for measuring distance. The other was a passenger car with a 1.3 litre engine. The researchers drove the equipped car ahead, with the subject-driven passenger car following behind.

2.2.3 Design and Procedure

Subjects were instructed by 2-way radio to follow the car ahead according to four separate guidelines.

(1) "Follow the car ahead at a distance which you feel is comfortable."

(2) "Approach until you begin to feel the distance is dangerous."

(3) "Follow the car ahead at the minimum safe distance."

(4) "Follow the car ahead at a distance which you feel to be neither too far nor too near."

Each subject performed each task four times at two different speeds: 50 km/h and 60 km/h, and eight times at the speed of 80 km/h over a period of approximately one hour, giving a total of sixteen separate trials per subject. The experiments were conducted only on non-rainy days.

After the field experiment, the following psychological tests were administered to each subject.

a. The Yatabe-Guilford personality inventory test

b. The aptitude test for drivers developed by Yamashita (1985). The basis of this test is the theory of attribution of responsibility.

c. The aptitude test for drivers developed by Nagayama which is based on Drake's theory (Nakayama Y, & Fujimoto T, 1971).

d. The diagnostic test of risk perception developed by Fukazawa (1983).

e. The experiment for measuring risk-taking level (Cohen, 1940).

f. Multiple choice reaction time.

2.3 Results

2.3.1 Three types of drivers classified according to car following behavior

Drivers can be classified into three types according to car-following behavior from the viewpoint of the relationship between driving speed and distance headway. Figure 5-Figure 7 give examples of these three types of drivers. Type 1 (Figure 5) is the driver who tries to maintain a constant time headway. Type 2 (Figure 6) is the driver who tries to maintain a constant distance headway. Type 3 (Figure 7) is the driver who does not sensitively change distance headway according to speed but changes his car-following behavior depending on the road type; in the present experiment drivers who are classified in this type category drove differently on the highway and on the local road in terms of distance headway.

2.3.2 Psychological basis for drivers' car-following behavior

Type 1 drivers display a wave of large amplitude with high frequency because they try to change their distance headway according to the changes in speed of the car ahead. Type 2 drivers display a flat wave (low amplitude, low frequency) because they try to maintain distance headway constant even if the speed of the car ahead changes. Type 3 drivers also

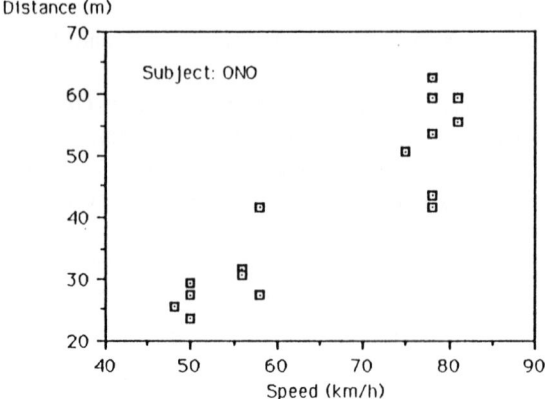

Figure 5. An example of Type 1

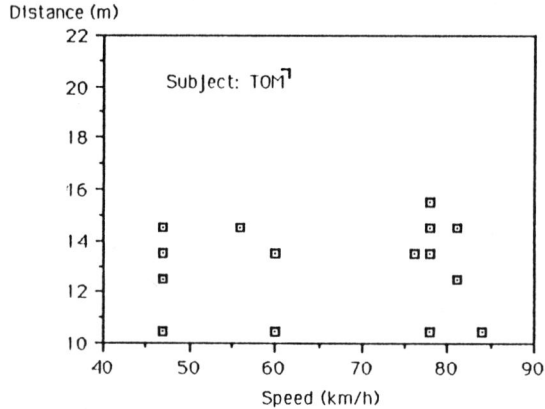

Figure 6. An example of Type 2

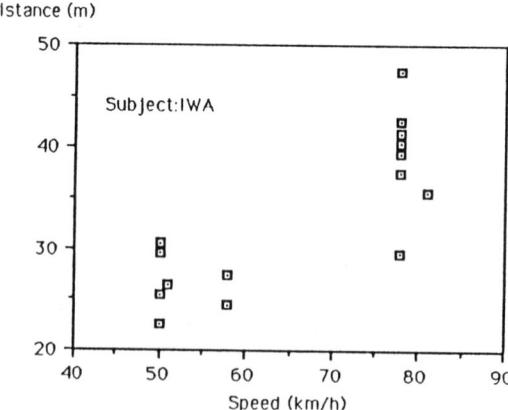

Figure 7. An example of Type 3

display the same kind of wave as type 2, but in observation of the overall wave shape for their driving on various kinds of road, it is seen that amplitude and frequency are both greater in comparison with type 2.

The degree of proximity in driving is understood by the time headway figure, which is calculated using speed and distance figures. The method of multi-variate analysis, quantitative theory 3 developed by Hayashi (1983), was used to clarify the individual patterns of proximity. Analysis was made of the relationship between the three different types of drivers mentioned above, as regards time headway, personality and safe driving attitude. Quantitative theory 3 is a type of factor analysis which may be used for the purpose of grouping variables whose raw data are categorical. As a preliminary procedure, values for each variable are categorized into two groups; subjects were divided into groups according to their scores for each variable. For the variable "Time Headway", subjects were divided into three groups. Time headway of the first group is less than 1.0 sec. For the second group it is between 1.0 and 1.6 sec. For the third group it is more than 1.6 sec. The distribution of time headway almost fits the Semi-Poisson curve as shown in Figure 8. The grouping of subjects according to time headway was carried out by referring to this distribution.

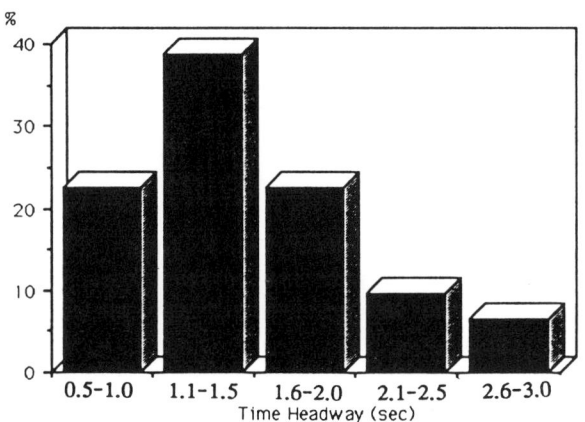

Figure 8 Distribution of time headway

After categorizing each variable, quantitative theory 3 was used to examine the relationship between these variables. The results of this analysis are shown in Figure 9; each variable is plotted according to first factor loadings and second factor loadings (the value of factor loadings are shown in Table 2). In Figure 9, the X axis can be interpreted as a dimensions of driver affect and the Y axis as a safety attitude.

The main variables which have plus values according to the first factor loading shown on the X axis in figure 9 are as follows:
    (1) Subjects who attribute the responsibility of accident to themselves.
    (2) Subjects with longer time headway.
The variables which have minus values on the same axis:
    (1) Type 2.
    (2) Confidence of drive technique.
According to the second factor (Y axis), the main variables which show plus values are:

(1) Subjects with unstable affection.
(2) Subjects with small time headway.
(3) Subjects with accurate mental activity.
The variables which show minus values are:
    (1) Type 1.
    (2) Subjects located around the mode level in the distribution of time headway.

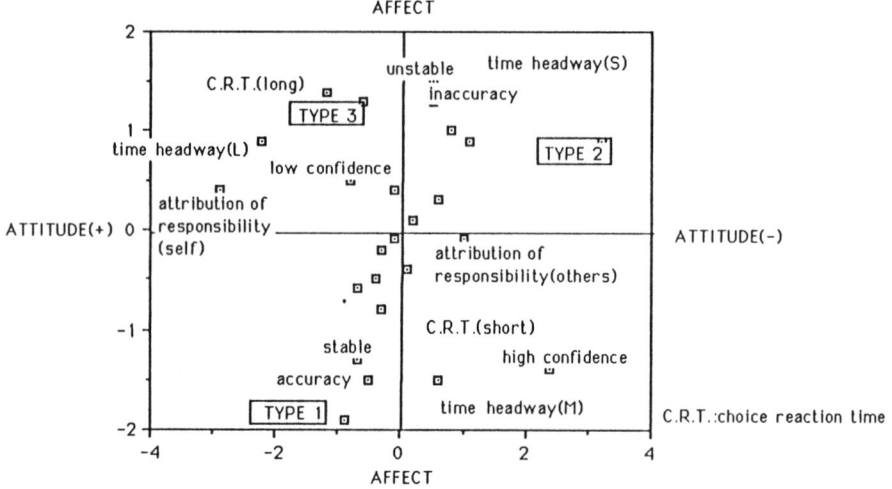

Figure 9 The result of quantification theory 3

3. DISCUSSION

According to Allport's double J curve theory, social behavior is influenced by both formal and informal norms. Individuals living in the same society or organization are forced to conform to the group's built-in norms. However, there are various kinds of individuals: Some people try to conform and some people do not. The distribution of social behavior, as a result, may be seen to resemble a mirror-imaged J curve on the X axis; with people on the left side displaying conformist behaviour and people who are on the right side displaying nonconformist behavior. The same range in social behavior is observable in car-following. Drivers can be considered to conform to both the formal norm (regulations and safety rules) and the informal norm (the stream of traffic flow). Some drivers seem not to want to comply with either formal or informal norms and may attempt to maintain a very short distance between themselves and the car ahead. Some drivers seem to wish to conform to the informal norm rather than the formal norm. Accordingly, they drive their cars at the most socially favourable distance. Other drivers seem to wish to maintain a sufficient distance between themselves and the car ahead for safety or some other reason. The greatest number of drivers fall into the second category. As a result, the distribution of time headway (calculated by speed and distance) displays the so called double J curve which is similar to the Semi-Poisson distribution.

Item	variable	factor 1	factor 2
Time headway			
	1. short	1.96	1.75
	2. medium	0.59	-1.53
	3. long	-2.20	0.92
Y-G personality test (affect)			
	4. stable	-0.69	-1.34
	5. unstable	0.74	1.43
Y-G personality test			
	6. introvert	0.56	0.34
	7. extrovert	-0.26	-0.16
Attribution of responsibility			
	8. to others	1.02	-0.14
	9. to self	-2.93	0.41
Confidence of driving			
	10. high	2.36	-1.43
	11. low	-0.82	0.50
Risk taking			
	12. high	0.09	-0.41
	13. low	-0.09	0.44
Choice reaction time			
	14. short	0.89	-0.99
	15. long	-1.23	1.37
Aptitude for safe driving			
	16. poor	1.11	1.87
	17. good	-0.70	-0.55
Rapidity of judgement			
	18. slow	-0.98	1.15
	19. quick	0.81	-0.95
Accuracy of judgement			
	20. poor	0.46	1.45
	21. good	-0.49	-1.55
Rapidity of action			
	22. slow	0.78	0.99
	23. quick	-0.37	-0.47
Risk perception			
	24. poor	-0.29	-0.83
	25. good	0.46	1.31
Attitude to risky situation			
	26. poor	-0.14	-0.06
	27. good	0.20	0.08
Relationship between speed and distance headway			
	28. type 1	-0.94	-1.91
	29. type 2	-0.62	1.34
	30. type 3	3.21	0.90
EIGEN VALUE		0.180	0.164
CUMULATIVE CONTRIBUTION (%)		15.75	30.09

Table 1 The result of quantification theory 3 (loadings regarding factor 1 and factor 2)

A similar matrix may be drawn (Figure 10) which shows a combination of the formal norm (safety rules regulations) and informal norm (traffic flow). Each cell in the matrix can be considered thus: Drivers in cell A attempt to conform to both the formal norm and the informal norm. They drive their car by maintaining the time headway which is greater than the mode value but not too deviant from it. Both safety attitude and stability of affect are thought to be best. They may be sensitive to changes in speed and adjust the distance according to speed. As regards Figure 9, these drivers belong to the third quadrant. Drivers in cell B try to conform to the informal norm more than the formal norm. Their time headway is around the value of mode of the distribution. Their safe driving attitudes are poor. However, they display stable affect. They made also be sensitive to speed.

Drivers in cell C try to conform more to the formal norm (safety). Their attitude regarding safe driving is highly developed although they display unstable affect. They do not comply with the informal norm because the distance headway is too small. They do not alter their distance headway according to speed, but they alter their time headway according to different kinds of roads, eg local roads and highways.

Drivers in cell D seem not to want to conform to either the formal or the informal norm. They try to maintain distance headway even if driving speed changes from 50 km/h to 80 km/h. Their time headway is very short. Their attitude to safety is poorly developed and they are unstable. The drivers in this cell may be considered the most dangerous.

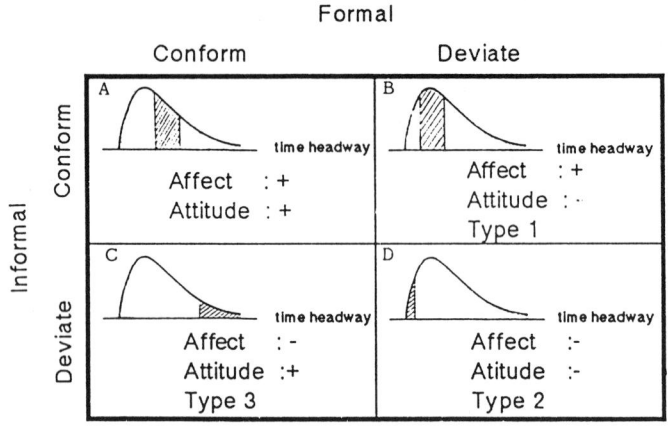

Figure 10 Using Allport's theory

REFERENCES

Allport F.H. (1934).   J-curve hypothesis of conforming behavior.   Journal of Social Psychology, 5:141-183.

Cohen J., Darnaley E.J., Hansel C.E. (1956).   Risk and hazard.   Operational Research Quarterly, 7(3).

Drake C.D. (194). Accident-proneness: a hypothesis. Character & Personality, 9:335-341.

Fukazawa N. (1983). On the risk perception. Japanese Journal of Applied Psychology, 8:1-12.

Hall E.T. (1966).   The Hidden Dimension (Doubleday & Co., New York).

Hayashi C. (1982). Quantitative Theory and Data Processing (in Japanese), (Asakura Publ. Co. Ltd).

Klebelsberg D. (1982). Verkehrspsychologie (Springer-Verlag, Berlin, Heidelberg, 1982).

Nagayama Y., Fujimoto T. (1971).   NF Safe Driving Aptitude Test (in Japanese), (Kigyohaihatsusenta).

Rockwell T.H. (1972). Skills, Judgement and Information Acquisition in Driving. In: Forbes, T.W. ed., "Human Factors in Highway Traffic Safety Research" (Wiley, New York). pp 133-164.

Yamashita N. (1985).   A study of attitude scale (1) - On a factor of attribution of responsibility. Reports of Chiba Institute of Technology, 21:81-88.

VISION IN VEHICLES – IV
A.G. Gale et al. (Editors)

VISUAL CUES FOR THE DETECTION OF IMPENDING COLLISION AT CROSSROADS: THE CASE OF CURVILINEAR SELF-MOTION

Catherine BERTHELON[1] & Daniel MESTRE[2]

[1]INRETS (MA), Salon-de-Provence, France
[2]University Aix-Marseille II & CNRS, Marseille, France

Abstract

It has been previously found that perception of the trajectory of a moving object (such as an approaching vehicle) is perturbed by the global optic flow motion resulting from the observer's rectilinear self-motion (e.g. when driving a car). In such a situation, the observer's perception relies on both global and local visual information, such as relative motion between the moving object and fixed elements in the environment.

An experiment is reported in which computerized car driving simulations were used to manipulate environment characteristics and vehicles' trajectories. Visual displays simulated the curvilinear approach of an observer to an intersection. An approaching vehicle, coming from the right of the curved road, was programmed to reach this intersection either 1 second before or after the observer. Visual displays projected on a TV monitor or on a large screen were stopped 2 seconds before the observer reached the intersection. Subjects had to decide whether they would have reached the intersection before, after or at the same time as the approaching vehicle. Overall, responses were correct in 62% of cases. A spatial reference point (road sign) near the intersection improved performance. However, judgements became increasingly difficult for small curvature radii where relative visual motion becomes ambiguous. Moreover, subjects appeared to rely more on local visual cues when visual information was presented on a TV monitor, and on global visual cues when a large-screen display was used.

1. INTRODUCTION

During motion, a car driver must not only control his/her trajectory but also anticipate the motion of other vehicles. In this respect, approaching an intersection is a frequent situation in which a correct evaluation of ongoing traffic is of vital importance. However, it is difficult to study this situation systematically and ethically in natural traffic conditions. Here, the use of graphics simulations of car driving counterbalances these problems reproducing road scenes with a good degree of realism (see figure 1). This enables the study of the role of visual factors in the perception and control of driving, by direct and easy replication of different potential sources of information.

Figure 1 : Example of a road scene taken for the study. Here, the approaching vehicle will reach the intersection 1 second after the observer's vehicle.

2. VISUAL ANALYSIS OF THE PROBLEM : OPTIC FLOW

The observer's self-motion in a stable environment produces an apparent visual motion or optic flow of all the physically static objects in this environment, in a direction running counter to that of the self-motion (Gibson, 1979). The importance of optic flow for perceiving the direction of self-motion and controlling the trajectories in a wide range of environments is well known (Lee and Lishman, 1977; Riemersma, 1982; Warren & al, 1991).

In this context, the visual motion of an object which is actually moving, as perceived by a moving observer, is the consequence of its objective motion and optic flow resulting from the observer's displacement. The moving object is therefore animated by a visual motion which differs from that of the fixed points in the environment. The latter assist detection of the moving object's presence but, perceptually, they may cause difficulty in analyzing its motion.   On the other hand, it is known that detection of a moving object by a static observer is enhanced by the presence of stationary references (Leibowitz, 1955). These references are even more effective, the closer they are to the moving object (Palmer, 1986). When an observer is moving, the detection of a moving object should therefore be improved, by the presence of a reference factor, e.g. a stable environmental point near the moving object.

These hypotheses have been tested for rectilinear self-motion (Berthelon and Mestre, 1990). Without a reference point near an approached intersection, an induction effect of the radiant global flow results from self-motion on perception of the motion of an object also moving towards the intersection. A reference point consistently improves this perception but it produces a localized induction resulting from the observer's analysis of the relative visual motion between the reference and the moving object.

The purpose of the present work was to test whether these phenomena can be found when the observer's motion is curvilinear, in particular on small curvature radii where there is evidence of trajectory control problems and under-estimation of curvature radii (Warren et al., 1991).

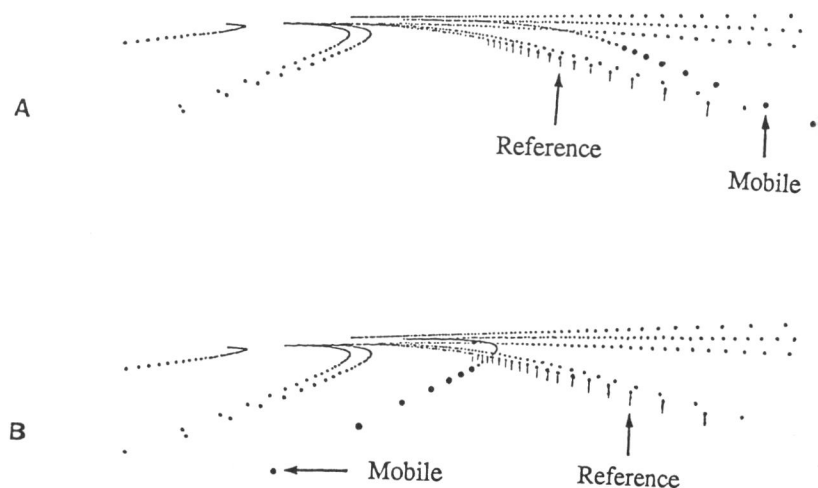

Figure 2 : Visual flow displays for a curvilinear motion to the left, parallel to the ground in a stable environment. A moving object arrives perpendicularly from outside the curvature and will arrive at the intersection A) one second after the observer, B) one second before the observer.

Moreover, for a curvilinear trajectory the optic flow is complex in that as the direction of motion no longer corresponds to a simple translation, as in a rectilinear trajectory, but also includes a rotation component (Gordon, 1966; Lee, 1980). The apparent movement of the object varies according to its position inside or outside the observer's trajectory (see figure 2). For a curved path to the left, the visual motion of a vehicle approaching from outside the trajectory and arriving at the intersection after the observer, is always in the same direction as that of the fixed environment points located outside the curvature. If it arrives at the intersection before the observer, the visual motion is inverted. From a direction that was initially similar to that of the environment points placed outside the curvature, it changes to the opposite direction (see figure 2). Moreover, if the approaching vehicle arrives at the intersection after the observer, it comes visually closer to a reference point located near the intersection and outside the curvature but never crosses the reference point before the observer reaches the intersection. Inversely, if it arrives before the observer, it always visually crosses the reference point before arriving at the intersection (see figure 2).

There would therefore seem to be two cues which make it possible to distinguish whether an approaching vehicle will arrive at an intersection before or after an observer: the inversion (or not) of its visual motion and the fact that it crosses (or does not cross) a spatial reference point located near the intersection. The effect of these cues on relative motion perception was examined empirically.

3. EXPERIMENTAL SECTION

3.1 General methodology
The visual sequences used for this experiment were displayed using an IRIS 4D/70 Silicon Graphics "3D surface" type unit. The "real time" image obtained was recorded onto a 3/4 Umatic video tape. Sequences simulated the self-motion of an observer on a curved road, approaching an intersection where another vehicle is arriving (see figure 1).

3.2 Experimental conditions
The subjects experienced curvilinear travel to the left, at 72 km/h. Their trajectory curvature radii were : 120, 240 or 425 m, starting 160 m before the intersection. Each visual sequence was interrupted two seconds before the subject reached the intersection. The approaching vehicle arrived rectilinearly from the right of the intersection, at 20 km/h. It could arrive at the intersection 1 sec. before or after the subject. In half of the sequences a road sign was placed near the intersection. Each sequence was shown five times at random, in the same order. There were therefore 60 visual sequences (3 radii, presence or absence of a road sign, 2 conditions of arrival of the approaching vehicle and 5 trials) which were shown to each subject both on a large screen and also on a TV monitor.

3.3 Visual motion analysis
First, it can be noted that, for a given speed, the smaller the trajectory curvature radius, the greater the rotational component in the visual motion of fixed points in the environment.

In our experimental conditions, when the approaching vehicle arrives at the intersection after the subject, it does not cross the reference point and the direction of its visual motion does not change. When it arrives at the intersection before a subject, who is approaching with a 120 m radius, the inversion of its visual motion is performed 1.7 seconds before arrival at the intersection. Hence it is not perceived as it occurs after the sequence has been interrupted (figure 3A). With a radius of 240 m, the visual motion is perceptibly inverted when the approaching vehicle crosses the road sign i.e. 2.4 seconds before arriving at the intersection (figure 3B). With a radius of 425 m, this occurs 3.3 seconds before arriving at the intersection viz. before the approaching vehicle crosses the road sign (figure 3C). The visual crossing between the vehicle and the road sign always occurs approximately 2.4 seconds before the observer arrives at the intersection i.e. 0.4 seconds before the visual sequences are interrupted, whatever the curvature radius of the motion trajectory.

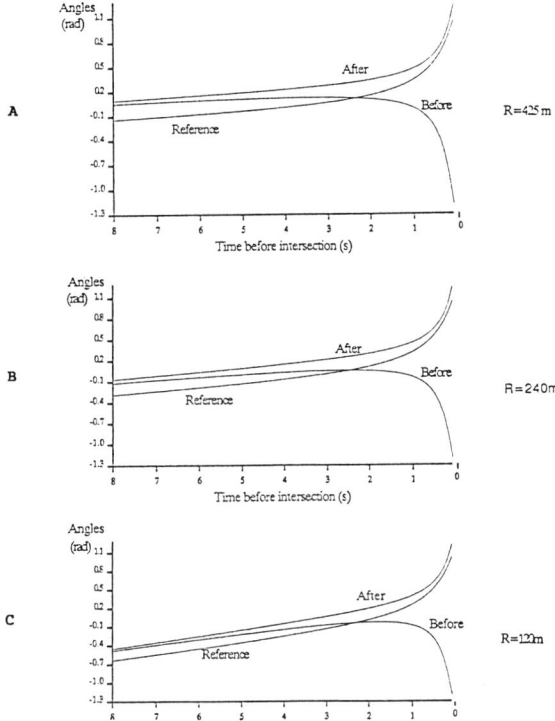

Figure 3 : Angular position of the visual scene features during a curvilinear motion towards the left as a function of time before the intersection. A) R=120 m, B) R=240 m, C) R=425 m.

3.4 The subjects

Twelve experienced drivers, with normal vision, acted as subjects in this experiment. They received payment. They were asked to judge whether the approaching vehicle would arrive at the intersection before or after as they would.

3.5 Results

62.5% of the responses from among all the responses given by the subjects were correct. The presence of a road sign improved performance from 59% correct responses to 65% correct.

Performance was lower with a 120 m radius (57% correct responses) than with radii of 425 m and 240 m combined (m=65% correct). This reduced performance is associated with a difficulty in recognising the condition where the approaching vehicle will arrive at the intersection before the subject. The percentage of correct 'before' responses was indeed lower for a 120 m radius (51%) than for the two other radii combined (70%).

The road sign and radius factors interacted essentially on the percentages of correct 'before' responses. Thus, with a road sign, these percentages were higher with a 240 m radius (80%) than for the two other radii (m=62%). Without a road sign, they are greater with 240 m and 425 m radii (m=68%), than with a 120 m radius (47%).

The way in which the information was displayed did not significantly influence subject performance (61% correct with the TV monitor, 63% correct on the large screen). However there were more correct 'after' responses using the large screen (67%) than with the TV monitor (54%) and inversely, there were fewer correct 'before' responses using the large screen (59%) than with the TV monitor (69%).

On the TV monitor, the radius had no significant effect but the presence of a road sign improved subject performance (65% correct with the road sign, 57% without it). Radius and road sign interact on the percentages of correct 'before' responses. With a road sign, more 'before' responses were correct with 240 m radii (88%), than with 120 m and 425 m radii combined (65.5%). In the absence of a road sign, they were greater with 240 m and 425 m radii combined (m=71.5%) than with a 120 m radius (52%).

On the large screen, subject performance was worse with a 120 m radius (57.5% correct) than with the two other radii combined (m=66% correct). This is linked to the fact that there were fewer correct 'before' responses with a 120m radius (46%) than with the two other radii combined (66.5%). The presence of a road sign did not significantly improve performance (65.8% correct with a road sign, 60.8% without it).

4. DISCUSSION

The purpose of this study was to investigate the accuracy with which an observer in apparent curvilinear motion is able to perceive relative movement of a vehicle whose trajectory intercepts his own. The results demonstrate the informative value of the visual information displayed and the observer's ability to analyze it thus confirming previous findings reported by Todd (1981). However, global optic flow seems to influence motion analysis of the approaching vehicle, particularly when the motion trajectory of the observer follows a sharp curve, as shown by the subject's difficulty in recognizing those situations in which an approaching vehicle will arrive at the intersection before they do.

Furthermore, whether the visual motion of an approaching vehicle inverts or not , relative to fixed environmental reference points seems to be a basic cue for the identification of its likely interaction with the observer. Thus, contrary to what occurs for 240 m and 425 m radii, when it arrived at the intersection before subjects travelling on a 120m radius, the inversion of its visual motion occurred after the visual sequences had been interrupted and the subjects showed special difficulties in analyzing its objective movement.

The presence of a road sign near the intersection consistently improved subject performance. By its apparent motion, a road sign makes it easier to distinguish the condition where the approaching vehicle arrives at the intersection before the subject (visual crossing with the road sign) from the condition where it arrives afterwards (no visual crossing). Thus, subjects could take the relative motion between the road sign and the approaching vehicle (motion parallax) into account when analyzing the actual movement. The "local" effect of the road sign seems to reduce the overall optic flow induction effect on perceived motion of the approaching vehicle.

In this respect, the cues provided by "visual crossing with road sign" and "inversion of visual motion of approaching vehicle" are complementary. Notably, with a 240m radius, the road sign makes it possible to recognise correctly the condition where the approaching vehicle will arrive at the intersection before the subject. Since in this condition the observer coincides with the approaching vehicle at the same instant that visual motion inversion takes place, the cue of 'visual crossing with road sign' assumes significance.

Finally, it can be noted that the optic flow and road sign effects are mediated by the information display mode. With a TV monitor, the road sign plays a significant part and the condition where the approaching vehicle will arrive at the intersection before the subject (in particular with 240 m radius) is better recognised than with a large-screen display. The local induction effect of the road sign is very clear and could be assimilated with effects predictable from a task involving distinguishing of object motion in a two-dimensional space (Gogel, 1984). By contrast, on a large screen, motion analysis of the other vehicle depends to a great extent on the curvature of the observer's approach trajectory and the condition where the other approaching vehicle arrives after the observer is recognised better than on a TV monitor. This suggests that subjects do not perceive the individual motion of the approaching vehicle but the overall motion or motion configurations in three-dimensional space. The substantial and global effect of optic flow would seem therefore to outweigh the "local" effect of the road sign.

This observed influence of information display mode is probably linked to the size of the visual stimulation, which enhances the sensation of self-motion (Berthoz et al., 1975) and also the perception of depth. This is in line with results obtained by Probst et al. (1986), which show that motion detection in central vision is more difficult when there is concurrent peripheral stimulation. It still remains to be shown that visual stimulation by a large screen produces phenomena similar to those which would occur in normal driving situations.

5. ACKNOWLEDGEMENTS

We wish to thank P. Gauriat (INRETS) for designing the displays and D. Benza (University Aix-Marseille II) for programming the visual motion analysis.

6. REFERENCES

Berthelon, C. & Mestre, D. (1990), Perception visuelle d'un mobile lors du déplacement : application à la conduite automobile. Le Travail Humain, 53 (1), 17-32.

Berthoz, A., Pavard, B., Young & L.R. (1975), Perception of linear horizontal self-motion induced by peripheral vision (linear vection): basic characteristics and visual-vestibular interactions. Experimental Brain Research, 16, 476-489.

Gibson, J.J. (1979, The ecological approach to visual perception. Boston: Houghton Mifflin.

Gogel, W.C. (1984), Le principe de proximité dans la perception visuelle. In C. Bonnet (Ed) La perception visuelle. Paris: Belin (Bibliothèque pour la Science).

Gordon, D.A. (1966), Perceptual mechanisms in vehicular guidance. Public Roads, 34, 53-68.

Lee, D.N. & Lishman, R. (1977), Visual control of locomotion. Scandinavian Journal of Psychology, 18, 224-230.

Lee, D.N. (1980), The optic flow field : The foundation of vision. Philosophical Transactions of the Royal Society of London, B 290, 169-179.

Leibowitz, H. (1955), Effect of reference lines on the discrimination of movement. Journal of the Optical Society of America, 45, 829-830.

Palmer, J. (1986), Mechanisms of displacement discrimination with a visual reference. Vision Research, 26, 1939-1947.

Probst, T., Brandt, T. & Degner, D. (1986), Object-motion detection affected by concurrent self-motion perception : psychophysics of a new phenomenon. Behavioral Brain Research, 22, 1-11.

Riemersma, J.B.J. (1982), Perception and control of deviations from a straight course: a field experiment. Report of the Institute for Perception TNO, Soesterberg, The Netherlands.

Todd, J.T. (1981), Visual information about moving object. Journal of Experimental Psychology : Human Perception and Performance, 7, 95-810.

Warren, W.H., Mestre, D., Blackwell, A.W. & Morris, M.W. (1991), Perception of circular heading from optical flow. Journal of Experimental Psychology : Human Perception and Performance, 17, 28-43.

VISION IN VEHICLES – IV
A.G. Gale et al. (Editors)
1993 Elsevier Science Publishers B.V.

THE INFLUENCE OF SIGHT DISTANCE ON SUBJECTS' LATERAL CONTROL: A STUDY OF SIMULATED DRIVING IN FOG.

Lisbeth HARMS

Swedish Road and Traffic Research Institute, VTIS-58101 Linköping, Sweden.

Abstract

A driving simulator was used for investigating the influence of sight distance on subjects' speed and lateral position on a simulation of a real road. The sight distance was varied by simulated fog delimiting the sight distance to approximately 480 m, 120 m, 60 m and 30 m. Sight distance was found to influence subjects' mean speed, but not their lateral position and lateral variation.

The correlation between lateral position in free-sight conditions and conditions of reduced sight (based on 100m intervals of the driving route) was positive but it declined with decreasing sight distance. This finding strongly suggested that the pattern of lateral variation differed between sight distances. Furthermore short sight distances resulted in a weaker relationship between the angular deflection of the road and lateral position than longer ones. The mean z-scores in 100-m intervals of the driving route indicated that lateral deviations were both less sensitive to road curvature and less consistent between subjects for shorter sight distances than for longer ones. This result may suggest that reduced sight increases the amount of random variation in the subjects' lateral positions.

1. INTRODUCTION

Reduced visibility poses a serious problem to car driving since both longitudinal and lateral control are probably based on environmental references (OECD, 1976). Most car drivers reduce their speed when confronted with sight restrictions, but their speed reductions are usually found insufficient to prevent their braking distance from exceeding their sight distance (Sumner et al. 1976, Hills, 1980 and Hawkins, 1988). Reduced visibility may also disturb drivers' lateral control by forcing them to adjust their lateral position on the basis of few, close and rapidly changing visual cues. Thus, under conditions of reduced sight lateral control can probably not be maintained without speed reductions.

Previously Tenkink (1988) demonstrated that the amount of lateral variation increased with decreasing sight distance when the speed level was held constant, whereas in free-speed conditions the increase in subjects' lateral variation was apparently compensated by speed reductions. However, it was also found that the speed difference between a straight road and a curved road was smaller for short sight distances than for long ones, and that the subjects lateral position in curves differed between sight conditions. Both these findings indicated that subjects' lateral control was actually affected by restricted sight.

If reduced visibility does force drivers to use different visual cues for their lateral control than they would use during free-sight, their pattern of lateral variations on a driving route may differ considerably between sight distances. The present study investigated subjects' speed and lateral position on a simulation of a rural road with different fog densities. The influence of reduced sight on subjects' pattern of lateral variation in 100-m intervals of the driving route was analyzed and compared between sight conditions.

2. METHOD

2.1 Apparatus and simulations

The moving-base driving simulator at the Swedish Road and Traffic Research Institute, was used for the experiment (see Nordmark et al., 1985 for technical specification of the driving simulator). The simulation of horizontal and vertical curvature was based on measures of the angular deflections in 12 m intervals of a 3.2 km long and 7 m wide section of a rural road. The road included 3 major curves: Two reverse curves with minimum radii of 250 m occupied a total of 1.2 km of the road section, and one reverse curve with a minimum radius of 430 m occupied 400 m. The mean angular deflection calculated for 100-m intervals of the driving route varied between -23 deg (left-hand angles) and +22 deg (right-hand angles). The angular deflection in "straight" sections of the road varied between 0-5 deg. Road markings followed Swedish standard with intermittent edge and centerlines.

"Fog" was simulated by continuous reduction of the chromatic value of display pixels as a function of their calculated distance from the driver. The maximum reduction, representing non-transparent fog, was obtained at distances of approximately 480 m (free-sight), 120 m, 60 m and 30 m (see Lidström, 1991 for specification of the fog function).

2.2 Procedure

Subjects participated in a comprehensive experiment including (1) driving on a real road, (2) driving on a simulation of the road and (3) driving on a simulated section of the road in fog.   This paper is concerned with fog-trials only. Subjects completed 24 fog-trials (six at each sight distance) each of 3.6 km.

Fog-trials succeeded no-fog trials of 7.6 km and included 400 m warm-up driving before the 3.2 km experimental driving. Speed and lateral position were registered in successive 5-m intervals of the driving route. Driving speed was measured in kilometers per hour and the lateral position was measured in centimeters from the (imaginary) left front-wheel to the centerline.

2.3 Subjects

Seven subjects participated in the experiment. They were aged 24-54 years with a mean age of 29.8 years. Their reported amount of driving was 10.000-35.000 km/year with a mean of approximately 14.000 km/year. They were trained in the driving simulator before performing experimental sessions. The order in which sight distances were tested was balanced across subjects and over successive sessions of individual subjects.

3. RESULTS

Table 1 presents the mean speed of individual subjects for the four different sight distances.

Table 1.: Mean speed (km/h) and standard deviations for the four   sight distances: 30m, 60m, 120m and 480m.

SIGHT DISTANCE								
	30m		60m		120m		480m (free sight)	
Subject	Speed	s.d.	Speed	s.d.	Speed	s.d.	Speed	s.d.
1	58.6	8.6	62.5	4.0	63.6	3.5	70.0	3.2
2	65.2	7.2	72.5	7.3	75.5	7.5	83.4	5.3
3	70.3	5.0	82.2	5.7	85.1	5.7	89.7	3.9
4	55.6	4.1	68.1	6.0	73.5	5.0	86.7	1.9
5	37.9	3.5	47.6	4.1	57.9	5.1	79.0	5.1
6	55.3	2.4	61.0	3.6	67.5	3.0	71.7	2.6
7	63.8	5.8	72.5	5.8	75.6	5.2	74.4	5.6
Across Ss	58.1	10.7	66.7	11.6	71.3	9.8	79.3	8.2

As can be seen the mean speed decreased with decreasing sight distance but both speed level and speed reduction varied between subjects. On average the mean speed for conditions with free sight was 79.3 km/h, mean speed for 120-m sight was 71.3 km/h and for the shorter sight distances of 60-m and 30-m the mean speed was 66.7 and 58.1 km/h respectively. Driving speed was subjected to a standard analysis of variance with subjects and sight distance as independent variables. Speed difference between subjects ($F(6,18)=11.16$, $p < .0001$) and between sight distances ($F(3,18)= 20.89$, $p < .0001$) both were found to be significant.

On average the lateral position for free-sight was .71 m. In conditions with reduced sight the lateral position was .71 m for 120-m sight and .70 m and 63 m for sight distances of 60 m and 30 m respectively. The mean standard deviation for free-sight conditions was .27 m.   For all other sight distances it was .23 m. The lateral position was subjected to a standard analysis of variance with subjects and sight distance as independent variables. The difference in lateral position between subjects was significant $F(6,18)= 42.00$, $p < .0001$) whereas the effect of sight distance was not ($F(3,18)=0.81$, $p > .5$).

Table 2 presents the distance to the centerline for individual subjects and its standard deviation. Both the lateral position and standard deviation varied between subjects, whereas the influence of sight distance on these measures was small and differed between subjects.

Table 2.: Mean lateral position (meters from centerline) and standard deviation for the four sight distances: 30m, 60m, 120m   and 480m.

	SIGHT DISTANCE							
	30m		60m		120m		480m (free sight)	
Subject	pos	s.d.	pos	s.d.	pos	s.d.	pos	s.d.
1	.79	.12	.82	.11	.85	.11	.84	.14
2	.41	.20	.52	.23	.52	.23	.59	.25
3	.55	.18	.61	.20	.68	.25	.69	.31
4	.78	.23	.75	.25	.74	.19	.74	.22
5	.66	.15	.63	.18	.66	.18	.63	.22
6	.92	.20	.91	.21	.88	.21	.91	.29
7	.64	.13	.63	.16	.63	.17	.59	.18
Across Ss	.68	.23	.70	.23	.71	.23	.71	.27

The lateral position in each 100-m intervals of the driving route was compared between conditions of sight for each subject individually. Table 3 presents product-moment correlations between   subjects' lateral positions in conditions with free sight and conditions of reduced sight. Generally the coefficients were positive and generally their numerical value decreased with decreasing sight. Also the correlation between the deflection angle of the road in 100-m intervals and the subjects' lateral positions declined with decreasing sight.

Table 3.: Product-moment correlations between lateral position in free-sight conditions and conditions of reduced sight based on 100-metres intervals of the driving route.

	SIGHT DISTANCE		
Subject	30m	60m	120m
1	.01	.48	.46
2	.04	.72	.86
3	.66	.91	.94
4	.22	.69	.86
5	.60	.69	.92
6	.25	.72	.82
7	.77	.85	.95
Mean	.36	.72	.84

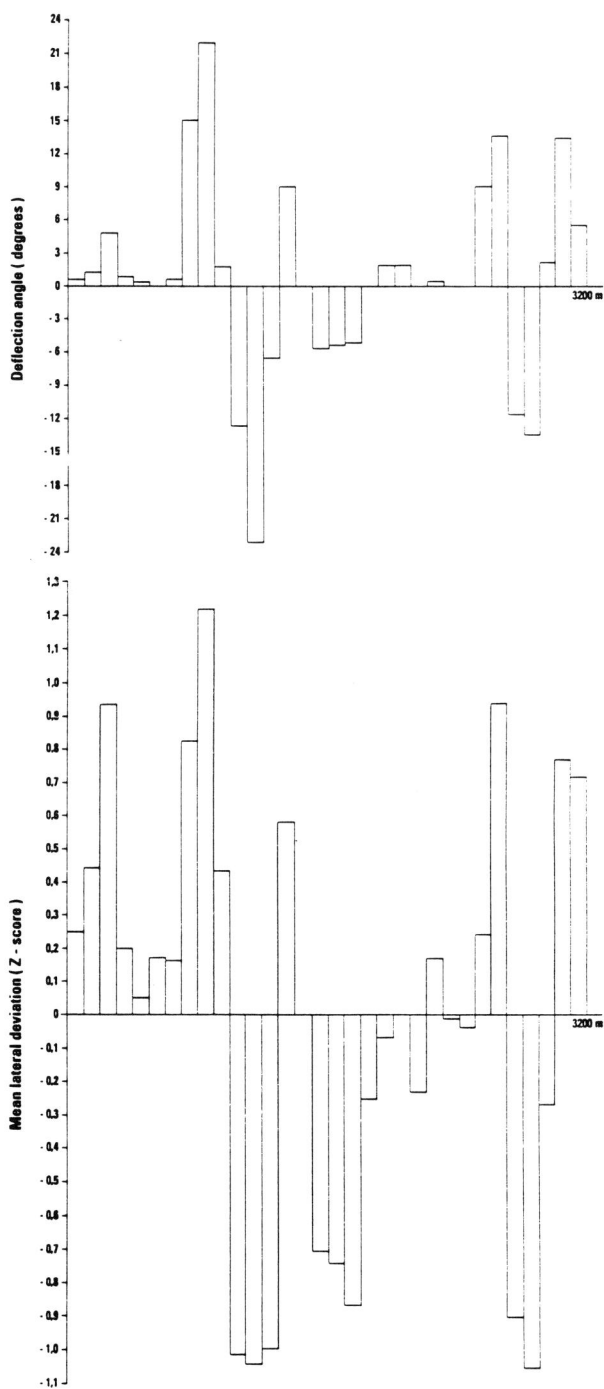

Figure 1: Upper: angular deflections (deg) in successive 100-metre intervals of the road.
Lower: lateral deviations (z-score) in the corresponding intervals in free-sight conditions.

The mean correlation between the horizontal angle of the road and the lateral position were .76 for conditions with freesight, .74 for 120-m sight, .58 for 60-m, and .20 for the 30-m sight distance.

The lateral deviation in successive 100-m intervals was estimated by converting the lateral position of individual subjects' to z-scores for each sight distance separately. Thus, the mean z-score in a 100-m interval reflected the average deviation from the mean in that interval within a certain sight condition. Figure 1 shows the angular deflection in successive 100-m intervals of the road (upper part) and the corresponding mean z-scores (lower part).

As can be seen in Figure 1 the z-scores followed the road curvature: Left-hand curves (negative angular deflections) were associated with negative z-scores indicating a displacement towards the center of the road, whereas right-hand curves were associated with positive z-values indicating a lateral deviation towards the road edge. Figure 2 presents the corresponding z-scores for each of the three sight distances: 120-m, 60-m, and 30-m.

Figure 2 illustrates the fact that the lateral deviations were more sensitive to road curvature the longer was the sight distance. Furthermore the pattern of z-scores

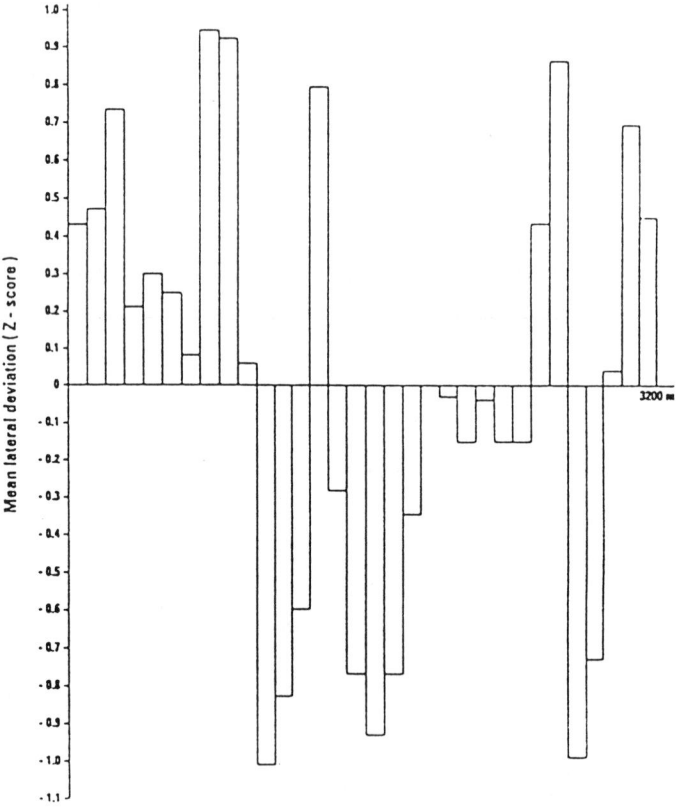

Figure 2a: The mean lateral deviation (z-score) in 100-m intervals of the 3.2 km road section in conditions with 120-m sight.

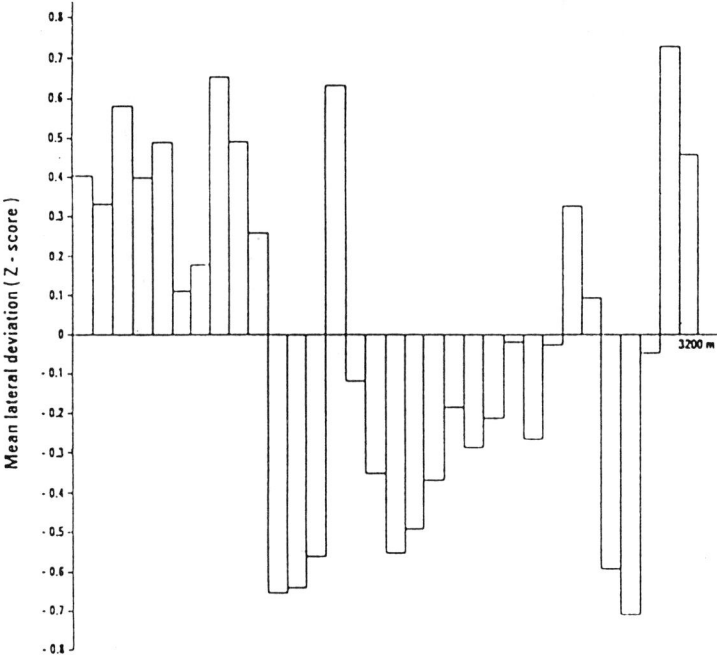

Figure 2b: The mean lateral deviation (z-score) in 100-m intervals of the 3.2 km road section in conditions with 60-m sight.

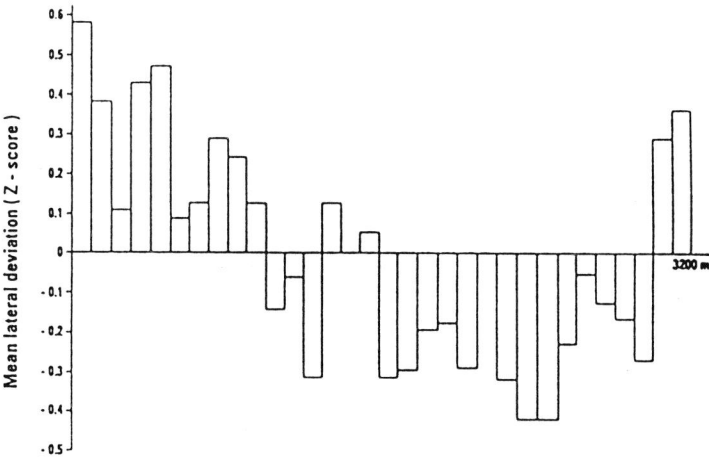

Figure 2: The mean lateral deviation (z-score) in 100-m intervals of the 3.2 km road section in conditions with 30-m sight.

demonstrated that the   lateral deviations were less consistent between subjects for short sight distance than for long ones. Thus, although the amount of lateral variation was rather unaffected by sight distance the different patterns of deviation on the driving route suggested a change in the efficiency of lateral control with sight distance.

4. DISCUSSION

The present study was consistent with previous studies in finding that a reduction in sight distance caused a spontaneous reduction of driving speed. The speed reductions were not sufficient to maintain a positive safety margin but they may have prevented reduced sight from increasing the amount of lateral variation.

The different patterns of lateral variation on the driving route, found in this study, suggested that subjects' lateral control was actually influenced in certain respects by sight distance. In free-sight conditions subjects consistently used their preview for compensating the road curvature i.e. their lateral displacements followed the direction of the curves. Sight reductions resulted in a gradual degradation of the visual references and apparently prevented the subjects from compensating road curvature by lateral displacements.

The change in the pattern of lateral deviations on the driving route between conditions of sight reflected both poorer sensitivity to road curvature for shorter sight distance than for long ones, and less consistent patterns of variation between subjects for short sight distances.

Thus, speed reductions may have prevented an increase in total amount of lateral variation on the driving route. Since reduced visibility deprived the subjects of visual references the amount   of random variation in their lateral positions on the driving route was apparently increased.

ACKNOWLEDGEMENT

This study was conducted with grants from The National Swedish Road Administration.

REFERENCES

Hawkins, R.K.(1988). Motorway traffic behaviour in reduced visibility conditions in Gale et al. (eds.) Vision in Vehicles II, North Holland, Amsterdam.
Hills, B.L. (1980). Vision visibility and perception in driving. Perception vol. 9, 183-216.
Lidström, M. (1991). R5/11 Fog effects, Version 1.0 91-03-12, (unpublished reference manual) VTI.
Nordmark, S., Jansson, H., Lidström M., and Palmkvist, G. (1985). A moving base driving simulator with a wide angle visual system. TRB 64. Annual meeting. TRB.
OECD (1976). Adverse weather, reduced visibility and road safety, driving in reduced visibility due to adverse weather, Road Research Report, OECD.
Sumner, R., Baguley, C. and Burton J. (1977). Driving in fog on the M4. Supplementary Report 281. TRRL.
Tenkink, E. (1988). Lane keeping and speed choice with restricted sight distances. In Rothengatter T. & deBuin R. (eds.) Road User Behaviour: Theory and Research.

5

VISUAL PERCEPTION
AND VEHICLE CONTROL:
VEHICLE SIGNALLING SYSTEMS

VISION IN VEHICLES – IV
A.G. Gale et al. (Editors)

AN EVALUATION OF REAR LIGHTING EQUIPMENT FOR VEHICLES

M. FOWKES and H.S. STOREY

Motor Industry Research Association, Watling Street, Nuneaton, Warwickshire, CV10 0TU, United Kingdom

Abstract
Lights fitted to the rear of a vehicle are used to convey a variety of information about that vehicle. This include information on whether the vehicle is braking, which direction it is likely to turn, whether it is likely to reverse or indeed just its physical position on the road. The success by which this information is perceived and acted upon by following drivers is therefore an important safety aspect of vehicle design. This paper assess the current practice within vehicle design by firstly giving an overview of the legislation that controls lighting equipment and installation. An experimental study is then described which employed driver response time measures to assess the effects of varying parameters associated with rear lighting layouts (light intensity, spacing and format of signal). This study involved the use of a secondary task technique and pseudo random presentation of rear lighting layouts. The subject test panel employed was chosen to improve the homogeneity of the sample, by selection of female drivers over the age of 50 years, as previous studies had suggested this to be the worst case subjects for this type of work. The results from this study are presented and the implications are then compared with current design practices on passenger cars.

1. INTRODUCTION

In situations of following traffic an important component of the visual information received by the driver is from the rear lights of the vehicle in front. Current rear lighting units on vehicles potentially convey a range of coded information on the present, or imminent, behaviour of that vehicle. Clearly any error in detection or interpretation of these signals by a following driver can increase the risk of an accident. In the most obvious case the non-detection and reaction to a brake light activation, and therefore deceleration, can obviously lead to a collision. Rear-end collisions of this nature account for a significant proportion of all road traffic accidents. Estimates of this proportion vary between countries and different operating environments. However, we can summarise by suggesting that approximately one in four road traffic accidents involve a vehicle-to-vehicle, rear end collision.

The identification of this type of accident has resulted both in considerable research and in some cases amendments to legislation affecting road vehicle design. An important example of this process was a programme of research in the USA that investigated the effectiveness of an additional high mounted brake light (HMBL) on reducing rear end collisions via a series of experiments and field trials. The conclusions from this programme eventually led to a change in US vehicle legislation that now requires the fitment of these devices. Legislation for vehicle design, construction and use is therefore an important facilitator in improving vehicle safety. This paper assesses some of the relevant research on the effectiveness of different parameters of vehicle rear lighting layouts. A review of the complex legislation applying to vehicle rear lights is given. A description is then given of the method and results from a recent laboratory study investigating rear lighting parameters and driver response time. Finally a brief summary is provided of current design practices on passenger cars.

2. LITERATURE SURVEY

Most vehicle rear light assemblies provide information on five basic functions. These functions are served by a variety of light sources namely, indication of presence (the rear or presence light), brake activation (the brake or stop light), intention to turn (the indicator or turn light), activation of reverse gear (reversing light) and the indication of presence in adverse conditions (rear fog or high intensity presence light). The variables open to manipulation are physical separation and geometric arrangement of light units, intensity and size of light units, colour coding of functions and the use of multiple light sources. Some of the published research literature is discussed below.

2.1 Separation of Lighting Functions
In an experiment which investigated the threshold for detecting separation between different lights at different distances, separations of 4, 6 and 8 inches under night time conditions were investigated and it was concluded that the best performance overall was noted from the widest separation between the lights, 8 inches in this experiment (Mortimer et al 1969). In a more recent experiment investigating the masking effects of high intensity rear lights on brake lights in fog, it was determined that a physical separation between the lights greatly aided detection of a brake signal. The largest recorded increase in improvement in this study was noted at the smallest separation distance (50 mm) with additional smaller improvements up to a separation of 150 mm (Helliar-Symons and Irving 1981).

2.2 Lighting Intensity
The visibility of rear lights at various levels of intensity has been investigated and observations that an intensity of more than 0.25 cd is required of a rear light to be seen at a distance of 73 m at night have been observed (Moore 1952) while in a later study it was concluded that visibility distance increased from 30 m at 2 cd to 73 m at 5000 cd in daytime fog conditions. This study went on to recommend that by increasing the intensity of rear lights to 1000 cd, the conspicuity of vehicles in fog would be improved (Moore and Smith 1966). The subjective noticeability of a flashing turn signal for intensities of 80, 120 and 200 cd has been addressed and it was observed that noticeability increased with intensity (Domas 1975) while other researchers have noted that as the ratio of brake light to presence light intensities increased reaction times of following drivers decreased (Rockwell and Safford 1966). A number of researchers have investigated the ability of

subjects to perceive different sorts of information from vehicle rear signals under different illumination conditions and found that increasing the intensity of indicator signals from 125 cd to 200 cd did not affect reaction times (Attwood 1977). However other research in this area indicates that increased intensity differences between lights can lead to a significant difference in the likelihood of correct identification and interpretation of a signal.

2.3 Additional Lighting Units

There has been considerable research into the potential benefits of an additional High Mounted Brake Lights (HMBL). A large scale field study into the effects of HMBL concluded that reductions of 44% and 58% in the rear end accident rate were noted for the two experimental groups of the study in comparison to the control group (Rausch 1982). When comparing response times of unsuspecting drivers to brake signals from a vehicle with ordinary rear lights and with an additional HMBL (both single and dual) it was observed that although the differences in mean response times of following drivers for different systems were not statistically significant, there was a considerable improvement in response rate for the experimental groups 55 % and 53 % response rates for the single and dual light systems respectively as compared to 31 % response rate for the control group (Sivak et al 1981). It has been estimated that 67% of all rear end accidents can be affected by an additional HMBL and the observation made that of these half would benefit from a HMBL (Digges 1985). It may be noted that subsequent legislation was introduced into the USA requiring fitment of these devices to all cars from September 1988.

3. VEHICLE LEGISLATION

Legislation controlling the design and installation of vehicle lighting exists across all world markets. This extensive, and increasing, body of legislation can be said to apply constraints upon:

a)   the characteristic of the light source
b)   the construction and performance of the light unit
c)   the installation of the light units on the vehicle
d)   the operation and activation of the lights when in use

The principal sources for this legislation in Europe are directives from the European Economic Community (EEC) and regulations from the Economic Commission for Europe (ECE). These separate bodies produce legislation that affects vehicle in different but overlapping territories. There is therefore a need for some agreement between the two bodies to produce compatible technical requirements. This has resulted in separately issued but comparable documents from each source. This legislation controls the design of bulbs, reflectors, filter materials and installation, by defining required photometric performance for intensity, spectral characteristics and visibility angles. A list of those items affecting rear lighting and signalling devices is given in Table 1.

North America, Japan and other markets have similar bodies of legislation which differ from Europe in details of technical requirements. Summarising such a complex body of legislation is difficult, however general comments on performance requirements for European market passenger cars are given below.

Table 1   Comparison of ECE Regulations and EEC Directives Affecting Vehicle Rear Lighting Layouts

ECE Regulation	EEC Directive	Topic
3	76/759	Reflex Reflectors
4	76/760	Number Plate Lamps
6	76/759	Direction Indicators
7	76/758	Side, Rear and Stop Lights
23	77/539	Reversing Lights
38	77/538	Rear Fog Lights
48	76/756	Lighting Installations

3.1 Brake Light

EEC/ECE requirements are for two 'red' brake lights. If brake lights are 'nested' with presence lights the luminous intensity ratio of the individual functions must be at least 5:1. Additional high mounted brake lights are permissible in some territories to operate together with the primary brake lights.

3.2 Indicator Lights

EEC/ECE requirements are for two 'yellow' lights for indicators. They may be grouped together with one or more other lights and the range of flash frequency permitted is 60-120 per minute. If the vertical separation between the presence lights and the indicator is <300mm, then the horizontal separation must be no more than 50 mm.

Table 2   A Summary of Angles of Geometric Visibility and Luminous Intensity Value, Requirements for Lighting Devices for 76/756/EEC

Light Unit	Angle of Geometric Visibility required relative to Reference Axis				Luminous Intensity in the Reference Axis (cd)	
	Outside	Inside	Above	Below	Min	Max
Rear indicator	80°	45°	15°	15°	50	200
Brake light	45°	45°	15°	15°	40	100
Additional HMBL	-	-	-	-	40	100
Rear Fog light	25°	25°	5°	5°	150	300
Presence light	45°	-	15°	15°	2	60 to front
					2	30 to rear

Note: 1.   Maximum 300 cd above a horizontal line passing through the reference axis, Maximum 600 cd below the line

3.3 Presence Lights

EEC/ECE requirements are for two 'red' lights for presence. In addition one or two higher intensity, or fog, presence lights are permissible which must be wired such that these may only be switched on when front headlights or fog lights are in operation.

Table 2 indicates the angle of geometric visibility and luminous intensity values specified for lighting devices on vehicles under 76/756/EEC.

4. AN EXPERIMENTAL EVALUATION OF REAR LIGHTING PARAMETERS

Clearly such detailed technical requirements for lighting units are not readily changed or amended without considerable justification based upon research and analysis. One such programme of research to examine optimisation of vehicle rear lighting arrangements within legislative restraints was described (Meatyard and Fowkes 1987) with this research programme being subsequently completed and is described below.

4.1 Experimental Approach

An experimental procedure was defined to examine the differences in driver response time to various rear light configurations. The method utilised subjects seated in a static instrumented test vehicle. Subjects were required to perform a simple continuous tracking task within this vehicle, by controlling the movement of a cursor on a VDU by means of steering wheel rotation (horizontal) and accelerator pedal (vertical) coordination to track a randomly moving target. During this tracking task subjects were also asked to detect 'signals' from the lights fitted to a mock-up of the rear of a car positioned 21 metres ahead of the subject car. Detection of these signals was signified by the subjects activating the brake pedal.

Subjects viewed the tracking task screen via a mirror placed in the location of the internal rear view mirror of the car to consistently present the intermittent rear light signals peripherally. Different configurations of rear light stimuli were presented within any one test session at between 15 and 30 second intervals. Within each experiment 20 brake stimuli were shown to each subject. Control of the activation of stimuli and measurement of reaction time and accuracy of the tracking task were under the control of a micro computer. In addition reaction times of longer than 3 seconds were recorded as 'missed' stimuli.

Each trial lasted for approximately 8 minutes and two ambient lighting conditions were used; "night" and "day" time. "Night" conditions were simulated by conducting trials indoors in blacked out conditions. "Day" conditions were carried out under uncontrolled external daylight. Ambient illumination was therefore constantly monitored during these latter trials. Eight subjects took part in the study all of which were female, aged over 50 and who held a current driving licence.

All light sources used in this programme were evaluated and calibrated for photometric output, warm-up time and drive requirement. All light sources prior to test were subject to a 12 hour run-in period to overcome initial ageing effects. Light sources were then installed in similar housings having illuminated areas of 100 sq. millimetres each.

The results were then analysed by examining response time of subjects (adjusted for light

M. Fowkes and H.S. Storey

source warm-up time), and instantaneous gap data on tracking task by the use of a generalised linear model to provide an "estimated mean response time". Missed stimuli data

Table 3 Summary of Results from Experiment 1, For Calculated Mean Response Time and Percentage Missed Stimuli.

Presence Light Intensity	Performance Measure	Time of Day	Spacing Between Presence and Brake Lights, mm				
			0 (Coincident)	0 (Abutting)	100mm	200mm	300mm
7 cd	CMRT (sec)	Night	0.65	0.64	0.63	0.61	N/T
	MSS (%)	Night	0	0	0	0	N/T
	CMRT (sec)	Day	1.30	1.08	1.01	1.12	1.15
	MSS (%)	Day	19.4	8.8	7.5	10.0	15.6
200 cd	CMRT (sec)	Night	N/T	0.90	0.82	0.77	N/T
	MSS (%)	Night	N/T	3.8	3.1	3.8	N/T
	CMRT (sec)	Day	N/T	1.60	1.21	1.20	1.07
	MSS (%)	Day	N/T	23.8	18.8	16.3	12.5

was treated separately and in both cases significance of differences were tested using Students t-test.

The mock-up of the rear of a car allowed mounting of numbers of light units at the same height (645mm) but at a range of varying horizontal separations. 'Coincident' light functions were also simulated, i.e. dual level/intensity from the same light units. Subsequent spacings evaluated were 'abutting', ie zero spacing and 100mm, 200mm and 300mm. High mounted lights were mounted at a height of 955mm for single units or 1185mm for dual units.

A sequence of experiments were then performed.

4.2 Experiment 1 : Horizontal Spacing Between Presence and Brake Lights.

Two intensities of presence lights (7 cd and 200 cd) were investigated with a single brake light intensity (66 cd). Horizontal spacings between presence and brake light functions studied were 0mm (both coincident and abutting) 100mm, 200mm and 300mm. The results for calculated mean reaction time (CMRT) and percentage of missed stimuli (MSS) for day and night time conditions are shown in Table 3.

4.3 Experiment 2 : Intensity of Brake Lights

Two intensity of presence lights were used (7 cd and 20 cd) and horizontal spacing to the brake lights set at 100mm as indicated by the results of experiment 1. Subjects were presented with brake lights at two intensities (32 cd and 120 cd) and during each trial the intensity of the presence lights remained fixed while the intensity of the brake lights were switched at random. For day time conditions a third presence light arrangement was used of "zero intensity" (ie a non-illuminated presence light). The results are given in Table 4.

Night time data showed no significant differences in mean response times for any of the tested brake light intensities against a 7 cd presence light. The 200 cd system indicated an improvement from a 32 cd brake to a 66 cd brake with a smaller improvement from 66 cd to 120 cd. The difference between the 32 cd and 66 cd response times was found to be statistically significant at the 0.1% level.

Table 4 Summary of Result from Experiment 2, For Calculated Mean Response Time and Percentage Missed Stimuli

Presence Light Intensity (cd)	Performance Measure	Time of Day	Brake Light Intensity (cd)		
			32	66	120
0	CMRT (sec)	Day	1.29	N/T	0.91
	MSS (%)	Day	17.5	N/T	4.4
7	CMRT (sec)	Night	0.63	0.63	0.63
	MSS (%)	Night	0	0	0
	CMRT (sec)	Day	1.51	1.04	1.02
	MSS (%)	Day	23.8	7.5	4.4
200	CMRT (sec)	Night	1.07	0.83	0.72
	MSS (%)	Night	8.8	3.1	0.6
	CMRT (Sec)	Day	1.48	1.22	1.14
	MSS (%)	Day	25.6	18.8	14.4

Table 5 Summary of Results from Experiment 3, For Calculated Mean Response Time and Percentage Missed Stimuli

Presence Light Intensity	Performance Measure	Time of Day	HMBL System				
			Control	Single 25 cd	Dual 25 cd	Single 45 cd	Dual 45 cd
7/73	CMRT (sec)	Night	0.64	0.59	0.54	N/T	N/T
	MSS (%)	Night	0	0	0	N/T	N/T
	CMRT (sec)	Day	1.33	1.09	1.09	1.05	1.09
	MSS (%)	Day	19.4	12.5	9.4	12.5	13.1
7	CMRT (sec)	Night	0.63	0.62	0.55	N/T	N/T
	MSS (%)	Night	0	0	0	N/T	N/T
	CMRT (sec)	Day	0.99	1.12	1.06	1.05	1.14
	MSS (%)	Day	7.5	5.6	6.3	3.1	5.0
200	CMRT (sec)	Night	0.83	0.79	0.65	0.74	0.66
	MSS (%)	Night	3.1	0	0	0	0
	CMRT (sec)	Day	1.21	1.30	1.27	1.17	1.14
	MSS (%)	Day	18.8	12.5	11.3	14.4	15.6

4.4 Experiment 3 : High Mounted Brake Lights (HMBL)

Four configurations of HMBL were tested. A single 25 cd, a single 45 cd, a dual 25 cd and a dual 45 cd and were tested displayed in addition to an ordinary pair of brake lights at "ordinary" height. Presence lights of 200 cd and 7 cd were examined with 66 cd brake lights 100 mm from the presence lights. A light system of 7 cd/73 cd was used to initiate a coincident presence/brake light signal. A 'control' condition of no HMBL additions was also used. Table 5 gives the results from Experiment 3.

Night time data for the 200 cd presence light systems indicated that all HMBL systems performed better than the control. Of these both the dual 25 cd and dual 45 cd systems were both showed significant improvements at the 0.1 % level while no other comparisons with the control indicated statistical significance. For day time conditions, only the 7/73 cd presence (coincident brake) system provided statistically significant data with all experimental configurations being better than the control group.

4.5 Experimental Conclusions

Subjects responded to brake signals faster in night time conditions than in day time, this better performance was also observed with missed stimuli data. Subjects also responded faster, and more frequently, to brake signals associated with a 'dim' (0 cd or 7 cd) presence light compared to a 'bright' (200 cd) fog light. Some horizontal separation between brake and presence light was shown to have a beneficial improvement in response time and frequency. The optimum spacing was 100mm.

Increasing brake light intensity from 32 cd to 66 cd gave a significant improvement on response time and rate. The addition of any HMBL system to the optionally separated brake/ presence light combination showed some improvement in driver response, particularly in day time conditions.

5. COMPARISON WITH CURRENT DESIGNS

A number of mass market European vehicles have recently undergone major facelifts with subsequent re-launchs of a number of models. It was decided to survey the rear lighting configurations of such vehicles and compare pre and post re-launch vehicles in terms of current research and the results of the 1987 TRRL report. Four different types of vehicles were surveyed, a small hatchback, a medium hatchback, a family saloon and a large family saloon and the surface area of each illuminated function of the rear lights was calculated and compared as a percentage of the total surface area of the lighting cluster. Results indicated that all of the vehicles surveyed, except the earlier version of the family saloon, had a common configuration of brake lights coincident with the presence lights. This function was found to be abutting in the earlier model of the family saloon and none of the vehicles surveyed had a physical separation between brake and presence lights.

6. SUMMARY

There are a number of inferences that may be drawn from the above conclusions. The results indicate that by increasing the brake light intensity, response times are improved and miss responses are reduced. There is a case for the implementation of dual intensity brake lights with 32 cd for normal use at night and 66 cd for daytime and at night when high intensity fog lights are in use. If this suggestion is unacceptable then thought should be given to increasing the minimum effective on-road brake light intensity to 66 cd.

Consideration should be given to requiring a minimum of 100 mm between brake lights and presence lights to improve response time and to reduced missed responses. It would seem to be acceptable for high intensity rear fog lights to be contained in the same housing as the presence lights and adjacent to the direction indicators if the spacing of 100 mm between brake lights and presence lights is maintained. The addition of high mounted brake lights appears to be advantageous particulary to vehicles with the common current configuration of brake lights adjacent to or coincident with presence lights. An examination of some recent models of passenger car shows a continuing prevalence of this arrangement of rear lighting function in Europe. An examination of some recent models of passengr cars show a continuining prevalance of this arrangement of rear lighting function in Europe.

7. REFERENCES

Attwood, D.A (1977). Automobile rear signal research I: Effects of signal colour and intensity, ambient illumination and driver age on laboratory performance. Tech memo No. RSV 77/3, Transport, Canada.

Digges, K.H (1985). The technical basis for the centre high mounted stop lamp. SAE report 851240.

Domas, P.A (1975). A subjective evaluation of turn signal effectiveness. In P.L., Olson, C.M. Jorgesson, J.K., Thomas, P.A, Domas (eds), Factors influencing the effectiveness of automobile rear lighting systems. HSRI, University of Michigan, Report No. UM-HSRI-HF-74-4.

Helliar-Symons, R.D and Irving, A. (1981). Masking of brake lights by high intensity rear lights in fog. TRRL Laboratory Report No.998.

Meatyard, A.G (1988). A study of the effectiveness of rear lighting arrangements for cars. TRRL Contractor report No.92.

Meatyard, A.G and Fowkes, M (1987). An Investigation into Rear Lighting Arrangements for Cars, In: Gale A.G. et al (Eds.) Vision in Vehicles II, North Holland, Amsterdam.

Moore, R.L (1952) Rear lights of motor vehicles and pedal cycles. Road Research Laboratory, Technical paper No. 25, London HMSO.

Moore, R.L, Smith, H.P.R (1966). Visibility from the driver's seat: The conspicuity of vehicle lights and signals. In Ergonomics and Safety in Motor Car Design, Institute of Mechanical Engineers, London.

Mortimer, R.G et al (1969). Automobile rear lighting and signalling research. GM Engineering Publication 3303.

Rausch, A (1982). A field test of two single, centre, high mounted brake light systems. Accident Analysis and Prevention, 14, 287-291.

Rockwell, T.H, Safford, R.R (1966). Comparative evaluation of an amber tail light system and the conventional system under night driving conditions, Ohio State University, Systems Research Group, Columbus, OH, Report No. EE5 272-1.

M. Fowkes and H.S. Storey

Sivak, M et al, (1981). Driver responses to high mounted brake lights in actual traffic. Human Factors, 23, 321-325.

VISION IN VEHICLES – IV
A.G. Gale et al. (Editors)

REAR LIGHT CONFIGURATIONS: THE REMOVAL OF AMBIGUITY BY A THIRD BRAKE LIGHT

S.P. AKERBOOM, H.W. KRUYSSE and W. LA HEIJ

Unit of Experimental Psychology, Leiden University P.O. Box 9555, 2300 RB Leiden, The Netherlands

Abstract

In two experiments, subjects were shown simulated rear-end configurations of cars on a vector display. They were asked to react to brake lights by pushing a button. In Experiment 1, we investigated the effect of the following variables on the speed and accuracy of these brake reactions: (a) the rear-end lights illuminated at the onset of a trial (only presence lights, presence lights with one fog light, presence lights with two fog lights), (b) configuration of presence and brake lights (coincident and separate), (c) contrast between presence and brake lights, and (d) delay between onset of the trial and the onset of the brake lights (0, 1400 and 2800 msec). The results show that the presence of fog lights in part of the trials resulted in two types of errors: false alarms (brake reactions to illuminated fog lights) and misses (no reactions to illuminated fog lights). The reaction time data were completely in accordance with these findings. In Experiment 2 we investigated whether the apparent ambiguity resulting from the use of fog lights in part of the trials can be reduced by an additional single high-mounted brake light. The results showed that a third brake light reduces reaction times in all conditions, almost completely eliminates the misses, but has no effect on the number of false alarms. It is argued that the number of false alarms will only diminish when a third brake light is used in all braking situations and not just in a subset of the trials.

1. INTRODUCTION

A considerable amount of car accidents are rear-end collisions. Although high speed or "tailgating" are conspicuous causes of this type of accidents, inadequate detection and interpretation of the braking or deceleration of the lead vehicle should be considered as psychological variables involved in rear-end collisions. It is conceivable that the present rear-light configuration, with fog and presence lights located in close vicinity of the standard brake lights, does not provide unambiguous information about braking under all circumstances.

A possible solution for this problem could be an additional center high-mounted stop light (Insurance Inst. Report, 1987, Malone, 1986). A number of possible advantages of such a light are mentioned in the literature (Sivak et al, 1987). First of all it is in the center of the visual field, secondly the information it provides is unambiguous and finally it may be detected by other drivers than the immediately following one, due to the so called "look-through" effect. However, studies on rear-light configuration of cars are not unanimous about whether or not the addition of a high-mounted stop light will increase safety. Some American and New Zealand large-scale field experiments do show a benefit of a single high-mounted stop light on rear-end collision numbers (Malone et al, 1978, McCormick & Allen, 1988, Rausch et al, 1982, Reilly et al, 1980), but these findings or their interpretations are questioned by others (Theeuwes, 1991). Some experimental studies found that the reaction times do not benefit from a single high-mounted stop light although they were more likely to generate a reaction (Sivak et al, 1981a, Sivak et al, 1981b). Furthermore some authors have argued that the positive effect obtained in the American field studies cannot be generalized to the European situation because of a difference in rear-end light configuration (Meatyard, 1988, Mulder, 1984).

We conducted several laboratory RT studies in order to investigate systematically whether or not a third high-mounted brake light reduces the ambiguity of rear light configurations (Akerboom et al, 1990). In these experiments, simulations of rear-end lights of cars were presented on a vector-scan display (Vector General). After displaying a fixation point a certain rear-end configuration was presented and, after an unpredictable delay, brake lights appeared in 80% of the trials. Subjects were instructed to react to the onset of the brake lights by pushing a button. The effect of the presence or absence of a third brake light was investigated under various lay-outs. In a series of experiments we investigated:

1.   The influence of distance between rear-end lights; that is, viewing distance.
2.   The relative position of presence and brake lights; that is, separate or coincident housing.
3.   The influence of differences in intensity between brake lights and presence lights.
4.   The influence of a second task; a letter detection task presented at the point of fixation.
5.   The delay of target onset; that is, a variable foreperiod between the onset of the trial and the appearance of the brake lights. It is important to note that this period was also reduced to zero seconds (the $t = 0$ or 'no delay' condition). Thus, at the start of the trial, subjects were given a configuration with illuminated brake lights. In this situation, subjects were not alerted by, or could not react to a sudden change in intensity of one of the lights during a trial; they had to make an absolute judgement. This condition is supposed to resemble a situation where the visual attention of the driver is momentarily directed away from the leading car at the moment of braking. As far as we know, this condition has not been examined in previous research.

The results of the first series of experiments showed that the presence of the third brake light at the point of fixation is a powerful factor in eliminating negative influences of other variables such as the coincident presentation of presence and brake light and a relatively small difference in intensity between brake and presence light. The beneficial effect of the third brake light was especially clear in the no-delay condition were an absolute judgement had to be made.

In this paper we present two experiments that were designed to examine a particularly ambiguous situation: one in which one or two fog lights are present in addition to presence lights. The first experiment was conducted to investigate the effect of one or two fog lights on subjects' brake reactions to a standard brake light configuration. The second experiment was conducted to investigate the effect of a high-mounted additional brake light on brake reactions to configurations with fog lights.

2. EXPERIMENT 1

The presence of two illuminated fog lights may result in an ambiguity leading to two kinds of errors. First, the initiation or even the presence of illuminated fog lights may be interpreted by the following driver as braking. This may result in an inappropriate brake reaction or false alarm. Second, in case the leading vehicle does not use fog lights, brake lights may be falsely interpreted by the following driver as illuminated foglights. In this case increased reaction times or even misses are to be expected.

2.1. Method
Subjects

Six male students from the University of Leiden, aged 25-38 years, served as paid subjects. None of them participated in a similar experiment before. All subjects had normal or corrected to normal vision.

Stimuli and design

Each subject received a total of 540 trials in two sessions. Each session of 270 trials consisted of 216 experimental trials (36 conditions x six replications per condition, and 54 (20%) catch trials). Trials were presented in a completely random sequence. Conditions were composed by the (factorial) combination of the following four factors:

1.   Three levels of attentional lights: presence lights without fog lights, with one fog light (at the left) or with two fog lights.
2.   Two brake light configurations: brake lights coinciding with presence lights or adjacent (inwards) to presence lights.
3.   Two levels of intensity of brake lights: a low contrast, ratio : presence lights to brake lights of 1 : 1.68 and a high contrast ratio of 1 : 2.21. Intensities of fog and brake lights are identical.
4.   Three delays between the presentation of the initial configuration and the onset of the brake lights: 0, 1400 and 2800 msec.

Apparatus

Stimuli were presented on a vector scan display. The presentation of the stimuli and the registration of the reaction times and errors were controlled by a PDP 11/34 computer. Reaction times were measured from the onset of the brake lights with an accuracy of 2 msec. Subjects were seated 90 cm from the Vector General screen. The horizontal size of the configuration was 13.1 degree of visual angle, corresponding to a following distance of 7 meters.

Procedure

Trials started with one of the following configurations: a fixation point with two presence lights, two presence lights and two fog lights, or two presence lights and one fog light. Thus presence lights were presented in all conditions (we chose this option because of the possible introduction of "Daytime Running Lights" in the Netherlands and because we were interested in ambiguous situations). After an unpredictable delay of 0, 1400 or 2800 msec brake lights were presented in 80% of the trials. These brake lights could be presented either adjacent to or at the same location as the presence lights and with different contrasts. As in previous experiments subjects were instructed to focus on the fixation point and to react as fast as possible with a push-button response (dominant index finger) when they detected the brake lights. Reaction times were measured from the onset of the brake lights.

2.2. Results and discussion

To evaluate the influence of fog lights on 'brake behaviour' mean reaction times (RTs) and error rates, that is false alarms and misses, were computed per subject per condition. False alarms are errors in which a 'brake reaction' is initiated before brake lights are

Table 1 Percentage false alarms and misses for the configurations without fog lights (P), with two fog lights (P,2F) and with one fog light (P,1F) dependent on delay (t = 0, 1400 and 2800 msec).

	delay	
	t = 0	t > 0
% false alarms		
P	-	2.6 (29% < 1000 msec)
P,2F	-	11.3 (84% < 1000 msec)
P,1F	-	4.2 (57% < 1000 msec)
% misses		
coincident housing		
P	6.2	0.35
P,2F	3.5	2.45
P,1F	7.0	0.35
separate housing		
P	25.0	0.35
P,2F	2.8	0
P,1F	4.9	0

presented; i.e. the fog lights are interpreted as brake lights. Misses are errors in which no brake reaction is given when brake lights are presented; i.e. the brake lights are interpreted as fog lights.

Table 1 shows the percentages false alarms and misses per experimental condition. It is not possible to make false alarms in the no delay condition. In this condition brake lights are illuminated at the start of the trial (t = 0). Furthermore, since false alarms indicate a reaction to a stimulus without brake lights, no distinction is made between coincident and adjacent brake light configurations and between low and high contrast.

The condition in which a lot of false alarms were made is the one with presence lights and two fog lights (P,2F): an inappropriate brake reaction was initiated in more than 10% of the trials. Apparently in this condition subjects mistake fog lights for brake lights. Although this kind of mistake is also present for the condition with just one fog light (P,1F) the percentage of false alarms is much lower.

Table 1 further shows that for the configuration with only presence lights (P), false alarms are nearly always slow reactions; about 70% are longer than 1 sec. However, in the other two conditions with fog lights, false alarms are mainly fast reactions. Thus, most of the inappropriate brake reactions are immediate reactions when one or two fog lights are presented.

Furthermore, Table 1 shows that nearly all misses were made in the conditions in which an absolute judgement (t = 0) had to be made. An analysis of variance (ANOVA) on the number of misses revealed that the interaction between the factors 'attentional lights', 'brake light configuration'and 'delay' was statistically significant ($F(20,20)= 2,89$, $p < 0.05$). In the condition without delay (t = 0) and presence lights adjacent to the brake lights, brake reactions were omitted in approximately 25% of the total number of trials. These misses were irrespective of the intensity of the brake lights: for low (27.8% misses) as well as high intensity ratios (22.2% misses) brake lights were falsely interpreted as illuminated fog lights. This ambiguity is also clear in the reaction time data.

Figure 1 shows the mean reaction times per experimental condition. An ANOVA on the mean reaction times with contrast, attentional lights, brake light configuration and delay as within subjects factors showed two statistically significant main effects, three significant first order interactions and one significant second order interaction. Respectively: Contrast, $F(1,5) = 14.14$, $p < 0.05$. Delay, $F(2,10) = 49$, $p < 0.001$. The interaction between attentional lights and brake light configuration, $F(2,10) = 4.89$, $p < 0.05$. The interaction between attentional lights and delay $F(4,20) = 4.34$, $p < 0.05$. The interaction between intensity and delay, $F(2,10) = 10.67$, $p < 0.01$. The interaction between attentional lights, brake light configuration, and delay, $F(4,20) = 4.34$, $p < 0.05$. When brake lights were spatially separated from the presence lights, and no fog lights were used (a condition that resulted in a lot of misses), reactions were extremely slow. Note that for this condition, unlike previous results (Akerboom et al, 1990), a separation between presence and brake lights now has a negative effect: separation increases the chance that brake lights will be mistaken for illuminated fog lights. A confusion resulting in a large number of misses and slow reactions.

The question that arises is how to improve the interpretation of brake lights in ambiguous situations. Obviously, not by manipulating intensity ratios or brake light configurations; remember that there is no longer a benefit of separated brake lights when in a sub-set of the trials fog lights are presented. In the next experiment we investigated the effect of an additional high mounted brake light.

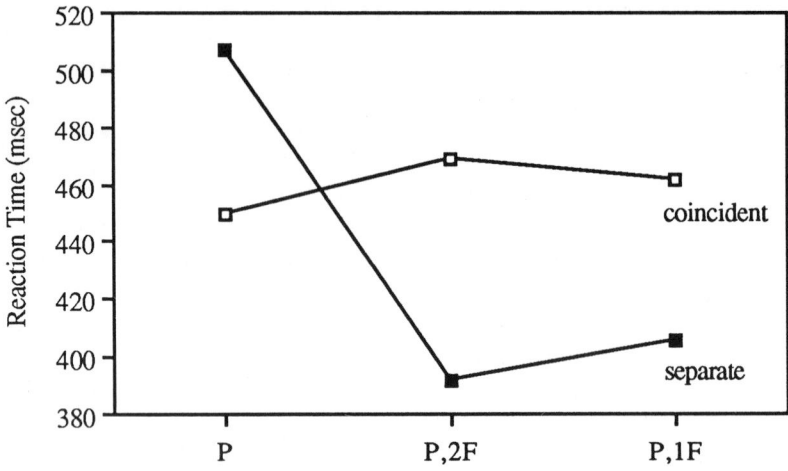

Fig. 1   The interaction between attentional lights (P= only presence lights, P,2F= presence
         lights + 2 fog lights, P,1F= presence lights + 1 fog light) and brake light
         configuration.

3. EXPERIMENT 2

To answer the question whether a third brake light improves the interpretation of rear
light configurations in ambiguous situations, the former experiment was replicated with a
few differences in order to simulate more realistically rear light configurations:

1.   In half of the experimental trials a single high-mounted brake light appeared in an
         isosceles triangular configuration with the standard brake and presence lights. The
         top angle of the triangle equaled 53 degrees.
2.   Intensity ratios of presence and brake lights were set at 1 to 2.9 and 1 to 6.2. The
         last ratio corresponds to the requirement in the Netherlands which is a minimal
         ratio of 1 to 5.
3.   On the vector display a picture of a car was presented. Its horizontal visual angle
         of 5.2 degrees corresponded to a following distance of 18m. Thus, information
         about where the rear lights appeared was given by the contour of this picture. The
         fixation point appeared in the low middle of the rear window of the car; this was
         also the position where the third brake light appeared. The distance between the fog
         lights and the other lights corresponded to the legal requirement of 10 cm.
4.   In case of separate presentation of brake and presence lights the arrangement could
         be either vertical with the brake lights above the presence lights, or horizontal with
         the brake lights situated on the inside of the presence lights.

3.1. Method
Subjects

Five female and two male students from the University of Leiden, aged 22-25 years, served as paid subjects. None of them had participated in a similar experiment before. All subjects had normal or corrected to normal vision.

Stimuli and design

Each subject received a total of 720 trials in two sessions. Each session of 360 trials consisted of 288 experimental trials (72 conditions x 4 replications per condition, and 72 (20%) catch trials). Trials were presented in a completely random sequence. Conditions were composed by the (factorial) combination of the following five factors:

1.   Two levels of single high mounted brake lights (SHMBL): present or absent.
2.   Three levels of attentional lights: presence lights without fog lights, with one fog light or with two fog lights.
3.   Two brake light configurations: brake lights coinciding with presence lights or adjacent to presence lights.
4.   Two levels of intensity of brake lights: a low contrast, ratio presence lights to brake lights of 1 : 2.9 and a high contrast, ratio of 1 : 6.2.
5.   Three delays between the presentation of the initial configuration and the onset of the brake lights: 0, 1400 and 2800 msec.

Apparatus and procedure

Apparatus and procedure were the same as in the previous experiment.

3.2. Results and discussion

As in Experiment 1, mean reaction times (RTs) and error rates (false alarms and misses) were computed per condition. Like in Experiment 1 still a lot of false alarms were made in the condition with presence lights and two fog lights. The percentages of false alarms in the experimental trials decreased in the following order of conditions: P,2F (two fog lights illuminated at the start of the trial: 16.7% without SHMBL and 15.6% with SHMBL), P,1F (one fog light illuminated at the start of the trial: 6.5% without SHMBL and 4.7% with SHMBL), and P (no illuminated fog lights present: 1.3% without SHMBL and 1.3% with SHMBL). If one realizes that false alarms are reactions to rear-end configurations in which no brake lights are illuminated, it is not surprising that there is hardly any difference between the percentages of false alarms in the conditions with and without SHMBL. We will return to this finding at the end of this section.

The overall percentage of misses was lower than obtained in Experiment 1, which may be due to the decreased ambiguity of the rear-end configuration by providing the outlines of the car and the more realistic intensity ratios. Nevertheless, in 2.6% of the trials in which lateral brake lights were illuminated at the start of the trial (the t = 0 situation) no reaction was given. This percentage of misses was reduced to 0.1% when a SHMBL was present, indicating that the addition of a third brake light indeed removed the tendency of subjects to interpret the illuminated braking lights as fog lights.

An ANOVA on the mean reaction times showed significant main effects of the factors presence or absence of a third brake light ($F(1,6)= 40.1$, $p < .01$, 370 and 479 msec respectively), low and high intensity ratio ($F(1,6)= 53.2$, $p < .001$, 464 and 385 msec respectively), coincident and separate housing (F(1,6)= 42.5, p < .01, 461 and 389 msec respectively) and delay (F(2,12)= 82.1, p < .001, 588, 346 and 341 msec for t = 0, t = 1400 and t = 2800 msec respectively). We will not mention all significant first, second and third order interactions involving the factor presence/absence of a SHMBL. It suffices to say that the benefit of a SHMBL was largest for conditions in which the reaction times were already high due to an ambiguity arising from factors like coincident presence and brake lights (an overall reduction in RTs due to the addition of a SHMBL of 28%, 538 versus 384 msec), low contrast between presence and brake lights (an overall reduction of 27%, 537 versus 392 msec) and the necessity to make an absolute judgement (an overall reduction of 34%, 707 versus 469 msec). One of the conditions in which the gain was especially high is the one in which only presence and brake lights were presented and subjects had to make an absolute judgement (t = 0) (see Figure 2). Like in the previous experiment subjects are not sure in this condition whether the lights they perceive are the brake lights or the fog lights; an uncertainty that results in relatively slow reactions. Finally, it should be noted that even in the condition in which the brake lights were spatially separated from the presence lights and a high contrast was used, the addition of a SHMBL resulted in a significant decrease in RT of 63 msec.

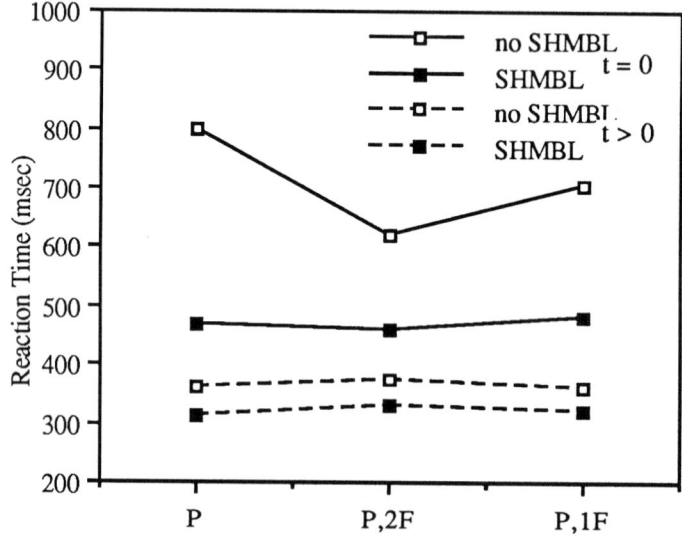

Fig.2   Mean reaction time to brake lights in the 12 conditions resulting from the factorial combination of the variables 'attentional lights', 'presence or absence of a single high-mounted brake light' and 'delay'.

The lack of an effect of the additional SHMBL on the number of false alarms, mentioned above, needs some further comment. This finding is most probably the result of the fact that in our present experiment a SHMBL was presented in only half of the experimental trials. Because of this, the lack of a SHMBL did not provide unambiguous information that no brake action was initiated. For that reason, it is to be expected that the number of false alarms will strongly decrease when the SHMBL is illuminated in all braking conditions. This leads to the following conclusions: (a) the behaviour of subjects is dependent on the total set of configurations that are presented within a certain experiment or real-life situation, and (b) if one would ever decide to introduce a third brake light, it would be much better to do this for all vehicles and not just for a sub-set. The latter may even lead to dangerous situations, in which drivers - expecting a third brake light - do not react, or react too slowly to the standard illuminated brake lights.

4. CONCLUSIONS

Experiment 1 showed that the presence of fog lights may introduce an ambiguity that leads to false alarms, misses and slow reactions. Experiment 2 shows that this ambiguity can largely be removed by the addition of a SHMBL. This benefit of the third brake light was especially clear in the no delay condition in which an absolute judgement had to be made.

The introduction of a third brake light did not reduce the number of false alarms to illuminated fog lights. However, it is likely that these false alarms will disappear in a condition in which all rear-end configurations are equipped with a third brake light.

REFERENCES

Akerboom, S.P., Kruysse, H.W. & La Heij, W. (1990) Achterverlichting nader bekeken. Leiden: Rijksuniversiteit Leiden, Werkgroep Veiligheid.

Insurance Institute for Highway Safety. Status Report, (1987), 22, (6), 4.

Malone, T.B. (1986) The centered high-mounted brake light: a human factors success story. Human Factors Society, 29, 1-3.

Malone, T.B., Kirkpatrick, M., Kohl, J.S. & Baker, C. (1978) Field test evaluation of rear lighting systems. Alexandria, VA: Essex Corporation. Prepared for NHTSA, U.S. Department of Transportation, Contract no. DOT-HS-5-01228.

McCormick, I.A. & Allen, K. (1988) The evaluation of single centrally mounted auxiliary stop-lights: a New Zealand field test. New Zealand Journal of Psychology, 17, 15-18.

Meatyard, A.G. (1988) A study of the effectiveness of rear lighting arrangements for cars. Warwickshire, England: The Motor Industry Research Association. Prepared for TRRL, England, Contractor report 92.

Mulder, J.A.G. (1984) Hooggeplaatste remlichten. SWOV R-84-49, Leidschendam: SWOV.

Rausch, A., Wong, J. & Kirkpatrick, M. (1982) A field test of two single center high mounted brake light system. Accident Analysis and Prevention, 14, 287-291.

Reilly, R.E., Kurke, D.S. & Buckenmaier Jr., C.C. (1980) Validation of the reduction of rear-end collisions by a high mounted auxiliary stoplamp. Alexandria, VA: Allen Corporation of America. Prepared for NHTSA, U.S. Department of Transportation, Contract no. DOT-HS-7-01756.

Sivak, M., Post, D.V., Olson, P.L. & Donohue, R.J. (1981a) Automobile rear lights: Effects of the number, mounting height, and lateral position on reaction times of following drivers. Perceptual and Motor Skills, 52, 795-802.

Sivak, M., Post, D.V., Olson, P.L. & Donohue, R.J. (1981b) Driver responses to high-mounted brake lights in actual traffic. Human Factors, 23, 231-235.

Sivak, M., Conn, L.S. & Olson, P.L. (1986) Driver eye fixations and the optimal locations for automobile brake lights. Journal of Safety Research, 17, 13-22.

Theeuwes, J. (1991) Center high-mounted stop light: an evaluation. Report IZF 1991-C3. Soesterberg: Institute for Perception TNO.

6

VISUAL PERCEPTION
AND VEHICLE CONTROL:
VISUAL INFORMATION ACQUISITION

TASK SIMULATOR FOR EVALUATING DRIVER INFORMATION ACQUISITION

J.J. COLLINS and M. McDONALD

Transportation Research Group & University of Southampton, England

Abstract

During the last five years a system for the evaluation of the visual acquisition of information by drivers has been developed at Southampton. This integrates a driving task activity and the use of eyemark camera equipment. The simulator is designed to allow for investigation of driver information acquisition tasks. The simulator provides a tracking task and information acquisition task which represent elements of the those tasks found in driving. Reading times are measured using eyemark camera equipment. This paper describes two experiments to determine the reading time of destination route signs and a recently completed experiment to determine the visual load required to read network information presented as maps. In the future it is intended to determine the reading times of in-vehicle route guidance displays. The driving task simulator provides a convenient means of evaluating the visual demand of many information acquisition tasks.

1. INTRODUCTION

Driving is a visually demanding activity. It is likely to become more demanding, with the introduction of Road Transport Informatics, and a greater need for network managers to communicate with the drivers via in-vehicle and external displays. Driving consists of a number of separate, but related activities, which are conducted concurrently. Perhaps the most important task which the driver must attend to is controlling the lane position of the vehicle. While conducting this tracking the driver selects information from the environment and makes decisions about the intended route. The driving task simulator provides a tracking task and an information acquisition task which represent elements of the those tasks found in driving. Using eyemark recording equipment the relative visual demands of different information acquisition tasks can be determined by measuring the required reading time.

2. EQUIPMENT

The main components of the driving task simulator are:

- Two carousel slide projectors each with separately controlled shutters.
- A back projection screen.
- A BBC microcomputer which controls the experiment and is linked to a large

monitor.
*   The front portion of a small car with steering wheel and indicator switch.

These are arranged according to the diagram in Figure 1.

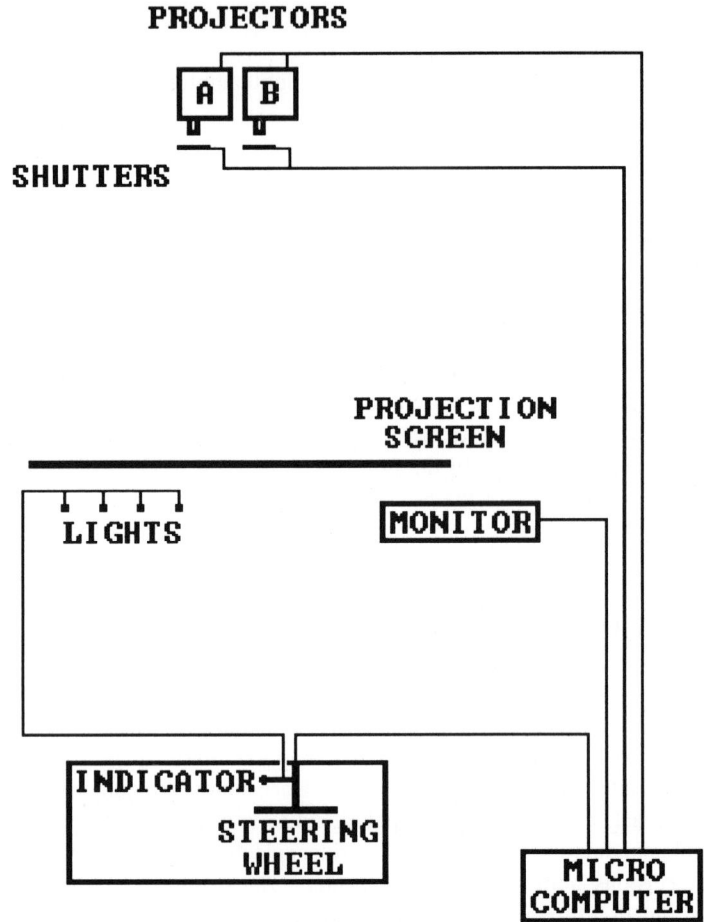

Figure 1, Layout of the Driving Task Simulator

The experiment is controlled by a program which runs in real time on the BBC microcomputer and displays a simulated road with the position of the car bonnet on the large monitor in front of the subject who is seated at the steering wheel in the car. The steering wheel is connected to the microcomputer and controls the position of the bonnet of the car on the road. The difficulty of this tracking task maybe controlled by setting the vehicle speed, steering lag, steering ratio, and visibility at the beginning of the experiment.

When the driver is off course an auditory warning is given.

The shutters and projectors are also connected to the microcomputer. When the subject is in control of the vehicle, stimulus slides may be presented to the subject on the back projection screen. The subject responds using the indicator switch which is connected to the four lights which are mounted on the edge of the back projection screen.

The subject wears an eyemark camera which records the scene in front of the subject, including the appearance of stimulus slides, the subjects visual behaviour and indicator switch responses via the lights on the projection screen.

3. USE

While using the driving task simulator the subjects wear an eyemark camera. Currently an NAC model V is being used. When correctly set up the output from the eyemark camera provides a video recording of the view in front of the subject, with two "eye marks" indicating where the subject is looking. Also superimposed on the video recording is a digital time base so that reading times may be determined.

So as to achieve minimum reading times the difficulty of the tracking task is adjusted such that it requires the subject's full attention. Preliminary trials with the task simulator were used to select the simulation parameters of speed, steering lag, steering ratio, and visibility. Immediately before each experimental trial subjects are allowed time to familiarise themselves with the tracking task and experimental procedure. The tracking task is very demanding so trials must be of limited length to avoid fatigue.

After familiarisation the eyemark camera is placed on the subject's head and is adjusted to an acceptable level of calibration. The experimental run may then begin. When the subject is in control of the tracking task, the program presents stimulus slides to the subject on the back projection screen for limited periods using the projectors and shutters.

It is important to know whether the subject has read the stimulus slide correctly. The subject therefore has to respond using the direction indicator on the steering column which is connected to the four lights on the back projection screen. This allows for four responses, of left, right, ahead (a forward push) and none of those (the horn on the end of the indicator arm). Stimulus slides must only allow for these four responses.

3.1 Reading Direction Signs

Hall et al (1991) used the driving task simulator to investigate the relationship between the time required to read a traffic sign, the quantity of information read and other parameters such as the layout and complexity. Four sets of 20 cross-road direction signs were read by each of 20 subjects which provided 1543 sign reading observations. Regression analysis was undertaken to relate the dependent variables using the GLIM statistical package (GLIM, 1986). The analysis provided predictive models of the reading time required for locating a given direction on the signs. These are given by:

Left and Ahead: $T = 0.784 + 0.064 N$

Right: $T = 0.451 + 0.064 N$

Missing: T = 0.784 + 0.167 N

Where T = Time required (seconds).
         N = Number of names on the direction sign.

These relationships are shown in Figure 2.

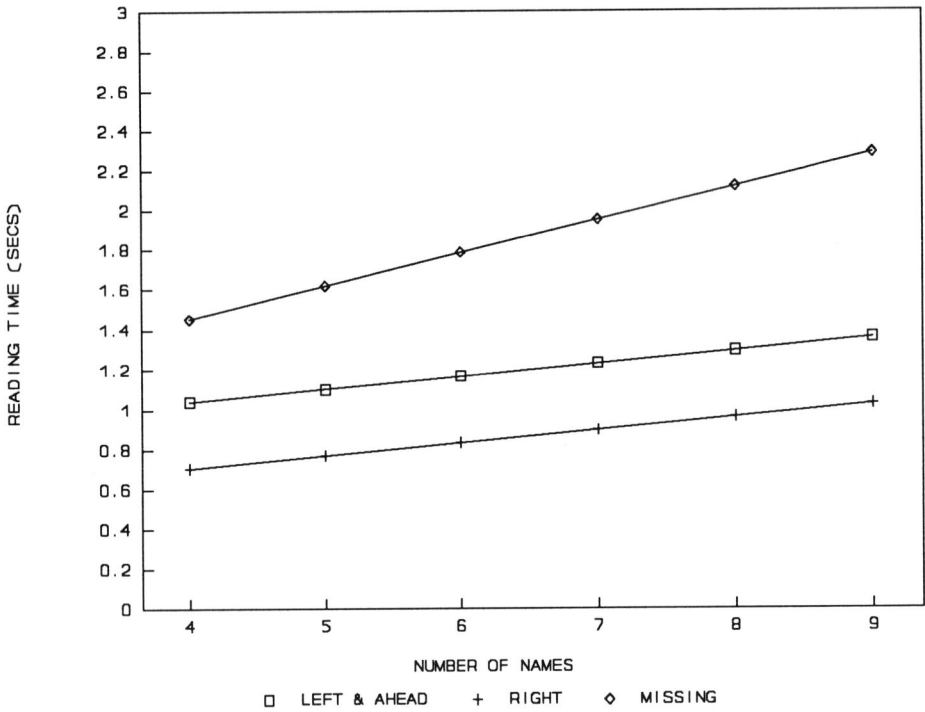

Figure 2, Predicted reading time of direction signs against number of names.

While Hall et al admit that the subject sample was small and not representative of the driving population as a whole, the results provide a useful guide to the minimum required reading time for direction signs. Required reading time for destinations on the right hand side of the sign were considerably shorter than for those ahead and to the left, perhaps indicating that direction signs in the are read from right to left.

3.2 Reading Obscured Direction Signs

A driver's view of a traffic sign or signal may be obscured by the presence of other vehicles in the traffic stream. In a similar experiment, to the one previously mentioned, Hall et al (1990) investigated the situation when a sign is obscured and whether an initial short viewing opportunity is of any value to the driver. Four sets of 25 direction signs were read by each of 24 subjects which provided 2328 sign reading observations. Four slide exposure conditions were used.

Condition (1)   6 seconds unobscured exposure.
Condition (2)   0.3 seconds exposure, 3 seconds obscuration, 4 second exposure.
Condition (3)   0.5 seconds exposure, 3 seconds obscuration, 4 second exposure.
Condition (4)   0.8 seconds exposure, 3 seconds obscuration, 4 second exposure.

Regression analysis provided predictive models of reading time for each of the exposure conditions. These are given by:

Condition (1) $T = 0.434 + 0.114 N$
Condition (2) $T = 0.323 + 0.114 N$
Condition (3) $T = 0.248 + 0.114 N$
Condition (4) $T = 0.287 + 0.114 N$

Where T = Time required (seconds).
            N = Number of names on the direction sign.

These relationships are shown in Figure 3.

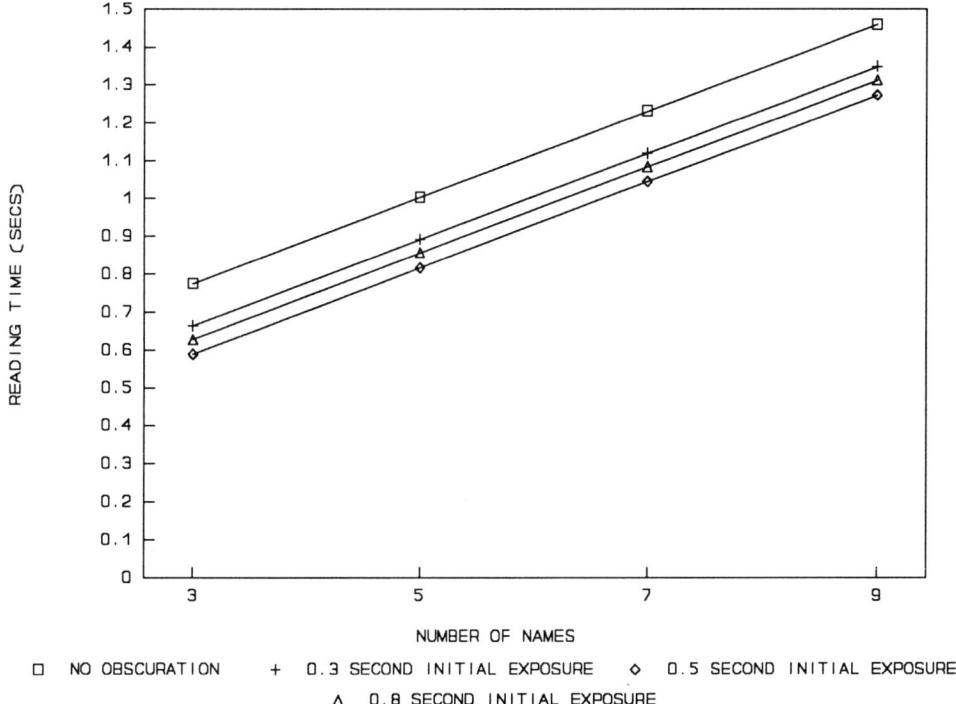

Figure 3, Predicted reading time of obscured direction signs against number of names.

It is clear that useful information can be gained from exposures as short as 0.3 seconds and that total reading time for obscured conditions is lower than that of unobscured.

3.3 Reading Network Maps

The introduction of Road Transport Informatics is likely to increase the demands made on the drivers visual sense. For route guidance and navigation, map based displays are rapidly becoming popular. A recently concluded experiment used the driving task simulator to investigate the relationship between the required reading time and map complexity and the location of the display. Subjects were required to find their way through networks presented on an in-vehicle display or on the back projection screen. Two sets of 24 maps were read by each of 10 subjects which provided 480 map reading observations. Figures 4, 5 and 6 show the first three levels of network complexity.

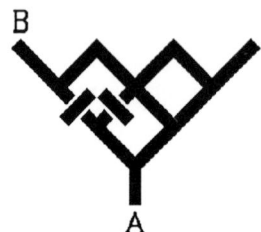

Figure 4, Network complexity 1.   **Figure 5**, Network complexity 2.   **Figure 6**, Network complexity 3.

Again, regression analysis provided predictive models of reading time for each of the exposure conditions. These are given by:

Internal display   T = 0.384 + 0.166 C
External display T = 0.515 + 0.166 C

Where   T = Time required (seconds).
        C = Complexity of the network.

These relationships are shown in Figure 7. It might be expected that the required reading time would be greater for in-vehicle displays as a reflection of the time required to re-accommodate the eye. However it is possible that a longer time can be taken for reading the external displays since subjects may be able to continue to monitor the tracking task using peripheral vision.

3.4 Future Uses

The latter experiment is part of a programme to investigate the safety aspects of the introduction of route guidance. The next stage of the programme will be to measure the required reading time of real route guidance and map displays.

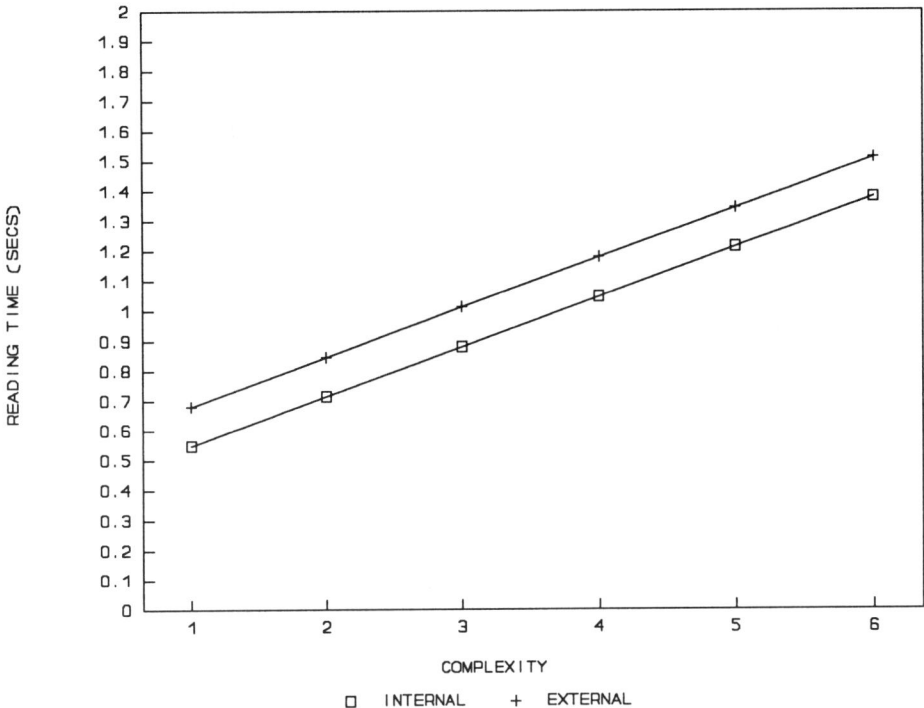

Figure 7, Predicted reading time of networks against complexity level.

4. DISCUSSION

The driving task simulator provides a controlled environment in which to evaluate a range of driver information acquisition tasks. It allows situations of maximum visual and cognitive load to be evaluated in safety.

It has been pointed out by Keilgast (1987) that the eyemarks of the NAC V eyemark camera tend to fall short of peripheral targets. The goggles of the eyemark camera also restrict peripheral vision which might lead to some changes in visual behaviour. The monitor used is perhaps large enough to allow for the tracking task to be attended to using peripheral vision but probably not to the extent that would be possible in actual driving. It is therefore intended to replace the monitor with a larger video projection screen. The control program uses the BBC microcomputer's memory to capacity which might limit future experimental design. To allow for more varied experiments the program is currently being rewritten for an IBM micro which has more memory.

The introduction of Road Transport Informatics is likely to increase the driver's visual load. The driving task simulator provides a convenient means of evaluating the visual load of many information acquisition tasks.

5. REFERENCES

GLIM - The Generalised Linear Interactive Modelling System (1986). Royal Statistical Society, Release 3.77, Numerical Algorithm Group Ltd.

Hall, R.D., McDonald, M., Rutley, K.S., (1990) Obscuration of signs by large vehicles, Transport and Road Research Laboratory, Department of Transport, Contractor Report 207.

Hall, R.D., McDonald, M., Rutley, K.S., (1991) An experiment to assess the reading time of direction signs, Proceedings Vision in Vehicles III, Pages 333-350, (North-Holland, Amsterdam: Elsevier Science Publishers).

Kielgast, K., (1987) Reliability of the NAC V - A preliminary test, Proceedings of the Third European Conference on Eye Movements, Pages 656-657.

VISION IN VEHICLES – IV
A.G. Gale et al. (Editors)

VISUAL SEARCH OF TRAFFIC SCENES:
ON THE EFFECT OF LOCATION EXPECTATIONS

Jan THEEUWES[1] and Marjan P. HAGENZIEKER[2]

[1]TNO Institute for Perception
P.O. Box 23, 3769 ZG Soesterberg, The Netherlands
[2]SWOV Institute for Road Safety Research,
P.O. Box 170, 2260 AD Leidschendam, The Netherlands

Abstract

The present study investigates top-down governed visual selection in natural traffic scenes. Subjects had to search for a target object (i.e., traffic sign, other road users) which was embedded in a natural traffic scene. Given a particular prototypical scene, the target was located either at a likely (expected) or unlikely (unexpected) position. The probability that a target object appeared at a likely location was varied between groups of subjects. The results showed the existence of scene dependent scanning strategies: search in the unexpected condition was significantly more error prone than search in the expected condition. This suggests that subjects strategically prepare for the upcoming stimulus and only search those locations which are likely to contain a target. If the target is not found at those likely locations, subjects tend to give a negative response. This effect remained after repeated presentation. The importance of these findings for search during actual driving is discussed.

1. INTRODUCTION

Although many conceptions of visual object perception (e.g., Marr, 1982) and visual search (e.g., Engel, 1977) primarily focus on the data-driven structural features (e.g., features, geons, location boundaries) of objects in their environments, it is well known that the meaning and the representation of the scene in relation to the object has an influence of speed and accuracy of both object search and identification. When considering visual selection in road scene environments, these contextual effects might be extremely important because driving, as an over-learned task, might rely on many sampling typicalities. In addition, since drivers are confronted with an enormous influx of visual information from which accurate and fast sampling is crucial, they will rely on rapid resource-inexpensive and conceptually-driven feature detection. Such type of processing will especially occur under conditions of visual and cognitive load and time pressure. Note that conceptually driven processing is only adequate if the expectations induced by the environment are correct. If expectations are incorrect and drivers rely on conceptually driven processing, severe errors might occur.

It is well substantiated that the processing of visual scenes is critically dependent on their spatial arrangement. A rearrangement of objects from their "natural" position impairs recognition of faces (e.g., Homa et al., 1976) and scenes (e.g., Biederman, 1972). On the other hand, the identification of objects is facilitated when objects are presented in a coherent scene (e.g., Biederman, 1972) but is inhibited if the objects violate their ordinary relation to the visual context (Biederman, Mezzanotte, & Rabinowitz, 1982). In visual search experiments similar findings are reported: search for an object located at an "unexpected" position is impaired relatively to objects appearing at their natural position. In addition, search for an object which is not likely to appear in a scene is slow and error prone (Meyers & Rhoades, 1978).

Biederman et al. (1982) give a list of five classes of relations which are sufficient to characterize the difference between a scene of unrelated objects and a well-formed scene. Support (i.e., objects appear resting on surfaces) and interposition (i.e., backgrounds should appear behind other objects) refer to general physical constraints of gravity. Probability, Position and familiar Size are semantic relations because they require access to the referential meaning of objects. Size is related to the size of a particular object relative to other objects appearing in the scene. Probability refers to the likelihood of a given object being in a scene. Position refers to the fact that objects which are likely to appear in a given scene often occupy specific positions in that scene.

The nature of contextual effects on the processing of objects in scenes is thought to be the result of an interaction between incoming perceptual information and higher level memory representations known as frames (Minsky, 1975) or schemata (Bartlett, 1932; McClelland & Rumelhart, 1981). For example, it has been argued that objects that are obligatory in the schema are encoded more or less automatically (with a minimum use of processing resources), whereas objects that do not fit in require more resource-expensive encoding processing involving active hypothesis testing (Friedman, 1979). Loftus et al. (1983) argue that scenes are processed in two stages. Holistic information is extracted first, followed by search for specific features. The holistic information can be assessed within a single fixation of the scene (Potter, 1975). This information is thought to activate the scene schema which is held in a presumed pictorial memory system (Paivio, 1971). A search is then initiated for specific objects as held in temporal storage.

The present study investigates the effect of contextual information on visual search of every-day life traffic scenes. More specifically, the study explores the effect of the object-context relation "position" as defined by Biederman et al. (1982). In contrast to earlier studies, we were interested in the effects of quite subtle violations to this relation. From an application point of view, examining this effect is particularly important because this relation might be violated in every-day life traffic situations. Perceptual errors might evolve when road users have wrong expectations regarding the location appearance of particular target objects. Thus, for example, traffic signs are not perceived adequately when they are located at locations which are unlikely given a particular scene.

Since it is not yet immediately clear how search objectives evolve during actual driving (for a discussion, see Theeuwes, 1991), in the present study, at the beginning of each trial, the search objective (target name: bicycle, traffic sign, car) was given to the subject. This was followed by a short presentation of the "precue" slide consisting of a traffic scene identical to the search scene, yet, without actually containing the target object. This combination of target object and to-be-searched scene was supposed to "prepare" the subject optimally for the upcoming scene in which subjects had to search for the target object. In the to-be-searched scene, there was a target object in 50% of the trials which could be at an expected or unexpected location. The short glance at the precue scene in combination with the target object was supposed to activate a scene specific schema which is assumed to contain knowledge about the typical makeup and contents of a scene being viewed. This scene schema will generate expectations about the locations of objects present in that scene. These expectations will bias search behavior towards those portions of the visual field which are supposed to contain maximum information (e.g., Biederman, 1972; Meyers & Rhoades, 1978). The present experiment investigates whether, dependent on scene-induced expectancies, subjects are biased to scan certain portions of traffic scenes.

2. METHOD

2.1 Subjects
Forty-eight subjects ranging in age from 19 to 55 years participated as paid volunteers. Twenty-four subjects each were randomly assigned to the "expected" and "unexpected" conditions. All had normal or corrected-to-normal vision and had their driving-license for at least 1 year.

2.2 Apparatus
An S-R interface with external clocks (accuracy of 1 msec) connected to an IBM AT-3 with video-digitizer (Matrox Inc.) controlled the timing of the events, generated video pictures, controlled slide projectors and recorded reaction times (RTs). The response panels consisted of left and right response keys (1 x 1 cm), which were mounted 1.5 cm apart.

The stimuli were projected by means of two Kodak carousel slide projectors (Kodak Carousel S-AV 2000) on a white screen (170 x 215 cm). Fixation point, target name and mask stimulus were projected on the same screen by means of a video projector (Barco data 400). Stimuli subtended a visual angle of about 18° in the horizontal and about 14° in the vertical direction.

Four subjects separated by wooden partitions were tested in a dimly-lit room. Subjects were seated approximately 365 cm from the screen. The center of the screen was located 185 cm above the floor of the room. An intercom was used for communication with the subject.

2.3 Stimuli
The search stimuli were 35 mm black-and-white slides of specific traffic scenes. The 44 traffic scenes used, were taken from a larger sample of scenes. Various types of traffic situations were used with the requirement that the traffic scenes were considered not too ambiguous and had at least some visual clutter. With respect to clutter this implied that scenes which did not contain many elements were not used. In addition, it was required that the target object (bicycle, car, traffic sign) was a naturally occurring

object in the specific scene. Target objects could either appear at an expected location or at an unexpected location (e.g. expected: traffic sign appearing at the right side of a crossing; unexpected: traffic sign appearing at the left side of the crossing). The expectancy judgement was made intuitively by two observers. Precue scenes were similar to the search scenes with the modification that the target object was not present in the scene. The masking stimulus was video-digitized by computer and consisted of a jumbled mixture of elements of various traffic scenes so that no single scene could be recognized.

The unexpected condition slides were, if possible, produced by presenting the photographed scenes mirror-reversed, and for the precue slide, the target object was photo-technically removed. This manipulation guaranteed that these slides were all identical with respect to light and local conspicuity. In other cases, expectancy manipulations were accomplished by changing the location of the target object in the actual scene. The distance from the center of the visual field to the target object located at an expected and unexpected location was more or less the same. This certified that differences in search times could not be attributed to differences in distances from the center of the visual field. The precue scene (the scene without the search target) and the scene containing the search target at an expected or an unexpected location were photographed within a rather short interval from the exactly same position implying that, besides very minor light differences, the slides were identical. Because target objects were never artificially inserted into the scene, the expectancy manipulations did not violate any of Biederman et al.'s relations which are supposed to define an object in a coherent real-world scene. Thus target objects rested on surfaces ('support'), were solid objects which could appear behind other objects ('interposition'), had the right size ('size'), and given a particular scene were likely to appear ('probability'). The only factor manipulated was 'position' suggesting that either the target object occupied a likely position (condition: "expected") or an unlikely position (condition: "unexpected").

Of the 44 trials, subjects searched 26 times for a bicyclist, 16 times for a traffic sign and 2 times for a car. In about half of these trials a target was present i.e., subjects searched 12 times for a bicyclist, 9 times for a traffic sign and once for a car, totalling 22 "target-present" trials. For each "target-present" trial, the "expected" and "unexpected" conditions were matched implying that for each scene there were two slides i.e., a slide in which the target object occupied an expected position and a slide in which the target object occupied an unexpected position.

2.4 Procedure

The sequence of events during a trial was as follows: initially, a target name (the Dutch equivalents for either traffic sign, "verkeersbord"; bicyclist, "fietser"; car, "auto") was presented for 2000 ms at the center of the screen. These letters were printed in lowercase black letters against a white background. This was followed for 800 ms by a black fixation dot at the center of the screen. Then, the precue slide was presented consisting of a traffic scene identical to the search scene without actually containing the target object. This scene was presented for about 500 ms followed by the masking stimulus which was presented for 1600 ms. Finally, the search slide was presented for a maximum of 5 sec until all 4 responses were emitted. Subjects did not receive performance feedback. Between trials there was a dark time of 3 sec. The sequence of events is shown by Figure 1.

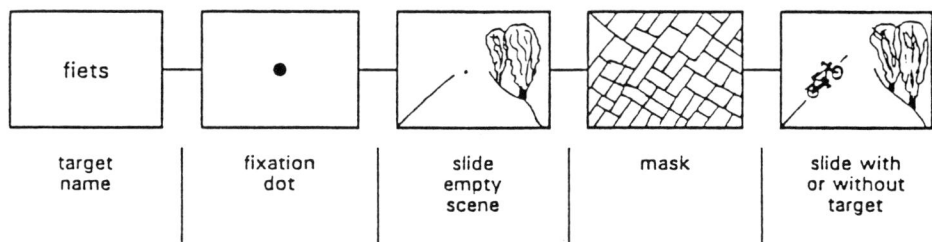

Figure 1 Sequence of events during a trial.

Two groups of 24 subjects were run. For one group of subjects the target object was consistently located at the "expected" location, whereas for the other group the target object was located at an "unexpected" location.

There were two random sequences of trial order presentations, which were counterbalanced between subjects. Each subject received two experimental runs of 44 experimental trials with a short brake of about 5 minutes in between runs. Each experimental run was preceded by 8 dummy trials to avoid start up effects.

Prior to the start of the experiment subjects received written instructions explaining the purpose of the experiment. They were not informed about the expectancy manipulations. Subjects were asked to search for the target object as fast as possible while minimizing errors. It was explained that the precue scene was similar to the search scene and that they should make use of this information to prepare for the upcoming search scene. When subjects thought that no target was present they pressed the "target-absent" button with their left thumb, and when they thought that a target was present they pressed the "target-present" button with their right. Before the experiment started subjects received ten practice trials.

3. RESULTS AND DISCUSSION

Mean RTs and error rates were computed for each subject in each condition. A separate analysis computing the mean error rate for each slide revealed that slide-number 1 in which a traffic sign was present produced error rates exceeding 85%. Inspection of the slide showed that the sign was too unclear to be perceived. Because this extreme high error rate the data of this slide were eliminated in the data analysis. In addition, RTs faster than 250 ms were considered guessing and therefore eliminated as well.

The mean RT for correct trials was submitted to an ANOVA with repetition (first time vs second time presented), expectancy (expected vs unexpected) and target presence (present vs absent) as main factors. There were main effects on RT for repetition ($F(1,46)= 46.9$; $p < .001$), and for target presence ($F(1,46)= 70.0$; $p < .001$). In addition, there was an interaction effect on RT of repetition and target presence ($F(1,46)= 15.3$; $p < .001$). The data indicates that, as expected, "target-presence" search was much faster than "target-absent" search (presence mean RT: 990.3 ms; absent mean RT: 1541.7 ms) indicating that search was self-terminating, i.e., search was terminated as soon as a target was found. The interaction between repetition and target presence indicates that the second time of presentation, search times were faster for trials in which a target was present than for trials in which a target was not present. This might suggest that subjects remember those trials in which a target was present better than the trials in which a target was not present.

The hypothesis that search would be faster for those trials in which the target appeared at an expected location is not confirmed by the present data: it was expected that for "target presence" trials a target located at an expected location would have been found faster than when the object is located at an unexpected location. Note that such an effect was not to be expected for the "target-absent" trials. Therefore, it was expected that the interaction between expectancy and target presence would have been significant. The results show that, albeit a trend in the correct direction, the interaction failed to reach significance ($\underline{F}(1,46)= 2.6$; $\underline{p} = .11$). Of additional importance is the finding that repetition did not interact with expectation ($\underline{F}(1,46)= .13$; $\underline{p} = .72$) suggesting that repeated presentation did not alter the effect of expectation.

In order to achieve homogeneity of the error rate variance, the mean error rates per cell were transformed by means of an arcsine transformation. The transformed error data were entered into the same ANOVA as performed on the response data. Again, there were main effects on error rate for repetition ($\underline{F}(1,46)= 17.1$; $\underline{p} < .001$), and target presence $\underline{F}(1,46)= 18.2$; $\underline{p} < .001$). In addition, again the interaction between repetition and target presence $\underline{F}(1,46)= 10.4$; $\underline{p} < .01$) was significant, indicating that subjects tend to make selectively make less errors when "target-present" trials are presented for the second time.

Contrary to the effects found on response times, the interaction between expectation and target presence for error rates was significant $\underline{F}(1,46)= 7.0$; $\underline{p} < .05$). Subsequent planned comparisons on the arcsine transformed error rates between expected and unexpected conditions show that there was a significant difference between the error rates of expected and unexpected conditions of the target-present condition ($F(1,46)= 6.3$; $\underline{p} < .05$). As expected this difference in error rates of the target-absent condition was not significant. The error data clearly indicate that when subjects search for a target located at an unexpected location they are more likely to respond "target not present" than when the target is located at an expected location. This suggest that subjects check those places which are likely to contain targets and when they do not find the target at the expected locations they are likely to give a negative response ("target-not-present").

The data on search times and error rates for target-present trials are summarized by Figure 2. The analyses show, as evident in Figure 2, that subjects apply different search strategies depending on the contextual cues available. Search in the expected location condition was to some extent faster than the search in the unexpected location condition. More importantly though is the finding that search in the unexpected condition was significantly more error prone than search in the expected condition. This indicates that subjects strategically prepare for the upcoming stimulus and search the scene based on the available contextual cues. If the target is at the expected location search is relatively fast and accurate; if the target is at the unexpected location search is somewhat slower and more error prone. Important is that this expectancy effect remains after repeated presentation. In addition, it appears that the subjects in the unexpected condition do <u>not</u> adjust their strategy over trials, i.e., it appears that subjects keep on preparing for the expected location even though for that group of subjects the target object never appeared at the expected location.

In an additional run involving another 24 subjects, 16 slides in which the target was located at an expected location were mixed with 6 slides in which the target was located at an unexpected location. This "mixed" condition provided a condition in which targets were usually at expected locations (in 73% of the target-present trials) and sometimes at unexpected locations (27% of the target-present trials). The results of the mixed condition substantiated the findings of the first run and confirmed the earlier conclusion that subjects use contextual cues to look at those places where target objects are likely to be found.

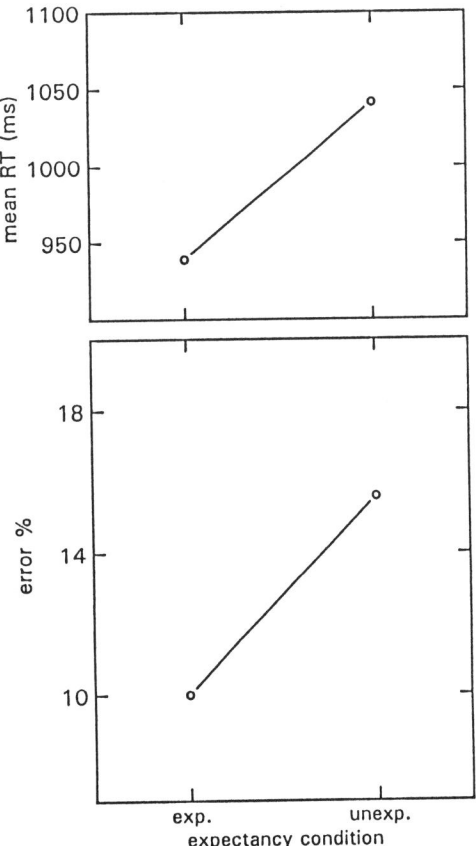

Figure 2 Mean RT and error rate for target-present trials in the expected and unexpected condition.

4. GENERAL DISCUSSION

The present study demonstrates the existence of scene dependent scanning behavior. Dependent upon the meaning and content of the scene in combination with the search objective, search behavior is biased towards certain portions of the visual field. In daily life people operate in a traffic environment which is reasonably predictable, and appear to rely on this assumption. The assumption is reinforced by a large number of times in which this inference is correct and it is supported by a common lack of feedback and/or penalties for detection misses. For typical traffic scenes, it appears that this search strategy is carried over into the laboratory and remains present after repeated presentation even in conditions in which the target object is presented consistently at unlikely positions.

The present results are in line with the findings of Meyers & Rhoades (1978). In their study, subjects searched for target objects in every-day life scenes (e.g., searching for a saucepan in a kitchen scene). They demonstrated the effect of location probability: searching for an object appearing at an "out of place" position (e.g., the saucepan under the kitchen table) was much slower than when the target object was at a likely position (e.g., the saucepan on the stove). In a mixed condition in which on half of the trials, the target object appeared at a likely position and on the other half on an unlikely position, search time was relatively short (similar to the "in-place" group) with a relatively high error score. Comparing the present results to Meyers & Rhoades' findings indicate that the present subjects in the unexpected condition had a search performance similar to subjects in the mixed condition of the Meyers and Rhoades study. In these conditions, subjects only search places that are likely to contain a target object, and when it is not found at that location, they give a negative (target-not-present) response. In Meyers & Rhoades' study, subjects in the out-of-place (unexpected) condition learned that context was not a useful aid in their search and adapted their strategy resulting in an accurate yet slow search. The present data do not suggest such a mechanism: subjects in the unexpected condition are somewhat slower; yet, the high error rate suggests that they do not adapt their strategy and have the tendency to remain searching for the likely positions only.

The present findings demonstrating the existence of scene dependent scanning behavior should be considered as quite striking given the real-life stimulus material used. Since the present study uses real traffic scenes, the possibilities of placing objects at "out-of-place" positions are rather limited. Unlike for example the stimulus material as used by Meyers & Rhoades (1978), traffic scenes have usually a clear 3-D perspective. This perceptive limits the possibilities of placing an object of a given size in that scene. In most cases one can only put the object at, for example, the right or left side of the scene. Putting the object at any given other location, might violate other relations defining a coherent scene such as "size" and "support". In addition, to ensure that search time differences reflect expectancy effects rather than conspicuity effects is was necessary to keep local conspicuity as similar as possible. For example, if an object on the right side of the road is located against an empty background and on the left side against a cluttered background, search time differences are more likely to reflect conspicuity differences rather than expectancy differences. The present experiment used black-and-white pictures rather than colored pictures, to further reduce the effects of conspicuity on search behavior.

Note that all these constraints were taken into account to increase the ecological validity of the present study. It should be realized that the effects of contextual driven search might be much stronger in real driving especially in conditions in which there is a relatively high visual load i.e., driving in busy traffic in urban environments, or under reduced sight conditions, for instance when driving in the dark or in twilight. The black-and-white pictures used in the experiment can be considered as simulating this kind of degraded visual circumstances. Especially in these situations, rapid resource-inexpensive and conceptually-driven feature detection is advantageous. The presently observed data suggest that objects at unexpected locations are not seen too late but, in most cases, not seen at all, i.e., when searching for objects at unexpected locations subjects tend to say "target-not-present". It is very likely that these type of errors also occur when searching during actual driving. In fact, accident data seem to confirm this notion: a large portion of drivers (about 37 %) involved in automobile crashes do not act too late but do not act at all to avoid the collision (Sussman, Bishop, Madnick, & Walter, 1985). Note that accidents do not occur often indicating that errors in visual sampling, i.e., detection misses, are not fed back to the driver. On the other hand, correct expectancies i.e., finding an object where you expected it, are consistently reinforced.

Given these considerations, it is clear that extremely dangerous situations may occur when the design of the traffic environment induces certain expectations regarding the spatial arrangement of objects in that scene, which are not correct. For example, car drivers approaching a typical crossing with a bicycle track tend to look only to the right side and stop searching when a bike is not found at that location. When at such a crossing, bikes approach from both directions, bicyclists coming from the left are likely to be missed. Because the lay-out of the bike path induced wrong expectations, drivers tend to look to one side only. In those circumstances, it would be better that the bike path does not resemble a bike path at all so that no expectancies are induced.

In which driving situations and under what conditions, expectancies are in operation is still very much unclear. As a first instance, Riemersma (1988a, 1988b) demonstrated that road users have different and more categories to distinguish traffic environments than there are distinguished officially. Future studies should identify the circumstances under which conceptually driven detection occurs, which elements of the environment induce expectancies, and what type of expectancies can be recognized. These findings may help in the design of safer road environments.

5. ACKNOWLEDGEMENT

This research was funded by the Dutch Ministry of Transport and Public Works.

6. REFERENCES

Bartlett, F.C. (1932). Remembering. Cambridge: Cambridge University Press.
Biederman, I. (1972). Perceiving real world scenes. Science, 177, 77-80.
Biederman, I., Mezzanotte, R.J. & Rabinowitz, J.C. (1982). Scene perception: Detecting

and judging objects undergoing relational violations. Cognitive Psychology, 14, 143-177.

Engel, F.L. (1977). Visual conspicuity, visual search and fixation tendencies of the eye. Vision Research 17, 95-108.

Friedman, A. (1979). Framing pictures: The role of knowledge in automatized encoding and memory for gist. Journal of Experimental Psychology: General, 108, 316-355.

Homa, D., Haver, B. & Schartz, T. (1976). Perceptibility of schematic face stimuli. Evidence for perceptual gestalt. Memory & Cognition, 4, 175-185.

Loftus, G.R., Nelson, W.W. & Kallman J.J. (1983). Differential acquisition rates for different types of information from pictures. Quarterly Journal of Experimental Psychology, 35A, 187-198.

Marr, D. (1982). Vision: A computational investigation into the human representation and processing of visual information. San Francisco: Freeman.

McClelland, J. & Rumelhart, D. (1981). An interactive activation model of context effects in letter perception; Part I. An account of basic findings. Psychological Review, 88, 375-407.

Meyers, L.S., and Rhoades, R.W. (1978). Visual search of common scenes. Quarterly Journal of Experimental Psychology, 30, 297-310.

Minsky, M. (1975). A framework for representing knowledge. In P.H. Winston (ed.): The psychology of computer vision. New York: McGraw-Hill.

Paivio, A. (1971). Imagery and verbal processes. New York: Holt, Rinehart & Winston.

Potter, M.C. (1975). Meaning in visual search. Science, 187, 965-966.

Riemersma, J.B.J. (1988a). Zonering en herkenbaarheid; een experiment. Report IZF 1988 C-2 Institute for Perception, Soesterberg, The Netherlands.

Riemersma, J.B.J. (1988b). Enkelbaans/dubbelbaans autowegen: beleving van de weggebruiker. Report IZF 1988 C-4, Institute for Perception, Soesterberg, The Netherlands.

Sussman, E.D., Bishop, H., Madnick, B. & Walter, R., (1985). Driver inattention and highway safety. Transportation Research Record 1047, 40-48.

Theeuwes, J. (1991). Visual selection: exogenous and endogenous control. In A.G. Gale et al. (eds.): Vision in vehicles III. Amsterdam: Elsevier Science Publishers B.V.

7

TRAFFIC SIGNS

TRAFFIC SIGN MEANING: DESIGNER INTENT VS. USER PERCEPTION

Alice A. THIEMAN and Lloyd L. AVANT

Departments of Human Development and Psychology, Iowa State University, Ames,
IA 50011 U.S.A.

Abstract

Subjects were presented traffic signs designed to communicate STOP, LEFT, RIGHT, and SLOW DOWN messages and asked to use their own criteria for grouping signs into groups that belong together. Probabilities of grouping according to the four intended meanings averaged .45, but probabilities of grouping as MERGE, KEEP, STOP,SLOW DOWN, and DO NOT ENTER averaged .67. These results indicate that the designer-intended priority message is comprehended by translations of the presented sign information through secondary mental operations.

1. INTRODUCTION

Effective traffic signing is critical to highway safety. According to a recent report (FHWA, 1989), $21 in accident costs is saved for every dollar spent on roadway signing. Thus, determining sign characteristics that produce faster and more accurate driver information processing should be of high priority. Many factors contribute to sign detection, recognition, and response selection. Our research has focused on the mental operations that process visual information from traffic signs prior to consideration of the situational factors that are intrinsic to actual driving.

Among the general determinants of the mental operations that process traffic sign information are the priority message the sign is designed to communicate, the format in which the message is presented, and the age or driving experience of the driver. In modern times, the increase in international travel has made it more important for drivers from one nation to be able to drive in countries where the language is unfamiliar; thus it is increasingly important to determine what sign parameters can optimize the mental operations that could use an international supralinguistic signing system for roadways (Krampen, 1983). Although exceptions are to be found, most studies that have addressed this issue have indicated that, generally, sign recognition and appropriate response are faster for symbol signs than for word signs (e.g., Collins, 1982; Ells & DeWar, 1979; King, 1975; Jacobs, Johnston, & Cole, 1975; Whitaker & Stacey, 1981). But, even when verbal signs produce faster latencies for correct responses than do symbol signs, the relationship usually reverses under degradation (e.g., increasing distance) of sign information.

Another important issue in signing research is the increasing age of the driving population. In the United States, it is estimated that by the year 2000, 13% of the population will be over age 65, and that percentage will swell to 20% by the year 2030

(U.S. Census Bureau, 1984). Given that the demographics of the population are changing and that there will be a substantial increase in the percentage of drivers who are at the upper end of the lifespan, researchers must determine how increasing age influences the mental operations that enable the older citizen to negotiate the environment on foot as well as operate a motor vehicle safely.

Previous research from our laboratory has addressed several general questions about how sign information is processed. This research has shown, for example, that the brain begins analysis of the action message communicated by the sign unconsciously and well before the viewer has conscious awareness that the sign is in the visual field. The research also indicates that Stop signs are more likely to be detected and recognized under difficult viewing conditions than are other familiar traffic signs. And, word signs appear to be detected more readily than symbol signs. The research has also shown recognition errors to be more frequent for some signs (e.g., Merge Right) than for others (e.g., Signal Ahead) (Avant et al., 1985; Avant et al., 1986).

The research suggesting the above conclusions used a set of 15 traffic signs and one non-regulation diamond shaped Stop sign. These signs were chosen as representative of four intended priority action messages (Stop, Slow Down, move Right, move Left) used by transportation engineers in the design of roadway signs. We have consistently used these four message categories in evaluating our data. However, John Groeger suggested that we might learn more about the meanings that drivers see in these signs if we asked drivers to simply sort the 16 signs into groups that belong together because they have the same or similar meanings. Such groupings might provide indications of the complexity and/or order of the mental operations applied to various traffic signs.

We conducted two experiments in response to Groeger's suggestion. In the first, we asked subjects to categorize signs into groups that belong together, using their own criterion for determining which signs belonged together. In the second, we provided subjects a choice among 11 possible driver actions and asked them to verbalize, as rapidly as possible, which action they would think of first when each sign was presented on a computer monitor. We recorded the subjects' action choices and the latency of those responses. We also recorded each subject's age so as to index, in a general fashion, the effect of age on response choices and latencies.

2. EXPERIMENT 1

The intent of Experiment 1 was simple and straightforward. It addressed the question: Do regular drivers categorize these sign meanings in accord with the Stop, Left, Right, and Slow Down meanings intended by sign designers?

2.1 METHOD
Subjects
Subjects were 43 student volunteers at Briar Cliff College and Iowa State University, all licensed drivers who had normal or corrected-to-normal vision.

Stimulus Materials

The sample of traffic signs is shown in Figure 1. The sample included four signs designed to communicate each of four driver action messages: Stop, Move Left, Move Right, and Slow Down. For each driver action, two variants of the message were used: Stop action messages were Stop and Do Not Enter; Move Left (Right) were Keep Left (Right) and Merge Left (Right); and Slow Down messages were Stop Ahead and Signal Ahead. Where possible, a word-only and a symbol-only sign presenting each message were selected; where this was not possible, the sign was identified as a word or symbol sign by the predominant property of the sign. The signs were photographed as 2" X 2" color slides.

Figure 1. Matrix of signs for detection, recognition and reaction experiments

Procedure

Subjects were presented the 16 pictures of the signs on a light box illuminating all signs at once. They were asked to simply sort the signs into groups that belong together, using whatever criterion they wished for the groupings. When each subject completed the sorting, he/she informed the experimenter and identified the criterion that had guided the groupings.

Design

Evaluation of the data was simple. The frequencies with which all 43 subjects grouped each sign with every other sign were tabulated, and these frequencies were converted to probabilities. These probabilities were examined in terms of two criteria: the first was probabilities of grouping by Stop, Move Left, Move Right, and Slow Down messages, and the second simply examined the groupings identifying highest probabilities of signs being grouped together.

2.2 Results and Discussion

The results were surprising. Probabilities of grouping signs according to the Stop, Move Left, Move Right, and Slow Down meanings were .34, .42, .41, and .61 respectively. However, when we listened to subjects' comments regarding their categories and paid attention to high probability groupings, we found that the highest average grouping probabilities were .74, .58, .61, .71, and .70, and the groupings were for Stop, Do Not Enter, Slow Down, Merge, and Keep messages respectively. We were surprised to find that subjects grouped Merge signs and Keep signs separately but, in each group, collapsed across the Left and Right directions in the signs. And, whereas we had previously grouped Stop and Do Not Enter signs as communicating the same priority message, probabilities of categorizing these signs together varied from only .05 to .33. Even within the Merge and Keep groups, there was a higher probability of placing word signs together (.79 to .81) and symbol signs together (.77 to .84) than there was of grouping the Left and Right directional signs together (.70 to .74).

The results of this sorting task indicate that, when asked to group signs according to their own meaning criteria, subjects do not categorize according to the priority messages intended by the designer. These data may or may not reflect the priorities that drivers give to various sign messages, but it seems appropriate to evaluate driver responses to test what messages have priority. For example, these data suggest that the priority the sign designer intends for the Left and Right messages are subordinate to the Keep and Merge meanings.

3. Experiment 2

3.1 Method

Prior research in our lab has shown that, when subjects were asked for button press motor responses to our sample of signs with response options limited to Stop, Left, Right, and Slow Down, Stop responses were faster than Left, Right, and Slow Down responses (1039, 1178, 1150, and 1144 ms respectively). And, mean response latency for word signs was longer (1141 ms) than for symbol signs (1116 ms), To extend the subject's options for making an initial response to the sample of signs, we considered the number of possible driver actions that might come immediately to mind when any traffic sign appears in the visual field. The options that we considered reasonable were the following 11:

Brake	
Steer Right	Steer Left
Turn Right	Turn Left
Let off gas pedal	Press down gas pedal

Change lanes	Check mirrors
Shift gears	Nothing

These response options replaced the Stop, Left, Right, and Slow Down options from our earlier research.   This many response options obviates the use of motor responses to indicate the subject's choice so subjects were asked to voice their choices.

Subjects
   Subjects were 50 students, staff, and faculty members at Iowa State University. Their ages ranged from 18 to 59 years.   All were licensed drivers and had normal or corrected-to-normal vision.

Procedure and Design
   Subjects were tested individually and were seated about 14" from a lab computer. The 16 signs were reproduced electronically on a Zenith 286 computer and presented on a VGA color monitor. The Micro Experimental Lab (MEL) program provided, for each subject, separate randomized orders for six replications of the 16 signs for a total of 96 trials for each subject. A voice-activated switch permitted the MEL program to also record the latencies of the subject's verbal response to each sign. Although all subjects received 96 trials, a programming error varied the number of times each subject saw individual signs from three to seven. The subject's responses were tape recorded as well as hand recorded by the experimenter. Subjects initiated each trial by pressing the keyboard space bar.
   At the beginning of the experiment, subjects were informed that traffic signs would be presented on the monitor and that their task was to speak, as quickly as possible, the driver action that first came to mind when each sign came into view. The 11 response options were placed in clear view below the lower left corner of the monitor. Subjects were instructed to avoid reading each sign; they were instructed to use, instead, one of the 11 response options listed just below the monitor to indicate what action they would first think of upon seeing each sign. Questions regarding what assumptions about a driving situation were appropriate were answered by telling the subject to make whatever assumptions he/she considered proper and to respond within the context of that situation. Responses other than the 11 posted options were scored as synonyms of those options or as Miscellaneous. The entire procedure took about 20 minutes.

3.2 Results and Discussion
   The first thing to note about these decision latencies is that they were all longer than those from our earlier experiment. These longer latencies clearly reflect the translation of decisions into a verbal, rather than motor, format in addition to any of the differential uncertainty about response options for the various signs suggested below.
   Response latencies from Experiment 2 were submitted to two different analyses of variance. Initially, the latencies were evaluated according to the four designer-intended messages (Stop, Left, Right, Slow Down).   The main effect of message was highly significant, $F(3,147) = 12.20$, $p < .01$, and mean response time for STOP signs (1507 ms) was clearly faster than for Left, Right, and Slow Down signs (1882, 1885, and 1803 ms respectively). The two variants for each sign message also produced a significant main effect, $F(1,49) = 76.94$, $p < .001$). Responses to Stop signs (mean = 1152 ms) were faster

than to Do Not Enter signs (1862 ms), Keep signs produced faster responses (1725 ms) than did Merge signs (2043 ms), and Stop Ahead signs prompted faster respones (1651 ms) than did Signal Ahead signs (1954 ms). Unlike the earlier study, this experiment did not show mean latency for word signs to be faster than that for symbol signs (but see discussion of age effects below).

These results replicate the major findings from the previous study in which subjects' responses were limited to four action decisions. In this replication, the Experiment 2 procedure offers the possibility of more sensitively indexing the mental operations that process traffic sign information than did the previous procedure.

A second analysis evaluated these response latencies when sign messages were those identified by the categorizing data from Experiment 1: Stop, Slow Down, Merge, Keep, and Do Not Enter. This analysis also addressed effects of subject age on decision latencies. Three age groups were identified: 18-25 (college-age subjects), 26-40 (young adults), and 41-59 (middle-age adults). The analysis also revealed a significant effect of the messages identified by subject-determined categories, $F(4,188) = 23.93$, $p < .001$. Stop signs were responded to faster (1146 ms) than any of the other signs (1802, 2047, 1709, and 1838 ms respectively) and, again, Keep signs produced faster responses (1709 ms) than Merge signs (2047 ms). Like the subject-determined meaning categories identified in Experiment 1, these latencies indicate that Keep and Merge messages are processed by mental operations unique to each message. And, contrary to the Left versus Right messages in designer-determined categories, latencies for these two messages differed very little (1880 and 1876 respectively). Do Not Enter and Slow Down signs produced roughly equivalent response latencies (1837 and 1801 ms respectively).

3.3 Other Informative Trends in the Data

Several other observations merit notice although they are not subject to statistical test. By and large, these observations concern the effects of age on the data even though none of our subjects could legitimately be considered elderly drivers.

One trend worthy of notice occurred in the ordering, from shortest to longest mean latency, of the five subject-determined meaning categories for the three age groups. For college-age subjects (18-25), the order was Stop, Do Not Enter, Keep, Slow Down, and Merge, with mean latencies of 1120, 1451, 1603, 1632, and 1853 respectively. This order differed for young adults (26-40), being Stop, Keep, Slow Down, Do Not Enter, and Merge with mean latencies of 1172, 1648, 1784, 1824, and 2048 respectively. For middle age subjects (41-59) the order changed to Stop, Keep, Slow Down, Merge, and Do Not Enter with mean latencies of 1114, 1681, 1841, 1956, and 1993 respectively. The general point made by these shifts in ordering of latencies for the various sign messages is that, as driving experience increases with age, the speed and/or uncertainty in mental operations applied to the various messages do not change uniformly; the single constant is that response to the Stop message is fastest for all ages and, in fact, changes very little across ages.

Age influenced mean latencies for other factors in a similar fashion. Thus, for the 18-25 age group, mean latency for word signs (1711 ms) was longer than for symbol signs (1611); for the 26-40 age group, mean latencies were nearly the same for word and symbol signs (1807 and 1845); the order for 18-25 year olds reversed for the 41-59 age group with symbol sign latency (1927) longer than word sign latency (1772). Similarly, latencies for Left and Right signs varied with age. For 18-25 year olds, latency for Right (1683) was lower than for Left (1772); for 26-40 year olds, latency for Left (1414) was considerably lower than for Right (1862); and for 41-59 year olds, the Left response (1728) was faster than the Right response (1919). Keep responses were faster for all age groups than Merge responses.

The relationship between age and response latency for each sign was also evaluated using correlational analyses. Age did not influence speed of response for the majority of the signs; only the latencies for Keep Right (Word), DNE (Symbol), Stop Ahead (Symbol), and Signal Ahead (Symbol) were significantly correlated with age ($r=.46$ ($p=.0008$), $.28$ ($p=.05$), $.30$ ($p=.03$), and $.32$ ($p=.02$), respectively). The important point to note is that three of the four signs are symbol signs.

Although many studies indicate that symbol signs are processed faster and more accurately than word signs, our data indicate that this conclusion may not hold for older drivers. Again, for the psychologist, these observations present the challenge of determining the ways in which the mental operations applied to the various signs are differentially modified by age and driving experience.

4. ACKNOWLEDGEMENTS

Experiment 2 was run using the MEL System, Psychology Software Tools Inc., licensed to Dr. Veronica Dark, Iowa State University. The authors are grateful to Dr. Leroy Wolins for assistance with the statistical analyses and to Dr. Veronica Dark for assistance with the computer programming.

5. REFERENCES

Avant, L. L., Brewer, K. A., Thieman, A. A., & Woodman, W. F. (1985). Recognition errors among highway signs. Transportation Research Record 1027, 35-42.

Avant, L. L., Thieman, A. A., Brewer, K. A., & Woodman, W. F. (1986). On the earliest perceptual operations of detecting and recognizing traffic signs. In A. G. Gale, M. H. Freeman, C. M. Haslegrave, P. Smith, and S. P. Taylor (Eds)., Vision in Vehicles. Amsterdam: Elsevier North-Holland.

Collins, B. L. (1982). The development and evalution of effective symbol signs. NBS Building Science Series 141. U.S. Department of Commerce, National Bureau of Standards. Washington, D.C.: U.S. Government Printing Office.

Ells, J. G. & Dewar, R. E. (1979). Rapid comprehension of verbal and symbolic traffic sign messages. Human Factors, 21(2), 161-168.

Federal Highway Administration (FHWA), 1989 Annual Report on Highway Safety Improvement Programs. Washington, D.C.

Jacobs, R. J., Johnston, A. W., & Cole, B. L. (1975). The visibility of alphabetic and symbolic traffic signs. Australian Road Research 5(7), 68-86.

King, L. E. (1975). Recognition of symbol and word traffic signs. Journal of Safety Research 7, 80-84.

Krampen, M. (1983). Icons of the road. Journal of the International Association for Semiotic Studies 43, 1/2.

U.S. Census Bureau. (1984). Projections of the Population by Age, Sex, and Race for the
    United States, 1983 to 2080. No. 952, Series P-25. Government Printing Office.
Whitaker, L. A. & Stacey, S. (1981). Response times to left and right directional signs.
    Human Factors 23(4), 447-452.

VISION IN VEHICLES – IV
A.G. Gale et al. (Editors)
1993 Elsevier Science Publishers B.V.

169

EFFECTS OF DELAY ON RECALL OF ROAD SIGNS: AN EVALUATION OF THE VALIDITY OF RECALL METHOD

Juha LUOMA

The University of Michigan, Transportation Research Institute,
2901 Baxter Road, Ann Arbor, Michigan 48109-2150, USA[1]

Abstract

This study was designed to compare the recall of road signs after two different delays. Three conditions were evaluated: a game crossing sign, a speed limit sign, and a control condition with no sign. Either immediately after passing a road sign or 670 m downstream, subjects in the sign condition were asked a question about the last road sign. The results showed that subjects recalled the speed limit sign regardless of the delay, but the recall of the game crossing sign decreased substantially when the inquiry was delayed. In both conditions, the other traffic in the vicinity decreased the recall percentage by more than half. The implications of this study are that the recall delay affects especially the recall of a road sign of subjectively minor importance and that a careful consideration of other traffic during the experiment is essential.

1. INTRODUCTION

This study concentrates on the recall method used in studies that have investigated the question of how drivers perceive and remember the information in road signs in real life. Drivers' recalls have frequently been studied by stopping vehicles that have recently passed a test sign and inquiring about the last sign they remember having passed (e.g., Hakkinen, 1965; Johansson and Rumar, 1966; Johansson and Backlund, 1970; Aberg, 1981). These studies conducted in Sweden and Finland revealed that, for example, 69-80% of drivers correctly recalled a speed limit sign, 61-77% a special police control sign, 46-67% a game crossing sign, and 18-39% a general warning sign.

This simple research method has obvious advantages. The number of drivers can be substantial, the drivers are unalerted when they are encountering the sign, and the results indicate at least something about how the drivers process information. However, the recall method has been criticized because of the potential effects of the delay between the passing of the sign and the inquiry, and the anxiety caused by a sudden request to stop by a policeman. On the other hand, Johansson and co-workers argued that it seems improbable that any driver who had read the police control sign would forget its message: (1) some of them were 'home made', (2) it must have been considered subjectively too important to forget and (3) it received reinforcement after a few seconds. Johansson and Backlund (1970) also collected half of the data when the vehicles were stopped by a policeman in uniform and the other half by a policeman in plain clothes. No differences were found.

Another possible way to study the recall of signs is to use subjects whose task is to answer questions concerning targets that they recently passed. The questions concerning road signs are included among questions concerning different kinds of targets (Luoma, 1991a). This modification of the recall method also allows recording of the driver's eye movements when the driver is encountering the sign. This method can avoid most of the potential effects of delay but the problems of having alerted drivers remain. Subjects may, for example, better obey traffic rules (Luoma, 1991b).

This study was designed to compare the recall of road signs after two different delays. The experimental set up was intended to replicate that used by Hakkinen (1965), Johansson and Rumar (1966), Johansson and Backlund (1970), and Aberg (1981), because these experiments were carried out in comparable circumstances. One of the main differences was that the previous studies used unalerted drivers, while the present study used alerted drivers. Another important difference was that in the present experiment the delay between the passing of the sign and the inquiry was varied.

2. METHOD

The experimental site was located on a Finnish secondary road, with a speed limit of 60 km/h and an average daily traffic of 2,900 vehicles. An experimental road sign was posted in a normal manner on a slightly descending left curve. Drivers were able to see the sign about 200 m away and there were no other road signs within about 1 km upstream and downstream from the experimental sign.

Three conditions were evaluated: (1) a symbolic game (animal) crossing sign with a supplemental 1 km sign, (2) a 40 km/h speed limit sign, and (3) a control condition with no sign. These signs were selected because previous studies have shown that the basic difference in the recall of signs is between warning signs and speed-restriction signs, with a lower percentage in the recall of warning signs. Moreover, on rural roads of this kind, the game crossing sign is rather common, but the speed limit of 40 km/h can be considered as an extreme restriction. Because the game crossing sign was supplemented with a 1 km sign, both signs were valid for a similar distance. The background of the sign was a forest.

The test vehicle was a small passenger car with a manual transmission. The car was equipped with a personal computer (Toshiba T3200) connected to sensors which recorded the actual distance and the actual speed of the car. The eye movements were recorded by an eye mark recorder (EMR-NAC Model 5).

The subjects included technical or secretarial staff of the Helsinki University of Technology and the Technical Research Centre of Finland. All were licensed drivers who volunteered for the study. Their ages ranged from 19 to 55 years and their vehicle kilometreage during the previous year ranged from 1,000 to 100,000 km. Most of them were unfamiliar with the test road. Eighty-six percent of them were men. None of them wore glasses.

The subjects participated in the experiment individually and only once. They were told that the purpose of the experiment was to analyze normal visual information acquisition during highway driving. Furthermore, they were told that their eye movements would be recorded, and that they would be asked some questions concerning what they had perceived.

Their task was to drive a route of 60 km as normally as possible, but following the experimenter's directions. They drove a practice route of 15 km without the eye mark recorder so that they could get used to the car.

After the practice session the eye mark recorder was placed on drivers heads and calibrated. After driving 10 km they passed the experimental site. Either immediately after passing a road sign or 670 m downstream, the subjects in the sign condition were asked one or two questions:

(1) What was the last road sign you passed?
(2) Was there anything else? (Only asked in the game crossing sign condition if Question 1 was answered correctly.)

In the nominally immediate condition, there was actually a delay of about 2 sec before the subject heard the first question. In the other condition, the experiment continued without interruption until the experimenter asked the subject to stop the car at a bus stop 670 m downstream from the experimental sign. After the stop the experimenter asked the same questions. Because subjects in different sign conditions were driving at different speeds after passing the sign, the longer delay averaged 49 sec in the game crossing sign condition and 56 sec in the speed limit condition.

The subjects were run on 28 days during a period of 53 days in the fall. Three or four drivers were run daily from 9 a.m. to 3 p.m. and one of those was a control condition with no sign. The type of sign was alternated after each 7 days of data collection. The tested delay was alternated after each 4 subjects.

The speed of the experimental vehicle was measured just before the driver was able to see the sign and about 200 m downstream from the sign.

A total of 102 alerted drivers participated in the experiment, but cases with an opposing vehicle, or a vehicle in front of the experimental vehicle with a gap less than 15 sec, during the section where the speeds were measured were omitted from the main analysis. The final data included 77 drivers without other traffic in the vicinity (14-18 cases in each sign/delay condition) and 25 drivers with other traffic in the vicinity. Except as noted, the following results do not concern the recall of the supplementary sign and the effect of other traffic in the vicinity.

3. RESULTS

Correct recalls were defined as answers in which the essential content of the sign was correct. In all cases, the road sign was correctly reported, if at all. The recall of the two road signs in the two delay conditions is given in Figure 1.

The results indicate that the subjects recalled the speed limit sign regardless of the delay (chi2(1) = 0.93, ns), but the recall of the game crossing sign decreased substantially when the inquiry was delayed (chi2(1) = 4.46, p<.03). When a question about the last sign was asked immediately, the difference in recall between the two road signs was marginally not significant (chi2(1) = 3.16, p<.08), but after the longer delay the difference was highly significant (chi2(1) = 12.59, p<.0004).

The results showed also that 50% of subjects who recalled the game crossing sign when

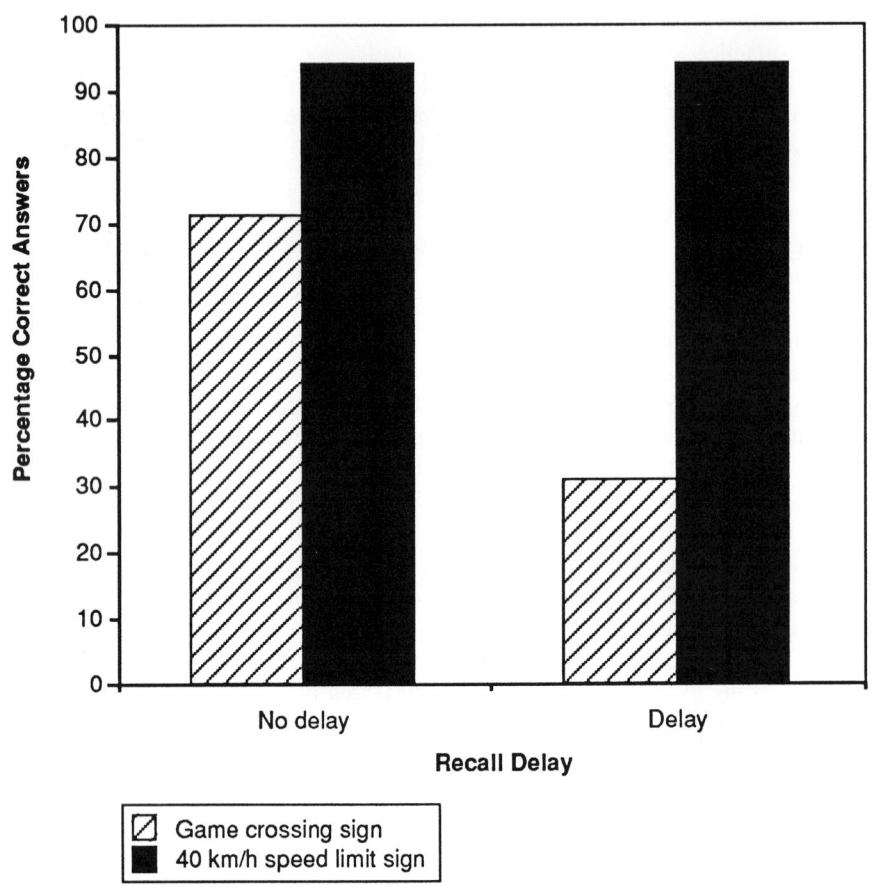

Figure 1   Correct recall of the road sign in the two sign and delay conditions.

asked immediately also recalled the supplementary sign. After the longer delay, it was recalled by 75% of subjects who recalled the game crossing sign. Four subjects recalled that there was a supplementary sign but did not recall the contents. These cases were coded as incorrect recalls of the supplementary sign.

Only one subject (in the game crossing sign and longer-delay condition) did not fixate on the sign. Drivers with eye fixations on the sign fixated it on average 2.9 times (s.d. = 1.5) and the mean fixation duration was 484 msec (s.d.= 246 msec). No significant differences were found between the sign conditions. The same result was found for the effects of number of eye fixations and fixation duration on recall of the sign.

Initial speed averaged 67.1 km/h. No difference was found for sign by delay conditions. However, speed changes differed significantly depending on the combination of sign, delay, and recall of the sign, $F(8,66)=28,21$, p<.0001 (Figure 2).

Scheffe's test (see Kirk, 1969) showed that the subjects in the speed limit condition who

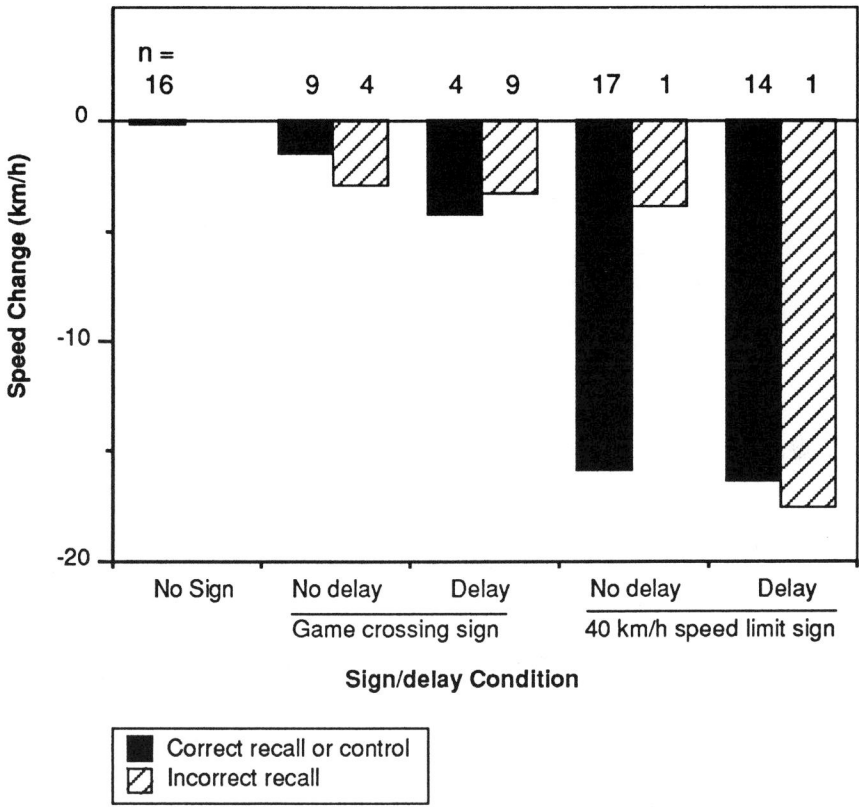

Figure 2 The average speed change depending on the sign, the delay condition, and the recall of the sign.

recalled the sign decreased their speed significantly more than the subjects who encountered the game crossing sign (whether they recalled it or not) or no sign. None of the other differences was significant.

The effects of the background variables on the recall of the game crossing sign were analyzed for each delay condition. None of the background variables was found to affect significantly.

Previous experiments concerning recall of a road sign did not control for traffic in the vicinity of the sign. The size of the present data set allows examination of only overall effects of other traffic on recall of the game crossing sign. The cases with other traffic in the vicinity were divided into three types: (1) one or more oncoming vehicles but no vehicle in front of the experimental car (43%), (2) one or more vehicles in front with or without an oncoming vehicle (43%), and (3) an approaching vehicle from the secondary road without vehicles in front or oncoming (14%). The frequencies of those types were quite similar in both delay conditions, and in all cases the subjects were able to see the sign. In cases when other traffic was present, 33% of the subjects recalled the sign if they were asked immediately and only 13% recalled it after the longer delay. In both delay conditions, the other traffic in the vicinity decreased the recall percentage by more than half.

4. DISCUSSION

This experiment was designed to evaluate the validity of the recall method. Specifically, the experiment compared the recall of road signs after two different delays, using the same experimental set up as the one used by Hakkinen (1965), Johansson and Rumar (1966), Johansson and Backlund (1970), and Aberg.

The results showed that when there was no other traffic in the vicinity, the subjects recalled the speed limit sign regardless of the delay, but the recall of the game crossing sign decreased substantially when the inquiry was delayed. Because the eye fixation patterns of the subject groups in different sign conditions did not differ, it can be concluded that the subjects detected the signs similarly.

In previous studies, recall of the game crossing sign after a delay has varied between 46% and 67%. The present figure of 31% is surprisingly small and it is difficult to suggest any particular reason for that except for the small number of subjects and random variation.

The speed limit sign was recalled better than in previous studies. There are three factors which probably explain the difference. (1) The drivers in the present experiment were subjects who have been found to behave differently from the unalerted drivers (Luoma, 1991b). (2) In the 1960s, when the other results concerning the recall of the speed limit sign were collected, there was no general speed limit system in Finland or Sweden. Nowadays drivers know that speed limits always exist, and so they may better observe them. (3) The main results of the present experiment included only drivers who had no other traffic in the vicinity. The present findings indicated that other traffic systematically decreases recall of a sign, and the previous studies did not control the existence of other traffic. Taking these factors into account may reconcile the results of the different studies. Similarly, immediate recall of the different signs is in good agreement with the findings of Luoma (1991a).

The main implication of this study is that recall delay has a different effect depending on the type of the sign. Johansson and co-workers evaluated the effect of delay on recall of subjectively important signs and found the delay of minor importance. This study suggests that delay is important and its effect appears in the recall of the road signs of minor subjective importance. Thus, using delayed recall to obtain information about driver information acquisition is questionable.

In addition, this study indicates that a careful consideration of other traffic during the experiment is essential. The lack of this control might explain a part of the variability in the results from previous studies.

Furthermore, the results showed that the subjects who recalled the speed limit sign decreased their speed significantly more than did the subjects who encountered the game crossing sign (whether they recalled it or not) or no sign. However, it is interesting to note that the subjects who did not recall the speed limit sign decreased speed differently. Although there were only two subjects in this group, it could be argued that the subject who decreased speed only slightly did not detect the sign well or immediately considered the message of the sign unnecessary and forgot it. On the other hand, the subject who decreased speed more substantially took the message of the sign into account but could not recall that the speed limit sign was the last presented.

With regard to the validity of the simultaneous measurement of recalls and responses, it is noteworthy that the question concerning the road sign presented immediately after passing the sign did not affect speed behavior. One would expect that the question would change the behavior of the driver, with the result that the measurements of speed behavior would be invalid. However, the present results did not indicate any such effect.

5. FOOTNOTE

Present address: Helsinki University of Technology, Laboratory of Industrial Psychology, Otakaari 1, SF-02150 Espoo, Finland.

6. REFERENCES

Aberg, L. (1981). The human factors in game-vehicle accidents. A study of drivers' information acquisition (Studia Psychologica Uppsaliensia 6). Acta Universitatis Upsaliensis. Uppsala.

Hakkinen, S. (1965). Perception of highway traffic signs (Reports from Talja No. 1). Helsinki: Talja.

Johansson, G. & Rumar, K. (1966). Drivers and road signs: a preliminary investigation of the capacity of car drivers to get information from road signs. Ergonomics 1(9), 57- 62.

Johansson, G. and Backlund, F. (1970). Drivers and road signs. Ergonomics 6(13), 749-759.

Kirk, R.E. (1968). Experimental design: Procedures for the behavioral Sciences. Belmont, California: Brooks/Cole.

Luoma, J. (1991a). Perception of highway traffic signs: Interaction of eye movements, recalls and reactions. In: A.G. Gale, I.D. Brown, C.M. Haslegrave, I. Moorhead & S. Taylor (eds.) Vision in Vehicles-III, Amsterdam, North-Holland.

Luoma, J. (1991b). Evaluations of validity of two research methods for studying perception of road signs. Ann Arbor, The University of Michigan, Transportation Research Institute. Report No. UMTRI-91-15.

VISION IN VEHICLES – IV
A.G. Gale et al. (Editors)
1993 Elsevier Science Publishers B.V.

DRIVER DETECTION OF LOCAL AND NON-PRIMARY DESTINATIONS ON DIRECTION SIGNS

M.C.M. DUNNE and P.B. LINFIELD

Ophthalmic and Physiological Optics Research Group, Department of Vision Sciences, Aston University, Birmingham, B4 7ET, UK.

Abstract

An investigation was carried out to determine to what extent colour coding of borders on direction signs optimised the detection of local and non-primary destinations. Both categories of destination were either presented together on a combined sign with a black border or appeared on separate signs. In the latter case, signs displaying local destinations were either colour coded with a blue border or the level of colour coding was enhanced by including a blue chevron.

The apparatus was designed for constant speed zoom presentation of stimuli. Reaction times, response accuracy and subjective confidence levels were recorded for 10 younger (mean age 22.3 ± 2.8 years), 8 middle aged (52.9 ± 5.4 years) and 10 older (73.7 ± 6.2 years) drivers.

All age groups responded better to combined sign arrays compared to separated sign arrays unless the level of colour coding for the latter was enhanced, in which case little difference was found between the two types of sign array. These results were, however influenced by the positioning of local destinations which always appeared below non-primary destinations in an array. Removal of this factor resulted in elevated performance levels as the level of colour coding was increased.

1. INTRODUCTION

Results presented in this paper are derived from data collected in the department of Vision Sciences at Aston University under contract to the Transport and Road Research Laboratory. The original study was designed to address the problem of overcrowding of direction signs at road junctions i.e. how direction signs found at roundabouts and T-junctions may be designed to optimise the detection of local and non-primary destinations. In the present study this data has been reanalysed in order to take a closer look at the influence of colour coding.

2. METHOD

Three flag-type direction signs (Circular Roads 7/75, 1975) were tested (signs 1 to 3) first of all. For sign 1, non-primary and local destinations were presented on separate boards; non-primary destination boards identified by a black border and chevron and local destination boards identified with a blue border and black chevron. The degree of colour coding was enhanced for sign 2 in that local destination boards were identified with a blue border and a blue chevron. Both sign types were compared to sign 3 in which non-primary and local destinations were presented on combined boards incorporating black borders and chevrons. Non-primary destinations always appeared above local destinations for all three sign types. Only signs 1 and 3 are currently used on roads in this country.

With the above sign types it was considered that non-primary and local destinations could have been detected by their relative positions alone. Therefore three extra sign types were tested (signs 4 to 6). In all of these, local and non-primary destinations were presented on separate signs which were placed side by side, pointing in opposite directions, instead of one above the other. This ensured that any position cues were removed. The level of colour coding was however varied. For sign 4, boards carrying either type of destination lacked any colour coding as both incorporated black borders and chevrons. Sign 5 colour coded local destination boards with blue borders whilst sign 6 enhanced the level of colour coding by including blue borders and chevrons on local destination boards. Two presentations of sign types 4 to 6 were made so that local and non-primary destinations appeared as often on the right hand side as on the left.

For each of the first three sign types, experimental runs consisted of 32 presentations per subject. This allowed a varying degree of sign array complexity to be incorporated. Here, 16 left hand signs (to simulate roundabout conditions) and 16 left/right hand signs (to simulate T-junction conditions) were included. The total number of destinations on each sign array varied between 3 and 12. Presentation times were also varied (1.5s, 2s, 4s and 6s) to simulate variable traffic windows, each duration being used equally for all sign arrays.

Experimentation was carried out on 10 younger (mean age 22.3 ± 2.8 years), 8 middle aged (52.9 ± 5.4 years) and 10 older (73.7 ± 6.2 years) drivers. The experimental design was as previously described by Linfield and Dunne (1988). Subjects were seated in a car which constituted the subject area (Figure 1). Direction signs were projected onto a 2.5m square beaded screen positioned 11m from the subject area. The projector used for this purpose (Figure 2) was designed to present a zoom image of the sign to be tested. By this means, the sign was initially seen at a visual angle corresponding to 102.6m, at which point the text required a visual acuity of 6/3.75 to be seen and was therefore not able to be read. The zoom time of 6.4s simulated a speed of 30 mph and resulted in the sign being magnified to a maximum of 6 times. At this maximum size, the visual angle represented a sign distance of 17.1m with a text size equivalent to 6/22.53 Snellen. Another projector, which produced pre- and post-stimulus masks, was positioned 4.5m from the screen. A BBC microcomputer controlled the pre-and post-stimulus mask projector, the stimulus zoom projector and recorded subject performance criteria.

Having described the different sign types to the subjects, with particular regard to the treatment of local and non-primary destinations, they were required to locate the position on the sign array of a target destination chosen randomly by the computer. Target destinations and categories (local or non-primary) were cued to the subject verbally by the experimenter during the pre-stimulus presentation. The name could also be read by the subject from a VDU situated directly in front of the car. Presentation of the stimulus then occurred followed by the post stimulus mask.

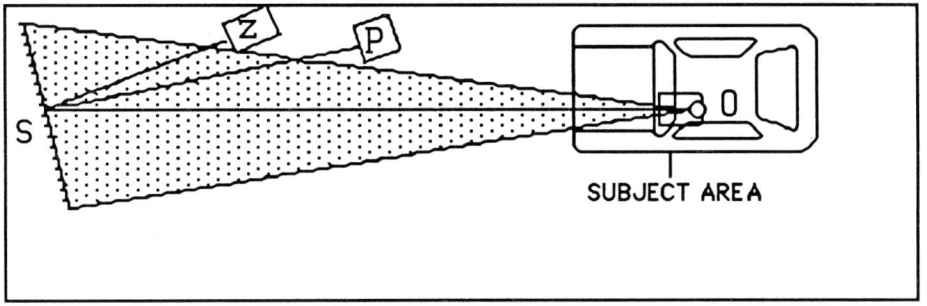

NOT TO SCALE

KEY	DESCRIPTION	DISTANCE (from screen)
Z	ZOOM PROJECTOR	3 m
P	MASK PROJECTOR	4.5 m
O	OBSERVER	11 m
S	BEADED SCREEN	–

Figure 1. Experimental area (after Linfield and Dunne, 1988)

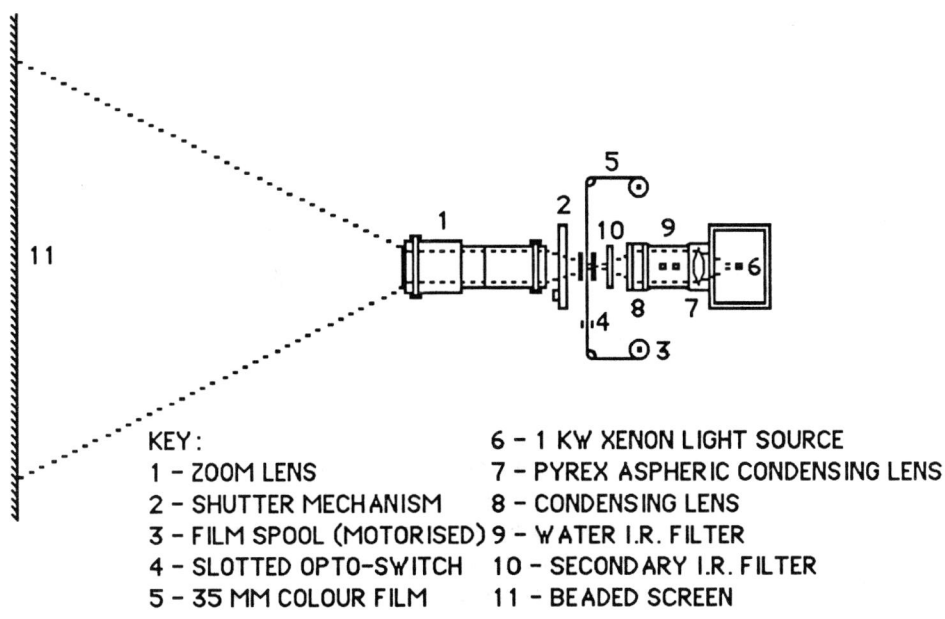

KEY:

1 – ZOOM LENS
2 – SHUTTER MECHANISM
3 – FILM SPOOL (MOTORISED)
4 – SLOTTED OPTO-SWITCH
5 – 35 MM COLOUR FILM

6 – 1 KW XENON LIGHT SOURCE
7 – PYREX ASPHERIC CONDENSING LENS
8 – CONDENSING LENS
9 – WATER I.R. FILTER
10 – SECONDARY I.R. FILTER
11 – BEADED SCREEN

Figure 2. Zoom, shutter and film loading mechanism (after Linfield and Dunne, 1988)

Subject responses were then made by means of three buttons mounted on the dashboard of the car. These were pressed depending upon whether the subject decided that the target name was on the right or left on the array. If the target name was not present, the centre button was pressed corresponding to "straight ahead". Absence of a target name occurred randomly 1 out of 4 presentations.

After the subject had responded to the sign array, their response times were automatically recorded by the computer which also recorded whether the response was correct. They were then asked to assess their confidence level on a four point scale (1-"no idea", 2-"not very sure", 3-"quite sure", 4-"absolutely certain"). These confidence levels were entered into the computer by the operator.

3. RESULTS

Figures 3 to 5 show performance levels recorded for each age group in response to sign types 1 to 3. The responses of each age group were averaged to give a condensed set of readings for each stimulus. Mean and standard error values were then calculated from 32 values per sign type. Performance levels indicated in the graphs are the percentage of correct responses (Figure 3), reaction times as recorded for correct responses only (Figure 4) and confidence levels also recorded for correct responses only (Figure 5). It was considered that incorrect responses most probably represented guesses made by individual subjects which would only have added meaningless noise to the results.

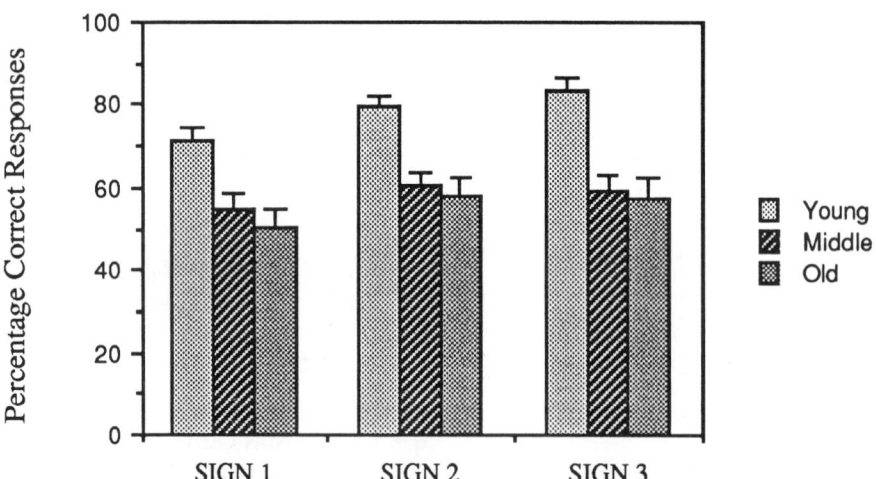

Figure 3. Mean and standard error values for the percentage of correct responses to sign types 1 - 3 recorded for 10 younger, 8 middle aged and 10 older subjects.

With a few exceptions, it was generally found that subjects responded with greater accuracy, speed and confidence when looking at combined signs (sign type 3) compared to separate signs with blue borders coding for local destinations (sign type 1). Performance levels were also greater for the separated signs when the level of colour coding for local

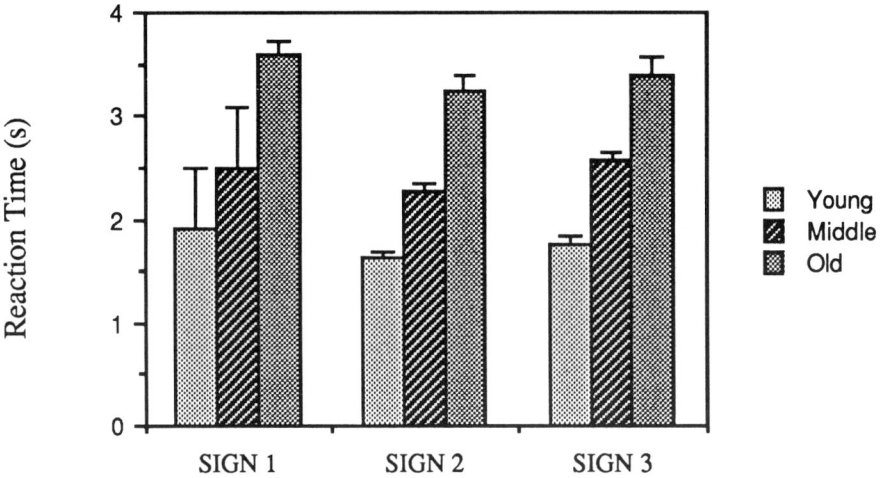

Figure 4. Mean and standard error values for reaction times (correct responses only) to sign types 1 - 3 recorded for 10 younger, 8 middle aged and 10 older subjects.

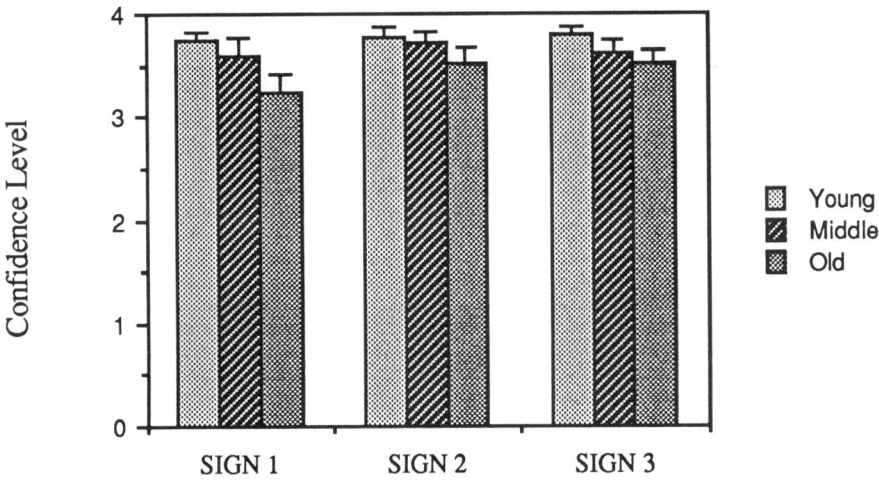

Figure 5. Mean and standard error values for confidence levels (correct responses only) to sign types 1 - 3 recorded for 10 younger, 8 middle aged and 10 older subjects.

destinations was enhanced by the addition of blue chevrons (sign type 2).

Performance levels fell as the mean age of the subject sample increased. Nevertheless, relative performance levels for different sign types remained fairly constant for the three age groups considered.

Figures 6 to 8 show performance levels recorded for each age group in response to sign types 4 to 6. Again, the responses of each age group were averaged to give a condensed set of readings for each stimulus. Mean and standard error values were then calculated from 8 values per sign type. As before, performance levels indicated in the graphs are the percentage of correct responses (fig 6), reaction times for correct responses (fig 7) and confidence levels for correct responses (fig 8).

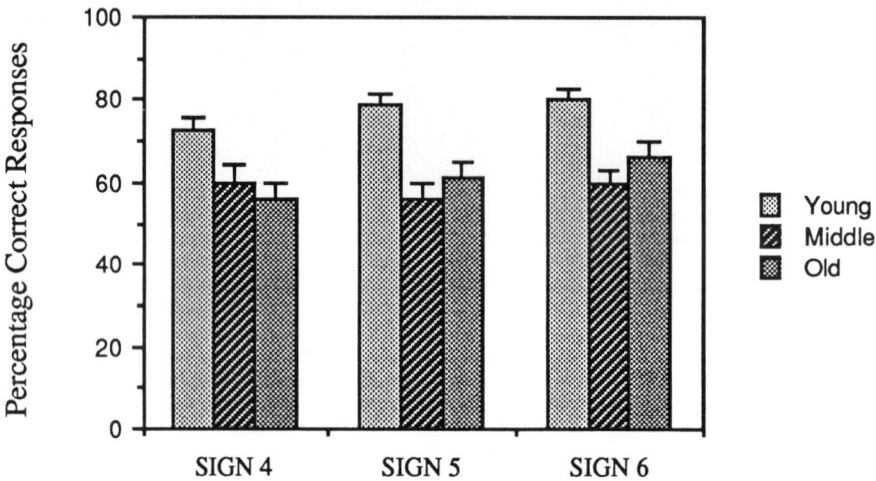

Figure 6. Mean and standard error values for the percentage of correct responses to sign types 4 - 6 recorded for 10 younger, 8 middle aged and 10 older subjects.

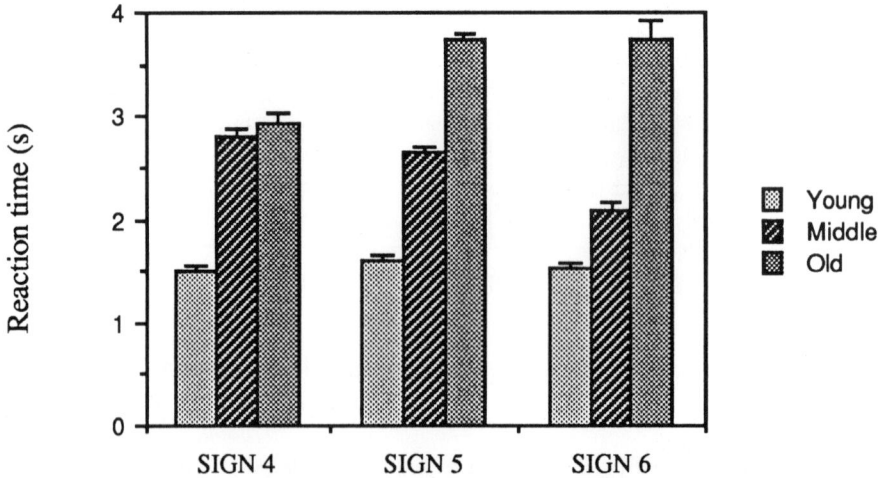

Figure 7. Mean and standard error values for reaction times (correct responses only) to sign types 4 - 6 recorded for 10 younger, 8 middle aged and 10 older subjects.

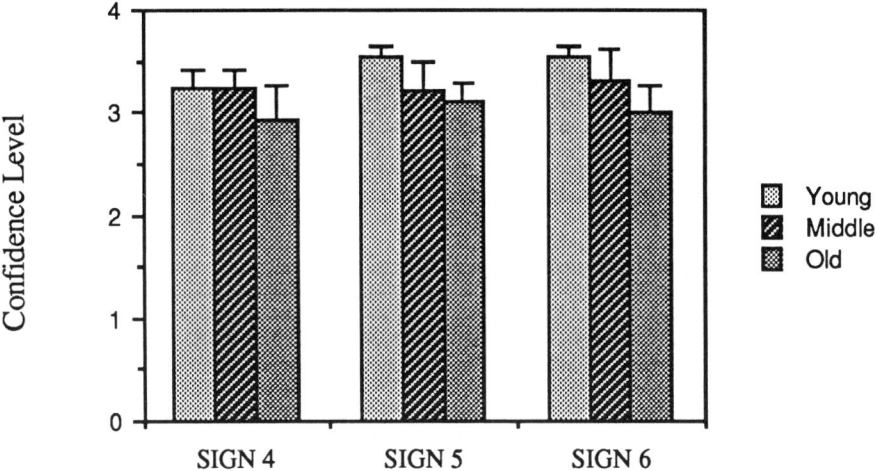

Figure 8. Mean and standard error values for confidence levels (correct responses only) to sign types 4 - 6 recorded for 10 younger, 8 middle aged and 10 older subjects.

As mentioned before, sign types 4 - 6 were designed to remove any positional cues to the location of local and non-primary destinations. Results were more variable with these signs as mean values were calculated from smaller samples. Nevertheless, there was an overall tendency for subjects to respond with greater accuracy, speed and confidence as the level of colour coding increased from none at all (sign type 4) through coding local destination boards with blue borders (sign type 5) to coding local destination boards with blue borders and chevrons (sign type 6). Again it was found that although performance levels fell as the mean age of the subject sample increased, relative performance levels for different sign types remained fairly constant for each age group.

To illustrate the principal findings of this study and facilitate statistical testing, all performance criteria were combined into a single value called the response factor (previously described by Linfield and Dunne, 1988). The response factor (RF) was developed along the lines that a good overall performance should be directly proportional to the percentage of correct responses (R) and the confidence level (C) whilst being inversely proportional to response time in milliseconds (T). The following approximate expression therfore arises :

$$RF = (10.R.C) \div T$$

A scaling factor of 10 times was incorporated into this expression in order to produce a response factor which varied between 0 units (poor performance) and approximately 4 units (very good performance).

As subjects of all ages responded in a similar manner to each sign type, the results were pooled. This had the additional effect of reducing the variability in the results by increasing sample sizes for each sign type by three times. Hence mean response factors shown in

Figure 9 for sign types 1 to 3 were calculated from 96 observations per sign. Likewise, mean response factors shown in Figure 10 for sign types 4 to 6 were calculated from 24 observations per sign. It is worth pointing out that each observation represented a mean value for 28 subjects.

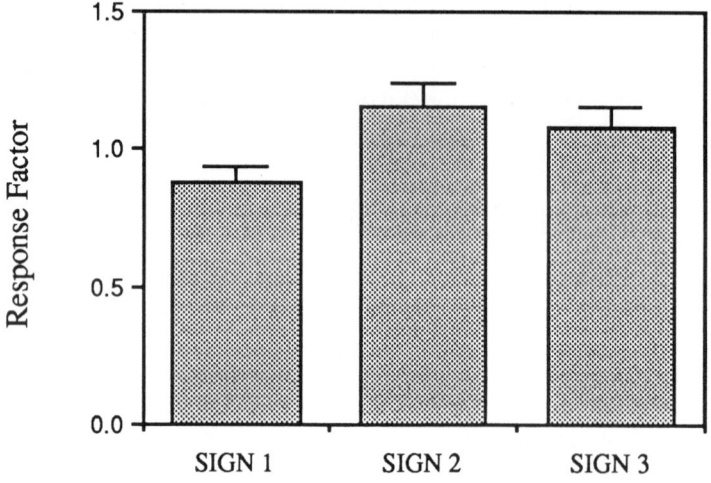

Figure 9. Mean and standard error values for response factors (correct responses only) calculated for sign types 1 - 3. Pooled data.

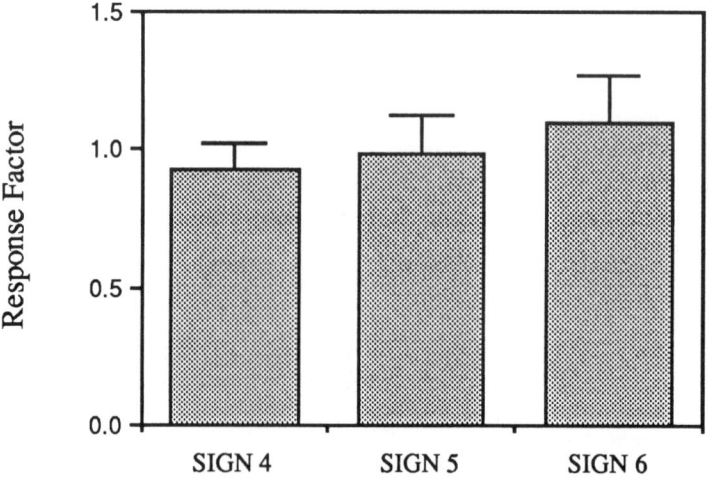

Figure 10. Mean and standard error values for response factors (correct responses only) calculated for sign types 4 - 6. Pooled data.

Figure 9 clearly indicates that subjects responded significantly better for combined sign arrays (sign type 3) compared to separate sign arrays carrying a blue border (sign type 1) for local destinations (paired t-test: t=-4.982; df=95; p<0.001). However, subjects also responded significantly better for separated sign arrays in which the level of colour coding was enhanced for local destination boards by the addition of a blue chevron (sign type 2) compared to levels normally used (sign type 1) for this type of direction sign (paired t-test: t=-4.280; df=95; p<0.001). No significant difference then occurred between separated sign arrays with enhanced colour coding (sign type 2) and combined sign arrays (sign type 3). Figure 10 reinforced the above findings. Here it was found that subjects responded better as the level of colour coding increased from none at all (sign type 4) through coding local destination boards with blue borders (sign type 5) to coding local destination boards with blue borders and chevrons (sign type 6). Neither of these observed differences, however, achieved statistical significance.

4. CONCLUSION

All age groups responded better to combined sign arrays compared to separated sign arrays unless the level of colour coding for the latter was enhanced, in which case little difference was found between the two types of sign array. These results, however, may have been influenced by the positioning of local destinations which always appeared above non-primary destinations in an array. Removal of this factor resulted in elevated performance levels as the level of colour coding was increased although these differences were not statistically significant.

5. ACKNOWLEDGEMENT

The results in this paper are based on data obtained in the course of a contract awarded to the Department of Vision Sciences at Aston University by the Transport and Road Research Laboratory, DTp. The views expressed are not necessarily those of the Department of Transport.

6. REFERENCES

Circular Roads No. 7/75 (1975), Size, design and mounting of traffic signs. HMSO, London.

Linfield, P.B. & Dunne, M.C.M. (1988), The effects of alcohol induced binocular instability on a driver's ability to correctly identify road direction signs, in: Gale, A.G., Freeman, M.H., Haslegrave, C.M., Smith, P. and Taylor, S.P., (eds.), Vision in Vehicles II, North Holland, Amsterdam, 75-82.

8

MEASUREMENT AND MODELLING

VISION IN VEHICLES – IV
A.G. Gale et al. (Editors)

TRAFFIC RELEVANT BEHAVIOR MONITORED BY THE ELECTRO-OCULOGRAM (EOG) AS A PSYCHOPHYSICAL MEASURING INSTRUMENT

Niels GALLEY

Psychological Institute, Universität zu Köln, Zülpicher Str.47, D-5000 Köln 41

Abstract

The Electro-oculogram (EOG) is widely used in the laboratory for measuring eye movements but seldom in the field. Some disadvantages of the EOG for measuring gaze behavior (for example lack of stability) can be overcome by using on-line computer identification of saccades and additional keyboard marking of relevant gazes by the experimenter. This uncovers the advantages of the EOG measuring precise fixation durations of gazes on defined instruments, activation decrements and increments of the driver due to time on task or mental effort (via saccadic velocity), and blink behavior as controlled interruptions of visual behavior. Three related studies of traffic relevant questions are examined for measuring the usefulness of the EOG-ON-LINE measuring device.

1. ANALYZING THE EOG ON-LINE

Gaze behavior searching stationary targets is realized in the main by saccadic eye movements which are characterized by their high velocity and their respectively short durations. The EOG is a conventional technique for measuring eye movements in the laboratory but is seldom used in the field (Galley 1988). Timing and amplitudes of saccades can be identified from the EOG by on-line computer programs (Königstein 1989) using a special instrument (manufactured by PAR-ELEKTRONIK in Berlin). The program identifies all saccades detected in the two dimensional EOG by their high velocity and identifies blinks from the vertical EOG channel. The program ignores all slow eye movements. Additionally, relevant gazes are marked on the keyboard by the experimenter, for example 'looking at the speedometer'. In this way it is possible not only to register global measures: histograms of all saccadic amplitudes, all saccadic intervals or blinking intervals but one can also monitor specific gazes at instruments or targets using the keyboard markers. With a dwell time of 1 ms the activation indicator 'saccadic velocity' of large saccades can be used: for example, saccadic velocity is diminished as a function of vigilance decrement, but is increased in the condition of mental effort (Galley et al. 1988). Until now this indicator of activation has been used only in psychopharmacological research (Galley 1989).

2. THREE STUDIES IN WHICH BLINKS AND SACCADES ARE IDENTIFIED

In three studies of traffic relevant behavior the advantages of the computer aided EOG are used to obtain information about looking behavior as well as activation changes. Also some problems with head movements are discussed. The studies are devoted to the following special problems of looking behavior in traffic relevant situations:

a) the comparative inspection time for different digital display technologies, namely; LED vs. reflexive vs. transmissive vs. transflexive LCD, here called the 'LCD study' (see figure 1).

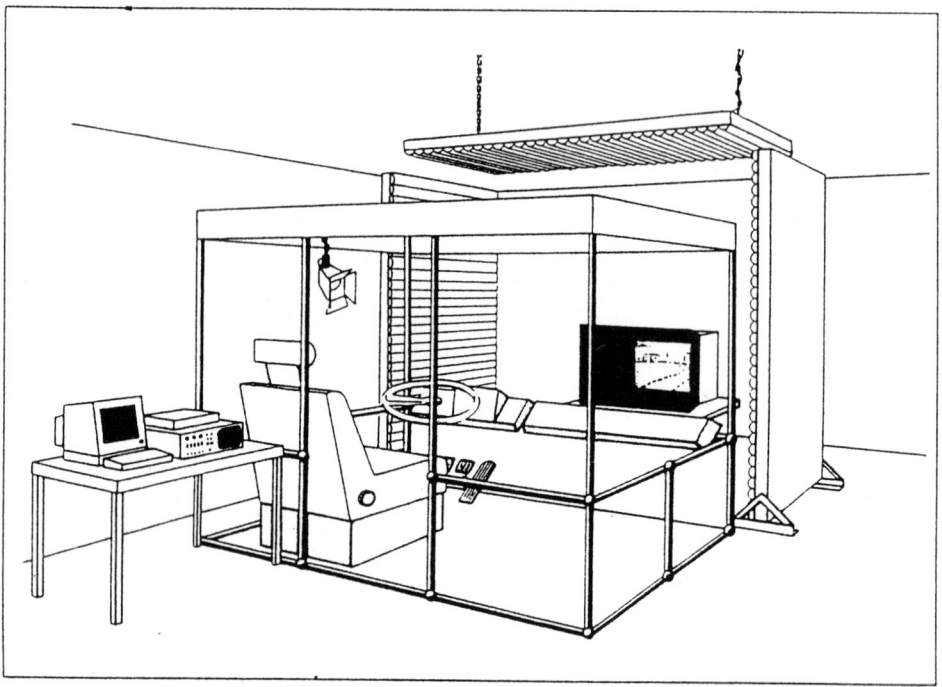

Figure 1 The setting of the LCD study. Subjects drive a car in a TV simulation. Additionally, they have to take notice of the instrument looking down at the panel. Driving behavior is monitored by the computer on the left table. Vertical and horizontal EOG channels store their eye movements on magnetic tape.

b) the inspection time of outside "rear-view-mirror-like" pictures through double-glazed side windows, which sometimes show disturbing reflexions, and also single-glazed windows without such reflexions. Sometimes there was a signal to be detected on the pictures or respectively no signal i.e. a noise condition which was not to be responded to. This study is called here the 'reflexion study' (a more comprehensive report is in press, Galley 1991).

c) In a field study inspection time was measured for reading speed information on a conventional speedometer vs. on a digital head-up-display, here called the 'head-up-display study'. In the three studies all saccades and blinks were identified and stored. Therefore, additional aspects of the data could be analyzed beyond the initial questions.

All subjects were experienced drivers between 22 and 65 years of age, 36 in the first, 32 in the second, and 37 in the third study. In the first two laboratory studies, subjects had to drive in a TV-simulation and during the racing game briefly <u>look down</u> in the first (see figure 2) and respectively <u>to the left</u> in the second study.

In the third field study, the subjects were required to look at the speedometer (conventional vs. head-up-display) several times, because the course contained different speed limits.

The two-dimensional EOG was stored on magnetic tape in the LCD study and saccades and blinks were identified off-line and respectively on-line in the reflexion study and the head-up-display study. In the head-up-display study the experimenter looked at the driving subjects via the rear-view mirror, scoring their gazes on the targets with defined keys on the computer keyboard. The speed of the car and the heart rate of the driver were monitored on-line, too, but not mentioned further here.

3. RESULTS

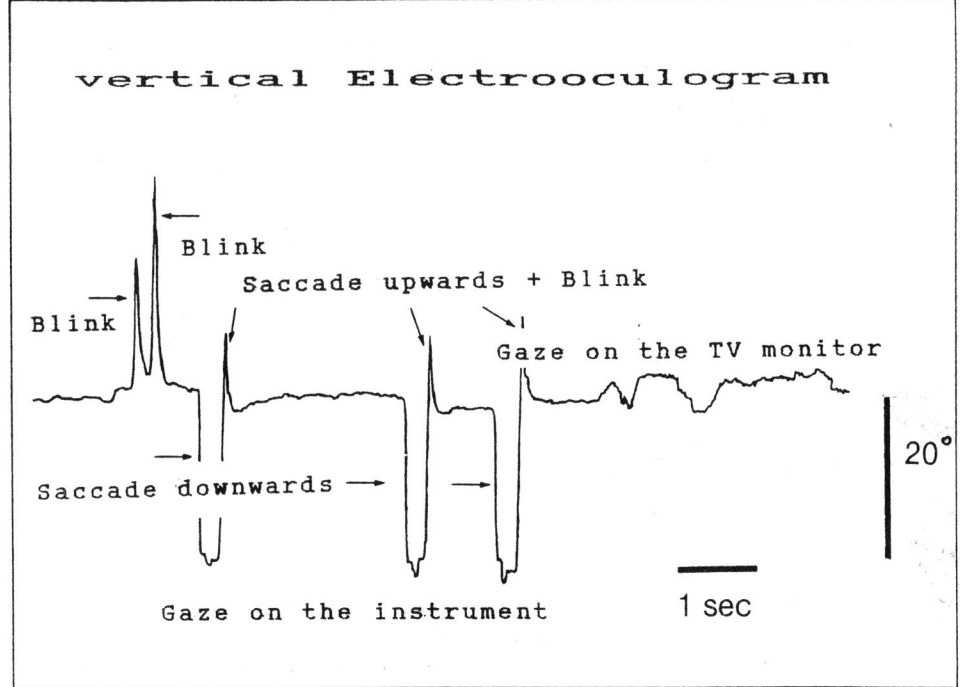

Figure 2 Original registration of the vertical EOG channel from the first study. Three times the subject looks down to the panel and back to the TV monitor. The time in between is the inspection time. In all three inspections the upward directed saccades are accompanied by blinks indicating the end of the cognitive task 'inspection of the instrument'.

Figure 2 shows an original registration of the vertical EOG channel from the LCD study.

One can see how the subject looked up and down leaving the racing game briefly for inspection of the instrument, which has a critical function in the game. One sees also his non-random blinking behavior, which coincides with the end of the inspection of the instrument and the upward directed saccade. In this case, which is frequent, only time information about the end of the inspection is caught, neither saccade-parameter nor blink-parameter could be separated.

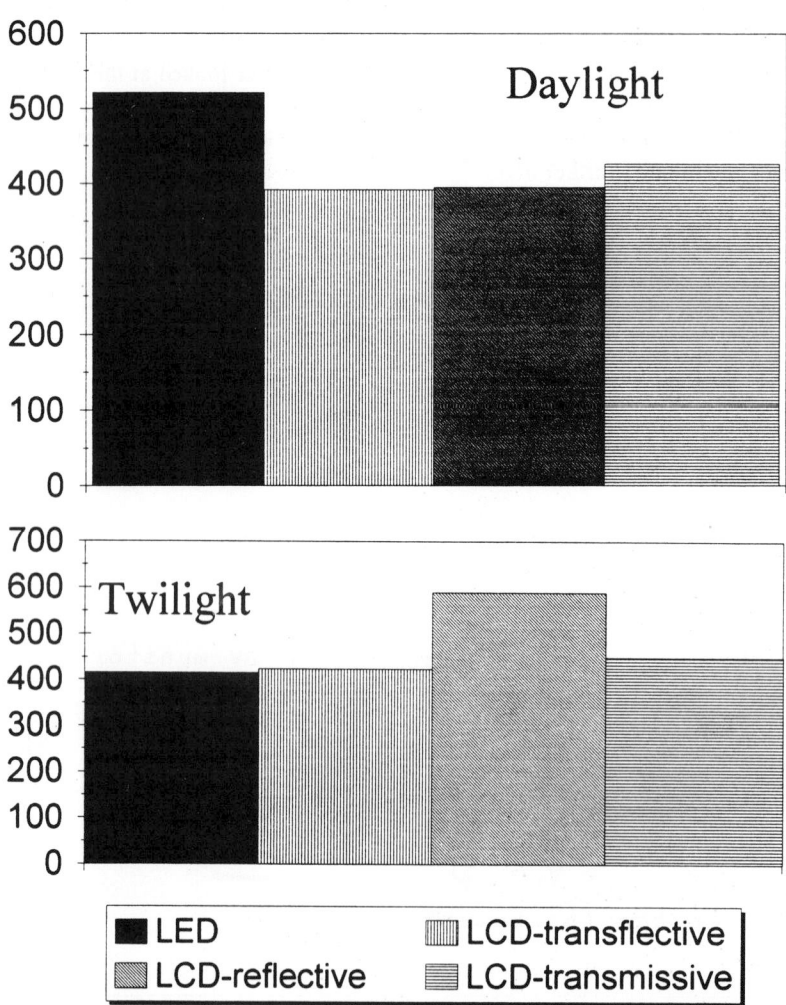

Figure 3 Inspection times on the digital displays in the LCD study. There are two extraordinarily long inspection times: the LED display in the daylight and the reflective LCD display in the twilight condition. The winner under both conditions is the transflective LCD display.

In all three studies the relevant glances to the targets had to be identified from all registered saccades. Identification of these relevant saccades to the targets were done by an off-line interactive search on all possible saccades, which were offered by the computer in special colours. For example a possible saccade to the target below the line of sight was coloured in violet, the respective saccade away from the target in olive-green. The operator can accept or refuse the proposal of the computer using context information, for example the keyboard inputs. By this method the secondary identification of the relevant saccades to and away from targets was done economically in a few minutes for a few thousand saccades made in the 90 minutes of driving, and respectively the roughly 80 minutes EOG registration in the head-up display study.

By this means it was possible to identify in this last field study 74 % of all scored gazes on the conventional speedometer and 63 % on the head-up-display, whereas the hit rate was more than 90 % in the two laboratory studies. The difference in the hit rate between field and laboratory studies is caused by the relative high per cent of concomitant head movements in the field and the optimal range of the targets (more than 20º)in the laboratory. In the field study the smaller hit rate of relevant gazes in the head-up-display condition is caused by the nearness of this target in relation to the further distance of the speedometer (8º vs 17º), which makes identification of the relevant gazes more difficult.

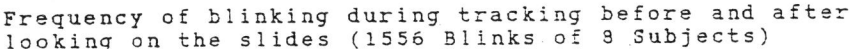

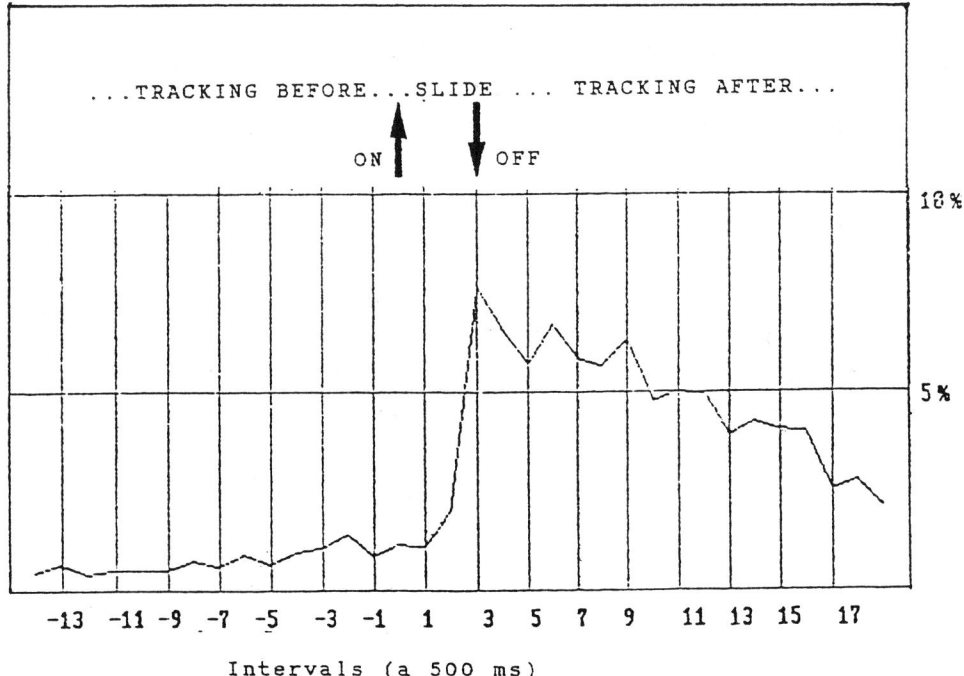

Figure 4 Blink probability in relation to the rear mirror inspection (from the reflexion study). When the secondary task is finished the blink rate goes up drastically.

Using the saccades reaching the targets and leaving them, it was possible to measure exactly the times on targets, which should be mentioned here briefly: the best in the LCD-display comparison was the transflexive and transmissive LCD with the shortest inspection times under daylight and night together.

In the second study the reflexions in the outside rear-view mirror through double-gazed windows added some additional 80 ms for the identification of the signals in the beginning but diminished to some 40 ms in the second half of the 24 minutes of the experiment. Thirdly the head-up-display spares some 50 ms if a small time window from 100 ms to 800 ms is used. Absolute values are 379 ms inspection time for the head-up-display and 429 ms for the speedometer. In all cases we suppose the higher contrast to be responsible chiefly for the shorter inspection times.

However it seems worthwhile to mention some other aspects of the data here beyond the target inspection behavior - because of the identification of all suprathreshold saccades and blinks we got a large amount of information about looking behavior. For example let us cast a glance at the blinking behavior. The blinking rate is high in some people and very low in

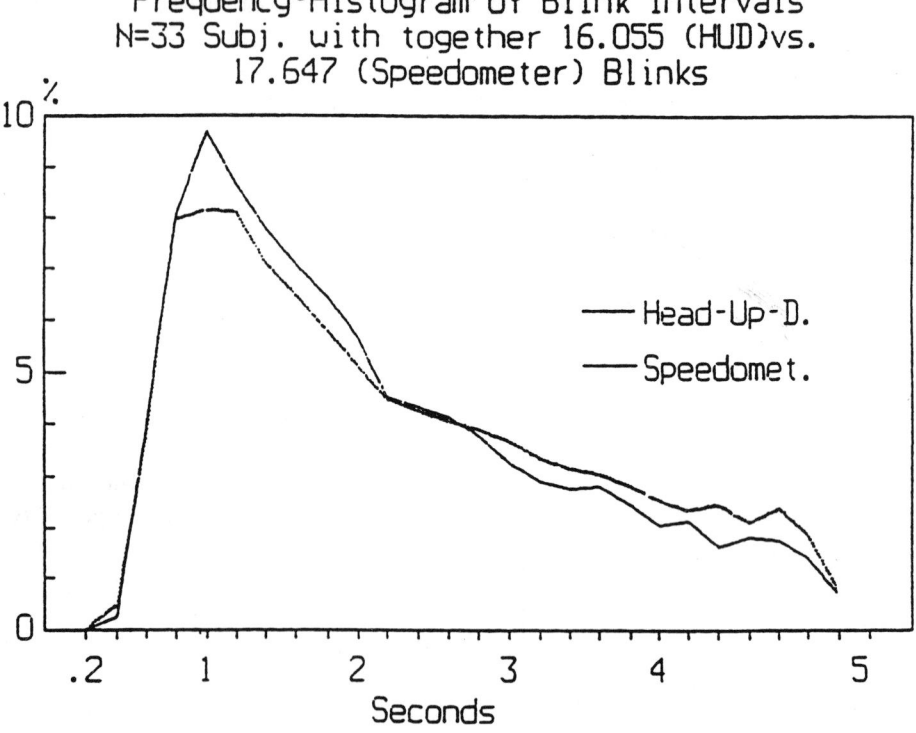

Figure 5. Histogram of blink intervals (from the head-up-display study). Two aspects are to be mentioned: firstly, the accelerated decreasing rate of long blink intervals, which indicates a normal high blinking rate of 1/sec as well as the occurence of very long intervals. Secondly, the head-up-display condition affects the blinking behavior in a consistent manner by favoring the longer blink intervals.

others. But the probability of a blink is very finely tuned to the end of the interfering inspection of the target field as shown in figure 4.

Our interpretation is that people suppress the blinking behavior the nearer the critical target period comes, and release the blink when the target identification is done. But what is to be expected from this blink releasing behavior as far as the blinking behavior of the head-up-display vs. speedometer drivers is concerned?

In Figure 5 we see histograms of all blink intervals of all drivers in the head-up-display study. One sees longer intervals in the head-up-display condition.

Our interpretation is that inspection of the speedometer distracts the looking behavior and facilitates some short interrupting blinks, whilst in the head-up-display condition blinks are more suppressed for more continuous monitoring of the visual scene.

The last aspect of the EOG data to be mentioned here is the saccadic velocity (the theoretical and methodological background of which we have reviewed elsewhere, Galley 1989). For example, in the reflexion study there was the question if the drivers were disturbed by the reflexions: we had heard that they needed a little more time for inspection, but in their saccadic velocity there was no difference between the double (= D) and single (= S) glazed target inspections. We had interpreted this lack of difference as a sign of not being disturbed; but this interpretation presupposes that saccadic velocity would be a sensitive indicator for activation. Therefore, we looked for vigilance decrements as well as for differences in saccadic velocity in the first tracking task and the secondary target inspection. As shown in table 1 all saccades from the target inspection task show higher velocities than to the target.

Condition	mean sacc.veloc.		signif.peak sacc.v.	sgn		
	to t.	from target		to t.	from target	
S-Signal	302	338	**	529	586	**
D-Signal	315	342	**	535	572	**
S-Noise	307	326	*	544	556	**
D-Noise	312	316	ns	526	555	**

Table 1. Comparison of saccadic velocities (in o/sec normalized on the same saccadic amplitude) to and from targets in the reflexion study. S = single-, D = double-glazed (i.e. with reflexions); *, ** = $p < .05$ resp. $< .01$ (WILCOXON).

We interpret this difference as an activation increment due to the greater difficulty of the secondary task. Furthermore, we found a decrement in saccadic velocity from the first to the second half of the task to be expected from habituation to and some monotony of the task (Galley 1991). We concluded that if there was a disturbance or a stress-like reaction we had to find it in the saccadic velocity; but we found no difference, therefore there was no suprathreshold stress reaction to the reflexions.

In the same manner we found an increase in saccadic velocity looking away from the speedometer and no such increase looking away from the head-up-display in the head-up-display study. We suppose that this difference should be interpreted as speedometer inspection being a more difficult task than head-up-display inspection.

4. CONCLUSIONS

In the field, saccades in the EOG are masked roughly to one-fourth by concomitant head movements and the most frequent very small saccades are not detected at all. But when some defined targets are used which are sufficiently apart from each other and the gazes on targets are scored by inspection to the keyboard additionally, the computer-identified saccades and blinks can unmask inspection times as well as vigilance decrements or increased mental effort via saccadic velocities. Frequency and timing of the blink seem to be an indicator for the interruption of the visual behavior.

5. REFERENCES

Galley, N. (1988). Erfassung von Blickbewegungen. In H. Kunert (Ed.), Die Orientierung im Straßenverkehr bei Nachtfahrten. Köln, TÜV Rheinland.

Galley, N. (1989). Saccadic eye movement velocity as an indicator of (de)activation. A review and some speculations. Journal of Psychophysiology, 3, 229-244.

Galley, N. (1991 in press). Leistung und Aktivierung - aus der Sicht eines Neuropsychologen. In W. Prinz (Ed.), Mensch und Technik

Galley, N., Boldt, M., Groetzner, Ch. & Strzeletz, P. (1988). Vigilance measurements on an eye movement task. In J. P. Leonard (Ed.), Vigilance: Methods, Models, and Regulation. Frankfurt/Main: Peter Lang.

Königstein, A. (1989). Die On-Line-Identifizierung sakkadischer Augenbewegungen aus dem Elektrookulogramm (Diplomarbeit). Bonn: Fachbereich Informatik der Universität zu Bonn.

A TOOL FOR SYSTEM ORIENTED ANALYSIS OF IN-VEHICLE EXPERIMENTAL DATA

Stefan BECKER[1], Eckhard BRUCKMAYR[1], Jörg SONNTAG[1], Arthur STEINEL[2]

TÜV Rheinland, Institute for Traffic Safety, Am Grauen Stein, D-5000 Cologne[1]
University of Mainz, Institute for Nuclear Physics, Saarstraße, D-6500 Mainz[2]

Abstract

Data analysis of real-life driving experiments is complicated by the multitude of driver, vehicle, and environmental variables. As an aid to overcome this problem a tool is suggested for time-synchronized presentation of video and numerical data on a high definition computer monitor. Data are displayed as graphs against time and as icons which change in real time according to changes of the measured values. The analyst would thus be able to recognize patterns related to interactions within the driver-vehicle environment system, to classify typical "tasks", and thereby to prepare qualitatively an effective quantitative data analysis.

1. INTRODUCTION

Driving experiments usually focus on the influence of selected driver, vehicle or environmental variables on driver behaviour. Typical examples are efforts to evaluate the impact of new driver information systems or drug use. Reductionist approaches, however, can not adequately account for the interaction of the multitude of variables that shape driver behaviour. Further progress can be expected from a method which is better suited to consider the complex interactions of driver/vehicle/environment system variables. A system approach has been advocated by several researchers (e.g. Klebelsberg, 1982; Fastenmeier, 1987; Möhler, 1988; Färber et al., 1988). The present paper is intended to make a contribution to this approach. It refers to experiments carried out in a PROMETHEUS project.

2. ON-LINE DATA AQUISITION

In real world driving experiments with an experimental vehicle data are obtained on driver, vehicle and environmental characteristics.

Driver:
- physiological (e.g. heart rate; cf. Verwey, 1990)
- overt behavioral (e.g. eye movements, handling of vehicle controls, vocal

utterances)

Vehicle:
> - vehicle position (e.g.lateral position, headway clearance)
> - vehicle dynamics (e.g. speed, roll angle)

Environment:
> - traffic scene ahead of the vehicle (video)
> - complexity of the traffic scene (Herberg & Becker, 1990) computed via digital
> image analysis
> - street dimensions, e.g. curvature and width
> (Hulse, et.al., 1989), obtained by digital image analysis)
> - in-vehicle physical environmental factors (e.g. temperature)

Pictures of the traffic scene ahead (driver's visual input) and the driver's face (for off-line analysis of eye movements) are taken by two synchronized CCD-micro-cameras. The two video pictures are mixed and stored.

The numerical data are stored on the hard disk of an on-board microcomputer. Pictorial and numerical data are time synchronized by a numerical time code written on the video tape as well as on the hard disk (Figure 1, top).

3. OFF-LINE DATA ACQUISITION

For simultaneous inspection a set of selected (video and numerical) data can be presented on a large high definition computer monitor.

To this end video tape and high capacity disk are transferred to the laboratory equipment (shown at the bottom of Figure 1). Video pictures and numerical data stored on the hard disk are again synchronized by the time code read out from the video signal by a time code reader. A frame grabber card is used for digitizing and positioning the video picture and also for combining it with the data displayed on the screen in alphanumerical and peferably in graphical format.

The screen is divided into four windows (Figure 2). The video picture is displayed in the top left part. Measured values are transformed into icons appearing in the symbol window beneath the video window. The icons change in real time according to changes of the measured values. Typical icons are simplified pictorial representations of steering wheel position, pedal position, or speedometer. Simple bar graph-like symbols for displaying actual lateral position on the road and headway clearance of the vehicle are superimposed on the video window. The diagram window is used for displaying temporal variation of variables within a defined period of time. Time windows as well as length, range and scale factor of the y-axis are chosen as required.   The alphanumeric window contains subject identification, time code, distance travelled, and additional information from secondary off-line analyses described below.   Selection and configuration of icons, graphs, and alphanumeric data can be determined according to the respective research question.

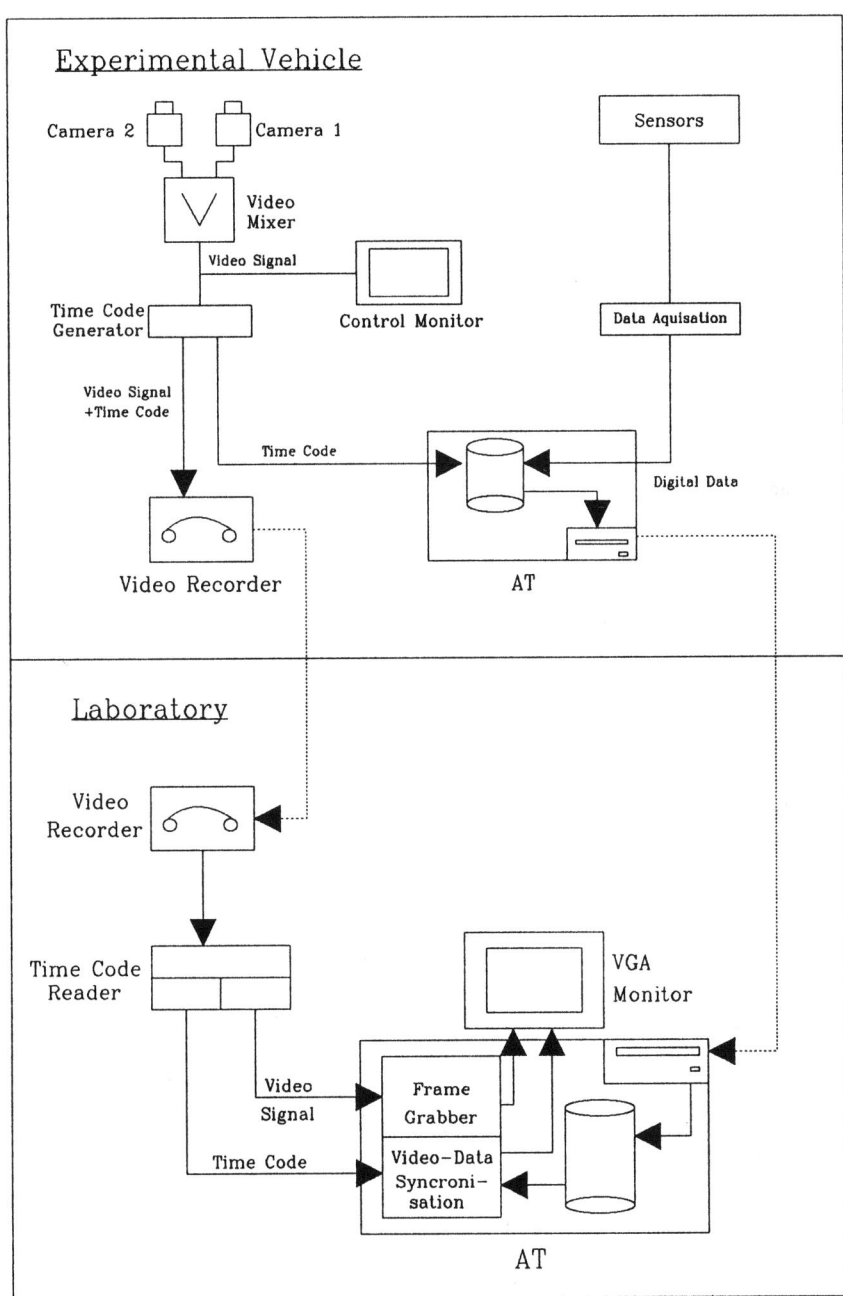

Figure 1 Vehicle and Laboratory equipment

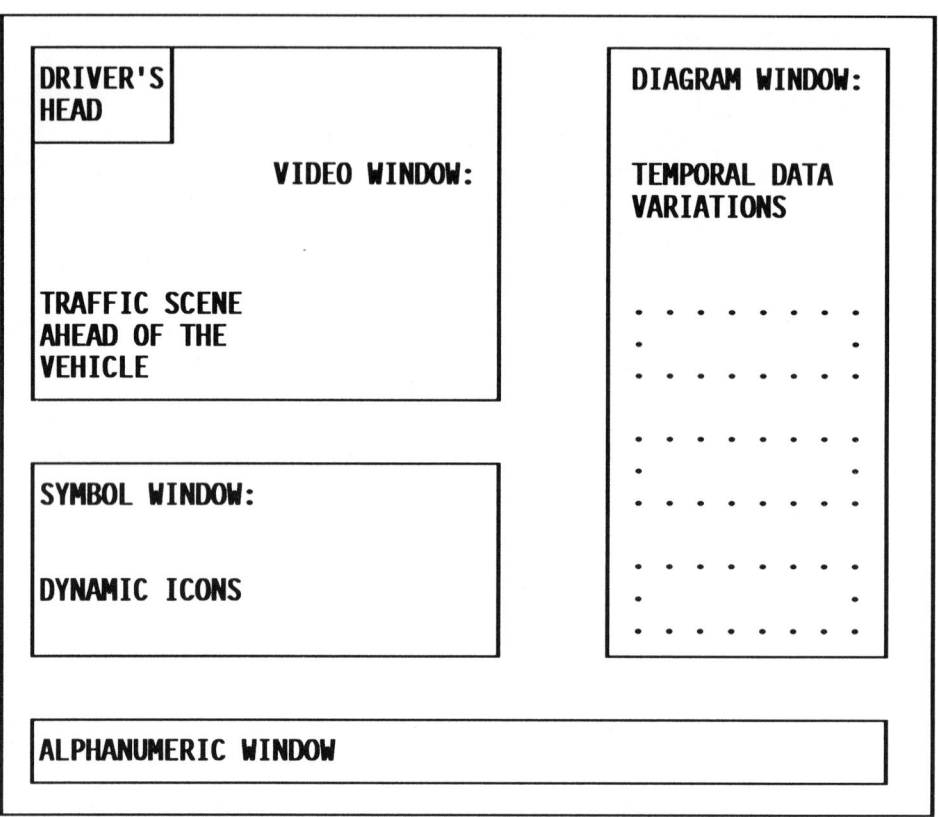

Fig.2 Configuration of windows on the computer screen

The recordings are viewed subsequent to the respective trials together with the subjects involved. Structured interviews are carried out during this session (cf. Parkes, 1989; Parkes et al., 1989) and interview data are entered as catch words into the alphanumeric window via a keyboard.

Post hoc ratings of the subject's experience during his travel are registered using a sliding potentiometer.   Both end-points of this device represent the extremes   on a psychological dimension such as arousal, load, or fear (comparable to a visual analogue scale, e.g. Nicholson, 1978; Pfendler, 1982). Ratings are shown on the display in an analogue form as points on a horizontal line.

As at present a non-obtrusive and reliable eye movement recording device for in-vehicle use is not available, the subjects' eye movements have to be coded (Snyder & Monty, 1986; Parkes, 1989; Parkes et al., 1989). This is done by allocating the gazes of the driver (shown in the video window) to a few gross areas of the field of view (dashboard, road ahead, rear mirrors). The codings are visualized by dot patterns or by percentages within a given time frame superimposed on the traffic scene shown in the video window (Kimmel, 1983).

4. QUALITATIVE AND QUANTITATIVE DATA ANALYSIS

Since in real-life driving experiments a multitude of sequences and combinations of tasks, situations and related requirements are met, it is necessary to identify and isolate typical recurring events, here called "situations" for short, in order to be able to relate driver performance to individual situations. By viewing the videotaped traffic scenes, these situations are identified by coding their respective starting and end points and by assigning each situation to well defined elements (tasks) of a rating system. Examples for tasks are; overtaking, headway clearance control, telephoning, and the like. Selected situations will be described in detail and content analysed in terms of sequence and interaction of the driver/vehicle/environment system components.

In a subsequent quantitative data analysis, indices (e.g. mean, time lag, first and second derivation) are computed for relevant variables within the defined situations. These indices become dependent variables in analysis of variance designs. The individual tasks are elements of the independent variable "task". On this basis univariate and especially multivariate comparisons between tasks can be computed for an individual index or a set of indices.

5. CONCLUSION

The particular strength of the described procedure is seen as being a tool for a qualitative analysis of driver/vehicle/environment interactions. In this capacity it can provide a sound qualitative basis for a sensible quantitative data analysis. Moreover, a major drawback of real-life driving experiments as opposed to simulator experiments, namely poor controllability of independent variables, can thus be compensated for.

The procedure described here will be evaluated within the PROMETHEUS project "The development of a practical method for assessing driver capacity".

6. REFERENCES

Färber, B.Ch., Färber, B.A. & Popp, M. (1988). Evaluation methods for traffic safety of new technologies in vehicles, in: Traffic safety theory & research methods, Session 5: Time dependent models. SWOV, Leidschendam.

Fastenmeier, W. (1987). Psychological investigations concerning man-machine interface design: analysis & assessment, requirements, Final Report, PROMETHEUS WP 31155, 31266. Lehrstuhl für Psychologie, Technische Universität München.

Herberg, K.W., Becker, S. (1990). Beziehungen zwischen der Informationsdichte von Straßenräumen und der Fahrgeschwindigkeit. Institut für Verkehrssicherheit, TÜV Rheinland, Köln.

Hulse, M.C., Dingus, T.A., Fischer, T. & Wierwille, W.W. (1989). The influence of roadway parameters on driver perception of attentional demand, in Mital, A. (ed.), Advances in Industrial Ergonomics and Safety: I. Taylor & Francis, London.

Kimmel, K.R. (1983). Visual scan and performance - indicators of man's workload?, in: Johannsen, G. & Rijnsdorp, J.E. (eds.), Analysis, Design and Evaluation of Man-

Machine Systems, Pergamon, Oxford.

Klebelsberg, D. (1982). Verkehrspsychologie, Springer, Berlin.

Möhler, W. (1988. Untersuchung der visuellen Wahrnehmung des Straßenraumes und dessen Einfluß auf das Fahrverhalten, Mitteilung Nr. 25, Lehrstuhl und Institut für Straßenwesen, Erdund Tunnelbau, RWTH Aachen.

Nicholson, A.N. (1978) Visual analogue scales and drug effects in man. British Journal of Clinical Pharmacology, 6, 3-4.

Parkes, A.M. (1989). Data collection techniques for the evaluation of micro-level driver behaviour. Report No: 18, DRIVE Project V1017 (BERTIE), HUSAT Research Centre, Loughborough.

Parkes, A.M., Ramsey, T., Holmes, D.R.J. & Fairclough, S. (1989). The mobile test facility developed by HUSAT. Report No: 20, DRIVE Project V1017 (BERTIE), HUSAT Research Centre, Loughborough.

Pfendler, C. (1982). Bewertung der Brauchbarkeit von Methoden zur Messung der mentalen Beanspruchung bei KfzLenkaufgaben. Zeitschrift für Arbeitswissenschaft, 36 (8 NF), 170-174.

Rompe, K., Heißing, B. (1984). Objektive Testverfahren für die Fahreigenschaften von Kraftfahrzeugen, Verlag TÜV Rheinland, Köln.

Snyder, H.L. & Monty, R.W. (1986). A methodology for road evaluation of automobile displays, in: Gale, A.G. et al. (eds.), Vision in Vehicles ,North Holland, Amsterdam.

Sömen, H.D.(1979). Die Forschungskonzeption der Bundesanstalt für Straßenwesen zum Problembereich Belastung und Beanspruchung des Kraftfahrers, in: Hoyos, C. Graf (ed.), Belastung und Beanspruchung am Steuer eines Kraftfahrzeuges - Untersuchungen mit Meßfahrzeugen, Bundesanstalt für Straßenwesen, Köln.

Verwey, W. (1990). Adaptable driver-car interfacing and mental workload: a review of the literature. DRIVE Project V1041, Generic intelligent driver support systems, Deliverable report GIDS/DIA/1, Traffic Research Centre, Haren.

VISION IN VEHICLES – IV
A.G. Gale et al. (Editors)

THE MEASUREMENT OF ROAD ENVIRONMENT APPRECIATION WITH A MULTI-SCALE CONSTRUCT LIST

Frank J.J.M. STEYVERS

Traffic Research Centre VSC, University of Groningen, P.O. Box 69, 9750 AB Haren (Gn), The Netherlands.

Abstract

The appreciation of the visual road environment may influence driving performance, especially on long trips in non-demanding situations. Effects like highway hypnosis may be due to too little stimulation from the road scene. In order to explore the drivers' experience and appreciation of the road environment, a rating scale was made from a list of constructs that were elicited from viewing environments on slides. This Road Environment Construct List (RECL) was applied to differentiate between the appreciation of two roads that had different relative accident rates. The roads were technically similar, but differed in their environmental setting. Therefore it was assumed that the context may cause a difference in appreciation, which in turn might contribute to accident causation. The roads were presented in two daylight and two traffic-density conditions. Two experiments were carried out: in the first experiment the roads were presented by slides, in the second they were presented by films. Principal Component Analysis showed that the scoring of the RECL was based on three factors, that were identical for the two experiments. The factors were labelled "hedonic value", "activational value" and "perceptual variation". Composite scores for these factors appeared to differentiate between the two roads, especially in the situation of low traffic density in daylight. Suggestions will be discussed to validate these factors with additional measures, such as eye movements and heart rate measures. Extension of the stimulus set and the presentation modes will be proposed as well.

1. INTRODUCTION

The appreciation of the visual road environment is an element that may contribute to the origin of driving behaviour. The building of anti-noise walls along many kilometres of highways may cause changes of driving behaviour, although the road on those locations is not changed technically (Jessurun et al, 1990). Also it is known (e.g. Rothengatter, 1988) that speed choice on highways is based largely on concepts such as 'driving pleasure'. Long trips in non-demanding situations may cause drivers to loose attention: this 'highway hypnosis' (e.g. Williams, 1963; see also Wertheim, 1978) may be an important cause in one-sided accidents. And route choice, especially with respect to tourist traffic, is sometimes entirely based on the 'beauty of the roadscape'. If we know what elements in the road environment cause this influence of driving behaviour a more explicit use of these elements may help to influence driving behaviour in a specific direction, such as less speeding or overtaking on locations where this is unwanted. Hence, insight in the appreciation of the road environment and its influence on driving behaviour may be an instrument for enlargement of traffic safety or guidance of traffic flow. However, before using the impact of the environment it has to be known how appreciations come into existence and how they may be evaluated.

This paper describes the development and use of a Road Environment Construct List (RECL), that can be used as a measurement scale for the evaluation of road environments in terms of appreciation. The RECL was constructed with respect to a practical problem. It was found that the relative rate of single vehicle accidents on 'polder roads' in The Netherlands is higher than on other roads, although the roads may be technically identical. Two roads were chosen as an example and were used as the main source of stimuli for the construction of the RECL. The roads in question were the N34 that runs through the Dutch province Drenthe, and the N305, that is to be found in the province Flevoland, in the polder: henceforth they will be referred to as Drenthe road and Polder road respectively. From these two roads slides were made at representative sections with comparable weather conditions. In order to be able to differentiate the impact of the road environment from other influences there were two lighting conditions (bright daylight and dusk) and two traffic conditions (with and without other cars). Figure 1 presents two slides from the daylight - no traffic condition, for the Drenthe road (upper panel) and the Polder road (lower panel).

There were 24 slides: 2 roads x 2 lighting conditions x 2 traffic conditions x 3 road sections at the same time.   Also at the same time films were made from these roads. The films were used in a final experiment, to replicate the earlier findings. There are three steps taken to construct the RECL: construct elicitation, construct selection and construct rating.

2. CONSTRUCT ELICITATION

In order to assess drivers' appreciation of a road environment it is necessary to know in what terms the environment is described. Therefore, subjects were asked to describe freely their impression when slides of the two road environments were shown to them. There were 24 male subjects between 22 and 37 years of age (mean 26.2), with a driver's licence for an average of 7.2 years (range 3 - 18 years) and an experience of 12800 km on average per year (range 4500 - 30000). The majority of the subjects were students, who were thought to be able to adequately verbalise their impressions. The subjects were randomly assigned to one of four subgroups. These subgroups had an identical treatment. The 24 slides were presented to them. During the presentation of each slide they were given ample time freely to write down their impressions.   Subjects' reactions were judged by five independent judges, all of whom were psychologists. The judges were asked to express in one or two words the various different impressions of each subject on each slide as succinctly as possible. The judges' summaries of the subjects' impressions were then compared. The five judges experienced little difficulty in condensing the impressions of the subjects. Their constructs were compared on a slide by slide basis, and a general construct was verbalised that covered the judges' summary of the subjects' impressions as closely as possible. In this way 26 constructs were elicited, 21 of which were used by all judges.

Figure 1: black-and-white copies of slides from each road for the daylight - no traffic condition. The upper panel shows the road in Drenthe, the lower panel shows the road in the polder of Flevoland.

3. CONSTRUCT SELECTION

A second group of subjects, with about the same qualities as the first group, served to select constructs for the RECL. Again for practical reasons the subjects were assigned to four subgroups with identical treatment. This stage of the construction of the RECL was done to assert that subjects are able to use the elicited constructs and that they interpret them in a similar fashion with a similar meaning. A Repertory Grid-like (see Kelly, 1955) way was used to present the slides. Subjects were shown the 24 slides in pairs: each pair consisted of one slide from the Polder road and one slide of the Drenthe road. Both slides were from the same lighting and traffic condition. Subjects were asked to compare the slides and to select from the construct list that particular construct that best described the difference between the two slides. The construct list contained the 26 constructs of the first stage. Additionally, for each construct subjects had to define a contrast. As contrast they were free to write down any word, or a word from the construct list. This provided an indication of differences between subjects about the meaning of the chosen constructs. After completion of the 12 pairs of slides the 12 construct-contrast pairs thus obtained were used as a five-point rating scale. From each pair of slides one slide was taken and presented to the subjects again. They had to evaluate the slide with all 12 construct-contrast pairs. In this way it was possible to assess the usefulness of the selected constructs in a rating scale.

Subjects apparently experienced little difficulty in selecting constructs and producing contrasts for these constructs. Some constructs were given very similar contrasts, e.g. 'changeable', 'monotonous', 'surveyable', 'boring', and 'safe'. Other constructs produced a large variety of contrasts: 'pleasant', 'activating', 'enjoyable', and 'encouraging speed'. And the contrasts for the remaining constructs suggest that the latter have two clearly different meanings, e.g. 'alertness' (attention and strain), 'spacious' (sufficient room and a pleasant feeling of space), and 'watchful' (attention and wakefulness). For the RECL constructs were selected that were chosen at least ten times by the subjects, whether as construct or as contrast to some other construct.

The completion of the rating scales were used to refine the initial selection of the constructs. It was found that some constructs were rated '3' (i.e. 'do not know') on the five-point rating scale when the slide was shown that was part of the pair of slides which previously caused the same construct to be selected as the best in describing the difference between the slides. Clearly such a construct was not very applicable, and hence it was not selected. In this way the 26 initial constructs were reduced to the 18 constructs that constituted the RECL.

4. APPLICATION OF THE RECL

The RECL was applied to assess the evaluation of the slides once more, but now with a new group of 84 subjects. The subjects had no experience with the stimuli and they had never taken part in research of this kind. The subjects were randomly assigned to one of three subgroups, which were given identical treatments. The RECL was presented as a six-point rating scale form. Subjects were instructed to imagine that they were driving on the presented roads. They had to indicate how much each construct was appropriate to describe their impression. Table 1 presents the constructs of the RECL. Each of the 24 slides were projected for 1 minute and 20 seconds. During this time, subjects filled in the form. In order to assess rating consistency, the presentation of the slides was repeated after a break.

The test/retest reliability of the 18 scales had a range from 0.80 to 0.90. Hence it was decided to average over repetition and road section per construct, per condition and per subject. In this way a data matrix of 18 constructs x 8 conditions per each of the 84 subjects was obtained. On this 18 x 672 matrix a Principal Component Analysis was carried out

Table 1: Constructs that were part of the RECL and were presented as six-point rating scales for the evaluation of subjects' impression of slides. Subjects had to imagine that they were driving and had to indicate how much each construct was applicable to the road environment shown. Rating classes were labelled: 'totally not applicable', 'almost totally not applicable', 'just not applicable', 'just applicable', 'almost totally applicable', 'totally applicable'. The original Dutch words are given in parenthesis.

---

1 Changeable	(afwisselend)
2 Increases alertness	(alertheidverhogend)
3 Increases attention	(attentieverhogend)
4 Threatening	(bedreigend)
5 Oppressive	(benauwend)
6 Increases concentration	(concentratieverhogend)
7 Dangerous	(gevaarlijk)
8 Demanding	(inspannend)
9 Irritating	(irriterend)
10 Monotonous	(monotoon)
11 Relaxing	(ontspannend)
12 Gives a good view	(overzichtelijk)
13 Enjoyable	(prettig)
14 Spacious	(ruimtelijk)
15 Peaceful	(rustig)
16 Boring	(saai)
17 Safe	(veilig)
18 Increases wakefulness	(waakzaamheidverhogend)

(SPSS/pc). This resulted in a three-factor solution. The eigenvalues of these factors were 9.335, 3.082 and 1.135 respectively, explaining 58.3%, 19.3% and 7.1% of the variance, which cumulates to 84.7% of the total variance. After Varimax-rotation factor loadings were obtained (presented in Table 2) constructs were assigned to a factor for which the particular constructs showed the largest loading. These are indicated in table 2 with a *. From these assignments the factors may be labelled. Factor 1 appeared to combine constructs with emotional connotations, hence it was called the 'hedonic value'. Factor 2 was made of constructs that indicated activity or effort, and was therefore called 'activational value'. The third factor appeared to consist of constructs that indicated environmental variation, and hence was called 'perceptual variation'. Cronbach's alpha for these factors was 0.97, 0.98 and 0.91 respectively.

Factor scores were obtained by averaging the rating score of the constructs that form each factor. For constructs with a negative factor loading the score was inverted (new score = 7 - old score) in order to preserve directional clarity. On these factor scores ANOVAs were carried out, with a 2 x 2 x 2 within-subject design. The results are summarized in table 3. The factor scores, averaged across subjects are presented separately for each factor in Figure 1.

Table 2: Factor loadings after Varimax rotation (6 iterations) for the rating-scale construct scores obtained in Experiment 1. The constructs which were assigned to a specific factor are marked with *.

Construct	Factor 1	Factor 2	Factor 3
1 Changeable	-.031	.113	-.866 *
2 Increases alertness	.330	.890 *	-.229
3 Increases attention	.336	.890 *	-.226
4 Threatening	.883 *	.287	-.034
5 Oppressive	.889 *	.154	-.020
6 Increases concentration	.453	.845 *	-.167
7 Dangerous	.887 *	.307	.000
8 Demanding	.782 *	.520	.039
9 Irritating	.820 *	.224	.165
10 Monotonous	.053	-.202	.924 *
11 Relaxing	-.759 *	-.497	-.039
12 Gives a good view	-.830 *	-.318	-.021
13 Enjoyable	-.795 *	-.420	-.203
14 Spacious	-.793 *	-.200	.009
15 Peaceful	-.755 *	-.226	.315
16 Boring	.008	-.124	.928 *
17 Safe	-.874 *	-.267	.011
18 Increases wakefulness	.393	.881 *	-.188

Table 3: Summary of the ANOVAs for the composite factor scores in Experiment 1. All df are (1,83). Abbreviations: * = p < 0.05; ** = p < 0.01 *** = p < 0.005; **** = p < 0.001.

Source	Factor 1 F	Factor 2 F	Factor 3 F
Road (R)	77.85****	3.97*	81.72****
Lighting (L)	204.10****	197.20****	3.23
Traffic (T)	41.92****	144.00****	135.67****
R x L	103.77****	76.30****	72.11****
R x T	128.40****	134.68****	47.82****
L x T	61.54****	73.15****	17.63****
R x L x T	<1.	23.55****	52.53****

Factor 1, Hedonic value, shows main effects and first-order interactions of all the independent variables. As can be seen in figure 3, this means that the Drenthe road has a higher Hedonic value than the Polder road, that the daylight condition is higher than the night condition and that the no-traffic condition is higher that the traffic condition. The difference in Hedonic value between daylight and night is larger for the Polder road than for the Drenthe road. This finding also holds for the difference between traffic and no-traffic. Finally, the difference between daylight and night is higher for the no-traffic than for the traffic condition.

Factor 2, Activational value shows all possible effects, although the main effect for road just reaches significance. There is a large difference in Activational value between daylight and night and between traffic and no traffic. Furthermore, the difference between daylight and night and between traffic and no-traffic is larger for the Polder road than for the Drenthe road. The difference between daylight and night is also larger in the no-traffic than in the traffic condition. Finally, the increment of the difference between no-traffic and traffic caused by lighting conditions is larger for the Polder road than for the Drenthe road.

Factor 3, Perceptual variation is influenced by all independent variables except for a main effect of lighting conditions. On the Drenthe road, there is more perceptual variation than on the Polder road and with traffic there is more variation than without traffic. The first-order interactions imply that the difference in Perceptual variation between daylight and night is larger for the Drenthe road than for the Polder road and also for the no-traffic condition than for the traffic condition. The difference between no-traffic and traffic is larger on the Polder road than on the Drenthe road. Finally, the second-order interaction may be explained by the finding that, for the Drenthe road, there is a larger difference in Perceptual variation between traffic and no-traffic in night as opposed to daylight conditions, whereas for the Polder road both night and daylight conditions reveal much the same difference between traffic and no traffic. More details of this study are to be found in Steyvers et al. (1989b).

The use of the RECL as a rating scale for the evaluation of road-environment experience has resulted in a solution of three factors that account for most of the variance (84%). It is likely that the factors represent the concepts Hedonic value, Activational value and Perceptual variation. A closer look at the meaning of the constructs suggests that factor 1, consisting of 11 constructs, is composed of two different sub-factors. However, this fails to emerge from the principal-component analysis, so that one cannot assume that subjects make such a distinction. On the contrary, it appears that subjects consider this group of constructs to be closely related in terms of meaning.

The Polder road gives rise to larger differences in evaluation scores than the Drenthe road on all three factors. These evaluations are not only dependent on the three independent variables, but the variables themselves appear to interact strongly with each other. This means that the experience of road environments cannot be regarded separately from aspects such as lighting and traffic conditions. The evaluation of the Polder road is more dependent on aspects other than the environment than is the case with the Drenthe road. With the former in contrast to the latter, it seems that the road environment itself does not make sufficient impact to establish a more or less stable experience. The daylight-no-traffic condition, in particular, reveals large contrasts: although is highly appreciated (has a high Hedonic value), it shows the lowest Activational value and Perceptual variation. It is this very condition that is most likely to elicit 'highway hypnosis' and it is remarkable that it emerges so clearly from rating-scale evaluation alone.

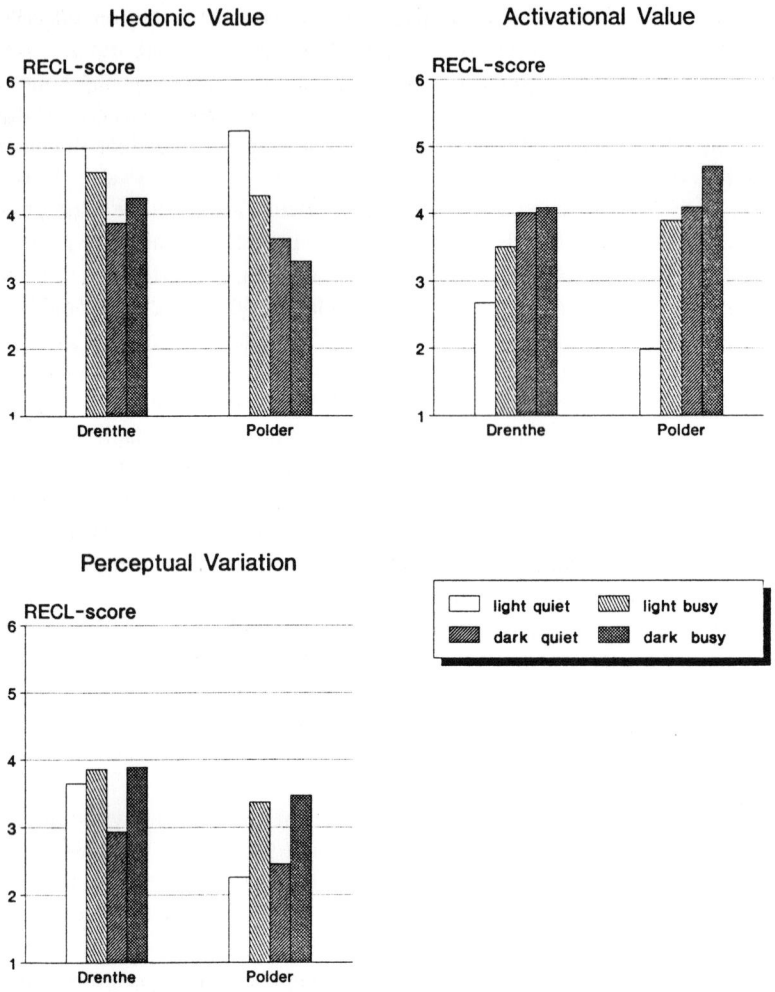

Figure 2: Factor scores separately for each factor, averaged across subjects, for each of the roads and conditions.

5. A REPLICATION STUDY

The application of the RECL was tested again in a similar experiment. This time the films of the same road environments were used. Also the RECL was slightly modified. Two constructs of the hedonic factor ('oppressive' and 'safe') were deleted, in an attempt to reduce the difference in size between the factors. Also two of the constructs of the activation factor were renamed ('increases' was changed in 'lowers') in order to get some variation in the direction of the constructs of that factor. In this study 64 subjects were asked to evaluate the eight films of the roads, using the modified RECL as a 16-construct six-point rating scale. Subjects were randomly assigned in eight groups, that received identical treatments: order of presentation of the films was balanced in a Latin-square design across subject groups. The instruction remained similar to that of the former experiment. The data analysis was done in the same way as described in section 4. The results were virtually identical to the results of the slide experiment. Again three factors were extracted from the PCA, that explained 66.8% of the total variation. The assignment of constructs to the factors resulted in an identical picture: the same constructs constituted the same factors. Cronbach's alpha for the three factors was 0.90, 0.84 and 0.85 respectively. After calculations of factor scores, the ANOVA of the 2 x 2 x 2 within-subject design (when averaged across presentation order, that did not show a main effect) gave a very similar result as in the slide experiment. The scores may be interpreted in a similar fashion. For further details see Steyvers et al. (1989a).

6. DISCUSSION AND CONCLUSIONS

The two experiments indicate that subjects are able to evaluate their experience of the road environment by means of the RECL used as a rating scale. The central finding to emerge from Experiment 1 was replicated in Experiment 2: the Polder road shows less Activational Value and Perceptual Variation, especially by daylight, while Hedonic Value is no less than for the Drenthe road. The difference in ratings between the Drenthe road and the Polder road for the various factors might be seen as lying at the root of effects such as 'highway hypnosis' and other undesirable effects of environment on behaviour. It could serve to explain the higher rate of one-sided, seemingly inexplicable accidents on the Polder road compared to the Drenthe road. In other words, the present findings can be interpreted as supporting the hypothesis that such accidents arise through sub-optimal attention and/or activation.

The emergence of a three-factor solution in a PCA of road environment evaluation, with Hedonic value and Activational value as the first and the second factor, may be compared to two IATSS (1982, 1983) studies. These used a rating-scale method to compare the appraisal of various highway scenes. This resulted also in three factors, the third of which was discarded because it contributed to less explained variance, according to the IATSS research team. Their 'emotional factor' and 'activational factor ' closely correspond with the descriptions of the first two factors in the present study. The Japanese IATSS study also used both slides and films for the presentation of the road environments. The IATSS-investigators found no differences between slide and film results. The present results are in general in accordance with this finding. The present results are also in accordance with the review of Berlyne (1971), who concluded that evaluations may be composed of a hedonic dimension, an intensity dimension, and a potency dimension. It is admitted, however, that equating 'Perceptual Variation' with a potency dimension is somewhat far fetched. However, the more perceptual variation an environment shows, the more potency an environment may possess.

The present results show that appraisal and experience of road environments may lead to differences in evaluation of road scenes. However, it would be valuable to investigate whether differences between Appreciation, on one hand and Activation Value and Perceptual Variation, on the other, emerge from measures other than ratings. Activational Value, for example, might be assessed using physiological measures, such as heart-rate, skin-conductance or facial muscular activity. Eye movements and fixations could be used to assess Perceptual Variation. Future studies should expand in two ways. On the one hand, they should use more and more normal, natural road situations in all their variety and complexity, and perhaps from all around the world. On the other hand non-existing or abstract road scenes with completely controllable elements should be used in studies with high-power graphic simulation equipment, in order to identify basic environmental features that contribute to the information processing of driving. Research of this nature is already in progress at the Traffic Research Centre. The ultimate goal of such research would be to develop a model of driving behaviour which takes account of the road environment and its perception and appraisal. When a road and its environment are being rebuilt or modified, such a model would be of value in offering the opportunity to examining the behavioural consequences of different alternatives when they are still at the design stage.

7. ACKNOWLEDGEMENT

The study of this paper was made in assignment of the Dutch Ministry of Transportation and Public Works, Transportation and Traffic Research Division, Road-scene and Aesthetics section, in Utrecht, The Netherlands.

8. REFERENCES

Berlyne, D.E. (1971). Aesthetics and Psychobiology. New York: Appleton-Century Crofts.
IATSS 423 project team (1982). Environmental influence on driving behavior. IATSS research, 6, 3-13.
IATSS 423 project team (1983). Roadscape - The analysis of visual-perceptual mechanism. IATSS research, 7, 3-14.
Jessurun, M., Steyvers, F.J.J.M., Waard, D. de, Dekker, K. & Brookhuis, K.A. (1990). [Experience, perception and activation during driving along a part of highway A2]. Haren (Gn), The Netherlands: Traffic Research Centre VSC. (In Dutch).
Kelly, G.A. (1955). The psychology of personal constructs. New York: W.W. Norton.
Rothengatter, J.A. (1988). Risk and the absence of pleasure: a motivational approach to modelling road user behaviour. Ergonomics, 31, 599-607.
Steyvers, F.J.J.M., Dekker, K., & Brookhuis, K.A. (1989a). [Aesthetic appraisal of the road - an empirical approach. Research results report 2]. Haren (Gn), The Netherlands: Traffic Research Centre VSC, University of Groningen. Report VK-89-16 (in Dutch).
Steyvers, F.J.J.M., Dekker, K., Hamacher, M. & Brookhuis, K.A. (1989b). [Aesthetic appraisal of the road - an empirical approach. Research results report 1]. Haren (Gn), The Netherlands: Traffic Research Centre VSC, University of Groningen. Report VK-89-08 (in Dutch).
Wertheim, A.H. (1978). Explaining highway hypnosis: experimental evidence for the role of eye movements. Acta Psychologica, 38, 235-256.
Williams, G.W. (1963). Highway hypnosis: a hypothesis. International Journal of Clinical and Experimental Hypnosis, 103, 143-151.

VISION IN VEHICLES – IV
A.G. Gale et al. (Editors)
213

VARIABLE VISUAL ACUITY FOR A DRIVER MODEL

Thomas JUERGENSOHN and Thiess-Magnus WOLTER

Technical University of Berlin, Institute of Vehicle Engineering, Sekretariat TIB 13
Gustav-Meyer-Allee 25, 1000 Berlin 65, Germany

Abstract
The Human-Machine Systems group at the Technical University of Berlin is working on
the implementation of an overall simulation of the driver, vehicle and the environment. The
driver's part of this model, called "Vehunculus", is divided into several modules. One of
these modules is the visual system which is able to simulate information processing taking
into account the variability of visual acuity as a function of location within the visual field.
It is shown how to use the rendering process of a graphic workstation to achieve a filtering
effect. Comparison with neurophysiological findings shows the similarity between the
"technical" solution and the properties of the human visual system.

1. INTRODUCTION

Traditional models of driver behaviour are dominated by the control theory approach
(Chenchanna, 1966; Mc Ruer, 1977; Blaauw, 1987) where characteristics of visual
perception are rarely considered. These models generally describe the driver's steering wheel
or car-following activities assuming that the driver has knowledge of relevant inputs such
as his heading angle and lateral position in relation to the road. Uncertainties are modelled
by the addition of white observation noise or a "Remnant". This approach is sufficient to
describe control behaviour. However, for high level information processing (such as decision
making) the specific influence of perception must be included. The close relationship
between the environmental conditions of visual perception and the ensuing eye movements
has been investigated by several groups (e.g. Mourant and Rockwell, 1979; Rockwell, 1972;
Cohen, 1985). Few researchers emphasize the difference between foveal and peripheral
vision (Bhise, 1971; Cohen, 1991). As yet there is no driver model which considers the
measurable decrease of visual acuity from the point of fixation to the edge of the visual
field.

2. THE IMPORTANCE OF EYE MOVEMENTS

Our driver model is aimed as a tool for the simulation of complex information processing
and as a means of understanding this processing. Therefore, it is necessary to create

quantifiable models for cognitive processes. Since high level information processing is very much dependant on individual characteristics of the driver, an adaptable model has to be generated in which the driver is described by a set of parameters. Two main problems of such a model are the selection of parameters and the validation. This can only be achieved by comparing the model's output with the reality. Since eye movements can easily be used to indicate information selection and the focus of attention, they play an important role in the model's validation. The visual system of a driver model has to imitate the variable visual acuity because these changes in acuity are the main reason for eye movements. Thus, it will be possible to simulate variable sharpness of sight on the driver's performance.

3. USING THE RENDERING PROCESS AS AN UNCERTAINTY FILTER

Obviously we will not be able to simulate the human's complex visual system. Moreover, our goal is to imitate the measurable dependency of the visual sharpness from the location within the visual field. There are a few different methods to determine visual acuity, but in any case the subject has to decide wether he is able to recognize a small structure (line, gap, edge) in a test pattern (see Figure 1).

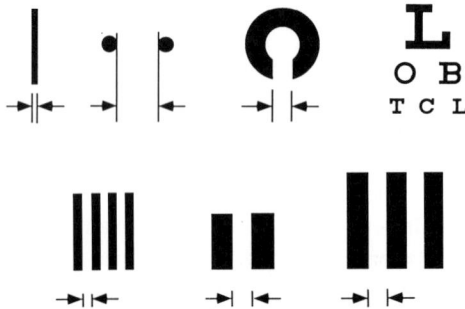

Figure 1: Some patterns used to measure visual acuity

The most common pattern is the Landolt-Circle which is used to determine the "Visus-function". This function is obtained by measuring the reciprocal angle at which the Landolt-Circle's gap is perceptible in dependancy from the distance of the point of fixation to the circle's location.

The "Visus" is the reciprocal to the angle a of the Landolt Circle which is yet recognizable at a certain point in the visual field.

The Visus-function shown in Figure 2 contains the entire processing chain from presentation up to assessment by the subject. For the visual system of a driver model this means: create a visual module in such a way that a pattern of a certain size is perceived only if its distance to the point of fixation lies below a certain radius. One possible way to

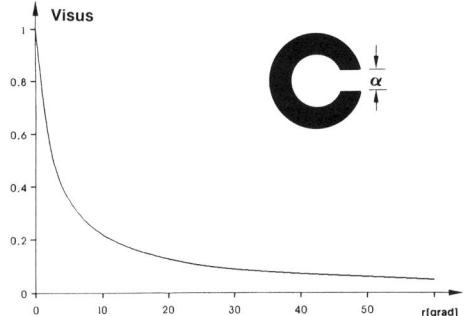

Figure 2: A typical Visus-function :

achieve this is to filter the visual field with a variable lowpass filter. The disadvantage of this approach is its high computational demand. An alternative approach uses the rendering processor of a graphic workstation. Since the workstation is required to simulate the environmental influence on the driver, it can also be used for filtering. One feature of the rendering process is the suppression of small structures.

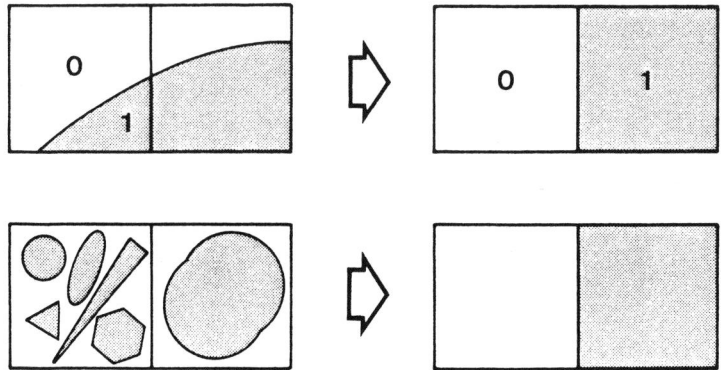

Figure 3: The rendering process: objects that are smaller than half a pixel are suppressed

Pixels have the same size everywhere but we need a filter with increasing size. One way to resolve this problem is to transform the image into a different plain. Instead of applying a rendering filter with increasing size we use an equal-sized filter on an image with structures of decreasing size. Figure 4 illustrates this process.

The effect of this process is shown in Figure 5. Here the limits of the perception of the gap are clearly recognizable.

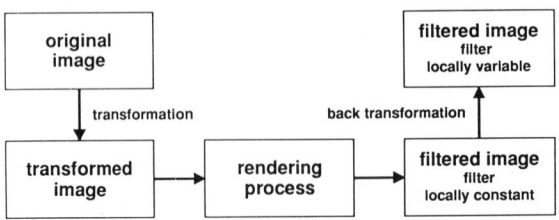

Figure 4: A locally variable filter effect is achieved with a locally independent filter by transformation of the original image

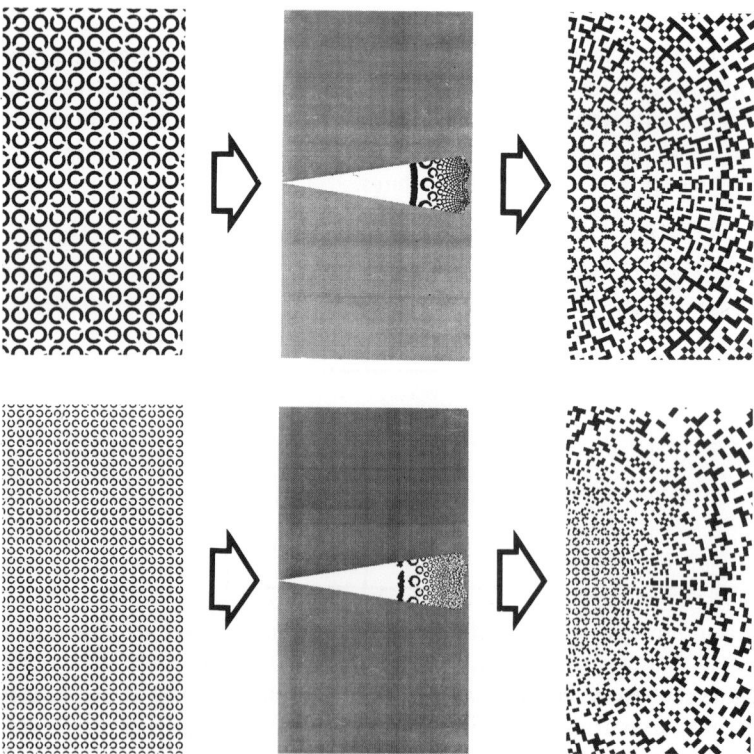

Figure 5: The effect of a locally variable uncertainty filter. Left: the original image, middle: the transformed image with decreasing structure size, right: the filtered image after rendering and back-transformation.

The transformation used in Figure 5 is a conformal mapping of the form:

$$w = c.z^{\,p},$$ w, z being complex and c, p being real.

The choice of c and p depends on the desired shrinking factor which is given by the shape of the Visus-function. If we assume that this function can be approximated by a power function $v(r) \approx r^k$ and that the shrinking factor is proportional to $v(r)$ it is possible to calculate the constants c and p.

4. SIMPLIFICATION OF THE IMAGE TRANSFORMATION BY USING STEPWISE APROXIMATED VISUS-FUNCTIONS

One disadvantage of the approach presented is that there is still much computation time needed for the complex transformation. This can be avoided if the transformation is simplified to $w = c_i.z$ (i.e. p=1) where constant c_i varies stepwise in the z-plane. The corresponding Visus-function is also stepwise constant. The effect of this filtering is shown in Figure 7, the corresponding Visus-function is presented in Figure 6.

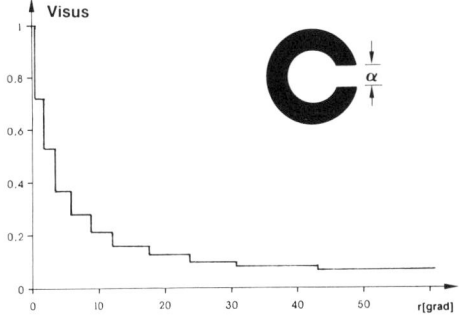

Figure 6: Stepwise approximation of the Visus-function

Since the conformal mapping degenerates to simple scaling and translating, the computation time decreases by a factor of 1000. Certainly, the mapping is no longer objective and the original image is split into different scaled overlapping subimages. So, we have to put each subimage onto a different plane and add the lost neighbourhood relation between the subimages by software. In Figure 8 the effect on a simple road scenario can be seen: the original image (top), the transformed image with the subimages (middle, 10x enlarged) and the resulting image after back-transformation (bottom). In order to show the effect of fuzzification the pixel size has been altered by a random factor. The point of fixation lies within the bottom part of the right front pile.

Figure 7: A pattern filtered using a stepwise approximated Visus-function. The areas of equal visual acuity are rectangles.

Figure 8: The effect of a descending acuity on a simple road scenario. The original image (top) is transformed (middle, 10x enlarged). In the back-transformed image (bottom) the effect of the rendering filter is recognizable.

As demonstrated the demanded locally variable visual acuity can be achieved by using the present approach. But it must be said that the back-transformed image will never be used by the driver model. It has been included for illustration. All modules of the driver model that process visual information will only use the mapped image (middle of Figure 8). Due to its similarity to the human visual system we called it the "area-17-image". The subsequent module searches through it for edges, gaps and corners. Here another side effect of the mapping appears: the reduction of the image to approximately 8% of its original size makes such searching considerably faster. So we are able to simulate the full range of the human visual sharpness up to visus 3.

5. CONCLUSION

It is obvious that the present approach can simulate only a few properties of the human visual system. Our goal was to generate a system which forces the driver model to change its point of fixation in order to solve the driving task in an optimum manner. The visual acuity of a given subject can easily be approximated or changed during a simulation run. By using the rendering processor of a graphic workstation and by using a stepwise approximated Visus-function the simulation can be virtually achieved in real-time.

6. REFERENCES

Bhise, V.D. and Rockwell, T.H. (1971). Role of Peripheral Vision and Time Sharing in Driving, paper presented at the American Association for Automotive Medicine, Colorado.

Blaauw, G., Godhelp, H. and Milgram, P. (1972). Optimal Control Model Applications and Field Measurements with Respect to Car Driving, Vehicle System Dynamics, 13.

Chechanna, D. (1966). Untersuchungen über das menschliche Lenkverhalten an Fahrzeugen bei verschiedenen Modellen für den Fahrer, Dissertation, TU Berlin.

Cohen, A. and Hirsig, R. (1991). The Role of Foveal Vision in the Process of Information Input, Proceedings of the Conference on Vision in Vehicles III.

Cohen, A. (1985). Visuelle Informationsaufnahme während der Fahrzeugsteuerung in Abhängigkeit der Umwelterkennung und der Fahrpraxis, Schweizerische Zeitschrift für Psychologie, 44, 4.

Mc Ruer, D.T. (1977). New Results in Driver Steering Control Models, Human Factors 19, 4.

Mourant, R.R. and Rockwell, T.H. (1979). Mapping Eye Movement Patterns to the Visual Scene in Driving: An Explanatory Study, Human Factors, 12, 1.

Rockwell, T.H. (1972). Eye-Movement Analysys of Visual Information Acquisition in Driving: An Overview, Australian Road Research Board, Paper No. 948.

9

TELEROBOTIC CONTROL
OF VEHICLES

VISION IN VEHICLES – IV
A.G. Gale et al. (Editors)
1993 Elsevier Science Publishers B.V.

HUMAN ENGINEERING EXPERIMENTS USING A TELEROBOTIC VEHICLE

K.-P. HOLZHAUSEN, F.D. PITRELLA and H.-L. WOLF

Research Institute for Human Engineering (FAT), Neuenahrer Str. 20, 5307 Wachtberg-Werthhoven, Germany

Abstract
Experiments were conducted recently to uncover ergonomic problems and to evaluate the effects of design alternatives on human performance when remotely controlling the teleoperated sensor-equipped EROS vehicle. Efforts were focused on the control and visual links between the operator and vehicle. Reported here are the results of experiments comparing the effects of mono- and stereoscopic visual links on remote operator performance with steering and approach-braking tasks.

1. INTRODUCTION

Operations in hazardous work environments require remotely operated equipment. Many such applications require not only a vision link into a dangerous area but a mobile platform with TV imagery that can move around in the work space providing visual information at the site from different viewpoints to inform the remote operator about the situation. Other applications include the transportation of material or the remote manipulation of tools.

The Robot Research Group at the Research Institute for Human Engineering (FAT) has built up a development and test facility for telerobotic systems. The first task of this facility was to design and build a telerobotic vehicle called "Experimental Robot System (EROS)". In addition, the telerobotic vehicle can be simulated on the computer. One or more simulated vehicles can be run alone or together with the operation of the real vehicle. This simulation capability is expected to be useful in determining the value of various system designs and automatic algorithms in achieving various levels of vehicle autonomy and supervisory control. When telerobotic development has gone beyond remote operation of a single vehicle and has progressed to some level of partial autonomy, an operator and supervisor team at a control station would be in the position to conduct multiple vehicle operation. The basic technical description of the EROS system is given in Holzhausen (1991).

During the last year experiments and development trials were conducted to uncover ergonomic problems and to evaluate the effects of design alternatives on human perfomance when remotely controlling the teleoperated sensor-equipped vehicle. Efforts were focused on the control and visual links between the operator and vehicle. Reported here are the results of experiments comparing the effects of mono- and stereoscopic vision systems on operator performance with steering and braking tasks.

2. MONO- AND STEREOSCOPIC REMOTE VISUAL LINKS

In co-operation with the Nuclear Research Facility in Karlsruhe (KFK) a stereoscopic viewing system was installed on the EROS vehicle. The two subminiature cameras were mounted on the vehicle pan and tilt head in a parallel assembly with a lens separation of 65 mm. This distance approximates the interocular disparity in humans. The cameras produce standard CCIR-TV signals. Figure 1 is a functional diagram of the visual links of the stereo system. The first half picture of the left camera and the second interlaced picture of the second camera were mixed together to form a standard TV pattern. The pattern was them transmitted using a 2.3 GHz transmission link with a bandwidth of 5 MHz. In the control station the video signal was further processed to separate the left and right camera information. The patterns were stored in video RAMs. The left and right video information was then displayed at a rate of 100 Hz. The operator used liquid crystal (LC) shutter glasses which were synchronized by a signal from the decoder. A mono display could be selected by switching to information from one of the cameras. The 100 Hz technique rendered a clear and flicker free view of either the mono or the stereo display.

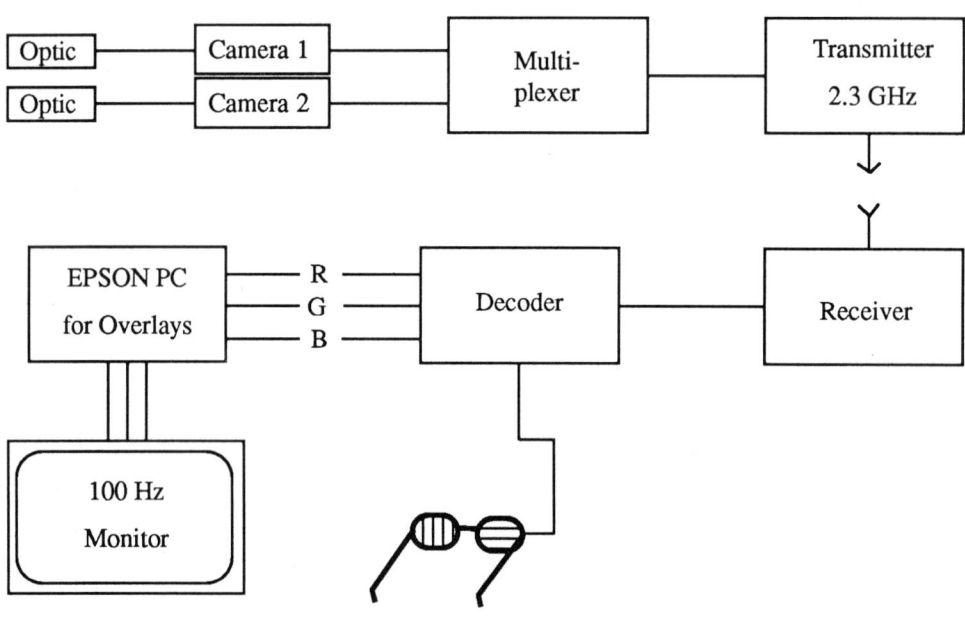

Figure 1: Monoscopic and stereoscopic remote visual link system

3. "S" CURVE STEERING TASK

The object of this task was to compare the effects of mono- and stereoscopic visual information obtained remotely and transmitted by communication links on the remote steering performance of the EROS vehicle. The vehicle was controlled using a spring centered displacement stick located on a control console. The left-right axis controlled the steering angle of the steering wheels. The task was to drive as fast as possible around a course layed out in the EROS research hall (see Figure 2) without touching any vertical cylinders used to mark the "S" curve part of the course. The large cardboard cylinders are 1.6 m high and have a diameter of 40 cm. The performance scores were elapsed times around the course. Any time the vehicle touched a cylinder led to an automatic braking of the vehicle. No times were recorded for such runs. Each of six driver/subjects performed four blocks of runs in a within subjects design. Half of the subjects started with the mono (M) display information in the first block and switched to stereo (S) and back again in a MSSM sequence to counterbalance learning transfer effects between display conditions. The other half started with stereo in a SMMS sequence. The goal in each block was to make as many runs as was necessary to achieve 6 runs without touching cylinders. However, with some subjects only 4 or 5 such error free runs were achieved. Consequently, only the last four runs were used for data analysis.

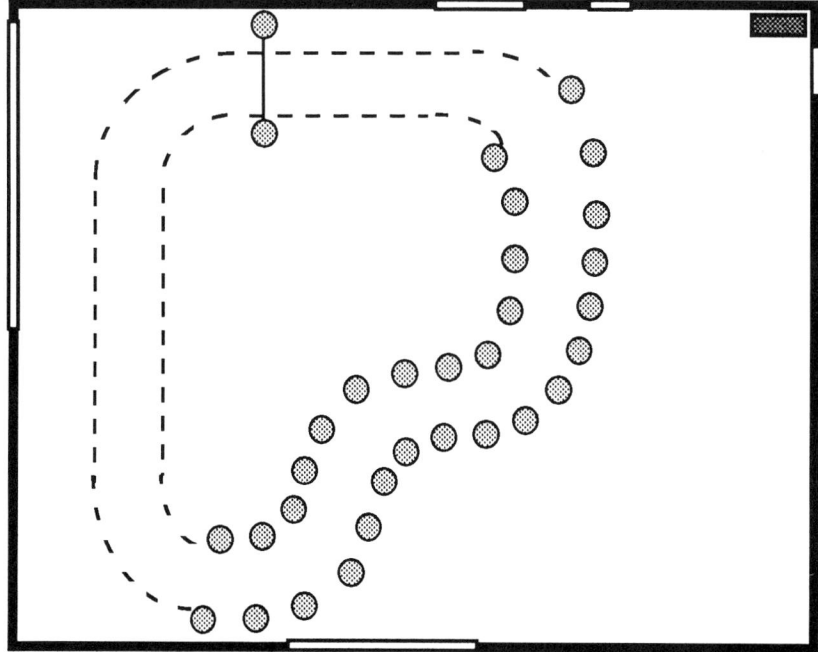

Figure 2: Driving Course for "S" Curve Steering Task

Since there were only 3 subjects in each order group, no comparisons could be sensibly made between mono and stereo within each group. Therefore, all mono blocks were pooled and compared with pooled stereo blocks. The results are shown in Figure 3. It is clear that the average group driving time of 35.2 s when subjects are using stereo display information is significantly lower than the 41.3 s when using mono information. This difference is statistically significant at the .0001 level with a one-tailed paired T-test. The better depth perception with the stereo display information permitted remote drivers to judge the position of cylinders better, which in turn allowed them to drive at higher speeds and resulting in shorter elapsed times around the course.

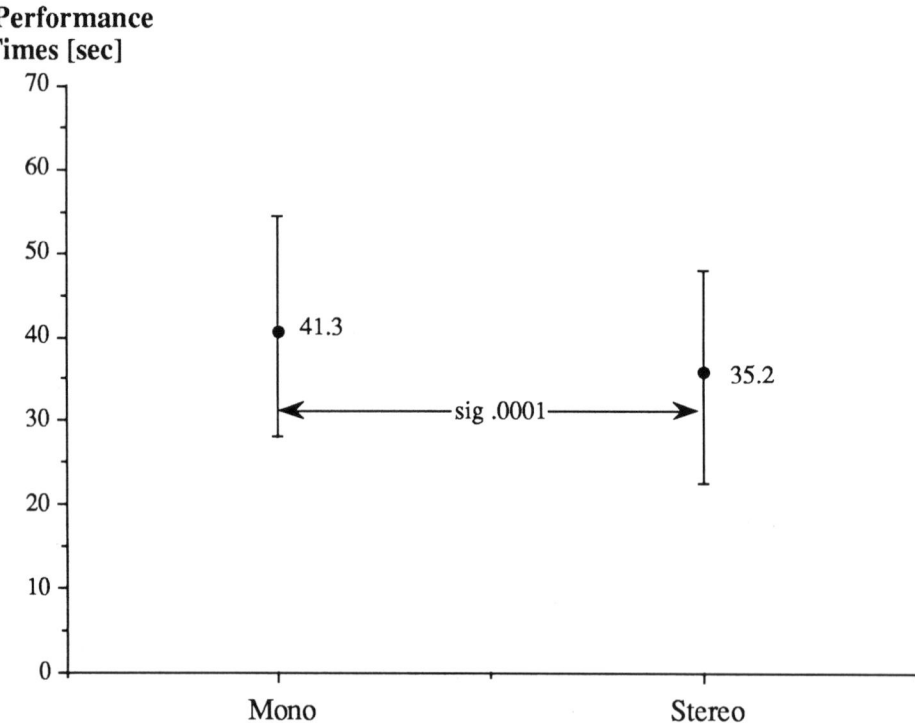

Figure 3: "S" Curve Perfomance Times Mono Versus Stereo

4. OBSTACLE APPROACH TASK

This task was concerned with how closely driver/subjects could remotely bring the EROS vehicle to a stop before an obstacle without hitting it, while using remotely sensed mono or stereoscopic display information. The same kind of large cardboard cylindrical objects used in the "S" curve experiment were positioned in the test hall to form a wall with a perceptually well-textured surface. The obstacles were easy to see with either the mono or stereoscopic displays. Each subject remotely drove the vehicle towards the wall (Figure 4) as slowly as necessary in order to stop at the closest remaining distance that they could judge with the available visual information without touching the wall. All trials in which the vehicle touched the wall were regarded as errors. Whenever the wall was hit another run was substituted so that all blocks would have 10 runs with stop distance scores. The vehicle was controlled as before using a spring centered displacement stick located on a control console. The left-right axis controlled the steering angle of the steering wheels. The forward-backward longitudinal axis controlled the driving speed in either direction.

Each of the 8 subjects carried out 10 experimental trials. The 8 subjects were randomly assigned to two groups of four. One group of driver/subjects used the mono viewing condition first and the other group started with the stereo system first. After the first 10 trials each group switched to the other viewing system and back again in an MSSM or SMMS order for a total of 40 trials per group.

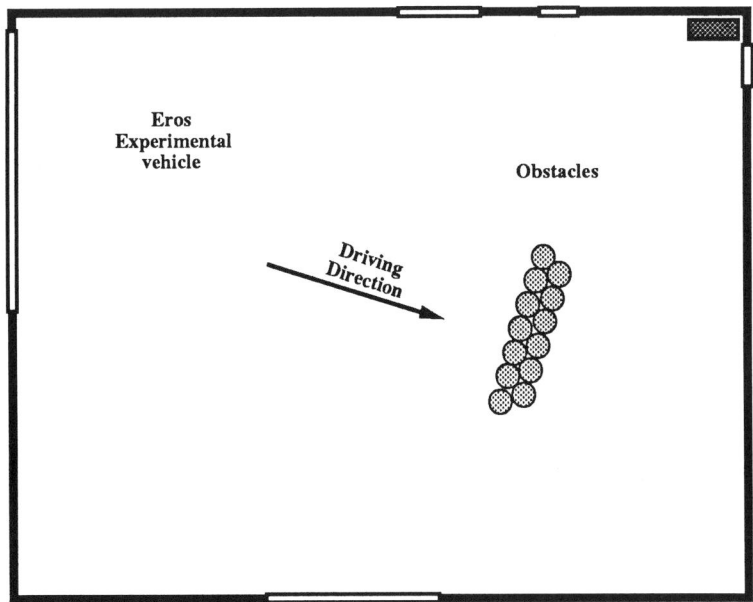

Figure 4: Experimental situation in the obstacle approach task

It was judged that sufficient data and subjects were available to examine the data within each group in order to determine in which direction learning transfers between display conditions may have occurred depending on which display condition subjects were presented first.

Figure 5 shows the stop distance results of this obstacle approach task. The vertical axis of the graph represents the group average of closest stop distances in cm. The horizontal axis represents trial blocks of both groups, each data point on the graph representing a particular display condition and presentation order. The first four points illustrate results of the mono-first group and the last four points of the stereo-first group.

The first data point (AMM) represents the results of the first mono block of trials of the "Mono First Group". The average stop distance to the wall is 48.4 cm. After switching to the first stereo block (ASM), group stop distance decreased significantly to 18.1 cm, the result of both learning and having better information. Stop distances decreased further in the second stereo block (BSM) to 15.8 cm due to learning, but was not statistically significant with only four subjects. After switching back to mono (BMM), stop distances increased significantly to an average of 30.1 cm in spite of still more training due to the loss of stereo depth cues. This performance in the second mono block of trials is not significantly different than performance in the first mono block showing a minimal learning effect.

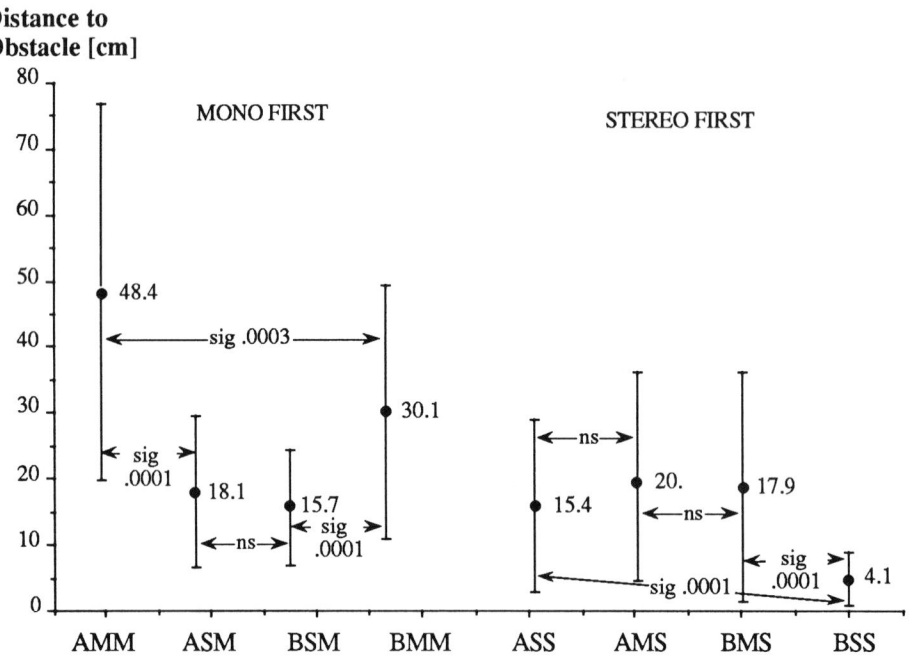

Figure 5: Stop Distances for Mono and Stereo Blocks

legend: A = The first block of trials for a specific display condition.
          B = The second block of trials for a specific display condition.
          M = As middle letter it means Mono Trial. As last letter, mono first group.
          S = As middle letter it means Stereo Trial. As last letter, stereo first group.

Average stop distance for the first stereo block of trials (ASS) of the "Stereo First Group" was 15.4 cm. After switching to the first mono block (AMS), stop distance increased somewhat to 20 cm due to the loss of stereo depth cues. As we shall see below stereo learning effects improved mono performance. In the second mono block (BMS), stop distance decreased slightly with a non significant learning effect to 17.9 cm. After switching back to stereo in the second stereo block (BSS) stop distance further decreased significantly to 4.1 cm.

In figure 6 is a comparison of the effects of all pooled mono and stereo display conditions for all 8 subjects. Average stop distance while using stereo information is only 13.3 cm compared to the 28.8 cm average stop distance with mono.

When considering error data (no. of trials where the wall was touched) it seems reasonable to predict that the closer to the wall (in stop distances) that subjects decide to stop, the higher are the chances that they will sometimes touch the wall. Error data results did show that there tended to be more error trials with stereo display information than mono. While the judgments of subjects with stereo brought them closer to the wall it improved the chances of occasionally touching it.

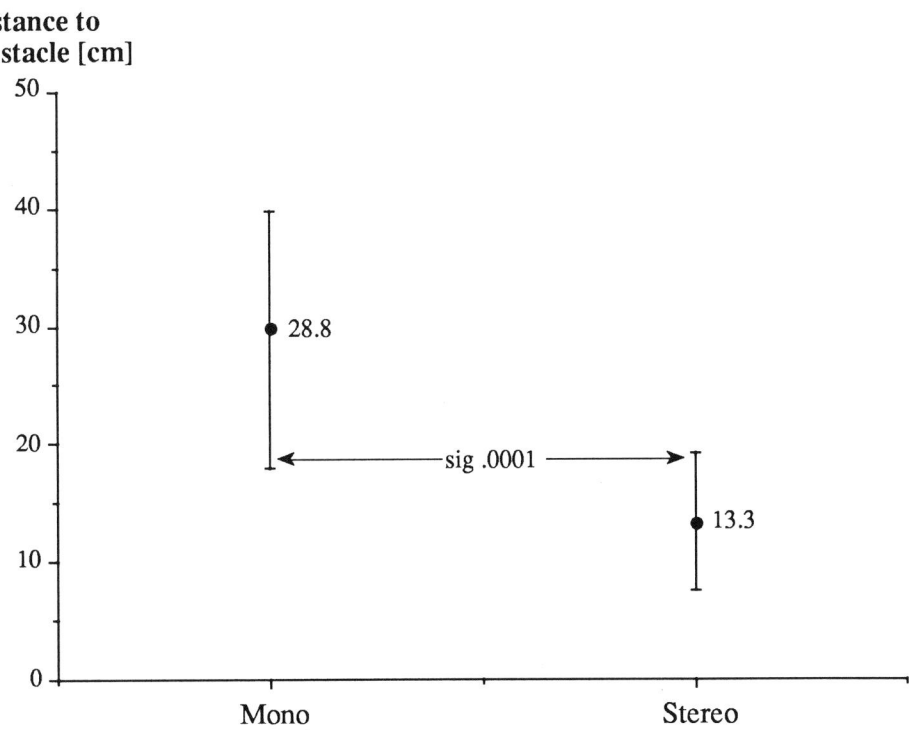

Figure 6: Average Stop Distances Mono Versus Stereo

There also is some evidence of asymmetric learning transfer effects between mono and stereo displays. Experience with the condition learned first will have either a positive or a negative influence on the ability to learn the following viewing condition. If the learning influences in either direction are approximately the same then transfer effects are equal or symmetric, otherwise they are asymmetric.

The performance between mono and stereo unconfounded with order or transfer effects can be seen when comparing the first trial blocks of the mono first (AMM) and stereo first (ASS) groups. Mono is clearly inferior with 48.5 cm to the stereo stop distance of 15.5 cm. When the mono first group switches to stereo (ASM) the performance is dramatically improved to 18.3 cm (33 cm less stop distance) but not significantly different than the 15.5 cm performance of the first block of the stereo first group. In other words there is no significant learning transfer from mono to stereo. When going from stereo (ASS) to mono (AMS) we would expect the mono to have about 33 cm greater stop distance if their are no learning transfer effects. In fact the mono stop distance is only about 5 cm greater than the beginning stereo performance, instead of the expected 33 cm greater stop distance. There was a large positive training effect when going from stereo to mono.

5. CONCLUSION

These experiments clearly show that stereo display information provides overall better performance than mono information in both steering and approach braking tasks. The superior depth information provided by stereo display information enhanced the ability of driver/subjects to judge distances to the obstacles. Furthermore, stereo experience provides a larger positive training effect on mono than in the reverse direction.

6. REFERENCE

Holzhausen K-P. (1991) Vision and Guidance of a telerobotic vehicle. In A. G. Gale et al. (Eds),Vision in Vehicles III Elsevier Science Publishers B.V. (North-Holland)429-436.

VISION IN VEHICLES – IV
A.G. Gale et al. (Editors)
1993 Elsevier Science Publishers B.V.

VISUO-COGNITIVE ASPECTS OF NAVIGATION IN REMOTE-CONTROL SITUATIONS

Evguéni A. LAPIN[*] and Patrick PERUCH[**]

[*] Institute of Psychology of the USSR Academy of Sciences 13, Yaroslavskaya Street, 129366 Moscow, USSR

[**] Université d'Aix-Marseille II, Faculté de Médecine, URA CNRS Cognition et Mouvement, IBHOP, Traverse Susini, 13388 Marseille Cedex 13, France

Abstract

Certain perceptual and cognitive aspects of navigation involved in remote-control situations were investigated. Central to this study was to determine how an operator converts visual flow transformations seen on a graphic display into egocentric "route knowledge," and then attributes this information to a path on the map. Another question was whether the non-correspondence between these two modes of spatial information presentation (i.e., misalignment) plays a role in this process. Two types of navigational problems were dealt with: direct answering (i.e., route memory from origin to destination) and reverse answering (i.e., route memory from destination to origin). The subjects were found to have difficulties in memorizing the visual flow and in using the perceived information to select the route on the map. The non-correspondence between egocentric and allocentric spatial information significantly influenced the decision time and success rate in direct answering conditions, but no misalignment effects were observed in reverse ones.

1. INTRODUCTION

Understanding the psychological processes involved in the control of a vehicle's displacement is of fundamental importance in remote-control situations. Analyzing perceptual processes and then spatial cognition is essential in the elaboration of the man-to-machine interface for use in a remote-control device. Such a design implies a working relationship between specialists in cognitive sciences and in robotics. Recent studies (e.g., Chavand et al., 1988; Mestre et al., 1990; ORIA-89, 1989) have revealed psychological problems in remote-control situations arising from the fact that the displacements of a remote-control vehicle are generally controlled by a stationary operator using a visual display as the main source of spatial information. In this situation, "direct" visual perception is replaced by images from video cameras on-board the mobile device (e.g., Holzhausen, 1991). Consequently, certain transformations of visual information are to be expected. It is essential to understand how an operator converts the visual flow transformations (Gibson, 1979) observed on a graphic display into egocentrically stored "route knowledge" (Shemyakin, 1962; Siegel and White, 1975).

Different types of spatial information about the vehicle's displacements are obtained from several sources: available spatial information presented on a display as visual-flow transformations which is egocentrically memorized, and analogic, allocentrically stored spatial information about the displacement (i.e., the path of the simulated vehicle) observed on the graphic map display. Thus, the operator has to establish the correspondence between these two kinds of spatial information. Spatial orientation requires the perception of the environment and spatial knowledge memorized in the form of a cognitive map (e.g., Thorndyke and Hayes-Roth, 1980). In such a context, spatial orientation may be described as a cognitive process establishing the correspondence between data from direct perception of the environment and memorized environmental knowledge and/or the information presented on a map which should be oriented in the same direction as the real situation observed by the subject. Several studies have demonstrated the misalignment effect on spatial orientation (Levine et al., 1984; Péruch and Savoyant, 1991; Shepard and Hurwitz, 1985).

When the operator has to find his way back to his point of departure, misalignment has often been observed to create difficulties in navigating. This misalignment corresponds to differences in the direction of movement and to the orientation of the real and/or mental map which make it difficult to remember the encountered points (i.e., right and left turns). The subject must then reverse this order to return to his point of departure (Passini et al., 1990; Heft and Wohlwill, 1987). The task is far more complicated for the operator seated in front of a screen, directing a vehicle back to its point of departure, because the right side of the vehicle may correspond to his left, and vice versa. The possible combinations of egocentric and allocentric modes of presenting spatial information not encountered in natural navigation situations may raise serious problems for the operator. This experiment aimed at analyzing certain perceptual and cognitive processes involved in orientation and navigation tasks, with regard to the influence of the non-correspondence between egocentric and allocentric spatial information when translating the perception of a visual flow into spatial knowledge.

2. METHOD

2.1. Material

A computer linked to a high-resolution graphic screen was used to produce a map and an animated sequence (i.e., films). The map was a 20-by-36 cm rectangle situated in the lower part of the screen and composed of 13 blue circles of 5 mm diameter, with a letter in each circle (see Figure 1).

The films simulated different routes followed on the map, and were presented at the top of the screen in a 36-by-4 cm rectangle. Each route included three 90-degree turns located directly before a circle, alternating with straight-line paths of equal length along which the circle increased to its maximum size. Turns and straight lengths were chosen on the basis of a preliminary study showing that the cognitive difficulty for this kind of task was not excessive. The films viewed by the subjects lasted about 45 seconds each. During the experiment the subject was seated in front of the screen at a viewing distance of about 80 cm, subtending horizontal and vertical visual angles of approximately 40 degrees.

2.2. Procedure

At the beginning of each trial, the map disappeared from the screen and a film was presented to the subject. Thus the only egocentric spatial information available was that associated with the displacements (i.e., visual flow transformations). Once the film had

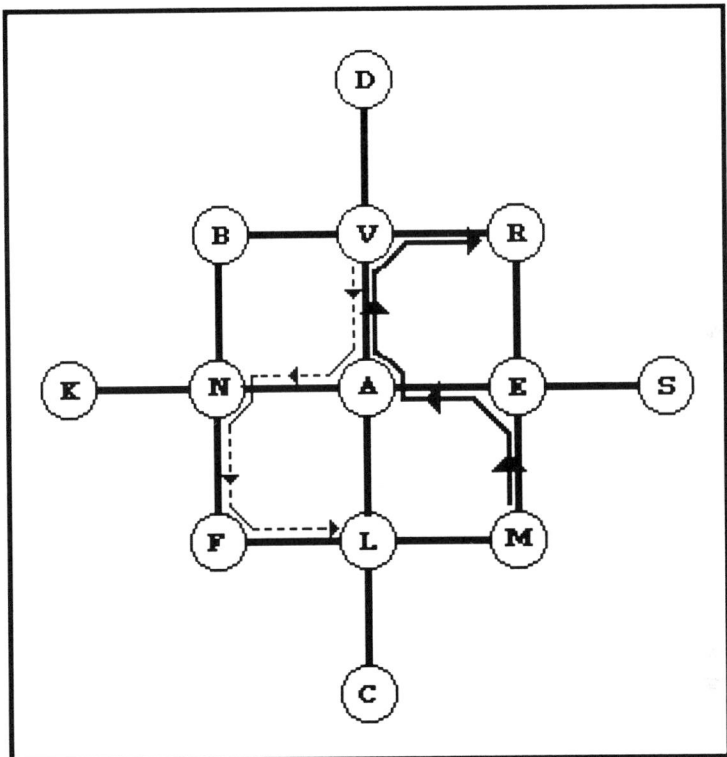

Figure 1. The map with two possible routes. From the starting point M the route is aligned with the orientation of the map, whereas from the starting point V the route is misaligned with the orientation of the map.

been shown, the map appeared in the lower part of the screen. The experimenter then indicated whether the letter corresponded to the starting or ending point of the route on the map. When the starting point was given, the subject was asked to enumerate aloud all the letters encountered along the route up to the ending point (i.e, direct answering). When the ending point was given, the subject was asked to enumerate aloud all the letters encountered from the ending point to the starting point (i.e., reverse order with regards to the film, or reverse answering). The subject was informed that from a given starting or ending point the film corresponded to only one possible route on the map, and that all turns were at right angles. Examples of routes are given in Figure 1. The time taken by the subject to answer the questions (i.e., naming each of the letters corresponding to a route) was recorded, but no time limitation was given.

2.3. Subjects
Six female and four male researchers or graduate students, from 20 to 45 years old, participated in a 30-minute experimental session. The subjects were accepted without considerations of age, gender, or background skills.

3. RESULTS

The films were presented in two different manners. The map was aligned when the direction of the route pointed upward on the screen, and misaligned when the direction pointed downward. According to Shepard and Hurwitz (1985), movements toward or away from the subject are interpreted on a map as upward or downward movements respectively. The subject was asked to find the solution for 12 aligned and 12 misaligned items, with an even split between direct and reverse answering.

3.1. Total time
A two-factor ANOVA (aligned/misaligned presentation in direct/reverse answering conditions) was computed for the mean total time (see Figure 2a). Total time was found to be significantly greater in misaligned conditions [F (1,9) = 6.71, p<0.05], and was greater in reverse answering conditions [F (1,9) = 9.59, p<0.025] ; no interaction effect was observed between these two factors [F (1,9) = 2.07, NS]. Moreover, subsequent ANOVAs of the misalignment effect showed a significant effect of the direct answering conditions on total time [F (1.9) = 19.25, p<0.05], but no significant difference was observed in the reverse answering condition.

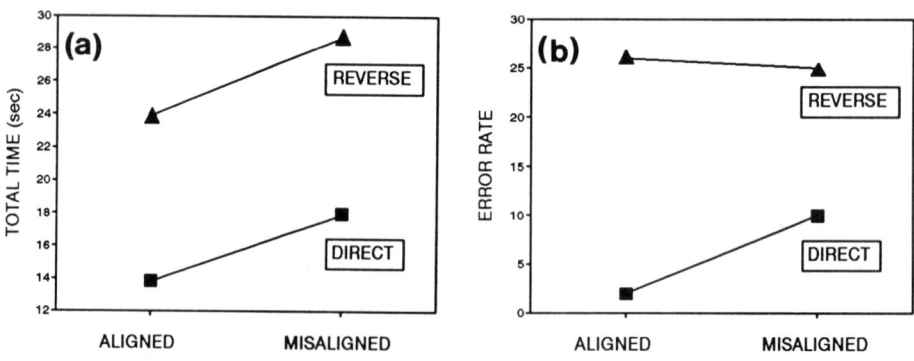

Figure 2. Total time (a) and error rates (b) for Aligned/Misaligned presentation conditions and Direct/Reverse answering conditions.

3.2. Error rates
An analysis of error rates (i.e., the total number of wrong directional answers given for the different decision points) was carried out for all test conditions (i.e., aligned/misaligned and direct/reverse - see Figure 2b). The rate was not significantly higher in misaligned

conditions, but was higher in reverse answering conditions [Chi2 (1) = 50.82, p<0.001]. Subsequent analysis of the misalignment revealed a significant impact of direct answering conditions on the overall error rate [Chi2 (1) = 5.91, p<0.02], but no significant difference was observed in reverse answering conditions. A significant correlation coefficient between the total time and the error rate [Rho (22) = .831, p<0.001] showed that the faster the subjects responded, the more accurate they were.

3.3. Strategies

Analysis of subject performance and post-experimental reports indicated two possible ways of solving the task: some "visual" subjects seemed to transform the direct-perception motion data into an image of the route, while other more "computational" subjects seemed to transform the data into verbal instructions (e.g. turn left, then right, and so on). However, in reverse answering conditions all the subjects solved the task by manipulating verbal information, indicating that in these conditions the subject required a higher level of mental abstraction in verbal processing.

4. CONCLUSIONS

The first question raised in this experiment dealt with the capacity of subjects to transform perception motion data into route knowledge, and then to establish the correspondence between egocentrically stored displacement information and allocentric information acquired from a map. The results showed that the subjects were able to carry out these kinds of spatial problems successfully, although their performance and post-experimental reports indicated certain difficulties in this process.

The second question was whether the non-correspondence (i.e., misalignment) between these two modes was decisive here. When the map was misaligned the subject might make use of a mental rotation, and misalignment mistakes would thus be expected. Indeed, the results showed that the subjects made more mistakes when the orientation of these two modes of spatial information differed. A significant misalignment effect was observed in the total time as well as in the error rates, but only for the direct answering tasks.

The third question concerned the influence of direct or reverse answering conditions on the decision process. The fact that the misalignment effect was observed only in the direct answering conditions indicates that the processes involved in the reverse conditions did not depend upon the orientation of the map.

These results could be taken into account by engineers in designing remote-control devices, and also in helping machine operators to establish a link between the egocentric and allocentric perception of information.

5. ACKNOWLEDGEMENTS

This research was conducted at the URA CNRS Cognition et Mouvement laboratory, and E.A. Lapin held a post-doctoral grant from Programme Diderot (Maison des Sciences de l'Homme, France).

6. REFERENCES

Chavand, F., Colle, E., Gaillard, J.P., Mallem, A. and Stomboni, J.P. (1988). Visual assistance to the teleoperator in teleoperation and supervision situations. Proceedings of the International Symposium on Teleoperation and Control, Bristol, 237-248.

Gibson, J.J. (1979). The ecological approach to visual perception. Boston: Houghton Mifflin.

Helft, H. and Wohlwill, J.F. (1987). Environmental cognition in children. In D. Stokols and I. Altman (eds.), Handbook of Environmental Psychology. New-York: Wiley, 175-203.

Holzhausen, K.P. (1991). Vision and guidance of a telerobotic vehicle. In A.G. Gale et al. (eds.), Vision in Vehicles III. Amsterdam: Elsevier, 429-425.

Levine, M., Marchon, I., and Hanley, G. (1984). The placement and misplacement of You-Are-Here maps. Environment and Behavior, 16, 139-157.

Mestre, D., Savoyant, A., Péruch, P. and Pailhous, J. (1990). In search for realistic visualizations for human computer interaction in spatially oriented process control. Proceedings of the Fifth European Conference on Cognitive Ergonomics (ECCE5), Urbino.

ORIA-89 (1989). Proceedings of the Conference "Remote control in hostile environment: cross technological experiences. Marseille: IIRIAM.

Passini, R., Proulx, G. and Rainville, C. (1990). The spatio-cognitive abilities of the visually impaired population. Environment and Behavior, 22, 91-118.

Péruch, P. and Savoyant, A. (1991). Conflicting spatial frames of reference in a locating task. In R.H. Logie and M. Denis (eds.), Imagery in Human Cognition. Amsterdam: Elsevier.

Shemyakin, F.N. (1962). General problems of orientation in space and space representations. In B.G. Ananyev (ed.), Psychological Science in the USSR, vol. 1. Washington, DC: U.S. Office of Technical Reports.

Shepard, R.N. and Hurwitz, S. (1985). Upward direction, mental rotation, and discrimination of left and right turns in maps. In S. Pinker (ed.), Visual Cognition. Cambridge: MIT Press.

Siegel, A.W. and White, S.H. (1975). The development of spatial representations of large-scale environments. In H.W. Reese (ed.), Advances in child development and behavior, vol. 10. New-York: Academic.

Thorndyke, P.W. and Hayes-Roth, B. (1980). Differences in Spatial Knowledge Acquired from Maps and Navigation. Cognitive Psychology, 14, 560-589.

VISION IN VEHICLES – IV
A.G. Gale et al. (Editors)
1993 Elsevier Science Publishers B.V.

VISUAL INTERFACES IN DRIVING REMOTE- CONTROLLED VEHICLES

Patrick PERUCH, Daniel MESTRE, Jean PAILHOUS and Alain SAVOYANT

Université d'Aix-Marseille II, Faculté de Médecine, URA CNRS Cognition et Mouvement, IBHOP, Traverse Susini, 13388 Marseille Cedex 13, France

1. INTRODUCTION

A great deal of research today is concerned with the study of the cognitive processes involved in the realization of spatial displacements. Some of the specific areas of interest are the conditions under which the necessary spatial representations for planning a displacement (for a review see Golledge, 1987) are elaborated and used, and the modalities in which a displacement is controlled visually (for example Gordon, 1966). The visual modality remains crucial for acquiring and processing spatial data. Gibson (1979), for example, indicates that the visual flow perceived by a moving subject contains all the information needed for analyzing and controlling a displacement (the position of objects in space, the direction and speed of the displacement, etc).

This argumentation mainly pertains to subjects moving in space in natural situations, i.e., subjects actively moving, as they are in locomotion, for example. In this case, the displacement can be controlled on the basis of visual and/or proprioceptive information (Lee, 1974): the visual flow subjects perceive generally corresponds to their expectations, since they are the ones creating the flow as they perform the displacement. However, natural displacement is not the only type encountered. For instance, there are many situations where a subject's access to the surrounding space is not as direct, and other situations where the subject him/herself does not actually move but controls the displacement of a mobile, as is the case in teleoperation. In such situations, interfaces are required for the control and command of the displacement.

In this article, we will analyze how the introduction of interfaces affects the conditions in which a displacement is produced and controlled. We will attempt to show that as the situation becomes less and less natural, the already important role played by visual information increases, and the ways in which visual information is presented on the interfaces change as the modalities increase in number. Our discussion will not only be supported by fundamental and/or applied research on the mental representation of space and the visual control of displacement, but also by the few available studies on teleoperated situations.

2. CONDITIONS OF DISPLACEMENT CONTROL

First, a subject can either move him/herself (locomotion or transportation) or move a vehicle. Second, he/she can either directly or indirectly perceive the space in which the displacement is being carried out. These two factors in combination define the conditions of realization for displacement, and describe the gradual transition from natural displacement to teleoperation.

2.1. Locomotion

The subject is moving in a space that he/she directly perceives (see figure 1): research on human locomotion has shown how important proprioceptive feedback and visual flow are to this kind of natural displacement.

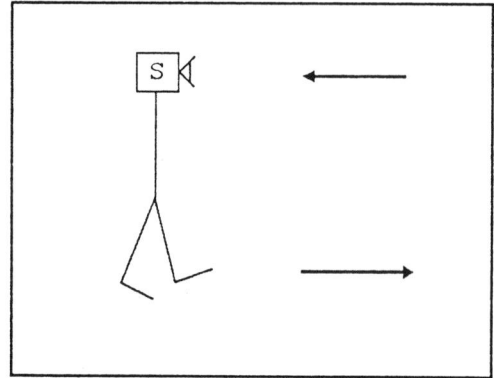

Figure 1. Locomotion: the subject ("S") moves him/herself under direct visual control.

2.2. Transportation

2.2.1. Direct perception of space

The transported subject directly controls and mechanically commands his/her displacement, as in vehicle driving (see figure 2a). In this situation, visual and labyrinthine information is available, but the subject no longer has proprioceptive feedback, and the command system of the displacement has been changed.

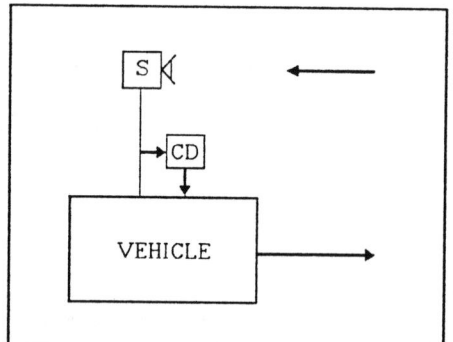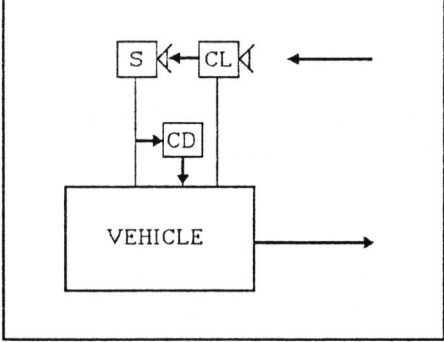

Figure 2. Transportation: the subject (a) directly or (b) indirectly perceives the displacement space (S = Subject; CD = Command; CL = Control).

2.2.2. Indirect perception of space

The transported subject controls his/her displacement by means of instruments, due for example to poor visibility (see figure 2b). When the space is perceived directly, the subject can be assumed to choose the information that is useful, but when the space is not perceived directly, the information provided by on-board instruments must be used. Thus, the loss of a direct view of the surrounding space makes the subject dependent upon the information supplied by interfaces. This already raises the question of their compatibility with the subject's functioning modes.

2.3. The subject controls the displacement of a mobile

2.3.1. Direct perception of space

Telemanipulation is the situation in which the subject controls a mobile's displacement in a directly perceived space (see figure 3a). The subject remains in the same space as the mobile thus its displacement is directly perceived, but neither labyrinthine nor proprioceptive information is available because the subject does not move. Although the size of the space is limited here, some problems may arise when the mobile comes back towards the subject, because at that time, the right side of the mobile corresponds to the subject's left side, and vice versa (contralignment). The problem of the mobile's return is a crucial one in teleoperated situations, and demonstrates the need to coordinate the spatial frames of reference of the subject and the mobile.

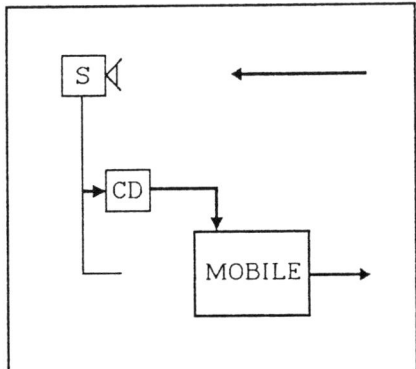 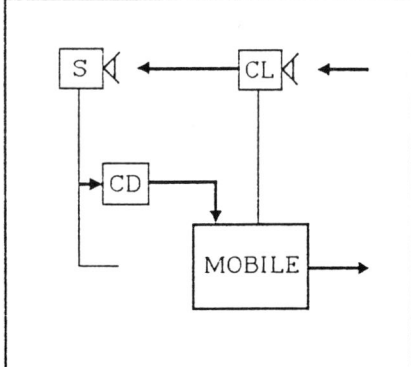

Figure 3. Remote control of a mobile under (a) direct and (b) indirect perception (S = Subject; CD = Command; CL = Control).

2.3.2. Indirect perception of space

Teleoperation is the situation in which the subject controls the displacement of a mobile in a space which is not directly perceived (see figure 3b). Using a mouse to control the displacement of a cursor on a computer screen is an example of this kind of situation, which combines the characteristics of both instrument piloting and telemanipulation, and thus poses certain important problems. Some of these problems are presented below.

3. VISUAL INTERFACES IN TELEOPERATION

3.1. Planning and control of displacement

The development of interfaces for displacement control requires knowledge of the perceptual and cognitive processes involved in these tasks, which therefore must be analyzed. From this point of view, any displacement can be divided into two phases: planning and control. Planning a displacement consists of determining one's location, the location of the goal (orientation, distance estimate, etc.), and a path linking the two. The control of a displacement consists of following the planned path (for example, establishing a sequence of intermediate goals) and the driving process itself (for example, keeping the vehicle within defined limits and on the correct trajectory). Displacement planning and navigation are generally studied in terms of spatial representation, while the control of displacement is generally investigated from a visual standpoint.

3.2. Spatial frames of reference

Research on the mental representation of space usually makes the distinction between an egocentric spatial frame of reference, in which the subject situates objects in space according to his/her own location, and an exocentric spatial frame of reference, in which the subject situates objects independently of his/her own location, such as on a map. Locating oneself in space consists of connecting successive viewpoints (egocentric spatial frame of reference) with the knowledge of the space in which the displacement is carried out (exocentric spatial frame of reference): "If I see this, I am here" (Levine, 1982). On the basis of this distinction, a method of analyzing the locating process was developed on an interactive graphic device (Péruch and Savoyant, 1991). The experimental situation is highly analogous to a teleoperation situation, because an (immobile) subject controls the displacement of a mobile object represented on a screen. The displacement is controlled via a mouse whose cursor indicates the mobile's location and orientation. Two important aspects of the remote control of displacement were investigated:

(1) The visualization system presents information about displacement in a "perspective" and/or "cartographic" mode. The perspective presentation mode is comparable to the scene subjects would see if they were actually moving in the space: in teleoperated situations, this information is given by one or more on-board video cameras. In the cartographic pre sentation mode, where the subject can see him/herself moving on a map, the computerized information is given on a graphic screen.

(2) The experimental device makes it possible to investigate the problems involved in the control of the mobile's displacement as it moves away from or towards the observer (robot coming back). In this case, difficulties due to the lack of a left-right correspondence between the mobile on the screen and the subject in front of the screen (contralignment) were analyzed in terms of conflicting spatial frames of reference. The results indicated that displacement control is more difficult (longer manipulation time, larger number of displacement errors) (a) when a map is lacking (egocentric presentation mode), and (b) when the spatial frames of reference of the robot and the subject do not correspond to each other (the right side for the represented robot on the screen

corresponds to the left side of the subject in front of the screen). This experiment shows that the relationship between information presentation mode and mobile displacement orientation is not simple. For example, the subject has to accept that a mobile moving upwards on the screen generally corresponds to its moving away from his/her own location, and vice versa. Moreover, in teleoperated situations, the subject usually functions from his/her own position in front of the screen, as if he/she were the mobile itself. Interfaces should take this aspect into account in selecting what information should be displayed.

3.3. The choice of information to display

What information should be displayed to help subjects make a displacement, and how should it be presented? For the visual control of displacement, research on computer aids for piloting large ships in harbor areas has shown that an egocentric presentation mode is superior to a cartographic one for the control of displacement (Bertsche et al, 1981; Péruch et al, 1984); in cartographic representation, location information cannot be limited to a single piece of information about the current position (a point on the map), but must also inform the subject about the orientation of the displacement. Also, performance with the perspective mode of presentation can be considerably improved if some dynamic cues necessary for the control of displacement are indicated: the stem and stem-mast of the ship, an indication of its rotational speed, its direction of heading (Mestre, 1988; Mestre et al, 1986). Lastly, other research has shown the value of combining the graphic (perspective and cartographic) and alphanumeric modes for presenting information (Schuffel, 1980).

4. CONCLUSION

With a few exceptions, the development of interfaces in teleoperation has not yet interested specialists in the study of human behavior. The tendency is to try to design real time "intelligent" interfaces, such as the ones which produce synthetic images (superimposed on the degraded video images that represent the ground or visually code the subject's effort (Mallem et al, 1989). The above research shows the need for, and value of, developing aids to provide dynamic information about the displacement, because in natural situations, subjects use this kind of information. However, the introduction of interfaces likely to help the subject sometimes has the opposite effect to the expected one, due to the fact that the subject's functioning modes are not sufficiently taken into account. The situations rapidly become very complex because the subject does not have the capacity to process the amount of information presented. This is the case, for example, in the situation described by Holzhausen (1991), where the five video cameras on-board the mobile platform can only be used separately. It is also true for the remote control of the Centaure robot in the French CEA where a co-pilot and a pilot must share tasks, the co-pilot handling displacement planning and the pilot handling control. This last example raises the issue of levels of compatibility: i.e., compatibility between the devices and the subject's (or subjects') functioning modes, between the various devices and the subject, and in some cases, between the subjects, for it is very difficult to separate control and command.

5. ACKNOWLEDGEMENTS

This work was partially supported by a PIRTTEM/Cognisciences grant from CNRS.

6. REFERENCES

Bertsche, W.R., Cooper, R.B., Feldman, D.A. & Schroeder, K.R. (1981) An evaluation of display formats for use with marine navigation piloting systems, United States Coast Guards, Washington DC.

Gibson, J.J. (1979) The ecological approach to visual perception, Houghton Mifflin, Boston.

Golledge, R. (1987) Environmental Cognition, in: Stokols, D. and Altman, I. (eds.), Handbook of Environmental Psychology, Vol 1, Wiley, New York, 131-174.

Gordon, D.A. (1966) Perceptual mechanisms in vehicular guidance. Public Roads, 34, 53-68.

Holzhausen, K.P. (1991) Vision and guidance of a telerobotic vehicle, in: Gale, A.G., Brown, I.D., Haselgrave, C.M., Smith, P. and Taylor, S.P. (eds.), Vision in Vehicles III, Elsevier, Amsterdam, 429-435.

Lee, D.N. (1974) Visual information during locomotion, in: MacLeod, R.B. and Pick, H. (eds.), Perception: Essays in honor of J.J. Gibson, Cornell University, Ithaca, NY, 250-267.

Le vine, M. (1982) You-Are-Here maps: Psychological Considerations. Environment and Behavior, 16, 139-157.

Mallem, M., Chavand, F. & Colle, E. (1989). Perception aids in remote control: Synthetic image superimposed on video image. Proceedings of the ORIA-89 Conference "Remote control in hostile environment: cross technological experiences", IIRIAM, Marseille.

Mestre, D. (1988) Visual Control of Displacement at Slow Speeds. Human Factors, 30, 663-675.

Mestre, D., Cavallo, V. & Péruch, P. (1986). Definition of an on-board visual aid for piloting large ships, in: Gale, A.G., Freeman, M.H., Haselgrave, G.M., Smith, P. and Taylor, S. (eds.), Vision in Vehicles, North- Holland, Amsterdam, 257-264.

Péruch, P., Cavallo, V., Deutsch, C. & Pailhous, J. (1984) Real-time graphic simulation of visual effects of egomotion, in: Green, T.R.G., Tauber, M.J. and Van der Veer, G.C. (eds.), Cognitive Ergonomics. Mind and Computers, Springer-Verlag, Heidelberg, 192-199.

Péruch, P. & Savoyant, A. (1991) Conflicting spatial frames of reference in a locating task, in: Logie, R.H. and Denis, M. (eds.), Imagery and Human Cognition, Elsevier, Amsterdam.

Schuffel, H. (1980) Some effects of radar and outside view on ship's controllability, in: Osborne, D.J. and Lewis, J.A. (eds.), Human factors in transport research, Academic, London.

10

IN-VEHICLE DISPLAYS:
EFFECT ON VISUAL WORKLOAD

VISION IN VEHICLES – IV
A.G. Gale et al. (Editors)

IN-VEHICLE DISPLAYS, VISUAL WORKLOAD AND USABILITY EVALUATION

S. H. FAIRCLOUGH, M. C. ASHBY & A. M. PARKES

HUSAT Research Institute, The Elms, Elms Grove, Loughborough, Leicestershire LE11 1RG UK

Abstract

Two field studies were conducted within the Driver behaviour and traffic safety research strand of the DRIVE programme. Both studies aimed to evaluate the visual attentional demand associated with the use of route navigation devices. Each study was conducted using members of the general public, driving specially adapted road vehicles in a real road environment.

The first experiment, conducted in Loughborough, was designed in order to evaluate the visual workload associated with two modes of route information presentation: paper map or text display on LCD screen. Twenty subjects were required to drive the experimental vehicle along two urban routes in low volume traffic conditions. The second experiment was conducted in Berlin in order to evaluate the visual workload associated with two real in-vehicle displays, the LISB and TravelPilot route guidance systems. Twenty three subjects took part in the study. The visual workload associated with each experimental session was measured in terms of glance frequency and glance duration spent viewing the navigation display. These results were used to formulate matrices of visual performance which assess the "visual cost" of an in-vehicle display.

1. INTRODUCTION

The proposed introduction of route information systems into the vehicle cockpit is representative of the 'first wave' of technological advancements planned for the conventional dashboard. Modern developments in information technology and microelectronics have created the potential to expand both the range and depth of driving-relevant information (from navigation information to real-time traffic congestion data) which may be presented via the 'dashboard of the future'.

The problems associated with the widespread introduction of these systems are rooted in the design of the technology rather than the 'hardware' components of the technology itself. The design of the in-vehicle display screen and the amount of information contained therein raises concern regarding traffic safety. Given that the driving task is essentially visual in nature, the driver is faced with an obvious source of 'resource competition' (Wickens, 1980) between the visual demands of the in-vehicle display and the external driving scene. Concerned professional bodies are looking to the human factors research community for answers regarding the probability and possible extent of these negative side-effects, both in human and economic terms.

Walter (1991) summarizes the goal of in-vehicle screen design. He states "from an ergonomic point of view, the instruments of a passenger car should be designed to an optimum in order to avoid an unnecessary increase of mental workload". Designers and researchers appear to agree that a minimum of visual distraction is an 'ideal' in terms of screen design. However, logic (if nothing else) dictates that some visual distraction is inevitable if the driver is to use the system at all. The problems for the human factors practitioner are (a) how to quantify this visual distraction and (b) how to test different designs prior to commercial exploitation.

These questions create an obvious role for Rockwell's (1988) conception of an in-vehicle display being accompanied by an associated 'visual cost'. The visual cost of an in-vehicle display is quantifiable in terms of the number of glances and the durations of those glances which the driver must perform in order to obtain his or her required information. Wierwille et al (1988) performed a detailed analysis of the visual demand associated with the conventional dashboard instrumentation compared to an electronic navigation display. This was an important study as it represents a first step at 'costing' conventional displays relative to to the visual demand associated with the in-vehicle display. Wierwille and his colleagues found that mean glance durations varied from 0.6 of a second to read the speedometer to 1.6 seconds in order to read a street name displayed by the electronic map display.

This paper is concerned with the quantificaton of visual cost as a measure of system usability. Two studies are described. The first compares navigation via a paper map with a simulation of a text-based electronic guidance device. The second study was conducted using two real route information devices in the city of Berlin.

2. STUDY ONE

2.1. Aim of the study

The aim of the experimental study was to compare driver behaviour whilst the subjects navigated an unfamiliar urban route using a paper map and a simulated electronic navigation device.

2.2. Apparatus

The experiment was carried out using the mobile test-bed facility installed in a Vauxhall Cavalier car. Video recording was obtained from three cameras (front, right-side and driver's face). Therefore the driver's eye movements, and information about the traffic situations encountered, were captured.

2.3. Subjects

Residents of the Loughborough area were recruited as subjects. The subject population contained ten males and ten females between 20 and 60 years of age with a range of driving experience (less than one year to over thirty years). All were paid for their participation.

2.4. Experimental conditions

The experimental conditions comprised of two methods of route navigation:

1. MAP - subjects navigated around the route via a detailed paper map taken from a local "A-Z" map. These maps were printed on A4-size sheets of white cardboard. The route was marked in green highlighter pen. The map was attached to the metal bracket via magnets sealed on the reversed side. The magnets allowed the subjects to rotate the map through 360° if required.

2. LCD/text - this navigation device consisted of a pre-programmed simulation which displayed text instructions running on a portable "Husky Hawk" computer. The screen was approximately the same size as an A5 piece of paper. The screen displayed royal blue characters on a light grey background. Text instructions were presented as a list of navigation commands in the form of instruction:destination eg   Turn Left: Colchester Road. The subjects could scroll through this list via the manipulation of an inverse video bar which highlighted the current instruction. The keyboard was covered by a cardboard overlay allowing the subjects to use two operational keys. These keys were UP or DOWN, which scrolled the highlight bar through the list of text instructions at a rate of one press per line.

The map or LCD was mounted on a specially-constructed bracket fixed to the centre of the dashboard, between the driver and front passenger seats.

2.5. Experimental design and procedure

The experiment was designed as a one-way repeated measures ANOVA. The nature of the experimental task (navigation) demanded that two experimental routes were designated. Order of route and condition were counterbalanced across all subjects.

The experimental routes were located in a suburban area just outside Leicester city centre. Traffic density was low during the experimental trials. All the subjects were unfamiliar with the area. The subjects were first given an opportunity to familiarise themselves with the vehicle instrumentation and controls whilst the car was stationary. The subjects were instructed to drive normally throughout the experiment and if at any point they felt uncomfortable or distressed by the experiment they were to stop the car. Subjects had to undergo a familiarisation period which involved a short drive using both navigation aids. The subjects drove each experimental route with a resting period between routes if required.

2.6. Experimental results

Glance duration and frequency were used to calculate the mean glance duration to both the LCD/text and the map display. The visual data was scored by hand from the video record to the nearest second. Table 1 shows the percentage figures for visual allocation over eight regions of the driving scene for both experimental conditions. Statistical testing was carried out via Wilcoxon test.

2.7. Discussion

The results reveal an increase in visual attention to the map display at the expense of visual allocation to other areas of the driving scene. The increase in visual allocation to the map was expected, the paper map being more visually complex both in terms of the amount of information it contained and the legibility of that information compared with the text-based LCD display.

	MAP	LCD/text
Navigation Information	22.1**	12.1
Roadway ahead	67.2	76.1**
Rear view mirror	1.7	2.3**
Dashboard	0.2	0.3
Left-wing mirror	0.1	0.2
Right-wing mirror	0.7	1.3**
Left window	2.9	2.9
Right window	5.2	4.9

Table 1. Percentage allocation of drivers visual attention over nine regions of the driving scene whilst the vehicle was in motion. The double asterisk (**) denotes a significantly higher score ($p<0.01$).

The increased visual demands in the paper map condition had a considerable impact on other regions of the driving scene, in particular the rear view mirror, the right-wing mirror and the roadway ahead. This data provides some circumstantial evidence for Rumar's (1988) argument that the visual overload associated with complex in-vehicle displays will impinge directly on visual resources usually allocated to the roadway and the vehicle's interactions with other road users.

In this case, visual cost was represented in terms of a percentage of the time spent mobile on the road. This measure proved sensitive enough to (a) differentiate between the paper map and the LCD/text display and (b) detect associated changes with regard to other areas of the visual scene. However measures of glance duration may be misleading. For example, Rockwell (1988) cites signing research which revealed a reduction in glance duration to road signs from 2 seconds in light traffic to 0.9 seconds in heavy traffic. Therefore reductions in glance durations to the mirrors and roadway ahead in Table 1 could be indicative of a strategic reduction of glance duration in order to cope with the demands of the paper map. The next step was to measure drivers' visual attention to real in-vehicle displays with regard to the evaluation of system usability.

3. STUDY TWO

3.1. Aim of the study

The aim of the study was to investigate changes in drivers' visual behaviour whilst navigating through the city of Berlin using both the LISB/ALI SCOUT and the TravelPilot route information systems.

3.2. Apparatus

The test vehicle was a BMW 518i fitted with both LISB and TravelPilot systems. Two

VHS video recording systems were installed in order to capture views of both the visual behaviour of the driver and the road ahead.

3.3. Subjects
The subject sample comprised of thirteen males and eleven females. All were residents of Berlin. The majority of the subjects had over five years of driving experience and two had used the LISB system before (though no more than once). All subjects were paid for their participation.

3.4. Experimental conditions
The two systems comprised the experimental conditions. A brief description of each follows;

1. The LISB system comprises an LCD display (45x55 mm) which shows direction arrows, lane recommendations, vector distance to the destination and a count-down to a guided manoeuvre. The display is supplemented by an alerting gong and a digitized male voice command from the rear, right loudspeaker.

2. The TravelPilot system uses a CRT green on black display (11 cm square) which shows graphical map information. The TravelPilot (henceforth referred to as TP) is a moving map display which shows the position of the driver on the road network. Whilst the vehicle is in motion, the driver is also presented with compass north, vector distance and direction to destination. In addition, the driver may request street names, alter the display scale and request an overview display which includes the destination position.

3.5. Experimental design and procedure
The experiment was a repeated measures design. The subjects drove to two destination points using each route information system. The two destination points were counterbalanced across the subjects. Both destination points were located separately in the heart of the city centre. Starting points and destination points were chosen so that the subjects' journeys should be mutually exclusive.

The subjects were familiarised with the controls of the vehicle and proceeded to drive a familiarisation route until they pronounced themselves satisfied with their ability to control the vehicle. The subjects were then given an introduction to the first route information system whilst the vehicle was stationary. The subjects then drove the vehicle on a second familiarisation route to the starting point of the first journey. The subject then completed the first experimental condition. An experimenter was present throughout the experimental trial sitting in the back seat. This procedure was repeated for the second experimental condition.

3.6. Experimental results
The visual data was scored by hand from the video record to the nearest half-second. Of the 24 subjects recruited, one refused to take part as she discovered that the spectacles she needed to view the route information systems adversely affected her distance vision.

	LISB	TRAVELPILOT
Navigation Information	9.2	12.9**
Roadway ahead	80.5**	76.1
Rear view mirror	2.4	1.9
Dashboard	0.9	0.8
Left-wing mirror	2.2	1.8
Right-wing mirror	0.5	0.4
Left window	1.5	2.5**
Right window	1.4	1.8

Table 2. Percentage glance duration for nine areas of the driving scene for both the LISB and the TravelPilot systems (n=21). The double asterisk (**) denotes a significantly higher score (p<0.01).

	LISB	TRAVELPILOT
Navigation Information	23.8	27.7**
Roadway ahead	48.9	49.1
Rear view mirror	8.7**	7.5
Dashboard	2.2*	1.8
Left-wing mirror	6.8**	4.7
Right-wing mirror	1.7	1.6
Left window	3.6	2.9
Right window	3.1	3.6

Table 3. Percentage glance frequency for nine areas of the driving scene for both the LISB and the TravelPilot systems (n=21). A single asterisk (*) denotes a significantly higher score at the 5% level (p<0.05) whereas a double asterisk (**) denotes significance at the 1% level (p<0.01).

Of the remaining 23, two subjects' video records were impossible to score due to problems with picture quality.

The one aspect of the study which could not be adequately controlled was the selection of the experimental route itself. When using the TP system, the decision was left to the individual driver whereas in the LISB condition, explicit instructions were given in accordance with real-time traffic information. In the case of one of the experimental destination points, the LISB system directed drivers to a stretch of urban motorway whereas the TP drivers drove along conventional two-way traffic roads. This led to a distortion in drivers' visual behaviour due to the different traffic environments for the first destination point. Fortunately, the journey to the second destination point were approximately equivalent in terms of road types and traffic density for both systems. Therefore the data for only one destination point is presented overleaf.

Visual cost was measured both in terms of glance frequency and glance duration (see Tables 2 & 3). Statistical testing was carried out using non-parametric t-tests.

3.7. Discussion

It was decided to split the visual data from the Berlin field study into separate indices of duration and frequency in order to assess the differences which might exist between the two, in terms of sensitivity to either system. The relative significance of visual regions to the left and right of the vehicle across the two studies are reversed as the second study was carried out in a left-hand drive car. The increased glance duration to the left window for the TP condition is indicative of the subjects ⊦ attempts to locate relevant street names (displayed on the screen) as pertinent navigational cues.

The glance frequency data deviates from the duration data in the sense that there are no differences between the number of glances to the roadway ahead. This is significant as it reflects the subjects' intentions to maintain an equivalent number of "visual checks" to the roadway ahead. However, Table 2 also indicates that, as glance frequency to the navigation display increases, the number of glances to the dashboard, rear-view mirror and the left-wing mirror all show a significant decrease. Again, this trend appears to support Rumar's (1988) argument regarding the side-effects of visual workload.

Rockwell (1988) distinguished between glance frequency and duration on the basis that "(the) average glance duration was sensitive to design. More glances can not make up for poor legibility." In most respects, the data presented in Tables 2 and 3 bear out his statement. However with respect to the glance frequencies to the navigation display (Table 3) one might add the caveat that whilst logically more glances may not make up for poor legibility, this would not necessarily stop the driver from looking to the illegible display more often.

It appears that glance duration and glance frequency are representative of two different (if not unrelated) aspects of driver visual behaviour. Glance duration appears to be more sensitive to the difficulty of information uptake from an in-vehicle display. This difficulty may be grounded in the legibility of the interface, its layout or the amount of information contained therein (as often these three features are related). Glance frequency represents the amount of visual activity in terms of "visual checking" behaviour. This visual checking may be carried out on the internal vehicle environment (i.e. monitoring speed via the dashboard) or the external driving environment (i.e. mirror checking).

4. CONCLUSIONS

The two studies have shown how the visual behaviour of the driver is sensitive to different types of route information presentation. The data trend appears to follow Rumar's (1988) argument that 'spare' visual resources are allocated to the display at the expense of other regions of the driving scene. This trend of visual distraction is rather unsurprising in itself. However the associated magnitude of visual distraction or the 'visual cost' of a system display might yield useful information for both designers and legislators in terms of usability and possible consequences for road safety.

The problem is not one of obtaining the data (as the two studies have shown) but one of interpretation of that data. For instance Zwahlen and his colleagues (Zwahlen et al, 1988) argue that glances in excess of 2 seconds to an in-vehicle display cause 'dangerous' lateral lane position deviations. In 1986, Hughes and Cole (1986) performed a study which categorised those objects in the visual scene which attracted drivers attention. They concluded that 30-50% of driver visual attention may be allocated to things unrelated to the driving task itself. Antin and his colleagues (Antin et al, 1990) found that subjects spent approximately 33% of the total time driving viewing an electronic, moving map display. Antin et al use the conclusions of Hughes and Cole in order to claim that 33% visual distraction introduced by a display is 'acceptable'. But how do we judge what is 'acceptable' and what is dangerous in terms of visual distraction? The problem of interpretation is not only one of setting up performance limits but also the way in which one quantifies visual workload. Obviously a minimum of visual distraction is the goal of good interface design and some testing standard or standard 'coinage' of visual workload is needed in order to generalise from existing research. In other words, how can we put a price on visual cost?

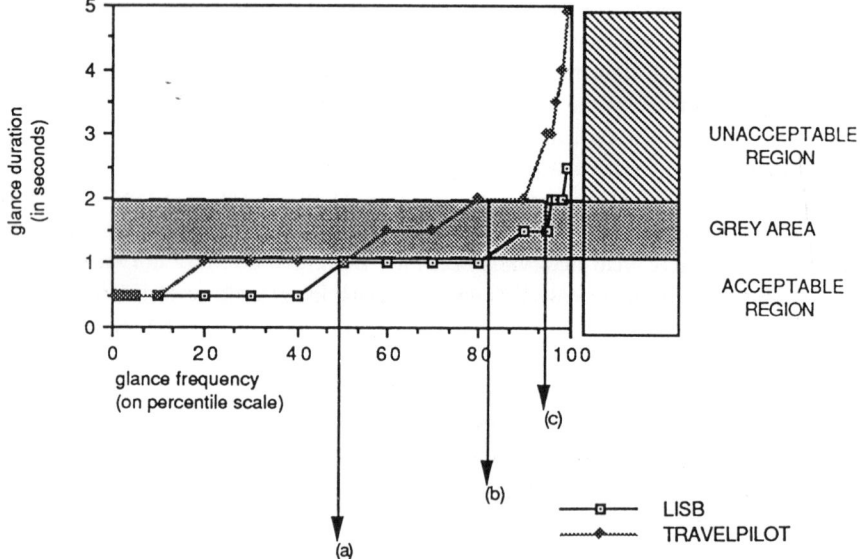

Figure 1. A culmative frequency distribution curve representing glance durations by glance frequency for both the LISB and the TravelPilot route navigation systems (n=21). Regions of acceptability/unacceptability are based on Zwahlen et al's (1988) paper.

(a) indicates the 50th percentile where glance durations to both systems are just outside of the 'grey area.'

(b) indicates approximately the 82th percentile where glances to the Travelpilot enter the unacceptable region.

(c) indicates approximately the 93rd percentile where glances to the LISB system enter the unacceptable region.

Great care must be taken when using these types of visual measures within the context of a field comparison. The data from study 2 indicated that both glance frequency and duration were influenced by demographic characteristics of the subject population (i.e. age, sex, driving experience) and the city locale/traffic environment. Given the sensitivity of the visual measures to these factors, data should only be compared which has originated from the same subject pool who have been tested within the same traffic locale under approximately equivalent conditions of traffic density. The sensitivity and validity of this type of comparison has its roots in the relative basis of the comparison.

The following method of scoring visual workload data is presented as a tentative first step towards some 'standard' of performance testing. Figure 1 represents the data originating from study 2. Glance duration and frequency for both systems are presented as a cumulative frequency curve on a percentile scale. Zwahlen et al's (1988) design guide forms the basis of the three areas of acceptability. This method of scoring the visual cost of an in-vehicle system places the emphasis on the probability of 'dangerously' long glance durations as opposed to gross measures of visual distraction per se. As may be seen from figure 1, approximately 18% of glances to the TravelPilot system were 2 seconds or more compared with 7% for the LISB system. The sequence of scanning which formed the y-axis of Zwahlen et al's original design guide has been discarded within the current formulation. The adoption of a percentile scale has been used to provide quantitative data which may be generalized across different studies. More research is needed as to what comprises a dangerous glance duration. Zwahlen et al (1988) based these figures on the probability of dangerous, lateral deviations of the vehicle. Other research conducted in the U.S. (Wierwille et al, 1988; Antin et al, 1990) report no differences in lane exceedences, brake actuations and accelerator measures when the subjects used a moving map display compared with either a paper map or a memorized route. However Antin et al (1990) report that steering wheel reversal rate decreased in the moving map condition. However these studies were conducted in the field (as were the two reported here), and it is imagined that research into the the consequences of 'dangerous' visual distraction on the driving parameters will be carried out within a simulator environment.

Finally we have concerned ourselves throughout this paper with the effects of introducing a route information display on the inexperienced system user. We acknowledge that future longitudinal research is required in order to assess how visual workload and its associated 'cost' might change with experience and practice.

5. ACKNOWLEDGEMENTS

The authors wish to acknowledge the contributions of Mike Maternaghan, Tracy Ross and Clare Davies to the U.K. field trial and the assistance of Kai Lorenz and the staff at BMW AG (EW11 and EW13), in particular Gabi Schrievers, with the German field trial. This research was carried out under the E.C. DRIVE programme (Project V1017 BERTIE).

6. REFERENCES

Antin, J. F., Dingus, T.F., Hulse, M.C. and Wierwille, W. W. (1990). An evaluation of the effectiveness and efficiency of an automobile moving map navigational display. International Journal of Man-Machine Studies , 33, 581-594.

Hughes, P.K. & Cole, B.L.(1986). What attracts attention when driving ? Ergonomics, 29 (3), 377-391.

Rockwell, T. H. (1988). Spare visual capacity in driving. In Gale A.G. et al (Ed.) Vision in Vehicles II , Amsterdam: Elsevier, 317-24.

Rumar, K. (1988). In-vehicle information systems. International Journal of Vehicles Design, 9 (4/5), 548-556.

Walter, W. (1991) Ergonomic information evaluation of analogue and digital coding of instruments in vehicles. In Gale A.G et al (ed.) Vision in Vehicles III , Amsterdam: Elsevier, 205-211.

Wickens, C. D. (1980). The structure of attentional resources. In Nickerson R. & Pews R. (Ed.) Attention and Performance , Englewood Cliffs, NJ: Prentice Hall, 239-275.

Wierwille, W. W., Antin, J. F., Dingus, T. A. & Hulse, M. C. (1988). Visual attention demand of an in-car navigation display system. In Gale A.G. et al (Ed.) Vision in Vehicle II ,Amsterdam: Elsevier, 307-316.

Zwahlen, H.T., Adams jnr. C. C. and DeBald, D.P. (1988). Safety aspects of CRT touch panel controls in automobiles. In Gale A.G. et al (Ed.) Vision in Vehicles II, Amsterdam: Elsevier, 335-344.

VISION IN VEHICLES – IV
A.G. Gale et al. (Editors)
255

EXPLORING MENTAL WORKLOAD VIA TLX: THE CASE OF OPERATING A CAR STEREO WHILST DRIVING

Patrick W. JORDAN[1] and Graham I. JOHNSON[2]

Department of Psychology, University of Glasgow, Adam Smith Building, Glasgow G12 8RT, Scotland[1]

Philips Corporate Industrial Design, Applied Ergonomics Group, Nederlandse Philips Bedrijven B.V., Building SX, P.O. Box 218, 5600 MD Eindhoven, The Netherlands[2]

Abstract

Various effects of using a high-end car stereo set on driving were investigated in the field. The experiment looked at driving with and without car stereo use.

An instrumented car was used to carry out the investigations. Comparisons were made of primary driving variables (such as speed), measures of performance with the stereo on pre-defined tasks, and the NASA Task Load Index (TLX). The TLX is an established subjective measure of mental workload (MWL). A further aim of the study was to investigate the effectiveness of the TLX as an MWL evaluation tool in a dual task situation involving driving. Focus of regard (direction of gaze) data were also collected.

The main conclusions were that driving performance is significantly affected by stereo operation, and that the TLX was a useful evaluation tool in this context, providing much insight into subjective MWL changes in an everyday situation, that of driving a car and operating a stereo system.

1. INTRODUCTION

The growth of in-car entertainment and information systems, both as a market and as an application of advanced technology, has meant that we are witnessing some end-user difficulties in the comprehension and operation of such systems. These systems include navigation and information systems, but do not exclude mass market products based upon the, once straightforward, car radio.

This paper reports an empirical field study of the usability of a "high-end" (expensive, multi-featured) in-car stereo (described in Jordan and Johnson 1991). The main objective of the study was to gain insight into the relationship between driving and stereo use. This paper reports on the aspects dealing with the concept of mental workload. The Task Load Index (TLX) was used as the measure of subjective mental workload (MWL), and its possible use with reference to usability appraisal in dual task situations was investigated.The International Standards Organisation (ISO), currently define usability as being a measure of "...the effectiveness, efficiency, and satisfaction with which specified users can achieve specified goals in a particular environment" (Brooke, Bevan, Brigham, Harker, and Youmans, 1990). This definition of usability was adopted for this study. Driving whilst using a car stereo is a dual task situation, where driving is the primary task and operating the in car stereo is the secondary task. The "specified goals" of the user, then, were to complete both the primary and secondary tasks as successfully as possible. Naturally, the priority during this study was explicitly directed towards safe driving.

The relationship between driving and stereo operation was addressed by measuring the mental workload (MWL) associated with using the stereo.

1.1 Mental workload (MWL)

Mental workload is a concept used by behavioural scientists in order to describe, predict, explain, and reflect performance of a human-machine system (Jordan, 1990). However the concept of MWL is somewhat unclear with various current definitions in use. Perhaps the clearest definitions are offered by Jahns (1973), who described MWL as being "...the extent to which an operator is occupied by a task, and Hart (1986) who described it as "... the integrated effects on the human operator of task-related, situation-related, and operator related factors that occur during performance of a task".

Although there may be little agreement on the definition of MWL, it is still reasonable to assume that it should be kept low in any potentially demanding situation (Meister, 1986).

There are a variety of methods for measuring MWL. The four methods used in this study were as follows: subjective measures (eg. Bortolussi, Kantowitz, and Hart, 1986),primary task performance measures (eg. Zwahlen, Adams, and Debald 1988), secondary task performance measures (eg. Lisper, Laurell, and Van Loon, 1985), and eye movements (eg. Unema, Rothing, and Luczak, 1988).

1.2 The TLX technique

The NASA TLX (Hart and Staveland 1988) is a multi-dimensional rating procedure, which provides an overall workload score based on a weighted average of ratings on six sub-scales:

Mental demand
Physical demand
Temporal demand
PerformanceEffort
Frustration level

Subjects mark rating scales between 0 and 100 to indicate the magnitude of the load on each factor. They then do a series of paired comparisons in order to determine the relative importance of each of the six factors (the weighting). The magnitudes and weightings are then combined to derive an overall TLX score, which is taken as a sound subjective measure of MWL.

2. METHOD

2.1 Apparatus and environment

The car stereo used in this experiment was installed in a Volvo 740 estate car that had been especially adapted for the experiment. Amongst the equipment that had been installed there were three cameras to monitor hand movements and eye movements, the pictures from which were mixed and then recorded on super VHS video tape. The driving trials of the experiment were carried out on an industrial estate. The experimental route contained a number of bends (some quite sharp), and straights of varying lengths. Although traffic was light, potential hazards included concealed entrances, parked cars, pedestrians, and cyclists.

2.2 Experimental design

Twenty subjects were used, divided into two groups of ten. One group performed tasks with the stereo whilst driving, and the other group performed the same tasks but in a stationary condition. Half the subjects in each group made inputs to the stereo using an infra-red hand-held remote control that was provided with the stereo (Jordan and Johnson 1991), whilst the other half used the conventional controls on the stereo itself. Those performing the experiment in the driving condition also performed control drives, during which no tasks were set.

Comparisons between MWL for driving and driving whilst using the stereo could then be made within subjects, and performance on the stereo whilst stationary and whilst driving could be compared between subjects. The measures of MWL taken were as follows:

Subjective measures: NASA Task Load Index (TLX) MWL questionnaire ratings (Hart and Staveland 1988). This was considered the main MWL measure.

Primary task measures: drive times (ie. mean speed).

Secondary task measures: percentage of stereo sub-tasks successfully completed.

Eye movement measures: percentage of drive time for which glance away from road.

2.3 Subjects

Subjects were chosen within criteria designed to minimise intra-subject variability. All subjects were aged between 20 and 45, male, holders of current driving licences, experienced with manual cars, had used a car stereo before, and had used a remote control before (although not in this context). None of the subjects had driven the experimental vehicle before, used the test stereo before, or been part of a similar evaluation experiment.

2.4 Stereo tasks

The task that the subjects were set with the stereo consisted of seven different sub-tasks chosen to cover use of the radio, cassette, and CD player. A maximum time to complete each of the sub-tasks was set according to the sub-task's difficulty. Each sub-task was classified as being within one of three bands of difficulty: easy, moderate, or difficult. A GOMS task analysis (Card, Moran, and Newell 1983) was used to rate sub-tasks. The greater the goal-stack, the more difficult the task was rated to be. Examples of sub-tasks are as follows: setting the radio's volume to the subject's preferred level (easy), returning to the start of a track playing on a cassette (moderate), and finding a specific track on a CD (difficult).

2.5 Procedure

The procedure was as follows.   After reading an introduction to the experiment and completing a personal details questionnaire, subjects were then allowed to familiarise themselves with the Volvo controls and drive around a car park at the beginning of the experimental route until they felt confident with the vehicle.Next, subjects drove twice around the experimental route itself. The first time around was for route familiarisation, and the second a timed control drive. During the control drive, hand and eye movements were recorded on video. Subjects were shown a map of the test route before this drive and were reminded of the route as they drove. On completion of the control drive the TLX questionnaire was administered, and subjective MWL ratings recorded.

After a period of familiarisation with whichever type of stereo controls the subject was to use, the drive was then repeated. This time subjects were asked to carry out some in-car sub-tasks with the stereo whilst driving - the "task drive". Before the task drive started, subjects were told which sub-tasks they were to be set, that they would have a set time to complete each sub-task, and that if they were having difficulty with a sub-task they should keep trying until the time limit had been reached. However, it was also strongly emphasised that the most important task was the driving task, and that this should always be given priority.As the drive progressed, subjects were told when they could start each sub-task. Each of these was set as soon as was convenient and safe after the last one had been completed. Sub-tasks were not set at what were considered to be difficult parts of the route (eg. bends) or when a demanding driving situation arose (eg. if a vehicle was turning in the road). As with the control drive, subjects were reminded of the route as the trial progressed. The experimenter gave no help or feedback with respect to the stereo tasks.

TLX ratings for performing three different sub-tasks whilst driving were then recorded separately - the mean of these ratings was taken as the TLX rating for driving whilst using the stereo. Subjects performing the experiment in the stationary condition did the same stereo task, and also completed the TLX questionnaire.

3. RESULTS

3.1 Subjective MWL measures

All subjects rated MWL for driving whilst using the stereo as being greater than that for driving alone. The mean TLX scores for the task and control drives were 57 (s.d. = 19) and 32 (s.d. = 14) respectively (where potential scores ranged from 0 to 100, and 100 represents the highest possible subjective MWL) . Using a Wilcoxon Signed Rank test, this difference proved statistically significant ($p < 0.05$). When the ratings for each subjective MWL component were looked at separately, a significant increase was found for each in the task drive, as compared to the control drive ($p < 0.05$), with the exception of physical demand. Figure 1 illustrates the difference in MWL component ratings between the control and task drives.

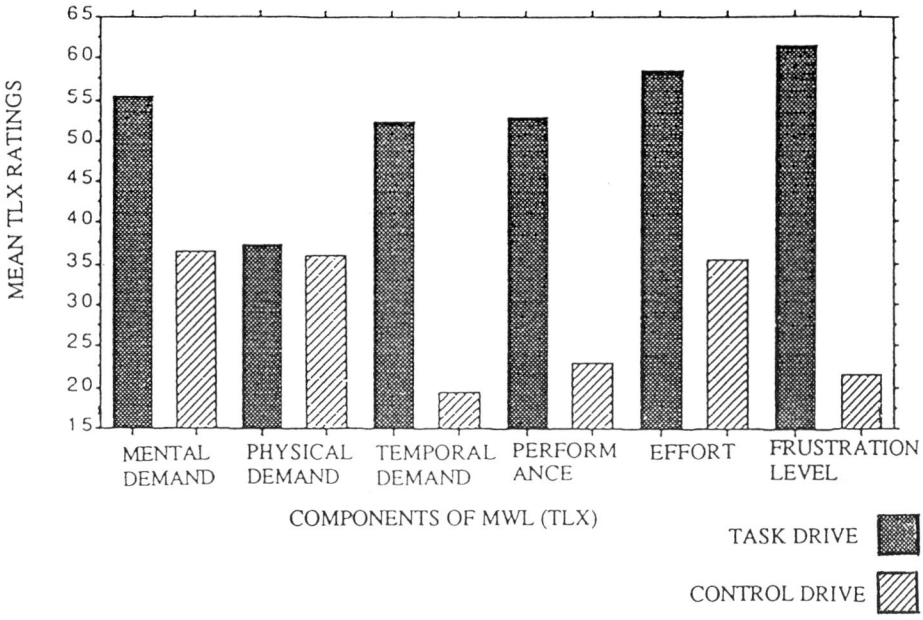

Figure 1: Subjective MWL component ratings (TLX) for task and control drives.

3.2 Primary task measures

All subjects took longer to complete the task drive than the control drive (mean difference = 53.9 seconds). The differences between task and control drive times were significant - a Wilcoxon signed rank test showed significance at $p < 0.05$.

3.3 Secondary task measures

Performance on the stereo tasks was not significantly different in the driving and stationary conditions. Table 1 lists the percentage of sub-tasks in the categories easy, moderate, and difficult that were successfully completed in the driving condition (mean percentage of sub-tasks completed in this condition was 66%).

TASK DIFFICULTY RATING	PERCENTAGE SUCCESSFUL COMPLETIONS
Easy	93%
Moderate	50%
Difficult	46%

Table 1: Percentage of sub-tasks completed in the driving condition, by task type.

3.4 Eye movement measures

Despite attempts to ascertain a global series of measures for direction of gaze, this did not prove especially successful. While two of the three in-car cameras focussed upon the the car stereo and the road view, the other attended to the gaze direction. The latter was positioned behind the driver, above his head, in order to pick up the reflection of the drivers' eyes in the rear view mirror.

Unfortunately, the video records of the control and task drives did not produce data of sufficiently good quality to enable the break-down of gaze direction aimed for. The fact that the mixing of the three views recorded occurred during the experiment meant that the view of the drivers' eyes occupied only a small part of the record. Furthermore, the direction of the camera (ie. face on to the mirror), and the under-estimation of head movement added to the difficulties in accurate recording.

We are able to recommend that a camera intending to record eye gaze (point of regard) be located at right angles to the drivers' normal viewing and that great tolerances are allowed for head movements whilst driving.

4. DISCUSSION

Many variables were measured, with the intention of examining various factors at play in situations where people drive and use a car stereo, the main ones being:

subjective MWL - TLX

(primary) driving performance - mean speed

(secondary) task influence - task completion measures

eye gaze - registration of gaze direction

In discussing the results of this investigation it is worthwhile considering the above four variables as they were seen to relate to the driving and stereo use task.

Firstly, subjective MWL, which we chose to measure using the NASA TLX, indicated that the differences between driving whilst operating and not operating a car stereo were, in this case, of statistical significance. Subjects were convinced that MWL increased whilst driving and operating the stereo. The TLX had thus proved itself, in the sense that it could discriminate between the conditions. This supports the findings of Fairclough, Ashby, Ross, and Parkes (1990), who employed the TLX in their evaluation of hands free telephone use.

Furthermore, the TLX could offer an insight into the various components of MWL (at least as decomposed by the TLX scales). This revealed that subjects considered themselves to have no (significantly) extra physical demands when operating the stereo in addition to driving, yet the other components - mental demand, temporal demand, effort, performance, and frustration level, were perceived as being greater in this situation.

In terms of the TLX as a tool in the evaluation of workload within this context, there are two apparent disadvantages and two practical advantages. The two disadvantages are that the TLX requires subjects to interpret the verbal descriptions and definitions of workload, as do other relatively sophisticated subjective MWL measures, and secondly that the report of the MWL for a given task or situation was (at least in this case) retrospective. The two advantages, which in our view outweigh its disadvantages, are that it need not be administered during the "task", and that the TLX offers ratings on separate useful components of MWL. As a result of our investigation with the TLX, and despite on-going debates about the nature and definition of MWL, we found the TLX extremely useful as a tool for the description of subjective experience in this context.

As far as the other recorded variables are concerned, we witnessed a statistically significant decrease in mean speed in the task drive, although the secondary task measures produced less than intuitively expected. These demonstrated that secondary task completion was not significantly different to that found in a stationary condition. It seems likely that, despite explicit instructions, the secondary task was not so secondary (the question of priority) and the "slowing down" by subjects was an attempt at holding perceived accident risk constant.

The eye gaze (point of regard) data was most disappointing. Even though pilot work had indicated that recording on video of the drivers' eyes, via reflection in the rear-view mirror, was likely to deliver interesting global information on gaze direction and frequency of glance, it proved not to be the case in the experiment itself. Camera position, size of mirror, angle of view taken by the camera, and the simultaneous mixing of a 3-view picture seemed to have contributed to the resulting data loss. The freedom of head movements also appeared to play a role in this.

One further lesson learned from this study was the difficulty and tediousness of dealing with video-based / derived data. We sought post-hoc, for example, for what we had considered to be possible (natural) embedded secondary tasks within driving. Two possibilities for analysis were gear change behaviour (frequency differences), and mirror use (frequency and duration differences). However, the former, whilst providing some indications of differences (see Jordan, 1990) did not offer significant ones, and the latter was fraught with the same problems as the point of regard data.

5. CONCLUSIONS

We can conclude from this study that the TLX as a measure of subjective MWL performed well in this context, as an evaluation tool. The results of the study indicated that subjective MWL was significantly higher for driving whilst using an advanced car stereo than for driving alone, and that this was associated with corresponding changes in driving performance.

6. ACKNOWLEDGEMENTS

At the time that this study was carried out, Patrick Jordan was a postgraduate student at the Centre for Ergonomics and Operational Research at the University of Birmingham, working under the supervision of Dr E.D. Megaw. Note that opinions expressed in this paper are those of the authors.

7. REFERENCES

Bortolussi M.R., Kantowitz B.H., and Hart S.G., (1986), Measuring pilot workload in a motion base trainer. Applied Ergonomics 17, 4, pp 278-283.
Brooke J., Bevan N., Brigham F., Harker S., and Youmans D., (1990), Usability statements

and standardisation - work in progress in ISO. In Human-Computer Interaction - INTERACT '90, D. Diaper et al. (eds.), (Amsterdam: North Holland).

Card S.K., Moran T.P., and Newell A., (1983), The Psychology of Human-Computer Interaction, Hillsdale, New Jersey: LEA Publishers.

Fairclough S.H., Ashby, M.C., Ross, T., and Parkes, A.M., (1990), Effects of driving behaviour on handsfree telephone use. Report no. 48, DRIVE project V1017.

Hart S.G, (1986), The relationship between workload and training: an introduction. In Proceedings of the Human Factors Society, 30th Annual Meeting, pp 1116-1120.

Hart S.G., and Staveland, L.E., (1988), Development of the NASA-TLX (Task Load Index): results of empirical and theoretical research. In P.A. Hancock and N. Meshkati (ed), Human Mental Workload, Amsterdam: North Holland, pp 139-183.

Jahns D.W., (1973), A concept of operator workload in manual vehicle operations. Forschungbericht 14, Meckenheim, FRG: FAT.

Jordan P.W., (1990), Driving and stereo use: a human factors evaluation MSc (Eng) report, University of Birmingham: Centre for Ergonomics and Operational Research.

Jordan P.W., and Johnson, G.I., (1991), The usability of remote control for in-car stereo operation. In E.J. Lovesey (ed), Contemporary Ergonomics 1991, London: Taylor and Francis, pp 400-407.

Lisper H.O., Laurell H., and Van Loon, J., (1985), Relation between time to falling asleep at the wheel on a closed track and changes in subsiduary reaction time to prolonged time on a motorway, Ergonomics, 29, 3, pp 445-453.

Meister D., (1986), Human Factors Evaluation, Amsterdam: (North Holland).

Unema P., Rothing, M., and Luczak, H., (1988), In A.J. Adams et al (ed) Ergonomics International 88, Proceedings of the 10th Congress of the International Ergonomics Association, London: Taylor and Francis, pp 463-465.

Zwahlen H.T., Adams, C.C., and Debald, D.P., (1988), Safety aspects of CRT touch panel controls in automobiles. In Gale et al. (ed), Vision in Vehicles II, Amsterdam: (North Holland).

VISION IN VEHICLES – IV
A.G. Gale et al. (Editors)
263

FEEDBACK MODALITY FOR NONTRANSPARENT DRIVER CONTROL ACTIONS: WHY NOT VISUALLY?

Michael M. POPP and Berthold FAERBER

Human Factors Institute, Faculty of Aerospace Techniques,
University of the Armed Forces Munich, Werner-Heisenberg-Weg 39, 8014 Neubiberg,
FRG.

Abstract
A well designed man-machine interface for control of a vehicle should give feedback to the operator to minimize his/her distraction from the main task, which is safe driving. Therefore, the present study investigates the effects of different kinds of feedback and different driving situations on driver behaviour in order to determine a suitable feedback modality. The research concentrates on nontransparent functions activated by the driver via voice control. In the experiments, four different feedback modes were used: a tone, visual feedback with and without acoustic announcement, voice feedback. The results show that the visual feedback information can be recommended for non-transparent driver actions.

1. INTRODUCTION

Voice control of functions in cars will be available in the near future. In addition to the technological requirements and traffic safety needs of such control devices (to ensure that they act with high reliability under all circumstances), there is the question of, which control actions are best suited to voice control. This question is related to a second one: since controlling vehicle functions by voice confronts drivers with a new way to perform actions which they previously performed manually. The normal way to control a vehicle is by pushing buttons, manipulating levers manually and operating pedals by the feet. This has established well defined relationships between the intended actions, the spatial location of the manipulations, and the reactions of the affected systems. (With modern electronics and remote control systems these relationships are sometimes 'hidden' in the car, but, the system remotely controlled is nevertheless associated with the system itself.) Imagine for instance the desire to listen to the radio news: the driver looks at the radio control panel and his/her hand reaches the button under visual (or at least visually initiated) control; turning on the radio gives a proprioceptive and tactile feedback via muscles and limbs, and an auditory feedback if the radio is operating correctly. The control of in-car functions by voice changes the eye-hand-arm control system into a voice control system. Differences between device locations and specific manipulations must be transformed into different verbal commands.

2. FEEDBACK INFORMATION

The general purpose of feedback after a voice input is, to inform the operator that a voice command has been detected and that the system is trying to act in accordance with this command.

2.1 Feedback and nontransparent driver control actions

A detailed investigation of feedback modality requires a further distinction to be made. A number of vehicle functions react to the control actions of the operator without latency and are clearly noticeable. Even when these functions are combined in the same control element (e.g. the wiper or washer functions, which are often positioned at the same stalk near the steering wheel), they do not need any additional feedback. However, there are also functions with long reaction latencies or hardly noticeable reactions (e.g. air-conditioning control). Manual operation of the air-conditioning system provides at least one clear feedback: the control has changed its position - a promise that the intended state of the system will come. After a verbal command, the operator can neither be sure that he/she gave the appropriate one nor that the system has interpreted it correctly. Therefore he/she has to wait until the system changes its state noticeably to confirm the successful operation. We will call these functions 'nontransparent driver control functions'. Examples of nontransparent control functions in cars are: control of the air-conditioning system, route guidance systems, and car phone.

Faerber, Popp & Stapf (1987) pointed out, that explicit feedback seems to be sensible for all voice inputs which activate nontransparent driver's control actions. In the study presented here, a series of different forms of feedback for those nontransparent control actions were compared.

2.2 Specific versus non-specific feedback

The negative effects of 'not completed actions' on memory and attention ('Zeigarnik-effect' of Zeigarnik (1927)) are well known to everyone from every day life. Applied to a driver's actions in a car, the psychological effect means that all actions once initiated are kept in mind until the operator is sure that the device has reached the intended state. The demand of the 'not completed actions' is mostly independent of the value or importance of the action. Even the interruption of totally unimportant actions like feeding the cassette player with a new tape seems to be difficult. The main task of safe driving seems to be pushed to the background while fumbling with the tape becomes the actual main task. From consideration of the Zeigarnik effect, it is possible to conclude that specific feedback to voice inputs is preferable. Specific feedback relieves the driver from the uncertainty of having performed the right action. On the other hand, the driver's workload should not increase by feedback to voice inputs, so that for this reason alone short and non-specific feedback might be better. In the case of 'nontransparent operator actions' we need both specific and quick indications about the success of the verbal commands. Only both qualities of feedback message seem to be able to switch the drivers attention back to the demands of vehicle control and secure driving. These two demands reflect some kind of speed-accuracy conflict which must be solved on an empirical basis.

2.3 Feedback modalities

Theoretically, all sensory modalities can be used to transmit information to the operator. But only some of them seem to be reasonable in any particular circumstance. Tactile and proprioceptive signals should be reserved for specific warnings (as recommended by Faerber et al., 1990). For that reason we decided to concentrate our research on the visual and the auditory channels.

2.4 Experimental questions

Summarizing the above arguments, the experiment has to answer two main questions:

1. Whether the different feedback messages (objective and subjective) affect the workload and the quality of driving performance.
2. Whether it is possible to come to a conclusion about the speed-accuracy conflict of the informational contents of well designed, adequate feedback messages for the two different modalities (visual, auditory).

Comparison between different feedback modalities only seems to be fair if the different forms of messages are indeed comparable. We decided to present the visual messages only in the same 'bandwidth' as that used for the acoustic ones. Therefore, we restricted the visual messages to short text strings. Their semantic content equals the content of the acoustic messages.

3. EXPERIMENTAL FEEDBACK MESSAGES

3.1 Acoustic feedback

Several forms of acoustic signal can serve as feedback. The coding of the intended message into pure tones or sounds is technically the simplest way, but the decoding needs training for the driver. If several acoustic signals are used, errors or mismatches are probable. Nevertheless pure tones should be investigated because the reactions to them are well known and they could be used as a baseline and link to other results in ergonomics. We decided to use an electronic three tone gong (duration 1 sec) as unspecific feedback to the control action.

Faerber & Faerber (1984) investigated voice warning systems in cars and made recommendations for the semantic and syntactic structure of these messages. In their experiments, short verbal feedbacks were formulated and stored after digital filtering. Each feedback is preceded by the three tone gong and informs the driver about the action he/she has initiated.

3.2 Visual feedback

It is important to keep in mind that the messages were to be presented for feedback purposes only. Therefore there was no need for highly sophisticated, fancy display messages. The feedback messages should only tell the operator that his/her command has been successfully received. Again, a balance has to be found between visual load and information about completed actions (as discussed in section 2.2.).

Presented in the central visual field, display messages are easy to detect and easy to read.

But this part of the dashboard display is reserved for many other functions. As a consequence, simple visual messages were presented in the periphery of the visual field of the driver. In the case of peripheral visual signals it is important to avoid sudden luminance and contrast changes. Otherwise the appearance of the feedback messages would drop an orientational reaction of the subjects. Since the experiment was performed during daytime the visual message was designed as a dark text on a light background. The luminance difference between the background of the display and the traffic scene was set to 1:4 (Krueger, 1980, 31ff).

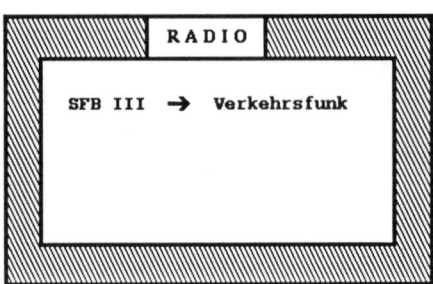

Fig. 1: Example of the visual feedback message when the operator has set the radio to receive the traffic message channel from the station SFB III.

4. EXPERIMENTAL SETTING AND DESIGN

The experiment was carried out in the interactive sight and motion simulator of Daimler Benz AG in Berlin (Drosdol and Panik, 1985). This moving base simulator is a tool to perform research in the field of man-machine-interface design. The possibility of varying traffic situations systematically and predictably, and the perfect retest reliability of the simulation guarantee reliable results. Driving in the simulated world imposes more mental load to the driver, than with driving in real traffic situations (Faerber, Popp and Stapf, 1988). But for investigating the effects of new installations in cars, this additional load is helpful in amplifying behavioural aspects which are too small or too infrequent to be observable under normal road conditions.

4.1 Driving task

Driving manoeuvres were simulated to systematically manipulate the driver's workload. The subjects drove on a straight road for about 40 km and were asked to follow two preceding cars with a constant speed. Whenever the preceding cars reduced their speed drastically, subjects were forced to pass or stop behind them. Variation of the three parameters: driving speed, manoeuvring space, and predictability of future traffic events results in apparently different, but equally loading, driving situations (see Faerber, Popp & Stapf, 1985).

4.2 Experimental conditions

Each subject performed two experimental blocks. Within each block, he/she went through 16 traffic situations of varying difficulty. In five of these situations they were asked to control different systems/functions via verbal command. After the control actions visual or acoustic (tone or voice output) feedback was given. Within one block, the nature of the message, although not its contents, remained constant.

4.3 Control functions

Subjects are asked (via acoustic instruction) to manipulate four different 'nontransparent control actions' with verbal commands. These were:

I   Car radio (Store new radio station)
II Air-conditioning (Increase fan speed, direct the stream of air onto the windscreen)
III Car radio (Receive only traffic information - 'dump switch')
IV Car phone (Call a previously stored number)

4.4 Feedback messages

The feedback messages were in the form of:

A   Signal tone without specific feedback about the action initiated.
B   Signal tone and voice output with feedback of the initiated action.
C   Peripheral display feedback of the initiated action in form of a short text string.
D   Same as C, preceded by a signal tone.

4.5 Dependent variables

We recorded the workload of the drivers, continuously measured by means of the cardiac R interspike interval pulse rate as described in Popp (1988) and the subjective ratings of the drivers at the end of the experiment. The performance of the drivers was measured by the parameters: speed, lateral distance, longitudinal distance to the leading car, acceleration in all axes, steering angle, heading angle and frequency of head movements of the drivers, (which was taken as a measure of the time and frequency of glances to the peripheral display).

4.6 Subjects

Twelve older (45-60 years) and 12 younger (20-35 years) subjects of both genders participated in the experiment. All of them were well trained drivers, but had not previously been tested in a simulator. The subjects were paid a fee for their time spent on the experiment.

4.7 Training, instruction, and experiment

The experimental sessions started with a training session. Subjects had to learn the whole set of possible voice commands used in cars. The commands actually used in the experiment were a subset of them. A learning criteria of 100% correct responses was used for the whole set. After this the subject was given a short training drive in the simulator.

The first experimental block started with an instruction about the feedback modality.

Then subjects drove 40 km on different road conditions passing 16 specific traffic situations varying with respect to their workload (as discussed above, Steiner, (1985)). In five situations, they had to perform different nontransparent control actions. Four of these situations imposed a high load on the driver. After a short rest the subjects drove the second experimental block, which was identical to the first except for the feedback modality.

5. RESULTS

Without exception, all feedback signals affected the performance and load of the subjects to some extent, but the results show no significant differences between the dependent variables and the four different forms of feedback messages. Only a few of the possible differences between parameters and experimental conditions were statistically significant (on the basis of t-test related samples or chi-square test in the case of the ratings).

In critical traffic situations, both forms of visual feedback produce longer reaction times than pure tone messages ($p < 0.05$, $p < 0.001$). Voice feedback produced longer reaction times than to the visual message preceded by a tone ($p < 0.05$). While overtaking drivers needed more lateral space when receiving voice feedback than when receiving visual feedback or the tone ($p < 0.05$). On the other hand, the pulse rate was higher if the subjects received the visual message with tone than with the pure tone alone ($p < 0.05$). In their ratings, subjects preferred the pure tone to the display message ($p < 0.01$). For the whole experiment, subjects estimated the pure tone messages to be best when compared with all other feedback messages ($p < 0.05$).

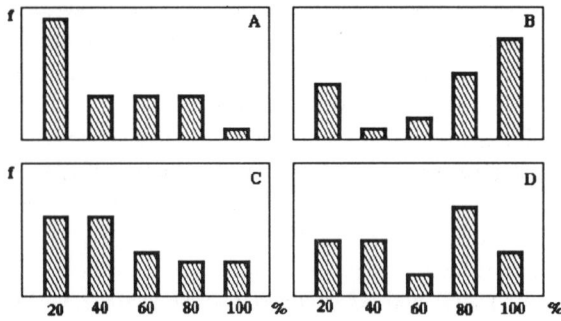

Fig. 2: Frequency distribution for the four different feedback messages over all performance parameters and mental load measured. Values are normalized on a scale of 0 - 100%; A) pure tone message, B) voice output message, C) visual display message, D) visual display message with preceding tone signal.

To answer the general question of which feedback form is better. The feedback messages can be arranged in order. The behaviour in critical traffic situations (with additional control action and feedback) of all parameters measured was combined in an overall frequency distribution using a common scale. First, all individual scales were normalized to the range of 0 - 100%. The percent values of the measurements of a scale were combined into classes of 20% width. Finally the number of occurrences of measurements in each frequency class were added for the four feedback modalities separately (as given in Figure 2).

The maxima of the four distributions give the hierarchy of the feedback messages. The summary comparison of all feedback signals shows a cumulative decrease of performance and a cumulative increase of mental load, if we arrange the feedback messages in the following order given in Figure 3.

```
mental load low - driving performance high
┌─────────────────────────────────────────┐
│               signal tone                 │
│             visual display                │
│      signal tone and visual display       │
│      signal tone and voice message        │
└─────────────────────────────────────────┘
mental load high - driving performance low
```

Figure 3: Relative order of feedback modalities in relation to workload and performance effects.

6. DISCUSSION

The simplest feedback without any specific information about the action initiated (A) was the clear winner in the comparison. The initially predicted favourite, the voice feedback message (B), was the loser. Both visual display versions take second and third place (C) and (D), in the comparison. It is necessary to consider why speech messages give such a poor response.   Whenever the operator initiated an action via voice, the car echoed this command back to him/her immediately. Voice output is a good solution if the message carries information of high interest, but the feedback messages do not. Furthermore, it is impossible to ignore speech messages. The result is an increase of irritation and subjective load, and a decrease in driving performance.

Are simple tones then suitable to feedback successful voice inputs? The answer is - in spite of the results - no! In the experiment there was only one source of non-specific acoustic signals - the voice recognition device, but high-tech cars with fancy electronics and devices beeping present a horror scenario. Visual feedback is an alternative. Both forms of visual display messages showed moderate results, but the display form which forced the driver to notice it (D) was worse. Operators seem to prefer to choose their own time to look at a display (C) rather than being forced to do so by an acoustic signal (D).

On the basis of our experiment, it is not possible to decide whether the nontranparent actions tested do have the effects of "not completed actions" predicted by Zeigarnik (as suggested in section 2.2) or not, but we are able to answer the initial questions. Our experiment shows that operators profit most if the feedback on voice commands is either 'quick and dirty' (that means very simple and unspecific), or non-insistent, and remaining waiting until the driver needs to refer to it.

ACKNOWLEDGEMENTS

We thank Daimler Benz, Dr. Ferdinand Panik, Peter Beck, and the simulator staff in Berlin for the possibility of using their equipment. Without their support, advice and help, the experiment reported would not have taken place.

REFERENCES

Drosdol J. & Panik F (1985). The Daimler Benz Driving Simulator: A Tool for Vehicle Development. Detroit, SAE Technical Paper 850334, Society of Automotive Engineers, Detroit.

Faerber B. & Faerber B (1984). Grundlagen and Moeglichkeiten der Nutzung sprachlicher Informationssysteme in Kraftfahrzeugen. Projektbericht, Universitaet Tuebingen.

Faerber B., Popp M.M. & Stapf K.H (1988). Erarbeitung von Gestaltungskriterien fuer Sprachdialogsysteme and Pruefung ihrer Auswirkungen auf die Verkehrssicherheit. Projektbericht I+II, Universitaet Tuebingen.

Faerber B., Faerber B.A., Godthelp J. & Schumann J 1990). State of the art and recommendations for characteristics of speed and steering support systems. Deliverable Report DRIVE V1041/GIDS-CON01. Haren, NL: Traffic Research Centre, University of Groningen.

Krueger H. (1980). Ophthalomological Aspects of Work with Display Workstations. In: Grandjean E. & Viglini E. (Eds.), Ergonomic Aspects of Visual Display Terminals, (London: Taylor & Francis), pp 31-40.

Popp M.M (1988). Zur Struktur and Funktion von Beanspruchungmassen in kritischen Situationen. In: Sicherheit im Sport - eine Herausforderung an die Sportwissenschaft. Dokumentation des 1. Internationalen Symposiums in Augsburg. Koeln, Sport and Buch, pp 161-171.

Steiner A (1985). Modellbildung and experimentelle Ueberpruefung eines Klassifikationssystems fuer Strassenverkehrssituationen, Diplomarbeit, Tuebingen, Psychologisches Institut der Universitaet.

Zeigarnik B (1927). Das Behalten erledigter and unerledigter Handlungen nach der Theorie Lewins. Psychologische Forschung, 9, pp 1-85.

VISION IN VEHICLES – IV
A.G. Gale et al. (Editors)

AN INITIAL MODEL OF VISUAL SAMPLING OF IN-CAR DISPLAYS AND CONTROLS

Walter W. WIERWILLE

Vehicle Analysis and Simulation Laboratory, Virginia Polytechnic Institute and State University, Blacksburg, Virginia 24061-0118 U.S.A.

Abstract

Recent research by a number of investigators has shown that there is a relatively consistent pattern in the way that drivers perform in-car tasks. This pattern involves time-sharing and visual sampling between the driving task and the in-car task. The pattern is a result of the need to attend to the primary task of driving while treating the in-car task as a secondary or subsidiary task. The visual resource must therefore be time-shared.

The pattern allows development of a model in which parameters area function of the specific type of in-car task and the current driving demands. Additional factors such as age, panel clutter, and legibility also effect parameter values. The model itself can be adjusted to account for such influences.

An initial form of model is presented, along with highlights of the supporting data and effects of various independent variables. The model provides insight into the way that in-car tasks should be designed.

1. INTRODUCTION

In driving, the primary sense modality for information gathering is visual. The driver views the forward scene, glances to either side when necessary and also watches the rear view mirrors and instruments (mainly the speedometer). While the driver does use auditory and other sensory cues such as feel in many situations, these play a minor role in information gathering. As a driver drives, the forward scene becomes the primary information gathering source. The driver may occasionally look elsewhere, but must still pay close attention to the forward scene. Another way of saying this is that attending to the forward view (and associated vehicle control cues) is the primary task of the driver. Because of the need for time sharing, instrument panel (IP) and other in-car tasks that require vision must be considered as secondary. When a driver performs an in-car task (a secondary task), that task must be time-shared with the driving task (the primary task). The driver has but one foveal visual resource which can only gather detailed information from a single source at any given time.

Drivers normally realize that they must not glance away from the forward view for too long a period of time. They also realize that they cannot accomplish the in-car task without vision. They therefore develop a time-sharing strategy, which meets a competing set of requirements. The strategy consists of employing short glances away from the driving task, to gather visual information associated with completion of the in-car task. The process of visual time sharing is relatively consistent and can therefore be modeled with reasonable accuracy.

2. BACKGROUND

Early work supporting sampling models of driving was directed toward understanding the attentional demand of driving. Senders et al. (1967), developed a theoretical model based on information theoretic concepts. Fundamentally, the idea was that drivers must sample the forward view and that between samples there is an uncertainty buildup with time. Eventually, an uncertainty threshold is reached and the driver must then glance to the forward view. The Senders et al work was demonstrated by using a vision occlusion device. This helmet mounted apparatus blocked the driver's vision on a periodic basis. The view and occlusion times could be adjusted. They found when using the device that there was indeed a minimum tolerable information sampling frequency for each given type of road and vehicle speed. If the sampling frequency was set below this minimum, drivers would immediately decelerate to compensate for lack of forward view information.

The Senders et al. work was directed at determining and modeling the attentional demand of driving, that is the primary task of driving. However, the research demonstrates that drivers must have samples of the forward view at approximately equally-spaced intervals. It also therefore helps to explain the visual time-sharing that takes place when drivers attempt to perform in-car tasks while driving.

One of the earliest studies to examine eye-fixations on in-car displays and controls was that of Mourant et al. (1977), (also Mourant et al. 1980). Their study compared five different types of stalk controls and three different types of panel controls. The results of the study indicated that the frequency of direct looks increased as the reach distance increased, and that direct looks were slightly longer for stalk controls than for panel controls.

In pioneering studies, Rockwell (1988) examined the in-car glance durations and number of glances for radio and mirror tasks. He used a cross section of drivers in traffic. He found that individual glance times into the car clustered around 1.25 seconds, and that for radio tasks such as tuning, four or five glances were required. Based on the results of the experiments, Rockwell concluded that there was a fairly consistent time-sharing strategy for performing IP tasks while driving, that individual glance length was relatively consistent, and that for complex tasks more glances were required.

Bhise et al. (1986) extended the work of Rockwell to a greater variety of tasks. In summarizing their results, they indicated that single glance times to the IP do in fact vary somewhat with the type of task, and number of glances varies greatly with the type of task.

Recently, Wierwille, Antin, Dingus and Hulse (1988), performed a study in which in-car conventional and navigational tasks were compared in terms of visual glance times and number of glances. This research was performed in an instrumented vehicle on public roads with an operational, computerized, moving-map navigation display. The results of their study show very clearly that total visual demand (the sum of individual glance lengths into the car) varies markedly with the task; it ranged from 0.78 second for reading speed up to 10.63 seconds for determining the name of the roadway at which the next turn was to be made in reaching a programmed destination. Of course, in most cases, drivers did not glance continuously. Rather, they sampled. Single glance lengths varied somewhat more than previous studies had indicated, with a range of 0.62 to 1.66 seconds. Also the average number of glances ranged from 1.26 to 6.64. This latter result is in agreement with earlier work, but is more comprehensive.

The results of these studies demonstrate several important relationships. First, they show the relatively narrow range of single glance times, and the relatively broad range of number of glances. The results also show that gathering information for several navigation tasks and certain other conventional tasks (radio tuning for example) results in large visual demands. Most importantly, drivers do not, on the average, allow their single glance times to exceed about 1.6 seconds, even for complex information gathering tasks. Instead, they return to the forward scene, attend to the driving task, and then return to gather additional in-car information. This process continues until the task is completed.

3. AN INITIAL MODEL

The process of time-sharing can be modeled rather simply (Wierwille, 1987). Consider that a driver is to perform a specific in-car task. Then, assuming the task requires vision, the driver samples the task until the necessary visual aspect is completed, as shown in Figure 1. The driver samples the task, returns to the forward view, samples the task, returns to the forward view, etc., until the visual aspect is completed. In some cases a single sample of the in-car task is sufficient. In other cases, more than one sample is required.

The model for visual sampling can be further specified as shown in Figure 2. This is a logic model and is based on the experimental data presented in the previous section. The model is a normative, deterministic model. Referring to Figure 2, when a driver begins to perform an in-car task he or she does so by glancing to the appropriate location. Information extraction begins as elapsed time passes. If the information can be chunked at about 1 second or less, the driver will do so and will then return glance to the forward scene. On the other hand, if chunking takes longer, the driver will continue to glance at the location for a bit longer. However, in doing so, the driver senses time pressure to return to the forward scene. If the glance to the in-car location continues up to about 1.5 seconds and the information cannot be obtained (or chunked), the driver will return glance to the forward scene anyway, and will try again later. On the other hand, if chunked information can be obtained within about 1.5 seconds, the driver will extract the information and return to the forward scene. Additional samples would be handled in exactly the same way, until all required visual information is obtained.

Given a free choice, drivers would prefer not to have to glance to the appropriate location for more than about one second. They will do so, however, under many circumstances if they must. They will not under most circumstances glance away for more than about 1.6 seconds (on the average). While the upper bound does vary somewhat with the individual driver and the driving conditions, there is nevertheless an upper bound for each driver. Time pressure and forward scene uncertainty build to the point that the driver is compelled

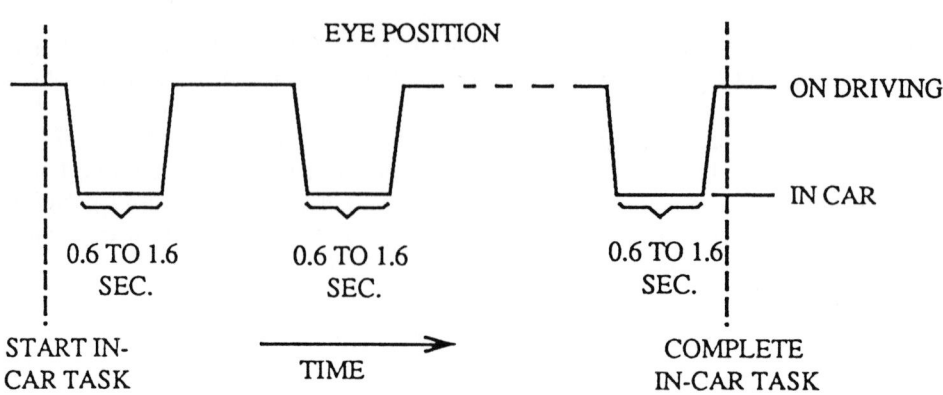

Figure 1. Elementary visual sampling model for in-car task performance.

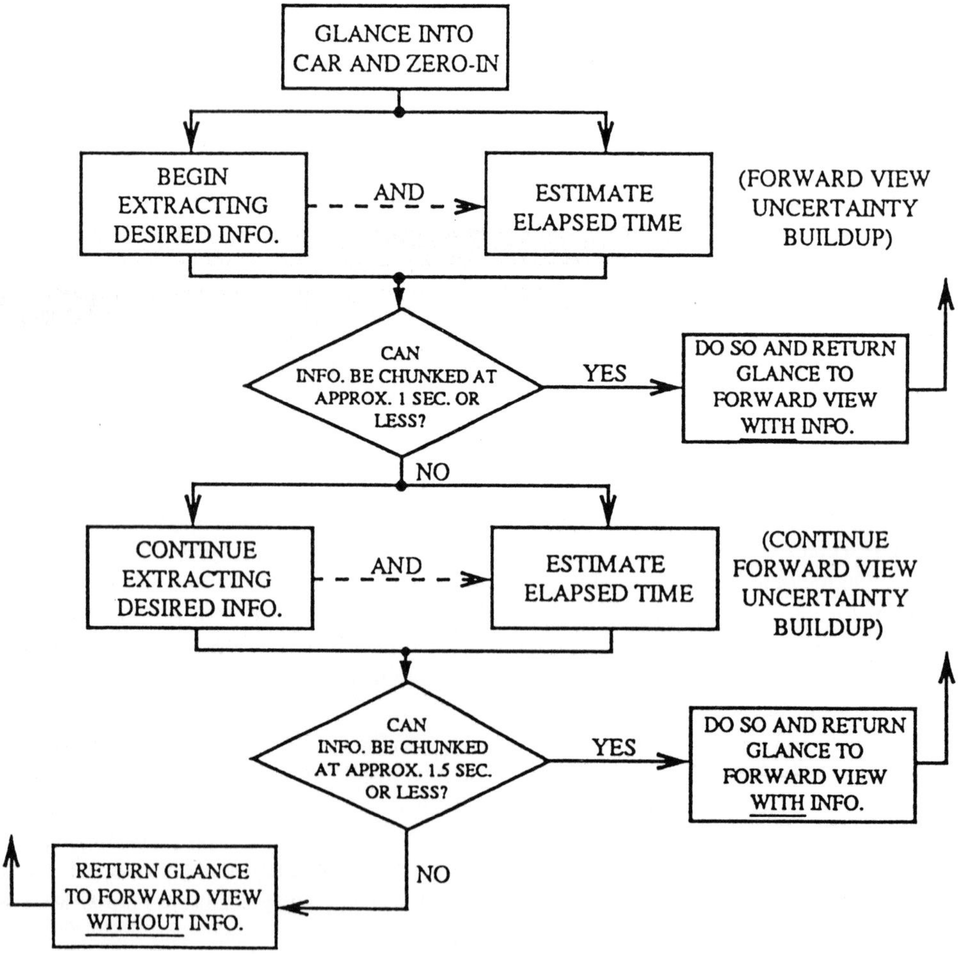

Figure 2. A more detailed model of visual sampling for in-car task performance.

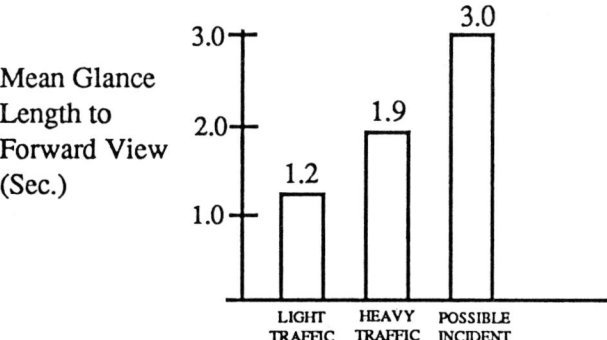

Figure 3. Glance length to forward view as a function of traffic type (Wierwille, Hulse, et al, 1988).

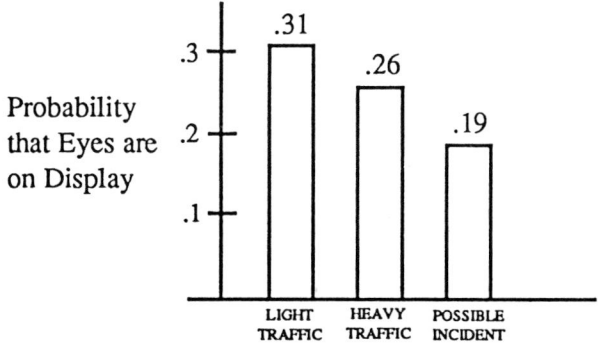

Figure 4. Probability that the eyes are on the navigation display as a function of traffic type (Wierwille, Hulse, et al, 1988).

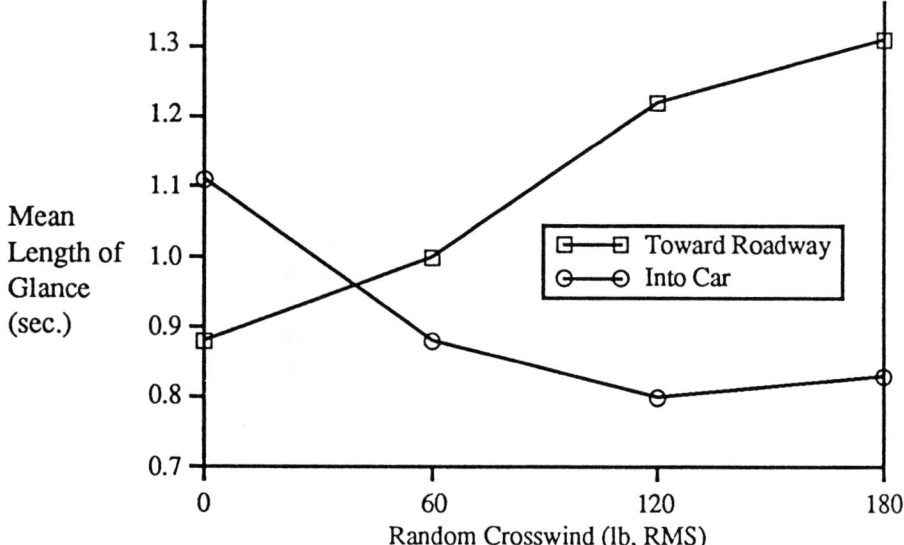

Figure 5. Mean glance length as a function of disturbance level (Kurokawa and Wierwille, 1990).

to return glance to the forward scene.

The model depicted in Figure 2 is admittedly too deterministic. Drivers do not measure elapsed time accurately and they do not consciously decide whether the available information can be chunked. Furthermore, they do not use the logic flow as specifically as it is shown. Nevertheless, the model does explain the processes that must be taking place that limit the lengths of glances into the car.

4. ADJUSTMENT OF PARAMETERS IN THE MODEL

There are sufficient data available to show how parameters in the sampling model vary as a function of several independent variables, including type of task, age, clutter, and forward view (primary task) demand. In addition to variation as a function of these independent variables, there is the usual inter- and intra-subject variability that always occurs when human beings perform tasks. Thus, the mean values and deterministic models can be enhanced or modified to account for a variety of influences.

Work has been done to determine the effects of driving task (per se) demand on the visual sampling process (Wierwille , Hulse, Fischer and Dingus, 1988; Kurokawa and Wierwille, 1990). The results of these studies show reliable adaptive trends by the driver as driving task demands increase. The following are general statements supported by the studies:

(i)   For drivers using an in-car navigation system and as roadways become more difficult to drive, the probability that the driver's eyes will be on the roadway increases, as shown in Figure 8 of Wierwille, Hulse, Fischer and Dingus (1988, Figure 8). Under the same conditions, the probability that the driver's eyes will be on the navigation display decreases by approximately the same amount, as shown in Wierwille, Hulse, Fischer and Dingus (1988, Figure 9).

(ii)   For drivers using an in-car navigation system and for varying traffic conditions, glance length to the forward view increases with traffic density and the possibility of an impending conflict (as shown in Figure 3). Under the same conditions, the probability that the driver's eyes will be on the navigation display decreases (as shown in Figure 4).

(iii)   As crosswind disturbance level increases while the driver performs various conventional in-car tasks, single glance length to the roadway increases and single glance length into the car decreases (as shown in Figure 5).

These results suggest that drivers undergoing increased visual loading due to (the primary task of) driving adapt their visual sampling strategy; they are under greater pressure to return their glance to the forward view sooner and to maintain it on the forward view for a greater proportion of total time. The models shown in Figures 1 and 2 do not presently account for this adaptation process. However, they certainly could be modified to include this as well as other adaptation processes. In Figure 2 for example, the pressure to return to the forward view could be included by shortening or lengthening the chunking times, or

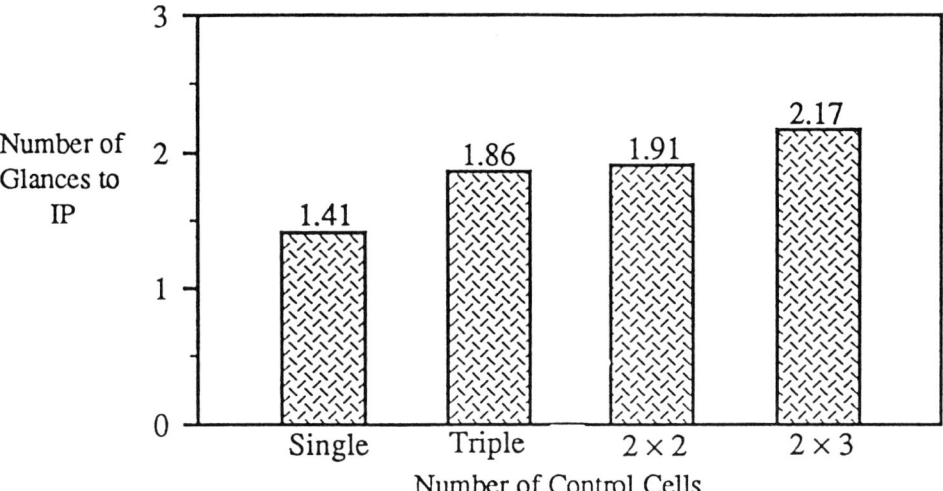

Figure 6. Effect of macroclutter on number of in-car glances (Kurokawa and Wierwille, 1991).

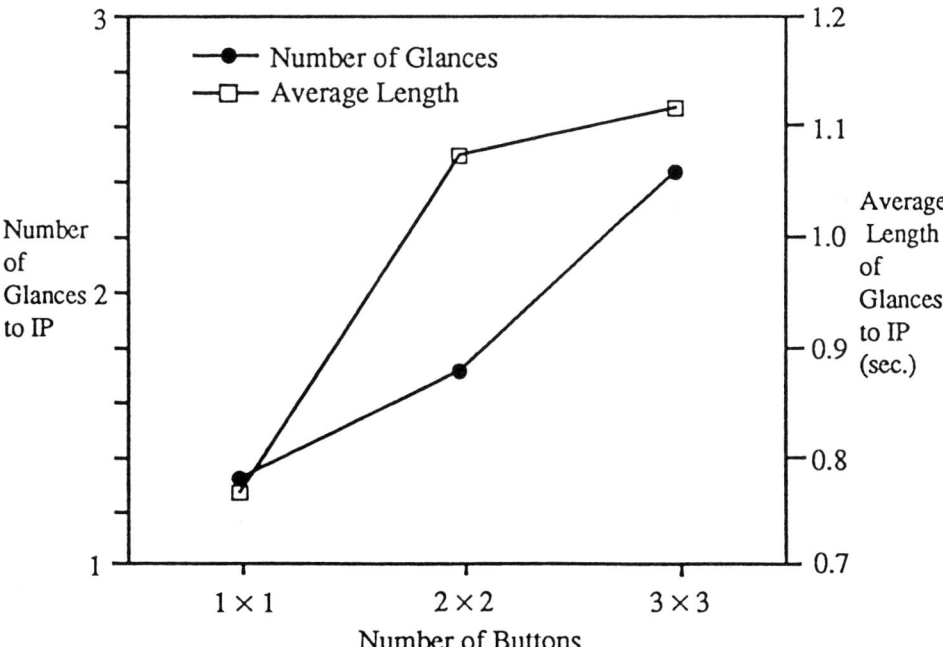

Figure 7. Effect of microclutter on number of in-car glances and single glance lengths (Kurokawa and Wierwille, 1991).

by replacing the decision model with a more complex one.

Several research studies have included measures of standard deviation or variance of single glance times. Such results allow specification of glance length variations. Generally, the distribution of glance times is truncated on the lower side and has a tail going toward long single glance times. Typical of these distributions are those shown in Rockwell (1988, Figures 1 and 2). Such distributions could be used to introduce variation in the logic model, through Monte Carlo simulation techniques for example.

A number of driving research studies involving in-car tasks have included age as an independent variable (Rackoff, 1974; Poynter, 1988; Hayes et al., 1989; and Imbeau et al., 1989). The results generally show that deterioration of vision and slowing of cognitive processes have an effect on in-car task completion times. Furthermore, if inadequate character size or contrast ratios are used in displays, even greater decrements will occur. With regard to glance times, there is strong evidence that in-car single glance times and numbers of glances increase with age. In addition, transition time between in-car task and forward view increases with age. (Figures 3 through 8, in the Hayes, et al. (1989) paper illustrate some of these effects for drivers performing conventional in-car tasks.)

Additional work recently completed (Kurokawa and Wierwille, 1991) shows that various types of instrument panel clutter cause an increase in the number of in-car glances. Figure 6 shows results for "macroclutter," when similar-appearing panels of controls are present. Figure 7 shows results for "microclutter," where similar-appearing individual buttons within a control panel are present. In the latter figure, both the number of glances and the single glance times increase with number of buttons present. Additional results of the Kurokawa and Wierwille (1991) work show that well-chosen abbreviations for labels provide shorter single glance times than do their fully-spelled counterparts.

The literature thus demonstrates the effects of several independent variables on the sampling process that occurs for in-car tasks. Not only do these results substantiate the model, but they also show how an appropriate model could be enhanced to account for a greater number of independent variables.

5. CONCLUSIONS

Research results demonstrate conclusively that drivers do use a visual sampling strategy to perform in-car tasks, that their behavior is relatively consistent, and that models can be developed that show the nature of the sampling process. In addition, a good deal is already known about how specific independent variables affect the visual sampling process. There are two areas where further research is needed. The first is in refinement and expansion of models of in-car task performance by the driver. This presentation has provided a simple model and a brief overview of the available data base. However, this is only the beginning. The models need to be improved in terms of accuracy, degree of generality, and determination of effects of independent variables. Also, a better understanding of what is causing parameter changes must be obtained. The second area of further research is development of better guidelines for in-car task communications with the driver and associated developments that allow minimization of demands on driver resources. Both of these areas of research represent great challenges, but promise substantial rewards in terms of driver-vehicle efficiency and accident prevention.

6. REFERENCES

Bhise, V. D., Forbes, L. M., and Farber, E. I. (1986). Driver behavioral data and considerations in evaluating in-vehicle controls and displays. Paper presented at the Transportation Research Board, National Academy of Sciences, 65th Annual Meeting, Washington, D.C., January.

Hayes, B. C., Kurokawa, K., and Wierwille, W. W. (1989). Age related decrements in automobile instrument panel task performance. Proceedings of the Human Factors Society 33rd Annual Meeting, Santa Monica, CA: Human Factors Society, 1, 159-163.

Imbeau, D., Wierwille, W. W., Wolf, L. D., and Chun, G. (1989). Effects of instrument panel luminance and chromaticity on reading performance and preference in simulated   driving. Human Factors, 31, 2, 147-160.

Kurokawa, K., and Wierwille, W. W. (1990). Validation of a driving simulation facility for instrument panel task performance. Proceedings of the Human Factors Society 34th Annual   Meeting. Santa Monica, CA: Human Factors Society, October, 1299-1303.

Kurokawa, K., and Wierwille, W. W. (1991). Effects of instrument panel clutter and control labeling on visual demand and task performance. Paper submitted for presentation at the Society for Information Display International Symposium.

Mourant, R. R., Herman, M., and Moussa-Hamouda, E. (1980). Direct looks and control location in automobiles. Human Factors, 22, 4, 417-425.

Mourant, R. R., Moussa-Hamouda, E., and Howard, J. M. (1977). Human factors requirements for fingertip reach controls. Technical Report DOT-HS-803-267, Washington, DC: U.S. Department of Transportation.

Poynter, D. (1988). The effects of aging on perception of visual displays. SAE Paper 881754, Warrendale, PA: Society of Automotive Engineers.

Rackoff, M. J. (1974). An investigation of age-related changes in drivers' visual search patterns and driving performance, and the relation to tests of basic functional capabilities. Proceedings of the Human Factors Society 19th Annual Meeting, Santa Monica, CA: Human Factors Society, 285-288.

Rockwell, T. H. (1988). Spare visual capacity in driving—revisited: new empirical results for an old idea. In A. G. Gale, et al, Eds., Vision in Vehicles II, North Holland Press: Amsterdam, 317-324.

Senders, J. W., Kristofferson, A. B., Levison, W. H., Dietrich, C. W., and Ward, J. L. (1967). The attentional demand of automobile driving. Highway Research Record, 195, 15-32.

Wierwille, W. W. (1987). Can dash instrumentation visual attentional demand be predicted using the design driver concept? Paper presented at the Transportation Research Board Annual Meeting, Washington, DC, January.

Wierwille, W. W., Antin, J. F., Dingus, T., and Hulse, M. C. (1988). Visual attentional demand of an in-car navigation display system. In A. G. Gale et al, Eds., Vision in Vehicles II, North Holland Press: Amsterdam, 307-316.

Wierwille, W. W., Hulse, M. C., Fischer, T. J., and Dingus, T. A. (1988). Strategic use of visual resources by the driver while navigating with an in-car navigation display system. SAE Paper 885180, XXII FISITA Congress Technical Paper; Automotive

Systems Technology: The Future, SAE P-211,   Warrendale, PA: Society of
Automotive Engineers, 2.661-2.675

11

IN-VEHICLE DISPLAYS:
EFFECTS OF DISPLAY TYPE AND LOCATION

VISION IN VEHICLES – IV
A.G. Gale et al. (Editors)

A COMPARISON OF THE EFFECTS OF AN ANALOG VERSUS DIGITAL SPEEDOMETER ON DRIVER PERFORMANCE IN A TASK ENVIRONMENT SIMILAR TO DRIVING

R.J. KIEFER and L.S. ANGELL

Human Factors Department, General Motors Systems Engineering Center, 1151 Crooks Road, Troy, MI 48084, USA

Abstract

This study investigated the effects of an analog versus a digital speedometer on driver performance. Younger and older drivers were asked to control the speed of a vehicle on a chassis dynamometer while detecting pedestrians moving out onto the simulated road of a filmed, computer-generated driving scene. For the speed control task, drivers were asked either to maintain a precise speed or to keep their speed within a 5 mph (8 kph) range. Drivers' speed control accuracy, ability to detect events on the roadway, and eye movement behavior were measured. The results from this study indicated an advantage for the analog speedometer, but further research will be required in order to conclusively recommend one speedometer format over the other.

1. INTRODUCTION

Only a few studies have compared driver performance with an analog speedometer versus a digital speedometer (Ishii, 1980; Simmonds, Gailer, and Baines, 1981). Results from the Ishii (1980) on-the-road study indicated that drivers fixated a digital speedometer for 70-100 ms less than an analog speedometer, regardless of road type and weather condition. Simmonds et al. (1981) made comparisons between digital and circular, analog speedometers in tachistoscope, simulator, and road studies. Results indicated a digital speedometer advantage for reporting absolute speed in all three studies, and a digital speedometer advantage for judging whether the current speed was beyond the speed limit in the simulator study. Results from the simulator study showed no difference between speedometer formats for the task of maintaining a constant speed. Several limitations of the Ishii (1980) and Simmonds et al. (1981) studies make it difficult to conclude whether an analog or digital speedometer format is the more appropriate means of presenting speed information to the driver. First, although average fixation time may be shorter for a digital than an analog speedometer (Ishii, 1980), a digital speedometer may increase glance frequency and total eyes-off-road time to the speedometer without necessarily increasing drivers' speed control performance. Second, these previous studies failed to measure the driver's ability to detect events on the roadway. Third, the digital advantage reported by Simmonds et al. (1981) in the absolute speed task may not generalize to the task of keeping speed within a certain range.

The purpose of the following research was to compare the effects of an analog versus digital speedometer on driver performance in a task environment similar to driving with a methodology that addressed the issues left open by the previous research. Younger and older drivers were asked to perform two tasks simultaneously which were critical to automobile driving: speed control and visual search. Performance was assessed for two different types of speed control tasks, maintaining a precise speed and keeping speed within a 5 mph (8 kph) range. This study was the first to compare these speedometer formats by simultaneously measuring drivers' speed control accuracy, ability to detect events on the roadway, and visual sampling behavior.

2. METHOD

The two female and fourteen male volunteer participants were personnel of General Motors Research Laboratories. Subjects in the younger age group were 23-35 years old, and subjects in the older age group ranged were 45-55 years old. All subjects had normal color vision, and better than 20/30 near and far acuity. Subjects experienced each speedometer format on two separate days of testing, with the order of speedometer format presentation appropriately counterbalanced.

A schematic representation of the experimental apparatus is shown in Figure 1. The two vehicles used in the experiment had identical powertrains with different speedometer formats. The analog speedometer was positioned to the left of the steering wheel, whereas the digital speedometer was positioned directly above the steering wheel. The mechanical, circular, analog speedometer had 10 mph (16 kph) increments indicated by a pair of numerals and a flanking marker. The numerals were approximately 4.75 mm in height and 4.25 mm in width, and the corresponding markers were 7.2 mm in height and 1.3 mm in width. Smaller markers (4.5 mm in height and 0.75 mm in width) were positioned midway between the larger 10 mph (16 kph). The numerals and markers were white, and the speedometer background was black. The seven segment, vacuum fluorescent digital speedometer had miles per hour numerals which were 25.5 mm in height.

The vehicle was secured in a chassis dynamometer, which allowed a driver to regulate the speed of the vehicle with the accelerator while the vehicle remained stationary (with corresponding changes in the driver's auditory and tactile information). In order to make the speed control task more difficult, grade/rolling friction forces of various quantities and durations were imposed on the vehicle, which caused the car to respond as it would when travelling up hills of various gradients.

A 19-inch (485 mm) color monitor displayed the driving scene to the subject, which appeared behind the windshield slightly above the front hood and directly in front of the seated driver. Six 5-minute driving scenes were filmed from a driving simulator. The driving scenes corresponded to the front view of a vehicle travelling at a constant speed down the center of a straight blacktop two-lane road (30 feet (9.1m) wide) with a broken white dividing line. The rest of the driving scene consisted of green ground, blue sky, and white pedestrians. A three-frame sequence of the driving scene is shown in Figure 1. The pedestrians appeared on the edge of the road as if they were about to cross the road. Once

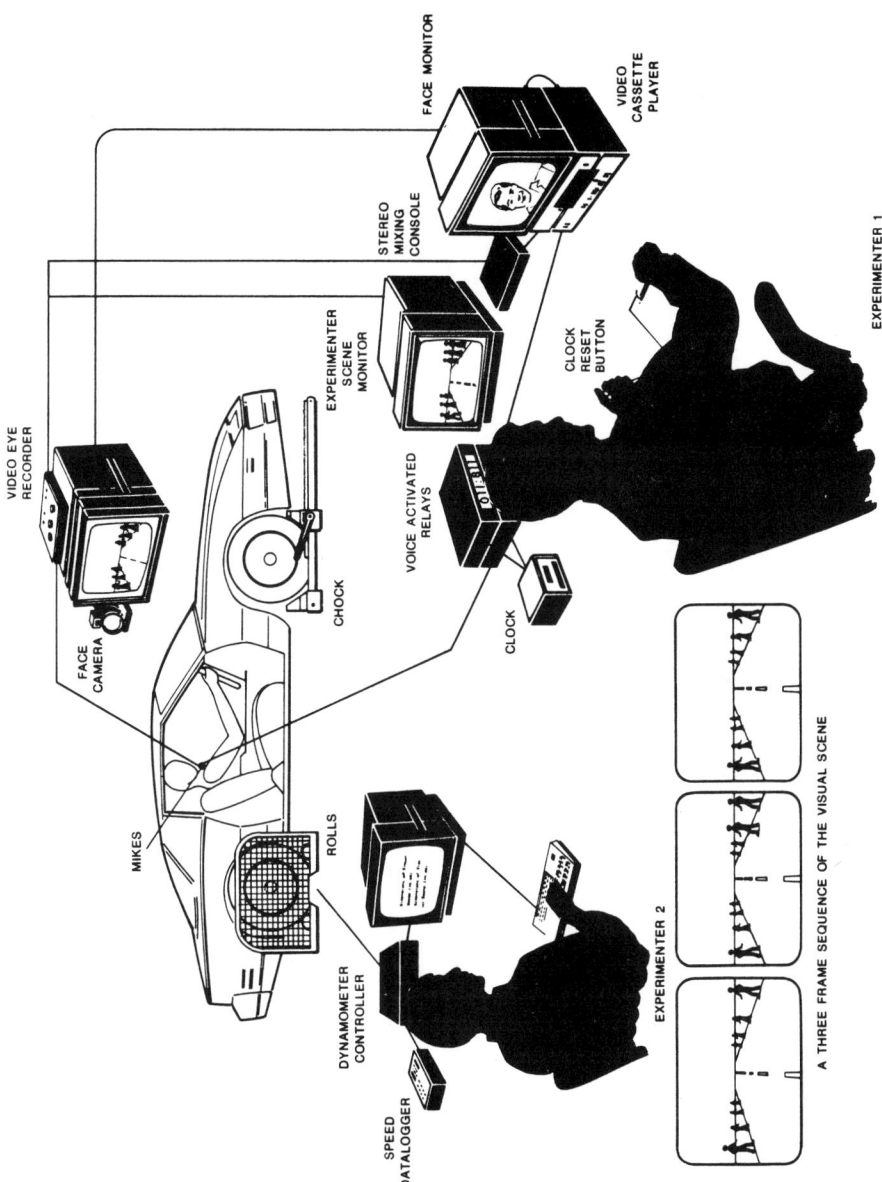

Figure 1. A schematic representation of the experimental apparatus

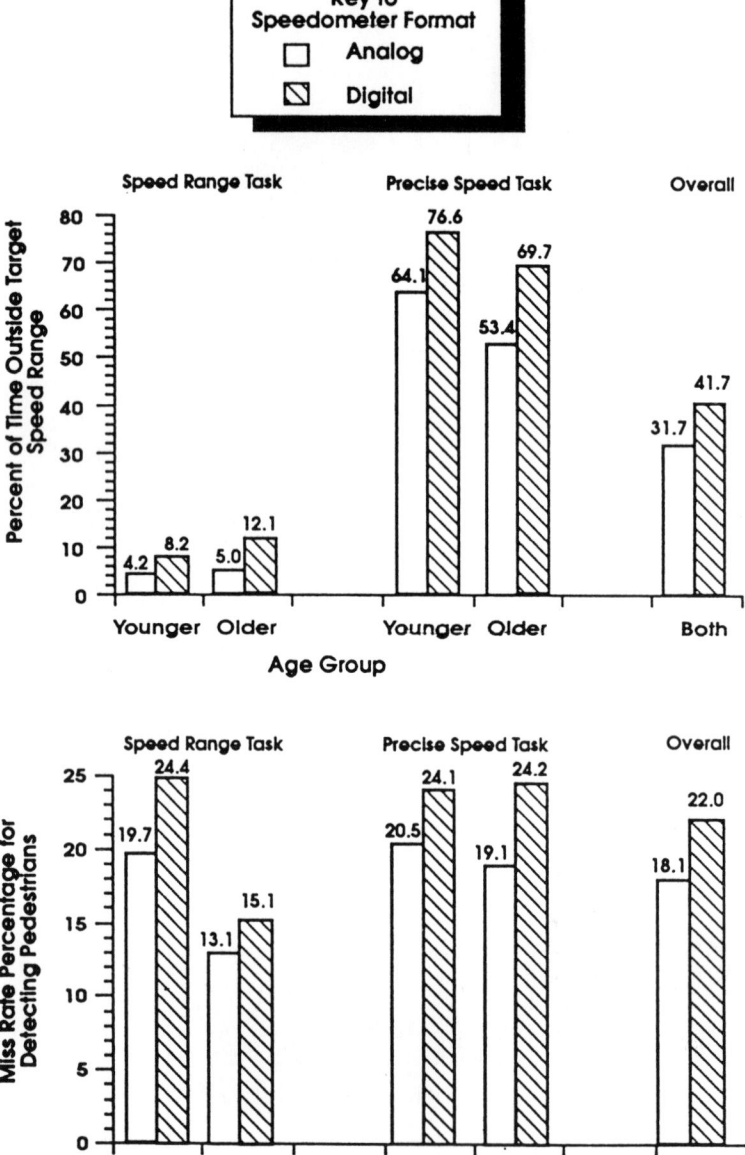

Figure 2. Speed control accuracy and pedestrian detection performance during dual task trials as a function of speed task, age and speedometer format.

every 4.85 seconds (on average), one of these pedestrians would jump out 8 feet (2.4m) into the road for a 50 ms duration, and then return to the side of the road. The time between any two pedestrians jumping on the road ranged between 0.85 and 10.85 seconds.

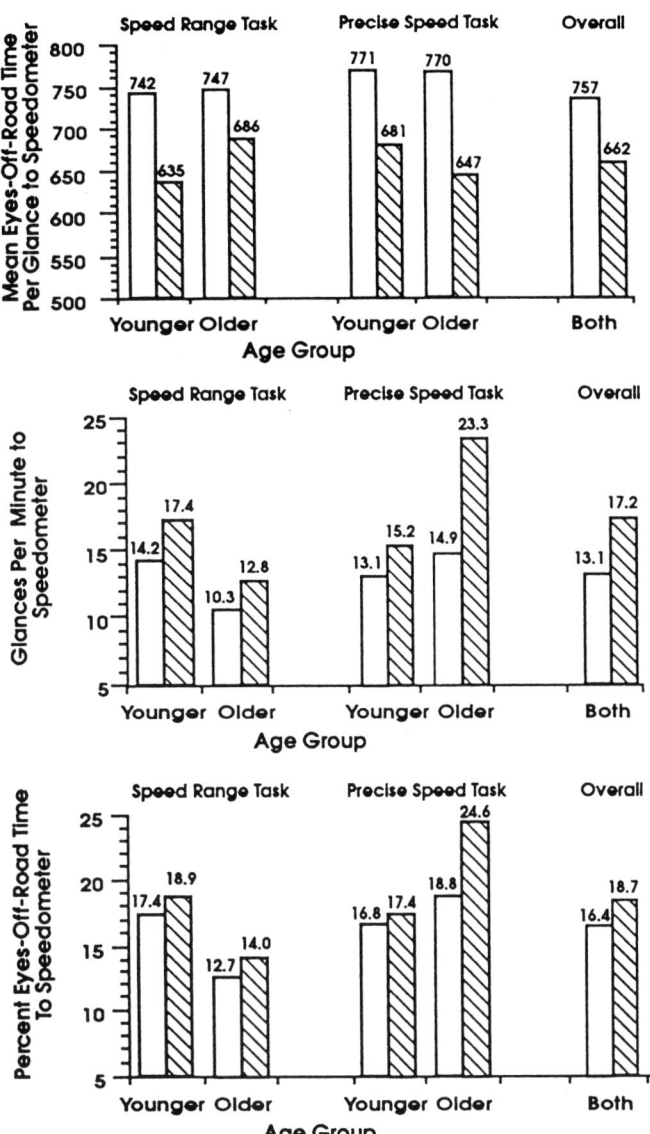

Figure 3. Eye movement behavior during dual task trials as a function of speed task, age and speedometer format.

Subjects were instructed to regulate the speed of a vehicle on a chassis dynamometer while searching for 'computer-generated' pedestrians jumping out onto the road of a filmed simulator driving scene, and were asked to treat each task as equally important. For the pedestrian detection task, subjects were asked to verbally indicate on which side of the road the pedestrian appeared. For the speed control task, half of the subjects in each age group were asked to perform a precise speed task, and half were asked to perform a speed range task. For the speed range task, subjects were asked to keep their speed between 35 and 40 mph (approximately 56.3 and 64.4 kph). For the precise speed task, subjects were asked to maintain speed at 40 mph (64.4 kph). For each speedometer, subjects experienced 7 five-minute trials. During the first two trials, subjects practiced performing speed regulation and pedestrian detection tasks separately. For the remaining five trials, referred to subsequently as dual task trials, subjects were asked to perform both tasks simultaneously. Performance during the first dual task trial was not used in the analysis.

Experimenter 1 recorded the subject's pedestrian detection responses and Experimenter 2 input the appropriate grade/rolling friction force levels imposed on the vehicle. A CSI 21x datalogger obtained dynamometer speed data at 2 Hz. A video camera was used to obtain drivers' eyes-off-road times to the speedometers (via frame-by-frame analysis).

3. RESULTS

Because real world driving requires performing several tasks concurrently, the key findings from this experiment come from analyses which compare the two speedometer formats during dual task performance. (Results from single task trials will not be discussed here.) To analyze dual task performance, a mixed factorial multivariate ANOVA was performed in which the within-subjects factors were speedometer format (analog and digital) and dual task trial (1, 2, 3, or 4), and the between-subjects factors were age (younger or older) and speed task (speed range or precise speed). The five dependent variables analyzed were pedestrian detection miss rates, percent of time spent outside the target speed range, glance frequency per minute to the speedometer, mean eyes-off-road (E-O-R) time per speedometer glance, and percent E-O-R time.

Pedestrian detection miss rates corresponded to the percentage of pedestrians which jumped out onto the road which the subject failed to detect. Speed control performance was evaluated by examining the percent of time spent outside the target speed range. To score the data from the speed range task the target speed was defined as 35.00-40.99 mph for the digital speedometer, since the speedometer readout would fall within the 35-40 mph range anywhere within this range. In order to equate for the size of this target range (6 mph, 9.6 kph), the target speed was defined during scoring as 34.50-40.50 mph for the analog speedometer. Similarly, for the precise speed task, the target speed was defined as 40.00-40.99 for the digital speedometer and as 39.50-40.50 for the analog speedometer. Eyes-off-road (E-O-R) time per speedometer glance refers to the time interval beginning when the subjects took their eyes off the road to look at their speedometer and ending when their eyes returned to the road after looking at the speedometer. Mean E-O-R time per speedometer glance refers to the average time for this interval. Percent E-O-R time refers to the total amount of time the subject had his/her eyes off the road (i.e., the sum of all E-O-R times to the speedometer) divided by the total amount of time the subject was engaged in the dual task.

Based on Wilk's criterion, the combined dependent variables were significantly affected by speedometer format, $F(5, 8) = 8.08$, $p<.01$, dual task trial, $F(15, 88.74) = 4.69$, $p<.0001$, speed task, $F(5, 8) = 28.72$, $p<.0001$, and the Test Run x Age x Speed Task interaction, $F(15, 88.74) = 1.98$, $p<.05$. Only results from the primary effect of interest, speedometer format, will be discussed here. To investigate this effect in more detail, follow-up univariate analyses were performed on the individual dependent variables. Univariate analyses revealed speedometer format to have had a significant effect on speed control performance, $F(1, 12) = 26.02$, $p<.0005$, mean E-O-R time per speedometer glance, $F(1, 12) = 9.50$, $p<.01$, glance frequency, $F(1, 12) = 11.00$, $p<.01$, and a marginal trend on percent E-O-R time, $F(1, 12) = 3.45$, $p<.10$. These results are shown in Figures 2 and 3, averaged across the four dual task trials. The percentages of time spent outside the target speed range for the analog and digital speedometer were 31.7% and 41.7%, respectively. Mean E-O-R times to the analog and digital speedometers were 757 and 662 ms, respectively. Glance frequencies to the analog and digital speedometer were 13.1 and 27.0 glances per minute, respectively. The percent E-O-R time for the analog and digital speedometer was 16.4% and 18.7%, respectively. Consistent with this latter finding, there was a marginal tendency toward lower pedestrian miss rates with the analog relative to digital speedometer, $F(1, 12) = 2.77$, $p<.15$. Pedestrian miss rates were 18.1% and 22% with analog and digital speedometers, respectively.

4. GENERAL DISCUSSION

The results indicated a consistent advantage for the conventional, mechanical, circular, analog speedometer over the digital speedometer. Results from dual task performance indicated that drivers were more accurate at controlling their speed with the analog speedometer while glancing less often at it. Although average E-O-R time per speedometer glance tended to be slightly longer for the analog speedometer, the tradeoff between average E-O-R time to the speedometer and glance frequency (as measured by percent E-O-R time to the speedometer) favored the analog over the digital speedometer. That is, the longer E-O-R time per glance to the analog speedometer was more than offset by the lower glance frequency to the analog speedometer, so that there was a trend towards a lower total E-O-R time to the speedometer with the analog format. This finding is consistent with the marginal trend indicating that drivers did a superior job of detecting targets with the analog speedometer. This pattern of results held for both age groups and for both types of speed task.

The observed advantage for the analog speedometer may be due to several causes. First, the analog format provides direct, continuously available information on the rate at which vehicle speed is changing and the direction in which vehicle speed is changing. In contrast, the driver can only obtain this same information from a digital speedometer by making a more difficult inference based upon successive speed digit readouts. Consequently, from a single glance at the speedometer, the driver may have more information on the rate and the direction of a speed change with an analog speedometer. A second possible reason for the observed results is that the analog format may provide more speed information in the driver's peripheral vision, such as the angle and movement of the speedometer pointer and perhaps a gross readout of speed information. In contrast, the only likely speed information available with digital speedometers in peripheral vision is the presence of some change in vehicle speed. The higher average eyes-off-road time for a single glance to the analog speedometer may have been due to the higher demands on driver visual acuity required for reading out speed from the analog speedometer, or to drivers prolonging their glances to the analog speedometer until rate and direction of speed information became available.

There are several reasons why we feel these results may generalize to real world driving. First, the positioning of the two speedometer formats in the test vehicles (noncentral for the analog, central for the digital) match their positioning in the majority of production vehicles. The observed advantage for the analog speedometer might be expected to increase with a central location. Second, these results were obtained with both a precise speed and a speed range task. Third, the overall 95 ms advantage in mean E-O-R time per speedometer glance found for the digital speedometer corresponds closely to the 70-100 ms overall digital advantage in fixation duration reported in the Ishii (1980) road study.

It is also worthwhile to address some of the limitations of this study. First, these effects may not generalize to experienced digital speedometer users or to older age groups. Second, there are a number of factors which play a role in optimizing speedometer displays (e.g., format, size, location, contrast, etc.). However, none of these factors would appear to be able to compensate for the inherent differences in the formats mentioned above. Third, it could be argued that the current experimental conditions artificially produced the observed results. Relative to the current experimental conditions, drivers in the real world have a larger amount of information available to determine both absolute and, more particularly, relative speed (e.g., vestibular cues, peripheral and central visual stimulation, angular velocities at various portions of the visual field). (For a more detailed discussion of the perception of forward speed during driving, see Riemersma (1984)). However, it seems likely that driver judgments about absolute speed (and to a lesser extent relative speed) depend at least partly on speedometer readings, particularly under degraded visibility conditions. Furthermore, it could be argued that driver workload is lower in the real world than under these experimental conditions. However, the practical consequences of speedometer format should be most evident under high workload conditions.

In conclusion, results from this study demonstrate a consistent performance advantage for the analog speedometer for the conditions studied. Further research will be required in order to recommend one format conclusively over the other. Most importantly, further studies should examine the consequences of speedometer format in real world driving.

5. ACKNOWLEDGEMENTS

This work was completed under a GM summer internship to the first author. We would like to give special thanks to Ronald J. Moller and Theodore P. Mugabi-Jordan for their significant contributions to this study.

6. REFERENCES

Ishii, I., (1980) Comparison of visual recognition time of analogue and digital displays in automobiles, SAE Paper 800354, Society of Automotive Engineers.

Riemersma, J.B.J., (1984) The perception of speed during car driving. Report No. IZF C-11. Soesterberg, The Netherlands: Institute for Perception TNO.

Simmonds, G.R.W., Galer, M., & Baines, A., (1981) Ergonomics of electronic displays, SAE Paper No 810826, Society of Automotive Engineers.

VISION IN VEHICLES – IV
A.G. Gale et al. (Editors)

VISUAL DETECTION OF IN-CAR WARNING LAMPS AS A FUNCTION OF THEIR POSITION

G. LABIALE

INRETS, 109 avenue Salvador Allende, Case 24, Bron cedex, France

Abstract

The aim of this study was to determine the optimum position of a warning lamp on a car dashboard on taking account of the performances of drivers in visually detecting the operation of the lamps, of their preferences and of the effects on the driving task. Tests were carried out with a Peugeot 405 car fitted with four flashing warning lamps, one fitted on the instrument panel and the other three along the top of the dashboard, one to the left, one in front and one to the right of the driver. Results showed that the optimum location of a warning lamp was at the top of the dashboard immediately below the windscreen and slightly to the right of the driver (viewing angle of 5 to 10 degrees) so that it was not obscured by the steering wheel. The results also suggested the concept of a "functional attention field.

1. INTRODUCTION

The technical development of motor vehicles should lead in the years to come to a transformation or even a complete rearrangement of the driving position and in particular of the way information is displayed on the dashboard. We know that it is, and will continue to be, of prime importance that the driver should be immediately informed of any mechanical failure of his vehicle (so that he can bring it quickly to a halt) or of any significant difficulties on the roads (so that he can alter his speed, trajectory or itinerary). We also know that, while an audible warning is detected more rapidly than a visual one (Panik, 1984; Bouis et al, 1979), such a warning can alarm the driver and disturb his driving task. Thus one solution aimed at reducing the high density of information presented to the driver on future arrangements of the dashboard would be to provide a single warning lamp that would be readily detectable in all driving situations. Operation of this lamp would be associated with the display of explanatory information (giving the reason for the warning) on a small screen which could be consulted later. The remaining problem is then to determine the ergonomic requirements for the warning lamp on the car dashboard, with a view to minimising the time taken by the driver to detect its operation.

A first ergonomic approach to this problem has already been made, where warning lamps were displayed at different locations on the windscreen and dashboard, has already been made (Labiale and Mamberti, 1989). Reflections of the illuminated warning lamps onto the wind- screen were considered to interfere with the perception of the road environment and to have a distracting effect on the driving task. The results of this first approach enabled us to decide on other possible locations for a warning lamp, namely in the zone where the windscreen meets the dashboard or on the instrument panel.

2. OBJECT OF THE RESEARCH

The object of this study was to determine the optimum location of the warning lamp. The tests that were carried out were accordingly concerned with locations of the warning lamp on the instrument panel and along the strip of the dashboard in front of the driver, immediately below the windscreen, with a view to determining:

- The performance of drivers in detecting the operation of the lamps.
- The subjective evaluations of the warning lamp displays by the drivers.
- The effects on the driving task.

3. TEST PROCEDURE

3.1. Subjects
A total of 36 subjects (22 men, 14 women) aged between 18 and 76 years participated in the tests.

3.2. Car and equipment employed
Tests were carried out with each of the subjects travelling on their own in a Peugeot 405 vehicle fitted with a system of four directly illuminated warning lamps. One of these lamps (E2) was fitted on the instrument panel and the other three (E1, E3 and E4) along the top of the dashboard immediately below the windscreen (see Figure 1).

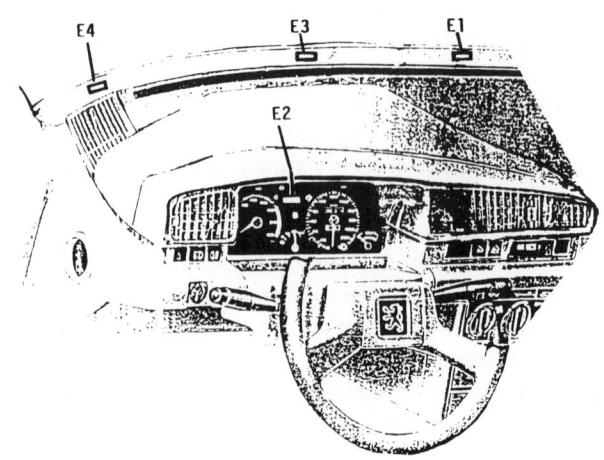

Figure 1 Location of the warning lamps within the test vehicle

The four warning lamps were connected to a Compaq 286, Portable III microcomputer located in the rear of the vehicle. This microcomputer controlled the operation of each warning lamp independently of the others, as well as the recording the time that each subject took to react to the operation of each warning lamp (using a response lever to the right of the steering wheel).

The performance of each driver during the test was recorded by means of a tape recorder and a camera.

The warning lamps were red, were 3.2cm wide by 0.9cm high and were each fitted with two 12v, 1.2W bulbs giving a luminance of 200 cd/m². The flashing operation of a warning lamp consisted of alternating periods of 350 ms on and 250 ms off.

3.3. Test course

The test course was 26 km long and ran mainly through town, where there was a constant density of traffic. It took about 45 minutes to drive around this course.

The tests were carried out during the day between 0830 and 1730 hours in both sunny and overcast weather conditions.

3.4. Experimental procedure

Each subject was alone in the vehicle and in a real traffic situation.

The maximum length of time for which a warning lamp remained on, if the driver failed to detect it and to operate the response lever, amounted to 15 seconds. The interval of time between the extinction of any warning lamp and the operation of the next one amounted to 150 seconds on average with a random variation of 30 seconds.

Just before starting the tests, the subjects were informed that a warning lamp would be illuminated at different locations in the vicinity of the driver. They were not told exactly where the lamps would be located but simply that they would be in their "field of vision".

The drivers were expected to operate a lever located to the right of the steering wheel as soon as they detected the operation of a warning lamp. The computer responded to this action by switching off the lamp concerned and recording the reaction time of the subject.

Three successive sequences of random operation of the warning lamps were executed during each test run. Only the second sequence was considered for analysis in order to avoid (a) the effects of surprise applying during execution of the first sequence and (b) the effects of the experience that would have been gained by the subject on executing the third.

At the end of the tests each subject completed a questionnaire concerned with their preferences, the subjective acceptability of the system and with any objectionable effects due to its operation.

Each subject was also subjected to two psychological tests:

-An Eysenk E.P.I. test which "determines the personality in terms of two dimensions which are generally independent of one another: extroversion-introversion (E) and neuroticism-stability (N)" and a Stroop stress test which "serves to predict the aptitude of a subject to maintain a satisfactory level of performance in a conflicting perceptive-cognitive situation".

3.5. Basis of the test procedure

We considered the following test variables:

- Location of the warning lamps (4 different locations).
-Individual driver variables such as age, sex, driving experience (number of years of holding a driving licence and distance covered per year) and the results of the psychological tests (Eysenk E.P.I. and Stroop tests).

The following was recorded or noted for each subject:

-The times taken in detecting the operation of a warning lamp.
-The subjective preferences (with regard to visibility and location of the warning lamps, the choice of system and the way in which the lamps were operated).
-Interference with the driving task (with regard to surprise reactions due to unexpected operation of the warning lamp, corrections to the driving trajectory, and any distraction or annoyance).

4. RESULTS

4.1. Visual detection times of the drivers

4.1.1. Recorded detection times
The average time taken for the visual detection of the warning lamps ranged from 2.09 to 3.62 seconds between locations and the individual times, again for all locations ranged from 0.76 to 13.90 seconds (As seen in Table 1).

Lamp and location	Reaction time (seconds)			
	Average	Standard deviation	Maximum	Minimum
E1 (to the right)	3.62	3.10	0.77	13.89
E2 (below)	2.09	0.99	0.76	4.95
E3 (in front)	2.32	1.17	1.37	6.76
E4 (to the left)	3.60	2.92	0.77	13.90

Table 1 Driver reaction times for each warning lamp location

4.1.2. Effect of the location of the warning lamps on the time of detection
The visual detection times clearly differ with the location of the warning lamps.
A one-way analysis of variance showed the significant effect of the location of the

warning lamps on the visual detection times of the drivers: $F_{(3.140)} = 4.54$, $p < 0.01$ (with or without equality of the variances).

Pair-wise comparisons of the average reaction times between locations of the warning lamps yielded the results given in Table 2, This Table shows that there were no significant differences between the average reaction times for warning lamps E1 and E4 (to the right and left at the top of the dashboard respectively) or for E2 and E3 (on the instrument panel and in the central position at the top of the dashboard respectively). On the other hand there are significant differences between the average reaction times of for warning lamps E1 and E2, E1 and E3, E2 and E4 and E3 and E4.

Lamp locations	t Student	d.f.	P <	Significant difference
E1/E2	3.04	35	0.004	+
E1/E3	2.64	35	0.01	+
E1/E4	0.4	35	0.96	0
E2/E3	− 0.85	35	0.39	0
E2/E4	− 2.98	35	0.05	+
E3/E4	− 2.32	35	0.02	+

Table 2 Comparison of the average reaction times as a function of the warning lamp locations

In other words, if we consider these results as a whole, we can say that there are two favoured locations for which the drivers were able to detect operation of the warning lamps more rapidly. These locations are on the instrument panel (lamp E2) and in the central position at the top of the dashboard (lamp E3). The locations to the right and left at the top of the dashboard are associated with longer reaction times.

4.1.3. Relationship between psychological characteristics of the drivers and the detection times

Studies of the statistical relationships (correlations and chi^2) did not revealed any significant effect ($p > 0.01$) of the following variables on the detection times: age, driving experience, level of study and the personality factors that were considered (dimensions of the Stroop and Eysenk tests) Nevertheless it was thought that it would be interesting to consider how these different variables were structured.

A Principal Component Analysis was performed to investigate the structure in relation to the following variables: age, driving experience, time of reaction to the operation of a

G. Labiale

warning lamp on the instrument panel, speed of response to the Stroop test and the introversion-extroversion dimension of the drivers. Three principal factors could be defined and these accounted for 84.2% of the explained variance: factor 1 which takes account of 43.4% of the explained variance on referring to the age of the drivers and their driving experience; factor II which takes account of 24.8% of the variance on referring to the time of reaction to the operation of a warning lamp and the speed of response to a Stroop test and factor III which takes account of 18% of the variance on referring to the psychological dimension "introversion-extroversion" of the drivers.

4.2. Subjective evaluations of the physical characteristics of the warning lamps

The drivers gave their subjective evaluations of the following characteristics of the warning lamps: visibility, preferred location, mode of operation.

4.2.1. Visibility of the warning lamps

Most of the drivers (As shown in Table 3) considered that the visibility of all four warning lamps was acceptable. It should be noted, however, that the location of lamp E4 (to the left at the top of the dashboard) was considered to be definitely less visible by 38.9% of the drivers (notwithstanding the fact that this lamp had the same luminance as the others).

Lamp and location	Visibility (%)		
	Good	Bad	No answer
E1 (to the right)	75	22.2	2.8
E2 (below)	75	22.2	2.8
E3 (in front)	94.4	2.8	2.8
E4 (to the left)	58.3	38.9	2.8

Table 3 Visibility of the warning lamps

4.2.2. Preferred locations of the warning lamps

Table 4 shows how most of the drivers preferred the location of the warning lamp to be either at E3 in the central position at the top of the dashboard (47.2%) or at E2 at a lower level on the instrument panel (38.9%): chi^2 = O.51, d.f.= 1, non-significant difference. Conversely the locations to the right and left at the top of the dashboard were rejected, particularly the location of lamp E4 which was never favoured.

4.2.3. Mode of operation and acceptance of the warning lamps

Most of the drivers (89%) preferred a flashing to a continuously illuminated lamp (11%). Some 78% of the drivers also thought that the warning lamp should be controlled in an automatic way by the system. Finally, it should be noted that 75% of the drivers who were questioned were prepared to accept this system based on the operation of a single warning lamp.

Lamp and location	Subjects preferring the location	
	Number	Percentage
E1 (to the right)	5	13.89
E2 (below)	14	38.89
E3 (in front)	17	47.72
E4 (to the left)	0	0

Table 4 Preference for location of the warning lamps

4.3. Subjective evaluations of interference with the driving of a car due to the operation of the warning lamps

According to the results given in Table 5, operation of flashing lights on the dashboard does not seem to interfere with driving whether this is a matter of control of the driving trajectory, interference with the perception of the external road environment or distraction of the attention needed for driving. However it should be noted that 8% of the drivers referred to the disturbing effect of the location of warning lamp E2 on the control of the driving trajectory. The basic argument of these drivers was that it was necessary to lower the eyes to the instrument panel in order to see this lamp and so to look away from the road. Finally it seems that the display of these flashing lights gave rise to a surprise effect for 36% of the drivers.

5. DISCUSSION AND CONCLUSIONS

In general the reaction times (between 2.09 and 3.60 seconds on average) that we recorded on operating warning lamps on the dashboard seemed to be longer than those mentioned in the literature (Olson, 1989), which report average reaction times of between 0.8 and 1.9 seconds for the visual detection of an event or incident on the road. A number

Effect	Subjects affected		Subjects unaffected	
	(N⁰)	(%)	(N⁰)	(%)
Surprised by operation of the lamp	13	36.1	23	63.8
Need to rectify driving trajectory	3	8.3	33	91.7
Disturbance to external perception	2	5.6	34	94.4
Distraction	4	11.1	31	86.1

Table 5 Numbers and percentage of drivers disturbed by the effects of the operation of a warning lamp

of reasons can be put forward in accounting for this difference:

- The task of detecting a warning lamp in the driving position is concerned with the peripheral vision of the driver and calls for the latter to direct his visual attention for a short instant from the road to the dashboard before deciding to operate the response lever.

- Our tests were not carried out on a test track or a road free of traffic but in urban driving conditions and we know that the more complex the road situation the greater the mental load on the driver and the longer his reaction times (Miura, 1986).

With our sample of drivers, Principal Component Analyses showed up three significant factors, namely factor 1 concerning driving experience, factor 2 concerning the speed of response and factor 3 concerning the psychological characteristics.

The central locations of lamps E2 and E3 in comparison with the side locations of lamps E1 and E4 generally correspond to the near, central vision and the peripheral vision zones of the drivers respectively and it should be noted that while drivers can carry out visual explorations within the whole of their visual field of view, they spend most of their time acquiring information within the central field. This explains why the best performances were obtained for the detection of the centrally located warning lamps. However, it would seem that we need to consider the results obtained for the location of lamp E2 (lower, centre) on the instrument panel, where the driver has to lower his direction of view by 20 to 25 degrees from the horizontal, in relation to other results. In fact everything indicates that it is the past experience of acquiring information from the instrument panel (exploration and attention) that facilitates the detection of this lamp E2.

The subjective preferences for the location of the warning lamps seem to be in agreement with the visual detection performances. It also seems that the drivers did not consider that operation of these lamps interfered with the driving task.

It is therefore suggested that the optimum location of a warning lamp would be on the dashboard, immediately below the windscreen and slightly displaced from the central position at a viewing angle of 5 to 10 degrees to the right. This slight displacement to the right would ensure that the lamp would not be obscured by the steering wheel.

This prompts us to put forward the concept of a "functional attention field" in order to be able to explain how information in certain "favoured" zones of the environment can be taken into account. This concept can be distinguished from those of the "visual field" and the "attention field". What we have described as a "functional attention field" accordingly corresponds to an attention field that has been structured for an task performed regularly. Thus, for a given visual field, the functional attention field will deal with the strategies for the acquisition of information taking account of particular zones, as well as with selective preparation routines and the search for information needed for the control of the task.

Thus, in the case of the task of driving a car, the "functional attention field" will include a definite and relatively stable configuration for the acquisition of information from the road environment and secondarily from the dashboard. The introduction of a new information system on the dashboard means that the driver will have to adapt or restructure his usual functional attention field. In this context, the frontal zone of the dashboard immediately below the windscreen could constitute the optimum location for the display of warning signals and could be included without any difficulties in the usual functional attention field of the driver.

6. ACKNOWLEDGEMENTS

Thanks are due to the JAEGER company (Studies and Research Department) who paid for this study contract.

7. REFERENCES

Bouis, D., Voss, M., Geiser, G. and Haller, R., (1979) Visual auditory displays for different tasks of a car driver. Proceedings of the Human Factors Society 23rd Annual Meeting, 35- 39.

Labiale, G., and Mamberti, M.L., (1989) Etude psycho-ergonomique de different voyants d'alerte dans le poste de conduite automobile, IRT report (JAEGER contract), NNV, 8901.

Miura, T., (1986) Coping with situational demands: a study of eye movements and peripheral vision performances, in Vision in Vehicles. Gale, A; et al. (Eds.) Vision in Vehicles, North Holland, Amsterdam.

Olson, P.F., (1989) Driver perception response time. SAE Paper, N° 890731, Society of Automotive Engineers.

Panik, F., (1984) Fahrzeugkybernetik. Papers for the XX FISITA Congress: Das Automobil in der Zukunft, SAE Publication P143, SAE Paper 8445101; 3,273-3,284.

VISION IN VEHICLES – IV
A.G. Gale et al. (Editors)
© 1993 Elsevier Science Publishers B.V. All rights reserved.   301

IN-VEHICLE DISPLAYS: HEAD-UP DISPLAY FIELD TESTS

Andreas SPRENGER

Forschungsgemeinschaft Auto-Sicht-Sicherheit e.V., Universitätsstraße 5, 5000 Köln 41,
Germany

Abstract
    The effects of a Head-Up Display (HUD) on drivers were tested under field conditions
and compared with those of a conventional instrument. The effects of stress, speed control
and monitoring the instruments on 36 male subjects were studied. Subjects were required
to drive twice along a test route of 87 km with identical VW Passats (VW Dasher), one of
which was equipped with a HUD. Eye movements were registered by an electro-oculogram
(EOG); speed and heartbeat rate were recorded simultaneously per computer.
    It was found that the HUD - a digital device - was read more often and faster than the
conventional speedometer - an analogue device. Reading of the speed from the HUD was
much easier than from the conventional speedometer, as was shown by parameters of the
eye movements and from subjective comments made by the subjects.
    The effects on speed control were insignificant. A slight reduction in frequency of
exceeding the speed limit was observed.

1. INTRODUCTION

    While driving, reading the speedometer is an action that is taken by the driver more or
less often. Normally, he or she has to glance away from traffic to an analogue speedometer
on the dashboard. Head-Up-Displays (HUD), which have been used for some time now in
aviation, have recently been applied to automobiles. Discussions of gains for traffic safety
and for the driver have been a matter of controversy.
    As a contribution to this discussion, the Forschungsgemeinschaft Auto-Sicht-Sicherheit
A.S.S.e.V. explored the effects of the HUD on eye movements, stress and behaviour as
regards speed.
    In July and August 1990, 36 subjects were required to drive along a test route which
included all types of streets:

- motorways with and without speed limits
- suburban roadways
- wide and narrow inner city streets

    Subjects were instructed to drive as usual, which meant not to drive fast or in an unusual
manner. They were also instructed that, in the event of being detected speeding by means

of radar, they would have to bear the consequences.

The experiment had to be constructed in such a manner so as to fulfill two requirements:

-        The test conditions should be comparable with normal conditions
-        Sufficient criteria were needed to register differences in behaviour in reading the two speedometers

2. TEST DESIGN

The test situation had to be similar to normal conditions of driving and reading an instrument. This can best be realized in field tests. These requirements produced the criteria which had to be fulfilled by the subjects.

1.   They had to be drivers of the test car model; i.e. they had to be drivers of a VW Passat (Dasher) model B3 with a petrol engine and gear transmission.
2.   They had to have had a minimum of five years driving experience. This requirement eliminated unnessesary eye movements common to beginners at driving (Cohen & Zwahlen, 1989).
3.   They had to be male. This requirement was based on experiments which showed different driving behaviour between the sexes (Hundhausen, 1991).
4.   They had to have a visual acuity of visus 1.0 at far distance.

These requirements reduced the group of prospective subjects. It was not possible to randomize age, height or annual driving mileage.

Criteria to be registered were eye movements, heartbeat rate and driving speed. For the registration of eye movements, a portable electro-occulogram (EOG) was used. Four electrodes connected to a preamplifier were attached by adhesive adjacent to the eyes of the subjects. The preamplifier was placed behind the headrest so that the subjects had no visual contact with the experimental equipment. The electric potentials from the eyes were transmitted to the EOG which was placed behind the driver. The EOG was connected to a portable computer in which the eye movement data was calculated and stored.

This measuring system verified by means of a scanning rate at 1000 per sec. whether the potential change in the electrodes was due to

-        an eye movement, i.e. saccadic movement;
-        a blink of the eye;
-        noise, an insignificant potential change; an involuntary quiver of the eye or nystagmus.

In the event of a saccadic movement or a blink of the eye, several data were registered, namely the exact time and locality of the start and ending point of the saccadic movement or blink of the eye.

In order to enhance the validity of the evaluation method, the experimenter observed eye movements of the subjects by means of the rear-view mirror. If the subject was observed making a reading, a registration was made on the computer record.

The adjustment of subjects to the electrodes adjacent to the eyes produced no problems.

Some people became so adjusted that at the end of the test they attempted to get out of the vehicle while still attached to the preamplifier

The heartbeat rate was registered once a second, and similarly the driving speed. Both vehicles were equipped with electronic speedometers so that the speed was recorded digitally.

The following vehicles were used: two VW Dasher B3, 1989 model with a 1.8l petrol engine, 100 kw (136 hp). Both vehicles were equipped with power steering, antilocking brake system and an air-conditioning system. The air-conditioning system was particularly useful in providing a comfortable atmosphere, as temperatures during the experiments were between 20 and 40 degrees Celsius.

The speedometer in the HUD is a reflection of digital speed data in a holographic mirror, a foil, which is placed between the two panes of the front windscreen. The distance from the virtual picture to the eye is about 280 cm in contrast to a distance of approximately 70 cm from the eye to the conventional speedometer on the dashboard.

The subjects were required to drive the route once with each vehicle. The order of usage and the time of day were selected at random. Following the first test drive, there was a pause of 30 minutes for relaxation.

The test route was made up of two sections: a training section and a test section. The training route led from the research institute over the motorway going north from Cologne to Leverkusen. Normally, it took approximately 25 to 35 minutes to travel this 19 km test route. The following 16 sections of the test route show the various characteristics:

- sections without speed limits were located on the A 59 motorway between Leverkusen and Düsseldorf with a length of 18.6 km.
- sections with speed limits were located at the end of the A 59 motorway, between Leverkusen and Cologne-North on the A 1 motorway and between Cologne-North and Cologne City on the A 57 motorway with a length of about 15.2 km.
- sections along rural highways from Düsseldorf to Monheim with a length of 4.8 km.
- sections with narrow city streets, having the added feature of parked vehicles along the way. The length here was 2,6 km.
- Wide inner city streets had speed limits between 60 and 100 km/h. Parts of these streets had two lanes in each direction. Their length was about 7.8km.

All sections of the test route had an equal traffic density independent of the time of day. The test condition "weather" was recorded, but was not varied systematically. During the tests there were four short periods of rain. Otherwise the weather was sunny or cloudy.

3. EVALUATION OF DATA

Some sections of the test route could not be used. Traffic jams, as well as problems with both vehicle and instruments, were responsible for reducing the sample size to 29 subjects for pair comparison.

Eye movements, registered by the instruments, were analysed in several steps. An interactive program made it possible to select those eye movements which were identified as a reading of the speedometer. Certain requirements had to be fulfilled:

- a saccadic movement from top to bottom in a precisely defined angle and amplitude; e.g.: an eye movement from the horizontal plane to the speedometer;
- eye movement back to the scene of traffic was one of the requirements which had to be fulfilled or there had to be a blink or a closing of the eyelids;
- the person conducting the test was required to register a mark in the test record which indicated a reading of the speedometer;
- readings which took less than 100 msec or more than 2000 msec were not included in the analysis.

All sections of the test route Length = 49 km, N = 29	Speedometer	Head-Up-Display	Level of Significance Wilcoxon-Test
Readings (registered by the person conducting the test)			
Mean	87.8	143.0	
Standard Deviation	59.4	88.2	
Median	79.0	106.0	
Minimum	11.0	36.0	0.0015
Maximum	206.0	358.0	
TOTAL	1843.0		
Movement to the speedometer			
Mean	37.8	58.0	
Standard Deviation	22.2	34.1	
Median	33.0	51.0	0.0025
Minimum	6.0	14.0	
Maximum	92.0	142.0	
TOTAL	1135.0	1972.0	
Movement to the speedometer in a time less than 800 msec			
Mean	25.0	44.3	
Standard Deviation	17.2	29.6	
Median	20.5	36.0	0.0008
Minimum	4.0	5.0	
Maximum	72.0	133.0	
TOTAL	749.0	1507.0	

Table 1: Frequency of readings

The heads of subjects were not held stationary, so that head movements were possible. The reading of the speedometer is a highly automatic action, so that head movements during the reading of the speedometer prevented the release of saccadic movements. For this reason some readings are missing.

More than 60 % of the readings which were registered by the experimenter conducting the test, could be identified as readings of the speedometer (given in Table 1). These readings made a precise evaluation possible. The data were treated at an ordinal level.

3.1. Frequency of readings

As the reading of the speedometer was rare, the readings for the entire test route have been summarised.

With the help of the Wilcoxon-test (ordinal level) it was found that the HUD was read more often than the conventional speedometer (p<.01).

Normally, the reading of a speedometer takes an average time of 450 to 650 ms (Färber and Färber, 1988; Bartholomäi et al, 1990). The analysis of readings, that took more than 100 msec and less than 800 msec revealed the same result, namely that the HUD is read more often.

Interpretations of the results may vary. To begin with, the effect of a new and unknown type of instrument may have influenced the driver. On the other hand, the HUD offers speed information close to the direct view as opposed to the conventional speedometer which requires a deliberate eye movement.

3.1.2 Display Recognition Time

Here, aggregated data shown in Table 2 was the basis for the following analysis: The mean and median of the display recognition time of each subject was used. The fact that some readings are missing is a result of the Wilcoxon-test for ordinal data. The time of fixation is, however, registered exactly so that Student's t-Test was also used.

The results for a time of fixation between 100 and 2000 msec indicate that it took more time to read a conventional analogue speedometer. It should be noted that some subjects may have read the other instruments on the dashboard which were not covered, in the interest of maintaining normal driving conditions. On the other hand, some subjects "inspected" the changing numbers in the HUD.

The results for fixations between 100 and 800 msec show nearly the same results. It should be noted here that readings of the speedometers were not under any time pressure and that subjects had the best driving conditions, such as daylight and mainly sunshine. Shorter periods of fixation may be expected in extreme situations.

It is considered that summation of all periods of fixation is not valid as a parameter for driving safety. There are two reasons for this. Firstly, all missing readings have to be considered, and secondly, it must be assumed that a driver will only read speed information when he considers the traffic scene not to be dangerous. The effects of different types of speedometers on a driver may be noticed in stress parameters and subjective opinions.

3.1.3 Parameters Of The Saccadic Eye Movement

Recent research on saccadic eye movement and the order of visual inputs indicates the importance of eye movements for solving cognitive tasks (Galley and Boldt 1985, Cohen

All sections of the test route	Speedo-	Head-up-	Level of significance (p)	
	meter	Display	Wilcoxon-Test	Students t-Test
Length = 49 km, N = 29				
Period of fixation Mean				
Mean	713.4	608.8		
Standard Deviation	144.9	140.4		
Median	711.0	618.5	0.174	0.011
Period of fixation Median				
Mean	619.5	511.5		
Standard Deviation	166.7	171.3		
Median	591.0	481.0	0.0202	0.020
Period of fixation less than 800 msec (Mean)				
Mean	446.5	410.2		
Standard Deviation	79.3	62.6		
Median	449.0	410.5	0.0504	0.038
Period of fixation less than 800 msec (Median)				
Mean	441.4	392.6		
Standard Deviation	102.6	81.7		
Median	447.0	404.5	0.0274	0.024

Table 2: Display recognition time

and Hirsig 1990). The speed of saccadic eye movement while reading an instrument may be considered as a parameter of activation and stress. The saccadic speed before looking at the speedometer was analyzed, as shown in Table 3, then the saccadic jump to the speedometer and back to the scene of traffic. As the HUD and the conventional speedometer had different locations and therefore different view angles, the saccadic speed was standardized at a saccade of 13°.

The last information input before reading the instruments is at a comparable level relating to saccadic speed. The eye movement from the scene of traffic to the conventional analogue speedometer occurs with a lower speed in comparison with the last information input and the eye movement back to the traffic scene. The reading of the HUD shows a contrary result, as shown by Figure 1. The levels of significance refers to the progress of eye movements and differ from those in Table 3.

A study of special sections of the test route, for example motorway sections with speed limit, shows the same effect in the reading of the conventional speedometer, but insgnificant changes in saccadic speed when reading the HUD.

All sections of the test route Length = 49 km, N = 29	Speedo- meter	Head-Up- Display	Level of significance (p)	
			Wilcoxon- Test	Students t-Test
Saccadic speed before reading (°s)				
Mean	298.5	290.2		
Standard Deviation	48.8	61.8	.3359	.549
Median	291.5	275.5		
Saccadic speed jump to the speedometer (°s)				
Mean	241.7	312.0		
Standard Deviation	71.7	88.2	.0002	.000
Median	222.0	300.0		
Saccadic speed jump back to traffic (°s)				
Mean	305.0	284.6		
Standard Deviation	84.9	63.5	.0571	.103
Median	281.0	281.5		

Table 3: Standarized saccadic speed at readings

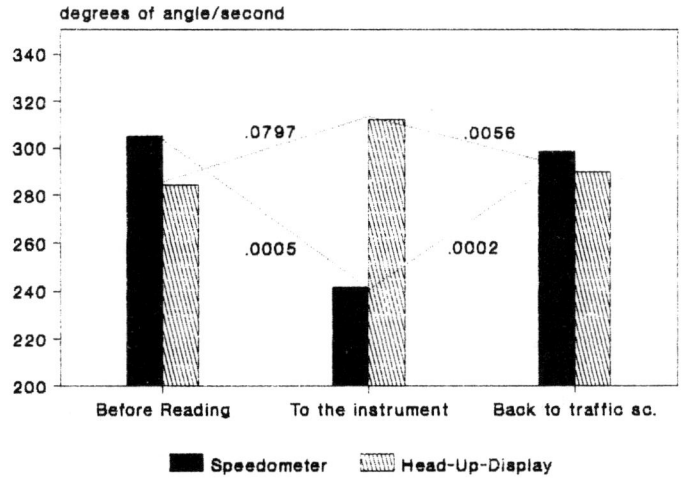

Fig. 1: Saccadic speed

The heart beat rate, as a parameter of physiological stress, showed no differences between driving in the two cars. Signs of fatigue could be seen in using the cars.

3.2. Effects on driving speed

The analysis of the driving speed with no vehicle in front revealed a slight trend to a less exceeding of the speed limit while using the vehicle equipped with the HUD. The results were insignificant.

3.3. Subjective rating

After completing the test route, subjects were requested to give their opinions in a semi-structured interview and to discuss their experiences with each speedometer. Among subjects, 80.6% noticed a shorter time for reading the HUD. while 77.4% maintained that it was easier to read the HUD than the conventional speedometer. Only one subject maintained that the HUD was disturbing, saying that it was as if a piece of paper was lying in front of his view. All other subjects thought of the HUD as a normal instrument. Sixty-nine percent maintained that it took less than 20 minutes to adjust to the HUD. The digital form of speed information highlights any exceeding of speed limits on inner city streets. Some subjects mentioned that they had a bad conscience with the HUD more often than with the conventional speedometer.

4. CONCLUSIONS

The field experiment showed that, in comparison with the conventional speedometer, speed information was read more often and in a shorter period of time with the HUD.

The eye movement data revealed a different quality of reading of the instruments. Cohen & Hirsig (1990) models of prediction for visual inputs while driving a difficult stretch of roadway. Thus, the order and the parameters of visual inputs are important. Galley (in press) suggests eye movement from the instrument back to the scene of traffic as a parameter for activation. It can be concluded that there is a higher activation and a higher degree of stress for the driver when reading the conventional speedometer than when reading speed information from the HUD.

Evidence from subjective statements support the psycho-physiological data. From this sample of drivers, it can be said that it is easier to read speed information from the HUD. It should be remembered that, during experiments in daylight, the conventional speedometer is placed against a darker background than the HUD which has nearly the same luminosity as the traffic scene. In addition, the HUD is placed 10° below the horizontal eyeline of the driver in comparison with 20° for the speedometer on the dashboard.

No effects bearing on driving speed could be observed by using vehicles with different speedometers. Only a slight trend to less exceeding of the speed limits was noticed with the HUD.

5. ACKNOWLEDGEMENTS

This study would not have been possible without the support of the Volkswagen AG, and in particular of Mr. J. Thomas and Dr. W. Zimdahl, both engineers as well as Dr. M.A. Beeck, physicist.

6. REFERENCES

Bartholomäi, G., Becker, O., Schneider, W. and Walter, W.,(1990) Ergonomische Bewertung der Ablesbarkeit digitaler Instrumente bei verschiedenen Lichtverhältnissen, in: Derkum, H.(ed.) Sicht und Sicherheit im Straßenverkehr, (Verlag TÜV Rheinland Köln), pp 7-12.

Cohen, A.S., and Hirsig, R., (1990) Zur Bedeutung des fovealen Sehens für die Informationsaufnahme bei hoher Beanspruchung, in: Derkum, H. (ed.), Sicht und Sicherheit im Straßenverkehr, (Verlag TÜV Rheinland Köln [Cologne]), pp 47-58.

Cohen, A.S. and Zwahlen, H.T., (1989) Blicktechnik in Kurven - Wissenschaftliches Gutachten, (bfu-Report 13, Bern).

Färber, B., and Färber, B., (1988) Grundlagen und Möglichkeiten der Nutzung sprachlicher Informationssysteme im Kraftfahrzeug - Hauptstudie, (Forschungsvereinigung Automobil Technik (FAT) Schriftenreihe, Heft 39, Frankfurt/M), p 120

Galley, N., Leistung und Aktivierung - aus der Sicht eines Neuropsychologen, in: Prinz, W. (ed.), Mensch und Technik (in press).

Galley, N. and Bodt, M., (1985) Short term performance and activation decrement in an eye movement task, in: Proceedings of the Workshop "Electro-encephalography in Transport Operations. Performance Decrement", (Interne Berichte der DFVLR [Internal report of the DFVLR], 1B-316-85-03 Köln).

VISION IN VEHICLES – IV
A.G. Gale et al. (Editors)

THE DRIVING SIMULATOR: AN AID FOR ERGONOMIC DESIGN OF CAR INTERIORS

Isabelle GUYARD

Renault, Research and Development, service 0076, Bernard Moteurs 2, 67 rue Galliéni, 92 500 Rueil Malmaison, France

Abstract

The driving simulator SCORE is designed to conduct human engineering studies on car interiors. It is a new means of testing to help ergonomists to assess the visual attention of drivers in connection with instrument scanning, and to measure any associated driving disturbance. The visual system simulates a sufficiently detailed road environment. The software can present any type of road scenery designed with the help of menus. Visual simulation is controlled by a mathematical model which describes the dynamic behavior of an automobile when the driver navigates through the visual database using traditional driving controls mounted inside a mock-up.

1. INTRODUCTION

The introduction of new types of instruments into cars has led to innovations in the data available to drivers concerning information on and monitoring of the vehicle as well as information about the road environment. However, these developments can result in an increased visual load with the attendant risk of distracting drivers from primary driving tasks (Guyard et al, 1989).

Faced with this problem, Renault identified the need for a design tool which would enable them to reproduce, for a representative population of drivers, a primary driving task (e.g. route-following or detection of external events) and to superimpose a secondary instrument-reading or use task upon it in order to measure the degree of distraction from the primary task caused by the secondary one.

The desire to be able to reproduce experiments exactly from one subject to another without danger and before the prototype could be installed in a vehicle, led Renault to develop SCORE [Simulateur de COnduite automobile pour Recherche en Ergonomie (ergonomic research driving simulator)] in 1987. Designed as a high-performance measurement tool using visual simulation but not as costly as moving base global simulators, SCORE was designed in collaboration with INRETS.

2. BACKGROUND

As the task of driving primarily involves the visual sense, it was this aspect which was given priority when designing SCORE. The aim was to provide a visual reproduction of road scenes in which drivers could operate in a realistic and interactive manner using conventional driving controls.

The simulation of a visual driving-workload had already been achieved in 1985 on a device called SMAV (Simulateur de Mobilisation de l'Attention Visuelle). This comprised a laser target describing random horizontal movements which was superimposed on a film of driving down a motorway, the camera being in the driver's position. Using a steering wheel, the subject was supposed to keep the target between two fixed limits representing the sides of the road. This electrical/optical equipment required a high-level of visual attention on the part of the driver, but since it was not synchronised with the film, did not allow for any anticipation of target movement.

However, it is clear that this ability to anticipate when following a route plays an essential role in driving and allows the driver to plan ahead of the current phase and not to respond with a simple reaction delay (Pham and Chatelet, 1973).

The emphasis was therefore placed on faithfulness of the reproduction in general. The specifications included:

- reproduction of a route-following task on a road with varying geometry.

- reproduction of a detection of simple events connected with traffic. These included:

> * following a vehicle with programmed indicators (brake lights, direction indicators).
> * overtaking.
> * oncoming vehicles.
> * obeying three-color traffic and road signals.

- demand for visual effort to accommodate the change from looking at the road to reading instruments.

- as faithful a reproduction as possible of the usable field of view in a light vehicle.

- reproduction of image resolution compatible with that of the eye.

- ensuring representative interaction between input driving commands and movements of the vehicle within the scene.

These specifications determined the design of the various elements of SCORE:

- a user-friendly data-base construction tool.

- real-time, high-performance visual simulation.

- A dynamic, real-time model, reproducing conditions in a light vehicle, including sound.

- A realistic and modular vehicle model.

3. DESIGN OF THE ROAD DATA-BASE TOOL

In order to provide display of existing or fictitious roads, or of projected roads, the technical solution for visual scenes was inclined towards three-dimensional synthesized image systems. This approach gives realistic reproduction of a scene and of any observer's eye position, useful for simulating different driving heights (from driving a light vehicle to an HGV) or for giving an aerial view of the road for use in navigation.

The data-base construction tool must be sufficiently "user-friendly" to allow a person who is not a computer specialist to be able to construct a road scene easily and quickly. This objective was attained with the concept of the data base in the form of a linear "strip of road" including in succession in a transverse section

> the road,
> markings,
> near-side hard shoulder.

The characteristics of geometry and arrangement of these elements are chosen from a tree-structure menu as shown in Figure 1. Equally, it is possible to insert a file into the route which produces the view of a junction of given complexity for which the user will specify the entry and exit point (eg round-about, crossing). Finally, when the ergonomist does not wish to reproduce a real route, it is possible to choose "random generation" of the route with an imposed minimum curve for bends. This type of solution allows for the instant generation of several kilometers of road.

Once this "strip of road" is created, a second phase consists of placing fixed objects in the scene (road signs, obstacles on the road, road construction works), in defining the conditions of visibility and colors along the route (good visibility, fog, day or night) and in specifying the scenarios of movements of the five mobile elements which can be included in the scene. Each mobile element, pedestrian or vehicle, is specified according to its path of movement, variations in its speed, the laws governing lighting of brake lights, direction indicators or traffic lights.

Entering the motion path for a mobile element is done by driving with the mouse and entering the "passage points" on the keyboard. This makes it extremely easy to simulate lane changes, avoiding of an obstacle, negotiating of a bend, fork or intersection. The software then interpolates between the input passage points. Entering other mobile element data is always done with the aid of menus and allows for construction of the following scenarios:

- The mobile element starts up at the same time as start up of the simulation or when the driver has reached a certain given distance, then continues its own evolution independently. This scenario makes it possible to impose strictly identical traffic conditions on different drivers.

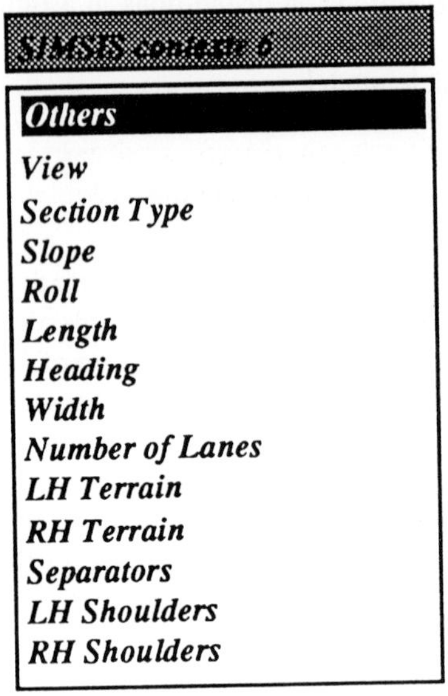

```
SIMSIS context 0

Others
View
Section Type
Slope
Roll
Length
Heading
Width
Number of Lanes
LH Terrain
RH Terrain
Separators
LH Shoulders
RH Shoulders
```

Figure 1. Main Menu

- Variations in the speed of the mobile element are unknown to the driver. The only indication given is approach or increasing of distance in relation to the vehicle. This allows for verification of whether a subject, when vision is removed from the road, retains visual awareness of the road environment and detects an approaching vehicle.

- The mobile element brakes for a given period and at a given rate of deceleration. Its brake lights are illuminated and its speed varies as a consequence. This makes it possible to see whether a driver detects a mobile element braking when following behind it. At present, triggering of braking depends only on a time setting. However, it could be triggered when the distance between the two vehicles drops below a threshold fixed by the controller of the experiment.

   All the scenarios have been defined in consultation with ergonomists, with the aim of imposing visual workload on drivers and estimating the level of visual awareness they retain of the immediate external environment (vehicle being followed, oncoming or overtaking vehicle) and of investigating the capacity of drivers for acquisition of "priority" information while reading instruments.
   To provide maximum flexibility, it is possible to associate different arrangements of objects and mobile-element scenarios on a given route. In particular, this allows ergonomists to take their subjects through the experimental route without traffic or obstacles during the familiarization phase and then to add the experiment scenario to start the measurement phase.

4. REAL-TIME VISUAL SIMULATION

4.1. Interactivity
Once the scene has been constructed with the tool described above, it is possible to move around within it using the workstation mouse or driving controls. In the first case, a sideways movement of the mouse on the pad simulates a change of heading for the vehicle and a longitudinal movement a change in speed. This solution is immediately active and gives an instantaneous dynamic view of the scene. The second case applies during the simulation phase. Then, the heading and speed data are transmitted directly from the model vehicle to the workstation, where they are interpreted for calculation of the image to be displayed.

4.2. Real-time
In both previous cases, a minimum image-refresh rate must be ensured to avoid the drivers' visual sense being affected. This basic requirement for ergonomic applications was taken into account by, on the one hand, limiting the complexity of the objects displayed and varying level of detail with distance from the observer, and, on the other hand, by systematic optimization in the software made possible by the architecture chosen for the data-base.

On most route simulations created by ergonomists, an image-refresh rate of 20 Hz can be provided and this is judged satisfactory. This rate remains closely linked to the type of machine used. A more recent version of the graphics hardware provides a refresh rate of 30 Hz for the same route. In this case, the normal video standard of presentation can be reproduced.

4.3. Resolution and field of view
The resolution of the image is another aspect of visual simulation vital for ergonomists and this also depends on the hardware used. Here a distinction must be made between calculated image resolution and displayed image resolution. The calculated image resolution depends on the size of the machine's pixel-plan and of the cone of vision defined when the image is generated. This latter parameter is calculated so as to represent as well as possible the field of vision delimited by the windshield of a light vehicle in real-time performance; the larger the cone, the better will be the subject's visual impression. However, the greater the number of objects to be displayed, the more the refresh rate will be degraded. The value of 60° in the horizontal plane, resulting from this necessity for compromise, gives, with the graphic station's 1280 pixels/line, a resolution of 3 minutes of an arc for the calculated image.

The resolution of the image displayed depends on its size. Use of a video projector provides an alternative to use of a monitor screen which requires more localized attention and limited movements of the eyes of an observer. In order to give the subject a feeling of reality, the image must be large. SCORE, with its 3m50 width image and 1280 pixels/line resolution at the graphic station, gives a displayed-image resolution of 2.7mm.

In order to obtain the calculated image resolution defined above, the vehicle mock-up has been positioned so that the observer's eye is at 3.2m from the projected image. This distance has been approved by the ergonomists whose aim is also to reproduce the effort of adjusting eye focus which is required during driving, looking from onboard instruments which are close to distant objects on the road.

5. ARCHITECTURE OF THE SCORE SIMULATOR

SCORE was designed as a mid-range simulator in order to produce an inexpensive tool for use by design departments. It was the visual simulation which required the largest investment, both for software and hardware. However, to attain a sufficient overall level of realism, it was necessary to develop, around the display system, other elements which consist of the host computer and sound reproduction system which complete the SCORE architecture, as shown in Figure 2.

5.1. The host computer
The main simulator functions are managed by a central or "host" computer which sends the commands to the different dedicated systems for visual and sound reproduction. Its tasks are as follows:

- control of simulation loop between driving input commands and the different presentations.

- acquisition of the steering wheel angle, travel of brake, accelerator and clutch pedals and gear lever position.

- animation of speed indicators and rev. counters.

- dynamic vehicle calculations.

- management of communications with graphics workstation.

- management of interface with sound sampler.

- storage of measurements.

Each of these points is therefore realized on a micro-computer, with standard boards and software interfaces.

5.2. Sound reproduction
The host machine calculates the various sound-simulation parameters and sends them via a MIDI interface to a sampler which stores real sound recordings. This makes it possible to reproduce engine noise, rolling noise, squealing of tires, noise of oncoming traffic and an alarm if the vehicle goes off the road.
These data are necessary for the driver to give a better impression of speed in the simulator and compensate for the absence of dynamic reproduction.

5.3. The driving cab
The driving cab for the SCORE simulator is designed to meet the following needs:

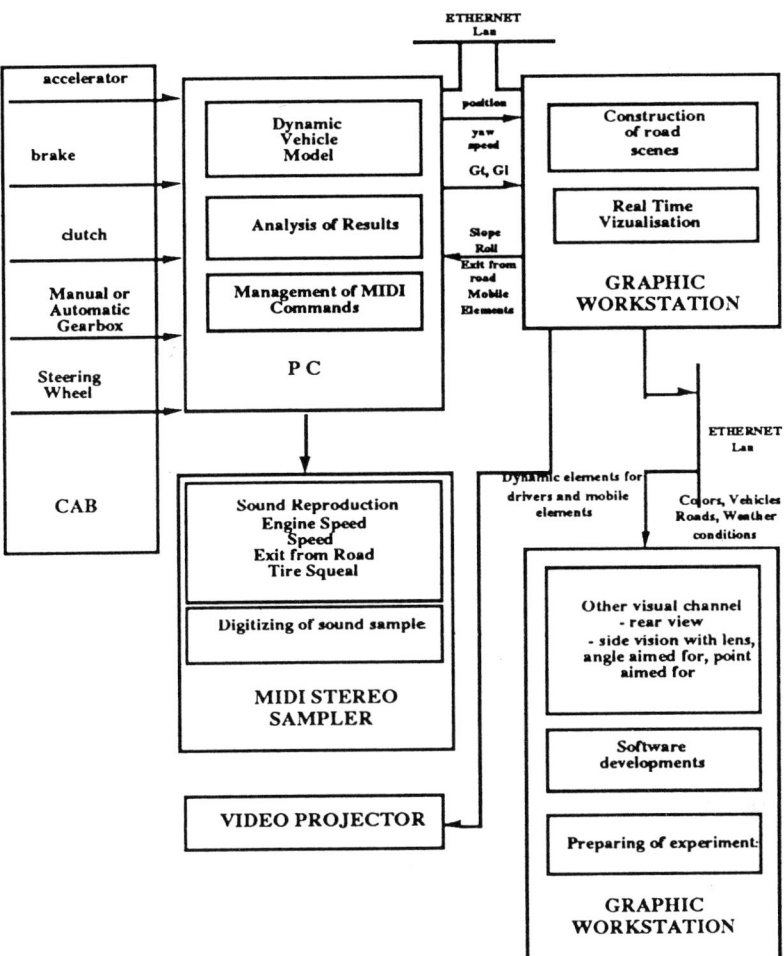

Figure 2 . Architecture of the SCORE simulator
changing of gear lever and clutch pedal when using automatic and manual transmissions.

- to house the driving controls which are the steering wheel and pedals, allowing for easy

- accurate reproduction of the relative positions of the pedals, seat and steering wheel as
well as the field of vision through the windshield of a given vehicle from the Renault range.

- rapid installation of instruments with precise positioning on the dashboard.

   A half-cab has been specially made from materials which are easy to work and to cut.
This respects the internal architecture of a future vehicle in the middle of the Renault range.
All of the meters and warning lights form an interchangeable block. The dashboard has

been cut out to allow for installation of a 9" (Macintosh SE format) screen at different heights in the central console. A support which can be masked has been installed in front of the passenger's seat to allow for the installation of equipment.

Finally the hood, mounted on castors and completely removable, allows for installation in the front part of the cab in which the simulator electronics are grouped.

This provides the ergonomist with a cab which is both modular and realistic in design in which the multi-function screen tools for creation of prototypes can be installed.

5.4. Measurement system

The SCORE simulator is a design study tool for ergonomists allowing for the creation of controllable and reproducible driving situations. SCORE has the additional advantage of facilitating collection of certain measurements which are more difficult to obtain in real driving conditions.

The measurements of relevance to ergonomists are those relating to route-following and detection of events in the external environment. The SCORE software allows for storage of the following parameters in a standard file:

- time
- steering wheel angle
- travel of brake and accelerator pedals
- position of gear lever
- vehicle speed
- engine speed
- various parameters linked to vehicle dynamics
- the absolute coordinates of the vehicle in the scene
- lateral deviation of route in relation to road center
- road camber
- leaving the road
- a reference signal triggered by the experiment controller
- the distance to mobile elements
- the status of mobile element lights
- speed of mobile elements

These parameters are important for analysis of:
- activity of driver controls
- driving performance
- response time to different signals

It is also possible to couple the SCORE simulator to different measurement systems, such as eye movement detection, so that the drivers' visual activity and driving performance can be analysed together (Kerihuel, 1989).

6. CALIBRATION OF THE TOOL

As we have already stated, the SCORE simulator is designed as a tool for the production of a visual workload for the driver. It is therefore logical to validate the system by quantifying the visual attention which it requires and by comparing the results with those obtained in real driving conditions (Laya and Neboit, 1983). Experiments are presently being conducted with this aim. Four positions have been defined for instruments in the model vehicle (Hella and Hartemann, 1982). A digital display device whose rate of display can be altered, is placed in each of the positions in in succession. The road scene which is being used is shown in Figure 3.

The driver, proceeding at a given steady speed, is instructed to remain on the road, driving in the right hand lane.   When he feels ready, the driver is asked to read aloud a pre-determined number of figures on the display, doing this in a single operation without looking back at the road.

On the simulator, the deviation in route is measured directly ; in real driving conditions, it is measured with the help of an optical system on a vehicle equipped with instruments. The aim of comparison is to calibrate the driving task on the simulator (by setting speed, width of road) to obtain performance levels comparable with those measured on the road. Once calibration is completed, the first experiments on a prototype instrument arrangement can be carried out on the SCORE simulator, for analysis and prediction of real driving conditions.

Figure 3. Example of road scene for calibration of the SCORE driving simulator

7. CONCLUSION

The SCORE simulator is presently providing Renault ergonomists with a tool for the first phases in development of onboard instruments. It is a useful complement to the expert knowledge and other methods employed in ergonomics as it provides "objective" measurement of interface compatibility in driving and of drivers' visual strategies. Its use makes it possible to forecast the results of tests in real driving conditions which will serve to conclude and confirm those made on SCORE.

Of course, it is clear that a simulator like this does not pretend to reproduce all the complexities of the environment and of the acquisition of information observed on the road and does not, therefore, replace the need for final tests in real driving conditions. Similarly, the absence of a moving base on SCORE and the low degree of complexity of the vehicle-dynamics model used limit its use simulation of steady driving conditions and to low dynamic workloads.

This is not an important constraint in the applications intended for SCORE, as most of the ergonomic protocols consist of creating "standard" motorway type driving conditions.

Finally, the complexity of visual reproduction assumed to be necessary for automobile simulation (unlike aircraft applications) has previously been a limiting factor in the development, but recent improvements in computer technology now make this accessible to an increasing number of users.

8. REFERENCES

Guyard I, Kerihuel H and Sfez E (1989). Etude ergonomique de l'utilisation d'un écran tactile en conduite automobile. Proceedings of XXV Congrès de la SELF, October 1989.

Hella F, Hartemann F (1982). Etude de la durée du regard pour prélever des informations à l'intétieur du véhicule. Rapport interne Renault, Décembre 1982.

Kerihuel H (1989). Présentation des outils de mesure des stratégies visuelles. Proceedings de XXVe Congrès de la SELF, Octobre 1989.

Neboit M, Laya O (1983). Etude de l'exploration visuelle du tableau de bord d'une automobile. Rapport final de contrat Renault/ONSER, Novembre 1983.

Pham AT, Chatelet A (1973). Dynamique du système Conducteur Véhicule. Ingénieurs de l'Automobile, Decembre 1973.

BREAKING UP OPEN-LOOP STEERING CONTROL ACTIONS
THE STEERING WHEEL AS AN ACTIVE CONTROL DEVICE

Josef SCHUMANN[1], Hans GODTHELP[2], Berthold FARBER[1] and Heinz WONTORRA[1]

University of Armed Forces Munich, Human Factors
Institute LRT 11, Werner-Heisenberg-Weg 39, 8014 Neubiberg, Germany[1]

TNO Institute for Perception, P.O. Box 23, 3769 ZG Soesterberg, The Netherlands[2]

Abstract

Active control devices have been used mainly in the field of aviation to reduce operator workload. At the handling level of car driving, the steering wheel can be used as an active control device to transmit relevant proprioceptive-tactual information cues for lateral control. To examine the use of proprioceptive-tactual information signals, an experiment was conducted in a fixed-base driving simulator. The driver had to initiate a lane change manoeuver, which can be described by an open-loop control behavior and during the manoeuver a warning signal could occur to inform the driver to stay in the right lane. This would break up open-loop control and transfer it to closed-loop control. Different proprioceptive-tactual signal cues via the active steering wheel (e.g. short vibrating torque shift, short steady torque shift) were compared with an auditory signal cue as the control condition. The results show, that proprioceptive-tactual feedback can be used to break up open-loop mode driving behaviour and that the steering wheel as an active control device supports the driver in his/her driving task.

1. INTRODUCTION

1.1. Active Control Devices

The present study focusses on the question of whether active control devices (i.e. an active steering wheel) may be useful at the handling level of driving in future cars (as suggested for example by Johannsen, (1990). The idea behind active controls is to reduce driver workload by using the steering wheel not only as control device but also as an information system for the driver. Active control devices convey relevant information of the controlled system to the driver and therefore concurrently serve as a proprioceptive-tactual display (Rühmann, 1981). The term 'tactual' is used in the meaning of Schiff and Foulke's (1982) definition in 'referring to active exploratory and manipulative touch'. The tactual sensation mainly consists of touch, pressure, and vibration transmitted by different cutaneous sensory receptors (for example Meissner and Pacinian corpuscles; (Sherrick & Craig, 1982). Through the action of the limbs, the proprioceptors - sense organs in the subcutaneous tissues of muscles, tendons, and joints - are activated simultaneously

(Geldard, 1972). From an information processing perspective, the employment of active controls is described within the concept of stimulus- response compatibility (Sheridan and Ferrell, 1974; Wickens, 1984), since the receptors of the information synchronously serve as effectors for an action proposed by the stimulus information. According to Sanders and McCormick (1987), compatibility links the relationship of stimulus and response to the driver's expectation and therefore can result in a reduced workload, faster response times, and fewer errors. Massaro (1990) terms this relationship 'perceiving-acting' compatibility, which will be supported by an active control device. Moreover, an active control can offer a meaningful interaction with the environment which helps to build up effective functional units of activity and facilitates compatibility matching, i.e. the assembling of intended driving control actions on the basis of displayed proprioceptive-tactual cues (as in the common coding approach in information processing of Prinz (1990).

1.2. The employment of an active steering wheel for lateral control

At the handling level of driving, the steering wheel is utilized for lateral control. Within an action-theoretic model of behavior, stabilization and steering tasks are performed by the driver on a partly automated sensorimotor level of control (Rasmussen, 1986). Signals having a direct impact on his level therefore can be transmitted by proprioceptive-tactual sensory modalities. As a consequence, the employment of active controls, transmitting feedback via these sensory channels, has been suggested mainly in aviation (see for example Gilson and Fenton, 1974; Jagacinski et al, 1983). Surprisingly, there have only been sporadic attempts to use them in automobiles, where the steering wheel has been substituted by a driver control-stick (Rule and Fenton, 1972). Only recently, through the implementation of computer technology into an automobile, (for example the design of 'drive-by-wire' steering), has active control technology also been considered in motor vehicle control (Hess and Modjtahedzadeh, 1990). As an active control device, the steering wheel conveys feedback concerning lateral control aspects to the driver and consequently serves also as a proprioceptive-tactual display. Sanders and McCormick (1987) suggest that tactual display have the advantage of the utilization of a different sensory modality which can result in less competition for information processing resources (see Farber et al, 1990). Burke et al, (1980) see a main disadvantage in tactual displays in the need for permanent contact between the hand(s) and such an active control device; however such a permanent contact is in any case assured in the case of the steering wheel for controlling driving actions.

In this approach, the regular steering wheel torque will be influenced artificially to transmit proprioceptive-tactual cues to the driver which signal an affordance to react to with appropriate steering actions (Gibson, 1979; Turvey et al, 1981) . With such an active steering wheel, the driver is not a passive receiver of information, but receives by means of active touch controlling aspects of the car, even in the absence of visual cues (Gibson, 1962).

Rasmussen (1986) emphasizes that humans are actively picking up the information that is relevant for their actions, a point also made by Gibson (1979) and Reed (1982). In this sense, an active steering wheel can offer relevant information about the lateral lane deviation to modulate the steering control actions. Specific signal cues have to be developed for the active steering wheel, which lead the driver to an appropriate initiation of a steering action in a certain direction, which then can be supported by visual stimuli.

Two vehicle motion characteristics - the lateral position y and the heading angle   ,
which is proportional to the lateral speed y - serve as the driver's input for the lateral
control task (Carson and Wierwille, 1978). From these variables the TLC-measure (Time
to Line Crossing) has been derived, representing the time necessary for the vehicle to reach
either the left or right edge of the lane (Godthelp et al, 1984). The control loop for an
active steering wheel supporting lateral control is depicted in Figure. 1.

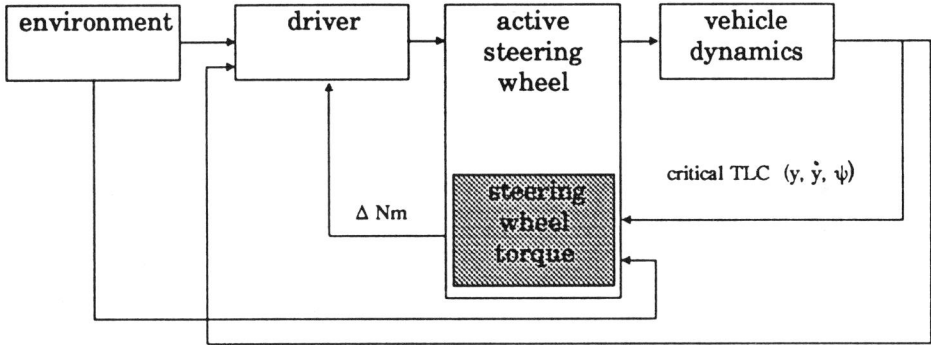

Figure 1. Schematic diagram of the man-vehicle control loop with an active steering wheel
providing proprioceptive-tactual feedback about the error between the actual lateral position
and some normative behavior (operationalized by a TLC-measure).

Proprioceptive-tactual feedback information may be employed in different ways during
the control activities of the driving task:

> during closed-loop control, in supporting information   from other sensory
> modalities (for example visual, auditory), in the meaning   of redundancy gain
> and/or as visual workload relief,

> during open-loop control (mainly without visual feedback), in breaking up open-
> loop control and transferring it to closed-loop control.

To examine this second point, an experiment was conducted in a fixed-base driving
simulator. The driver had to initiate a lane change manoeuver which is performed in an
open-loop control mode (as suggested by McRue et al, (1977) for example). During the lane
change manoeuver a warning signal via the active steering wheel should enable the driver
to react immediately to break up his/her manoeuver and to stay in the right lane of the
road. The warning signals will be generated by changing the steering wheel torque. This
torque change may lead to critical situations during driving, if for example a sudden, strong
steering wheel torque change startles the driver who then jerks the steering wheel.
Psychophysical threshold experiments were conducted (Schumann et al, 1991) to determine
small torque changes, which would be perceivable at the steering wheel by the driver. The

level of these steering wheel torque shifts serves as a basis for the shaping of different steering wheel signals for the following experiments.

2. METHOD

2.1. Task and stimuli

The driver had to perform a lane change manoeuver on a two lane rural road as depicted in Figure 2.

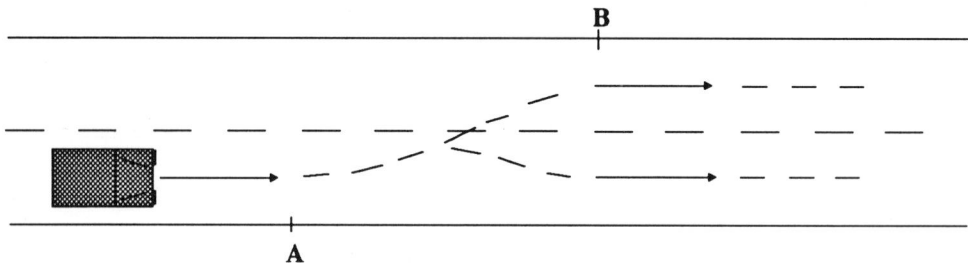

Figure 2. Path of the lane change manoeuver, with and without warning (A: start of lane changing, B: lane barricade).

The driver started in the right lane at a predetermined fixed speed (100, 80, 60 km/h). Passing point A (see Fig. 2), the driver had to initiate a lane change manoeuver to the left lane. At A, which was always located at seven seconds before B, the visual scene was occluded for a short (0.5 sec) period. This served as a cue for the driver to intiate the lane change manoeuver. After this initiation cue, two conditions could occur:

(1)   a 'no occlusion' period, where S could perform the lane change manoeuver with complete vision.
(2)   a 'with occlusion' period, where the visibility stayed occluded for an additional 2.5 sec. In most of the runs, the lane change manoeuver could be carried out without problems, (i.e. with a lane closure at B becoming visible in the right lane). However, in one third of the runs S was warned not to leave the right lane because of an unexpected shift of the lane barricade to the left lane. The warning signal was given at a TLC distance of 2 sec from the center lane. As described earlier, TLC represents the Time-to-Lane-Crossing, i.e. the time until the left fender of the car would cross the center line. At 1.5 sec after this TLC instant, the lane barricade became visible at the corresponding closed lane for that particular run. After point B, the subject had to drive for three more seconds in his respective lane. Different signals were introduced to indicate that the driver should stay in the right lane (see Table 1).

Table 1: Warning signals used for the lateral control task

SIGNAL	CHARACTERISTIC
Auditory Signal 0	short (0.5 sec) tone
Tactual Signal 1	implemented at the steering wheel as a short (0.5 sec) vibrating (10 Hz) torque shift (level 1.2 Nm)
Tactual Signal 2	implemented at the steering wheel as a vibrating (10 Hz) torque shift (level 1.2 Nm), continuously on until lateral speed to the right $\geq$ 1m/sec
Tactual Signal 3	implemented at the steering wheel as a short (0.5 sec) steady torque shift to the right (level 2.4 Nm)

2.2. Apparatus

The experiment was carried out in the fixed base driving simulator of the TNO Institute for Perception. This simulator contains a Volvo 240 mock-up, with regular steering wheel and pedals. The steering wheel linkage is connected to a potentiometer which measures the steering wheel angle. Steering force is generated by means of an electric torque motor (Axem MV 19), mounted in the steering axis. The perspective view of the outline of the road is electronically generated by an Evans and Sutherland PS300 system and projected in front of the mock-up with a horizontal field of view of 50º.

2.3. Subjects

Eight male subjects participated in the experiment, all of whom had previous experience with the driving simulator. All Subjects had had their driving license for at least five years with driving experience of at least 10000 km per year. Age varied between 23 and 38 years. They were paid for their services.

2.4. Experimental Design and Procedure

In the driving simulator, subjects performed a lane change manoeuver (lateral control). In a within-subjects design, Subjects participated in four sessions with the different warning signals. The order of presentation of the signals was in accordance with a digram-balanced 4*4 Latin-square (as given in Wagenaar, 1969).

At the beginning, each subject was given written instructions about the experiment. After a short introduction by the experimenter, the subject entered the mock-up. The experimenter always informed the subject about any change in the experimental conditions (for example occlusion off/on). Each subject had four sessions of runs, with a different warning signal each time. A session lasted about 30 minutes with a special training period at the start. Subjects alternated their sessions, giving each subject a break of about 30 minutes between sessions.

Training period

The training for the first session of warning signals consisted of 39 runs. It started with 13 runs at the slowest speed (60 km/h). The first seven runs were without occlusion (first four runs without a warning), followed by six runs with occlusion (first three runs without a warning). After that, 13 runs were made at each of the higher speed (80 km/h and 100 km/h. The training in the following sessions of warning signals consisted only of 12 runs each (speed in ascending order; two runs with warning signals without occlusion, two runs with warning signals with occlusion).

Experimental session

In each session the subject made 54 runs, i.e. three sets of 18 runs with a constant speed of 60, 80, or 100 km/h. The sequence of speed sets was randomized. In a set, the first nine runs were without occlusion, to acquaint the driver with the steering actions for his lane changing manoeuver. In three randomly chosen runs a warning signal was assigned to indicate that the subject should stay in the right lane. During the following nine runs with occlusion again, three runs occurred with a warning.

2.5   Data analysis

Data storage started at point A with a sampling rate of 10 Hz. The following signals were recorded (see Figure 3):

δ_s	steering wheel angle
y	lateral position
OCC	occlusion
tw	time distant of warning
ψ	heading angle

From these signals the subsequent measures were calculated:

δ_{sl}	maximum steering wheel angle to the left
$\dot{\delta}_{sl}$	maximum steering wheel velocity to the left
δ_{sr}	maximum steering wheel angle to the right
$\dot{\delta}_{sr}$	maximum steering wheel velocity to the right
$|\dot{\delta}_s|_{3\text{-}7}$	mean absolute steering wheel velocity between time instant 3 (occlusion ends) and time instant 7 (passing the barricade at point B).
$|\dot{\delta}_s|_{7\text{-}10}$	mean absolute steering wheel velocity between time instant 7 (passing the barricade at point B) and time instant 10 (end of the run).
y_{min}	minimum lateral distance to the center line
rt	response time to warning signal, activated at a steering angle deviation $> 2^{\circ}$.

Differences between warning conditions were tested by means of an analysis of variance (ANOVA, within-subjects design), which contained of the following main factors: warning systems on four levels, speed on three levels, and occlusion (OCC) on two levels.

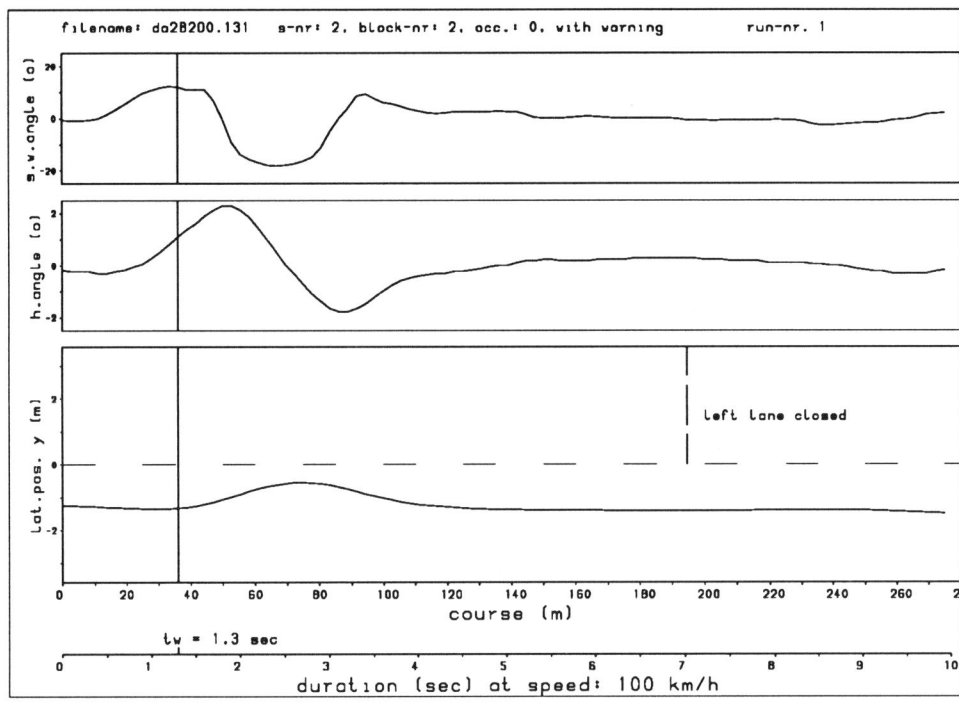

Figure 3. Data storage for one experimental run (lateral position y, heading angle (ι), steering wheel angle (δ_s), time instant of warning (tw).

3. RESULTS

The ANOVA revealed no significant differences between the warning signals on the following measures:

maximum steering wheel angle to the left and to the right,
maximum steering wheel velocity to the left and to the right.

This seems to indicate that warning signals via the steering wheel (proprioceptive-tactual) do not disturb the steering control actions any differently from an auditory warning signal. Also, no significant differences were found in the mean absolute steering wheel velocity for the two defined areas after the warning signal. Proprioceptive-tactual warning signals do not seem to influence steering control behavior compared with an auditory warning signal.

There were however significant effects for the remaining two dependent variables, i.e. ymin (minimal lateral distance to the center line) and rt (response time to warning signal). Figure 4 shows the minimum lateral distance to the center lane for the different warning signals.

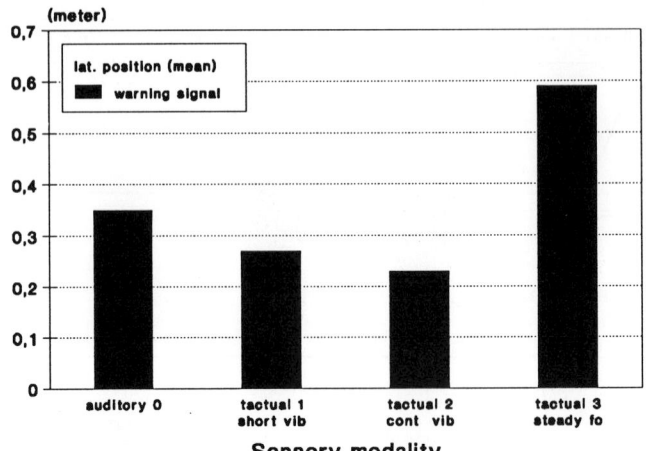

Figure 4. Minimum lateral distance to the center line for the different warning signals

The diagram reveals a significant difference between warning signals (F= 9.06, df= 3,21, p≤ 0.001). An additional contrast analysis (Dunnett's test, as in Kirk, (1982), where each proprioceptive-tactual signal was compared with the auditory warning signal (as control condition), indicated   that the significant effect of the factor warning signal can be put down to the fact that only the steady force warning signal (tactual   signal 3) leads to significant differences between pair of means (tD'= 3.26, df=21, p≤ 0.01). There was also a significant interaction effect between warning signal and occlusion (F= 4.29, df= 3,21, p= 0.016). This can be seen in Figure 5. A post-hoc analysis (Tukey HSD test, as in Kirk, (1982) showed significant differences between pair of means (abs. diff >> 0.21, p= 0.05) between the interaction conditions occlusion, the auditory and two vibrating proprioceptive-tactual warning signals (auditory 0, tactual signals 1 and 2).

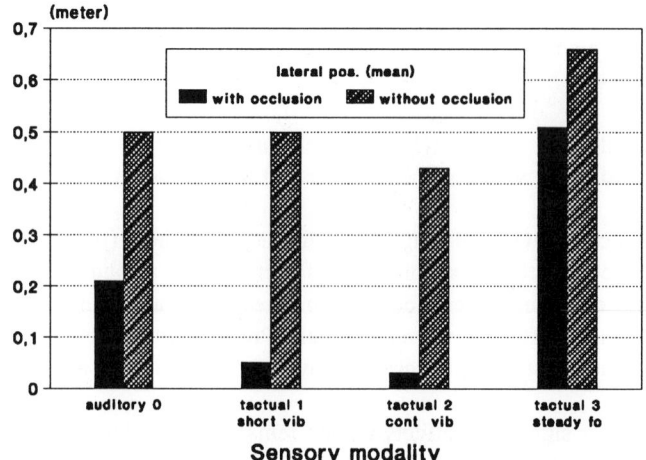

Figure 5. Minimum lateral distance to the center line for the different warning signals, with and without occlusion.

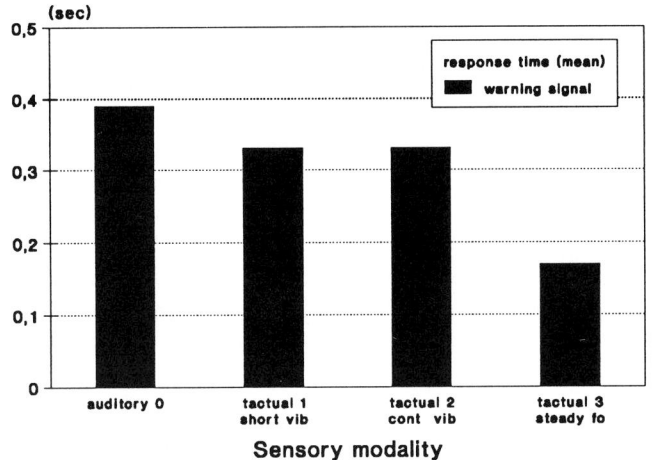

Figure 6.   Response times for the different warning signals.

Figure 6 shows the response times to the different warning signals. Again, this diagram indicates the significant effect of the different warning signals (F= 26.79, df= 3,21, p << 0.001). The significant effect can be explained mainly by the short response time to the steady force warning signal (tactual signal 3) (Dunnett's test; tD'= 7.62, df= 21, p<< 0.01). The results of the ANOVA also show a nearly significant interaction effect of the factors warning signal and occlusion (F= 2.84, df= 3,21, p = 0.062). The differences can be seen in Figure 7.   The trend in this figure shows the highest response time difference   in the interaction conditions with the two vibrating proprioceptive-tactual warning signals (tactual signals 1 and 2).

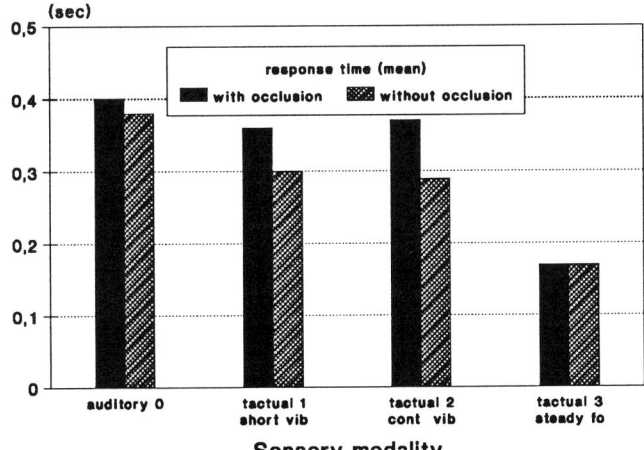

Figure 7. Response times to the different warning signals, with and without occlusion.

4. DISCUSSION

The results seem to support the hypothesis that proprioceptive-tactual warning signals can be employed to interrupt an intended lane change maneouver and to cause the driver to stay in the right lane. The performing of such a lane change manoeuver can be described in an open-loop steering control mode (McRuer et al., 1977). The warning signals were successful in breaking this open-loop control mode and transferring steering back to a closed-loop control mode, which should be supported by visual stimuli. Comparison of proprioceptive-tactual warning signals with an auditory warning signal shows that the auditory warning signal as well as the proprioceptive-tactual signals seem to be effective (see Figure 4). The need for visual stimuli after the warning signal can be seen in the high differences between the occlusion conditions (with and without visual support) for the minimum lateral distance to the center line (see Figure 5). The significant effect of the steady force warning signal (tactual signal 3) can be explained by the reduction of the response time to such a signal (see Figure 6), since a direct and immediate intervention of the system (the active steering wheel) occurs which starts to turn the steering wheel into the right direction. The shorter reaction times for the proprioceptive-tactual signals can also be explained in the sense of a stimulus-response compatibility or so-called 'perception-action' linking.

As the results show, the steady force warning signal gives the best results (Figures 4 and 6). Nevertheless the choice of the most appropriate proprioceptive-tactual warning signal is still open at this stage of research, since a pure warning signal, such as for example the short vibrating proprioceptive-tactual signal, is also effective. There can be different situations during lateral control where a warning signal alone might not be sufficient and a direct intervention of the system should occur. An example is driving on a curve, where a steady force warning via an active steering wheel into the appropriate direction might be the most informative signal in such circumstances. In the case of breaking up an open-loop control mode a short vibrating proprioceptive-tactual warning signal can be - as the results show - an appropriate choice.

Furthermore, the compatibility of an active steering wheel should be tested with other active control devices (for example an active accelerator, as discussed in Godthelp and Schumann, (1991). In addition to the simulator studies carried out thus far, field experiments are needed to evaluate the effectiveness of active control devices.

5. ACKNOWLEDGEMENT

This study was carried out as part of the DRIVE project V1041 on Generic Intelligent Driver Support systems funded by the Commission of the European Communities.

6. REFERENCES

Burke, M.W., Gilson, R.D. and Jagacinski, R.J. (1980). Multi-modal information processing for visual workload relief. Ergonomics, 23, 961-975.
Carson, J.M. and Wierwille, W.W. (1978). Development of a strategy model of the driver

in lane keeping. Vehicle System Dynamics, 7, 233-253.

Farber, B., Farber, B.A., Godthelp, J. and Schumann, J. (1990) State of the art and recommendations for characteristics of speed and steering support systems. Deliverable Report DRIVE V1041/GIDS-CON01. Haren, NL: Traffic Research Centre, University of Groningen.

Geldard, F.A. (1972). The Human Senses (2nd ed.). New York: John Wiley.

Gibson, J.J. (1962). Observations on active touch. Psychological Review, 69, 477-491.

Gibson, J.J. (1979). The ecological approach to visual perception. Boston: Houghton Mifflin.

Gilson, R.D. and Fenton, R.E. (1974). Kinesthetic-tactual Information Presentations - Inflight Studies. IEEE Transactions on Systems, Man, and Cybernetics, 4, 531-535.

Godthelp, J., Milgram, P. and Blaauw, G.J. (1984). The development of a time-related measure to describe driving strategy. Human Factors, 26, 257-268.

Godthelp, J. and Schumann, J. (1991). The use of an intelligent accelerator as an element of a driver support system. In Proceedings of the 24. ISATA Conference, Florence, 20.-24.5. 1991.

Hess, R.A. and Modjtahedzadeh, A. (1990). A Control Theoretic Model of Driver Steering Behavior. IEEE Control Systems Magazine, 10, 3-8.

Jagacinski, R.J., Flach, J.M. and Gilson, R.D. (1983). A comparison of visual and kinesthetic- tactual Displays for compensatory Tracking. IEEE Transactions on Systems, Man, and Cybernetics, 13, 1103-1112.

Johannsen, G. (1990). Fahrzeugfuhrung. In C.Graf Hoyos and B.Zimelong (Hrsg.), Ingenieurpsychologie (S.426-454). Gottingen: Verlag fur Psychologie Hogrefe.

Kirk, R.E. (1982). Experimental design: Procedures for the behavioral sciences (2nd ed.). Pacific Grove: Brooks/Cole Publishing Company.

Massaro, D.W. (1990). An Information-Processing Analysis of Perception and Action. In O. Neumann and W. Prinz (Eds.), Relationships between perception and action. Berlin: Springer-Verlag.

McRuer, D.T., Allen, R.W., Weir, D.H. and Klein, R.H. (1977) New results in driver steering control models. Human Factors, 19, 381-397.

Prinz, W. (1990). A Common Coding Approach to Perception and Action. In O.Neumann and W.Prinz (Eds.), Relationships between perception and action. Berlin: Springer-Verlag.

Rasmussen, J. (1986). Information processing and Human-Machine Interaction. An Approach to Cognitive Engineering. Amsterdam: North-Holland.

Reed, E.S. (1982). An Outline of a Theory of Action Systems. Journal of Motor Behavior, 14, 98-134.

Ruhmann, H. (1981). Schnittstellen in Mensch-Maschine-Systemen. In H.Schmidtke (Hrsg.), Lehrbuch der Ergonomie (2. Aufl.) (S.351-376). Munchen: Hanser.

Rule, R.G. and Fenton, R.E. (1972). On the Effects of state Information on Driver-Vehicle Performance in Car following. IEEE Transactions on Systems, Man, and Cybernetics, 2, 630-637.

Sanders, M.S. and McCormick, E.J. (1987). Human Factors in Engineering and Design (6th ed.). New York: McGraw-Hill Book Company.

Schiff, W. and Foulke, E. (Eds.) (1982). Tactual perception: a sourcebook. Cambridge:

Cambridge   University Press.

Schumann, J., Farber, B. and Wontorra, H. (1991). Das Lenkrad als propriozeptiv-taktiles "Display". Vortrag zur 33. TeaP, Gießen 24.-28. 3.

Sheridan,T.B. and Ferrell,W.R. (1974). Man-Machine Systems: Information, Control, and Decision Models of Human Performance. Cambridge, MA: The MIT Press.

Sherrick, C.E. and Craig, J.C. (1982) The psychophysics of touch. In W.Schiff and E.Foulke   (Eds.), Tactual perception: a sourcebook. Cambridge: Cambridge University   Press.

Turvey, M.T., Shaw, R.E., Reed, E.S. and Mace, W.M. (1981). Ecological laws of perceiving and acting: In reply to Fodor and Pylyshyn (1981). Cognition, 9, 237-304.

Wagenaar, W.D. (1969). Note on the construction of digram-balanced Latin squares. Psychological Bulletin, 72, 384-386.

Wickens, C. (1984). Engineering Psychology and Human Performance. Columbus, OH: Merrill.

12

POSTERS AND WORKSHOP REPORT

VISION IN VEHICLES – IV
A.G. Gale et al. (Editors)
335

PERCEPTION, ACTIVATION AND DRIVING BEHAVIOUR DURING A RIDE ON A MOTORWAY

M. JESSURUN, F.J.J.M. STEYVERS and K.A. BROOKHUIS

Traffic Research Centre, University of Groningen, P.O. Box 69, 9750 AB Haren, The Netherlands

Abstract

The present study investigated the comparability of two types of road presentation with respect to perception, activation and driving behaviour. It appeared that the perception of important aspects of a road environment did not differ between a scale-model in a visual road simulator and the real road. Driving behaviour and activation, on the other hand, differed between both types of presentation. It should be noted, however, that this simulator was not designed for such purposes.

1. INTRODUCTION

To reduce the sound nuisance caused by motorways, constructions have been built to keep out the noise, the so-called noise barriers. These constructions are more or less a salient feature of a road environment. A certainly conspicuous construction is a noise barrier situated along the A-2 motorway in the Netherlands. The striking thing about this noise barrier is that, while driving in the northern direction, the distance between barrier and motorway first diminishes until the barrier is very near the road. Then, the distance quickly becomes larger again. As you can see in Figure 1, this noise barrier consists of transparent pieces. The function of these pieces is to prevent the impression of something that is closing in on you.

From this part of the A-2 motorway, a scale-model (1:100) is available which was used in a visual road simulator during the design work. The merit of this simulator is that it presents, on a monitor, the image of the road environment the way it would be seen by a driver. So, you have the impression that you are actually driving on the road, with the view coming through the windscreen. The assumption made, when using this visual road simulator, is that the impression of the modeled road closely resembles the impression of the road in reality. To test this assumption, the present study investigated the impact of both types of road presentation on the perception, activation and driving behaviour of road users. The principle objective of the study was to find out whether differences existed between both types of presentation.

2. METHOD

Twenty-two male subjects were asked to "drive" twice in the scale-model and twice on the actual road in a specially instrumented test-vehicle. During the second ride in the scale-model as well as on the real road, a special apparatus for the recording of eye movements was attached to the head of a subject (the NAC eye mark recorder model V). By using the eye mark recorder, it was possible to investigate looking behaviour in terms of number and duration of eye fixations (central vision). During the ride, heart rate and driving behaviour were measured as well. Parameters of driving behaviour were speed, steering movements and lateral position on the road.

Figure 1. The noise barrier alongside a part of the A-2 motorway.

3. RESULTS

On the real road a shift of lateral position to the left was found, coinciding with the presence of the noise barrier. However, this effect was not present in the scale-model. Furthermore, on the real road the noise barrier led to an increment in mental effort as was indicated by the measures of heart rate. Analysis of the looking behaviour revealed that the eye fixations do not offer an explanation for the above-mentioned differences. The noise barrier was being fixated for the same amount of time, regardless of the type of road presentation. On the other hand, differences in looking behaviour did occur with respect to other objects of attention. These differences could, however, be explained partly by the inexperience of subjects as far as driving in a model is concerned.

4. CONCLUSION

Based on the above-mentioned results, two major conclusions can be drawn. In the first place, it is shown that the visual road simulator can be used for research on the perception of important features of a road environment. Secondly, it can be concluded that this simulator is less suitable for checking the impact of a future road on driving behaviour and on the state of activation of a driver. However, the visual road simulator was not designed for such purposes in the first place.

ACKNOWLEDGEMENT

The research was commissioned by the Dutch Ministry of Transport, Transportation and Traffic Research Division.

VISION IN VEHICLES – IV
A.G. Gale et al. (Editors)
1993 Elsevier Science Publishers B.V.

A SAFETY INTEGRATED FISHING VESSEL

J.A. STOOP

Safety Science Group, Delft University of Technology, Kanaalweg 2b, 2628 EB Delft, The Netherlands

Abstract
Accident analysis of 59 collisions on the north Sea in which fishing vessels were involved revealed a number of problems. Optimization of the design of the bridge and equipment was required with respect to mental load, human error, internal and external vision and the conditions under which the different tasks had to be performed (Figure 1).

ACCIDENT TYPE	USE SCENARIO				
	normal	fog	poor visibility	dense traffic	
1. sailing free	7	1			8
2. fishing in TSS		4		5	9
3a. sailing in TSS		5	4	10	19
3b. sailing near ports	2	3			5
4a. capsize fishing	4				4
4b. sinking	5				5
5. stranding	3		2		5
6. occupational	4				4
	25	13	6	15	59

Figure 1. Accident Analysis

340 J.A. Stoop

The results laid the basis for the redesign of the bridge with respect to the structure and the presentation of the flow of information, the layout of the bridge as well as the equipment.

1. INTRODUCTION

The redesign of the bridge is anticipating on the trend to the bridge as the operational centre of the vessel and fits in with the project 'Beamer 2000', an innovative fishing vessel design for the year 2000.

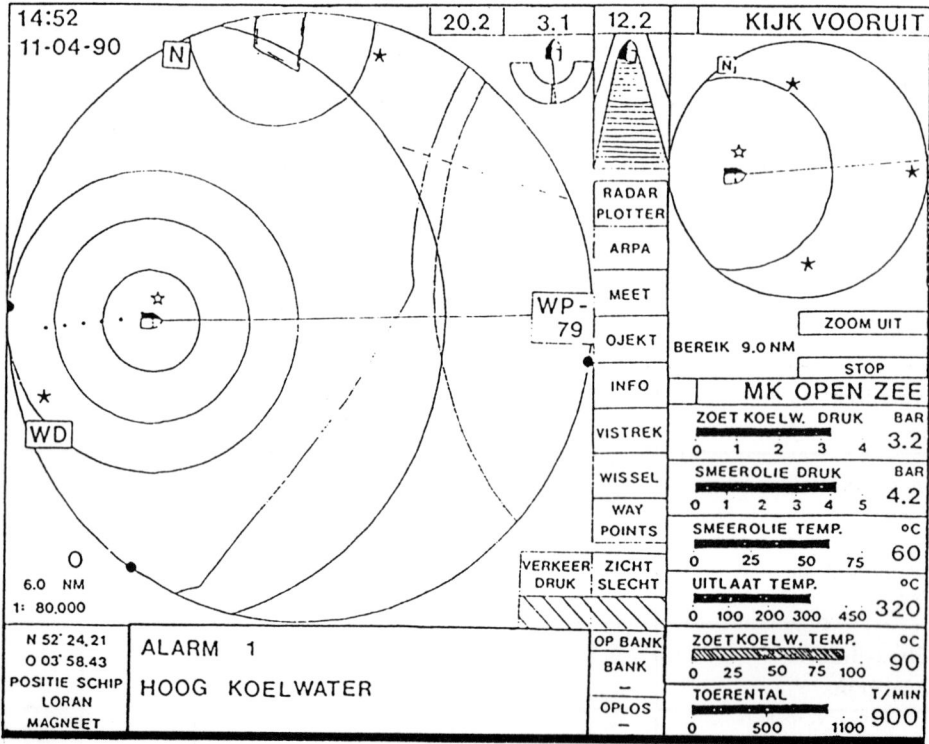

Figure 2. Navigation Unit

A design module focussing on mental load demonstrated the potential for the presentation of the required information on one integrated display; the navigational unit (Figure 2). The alteration of the bridge layout led, in a step by step approach, to a new bridge concept; the Beamer Bridge 2000 (Figure 3). This layout not only improved vision with respect to the maritime traffic situation, but improved vision to gear handling activities on the fishing decks as well (Figure 4).

The design was evaluated with respect to residual risks and additional risk reduction strategies of a non-technical nature such as training and qualification.

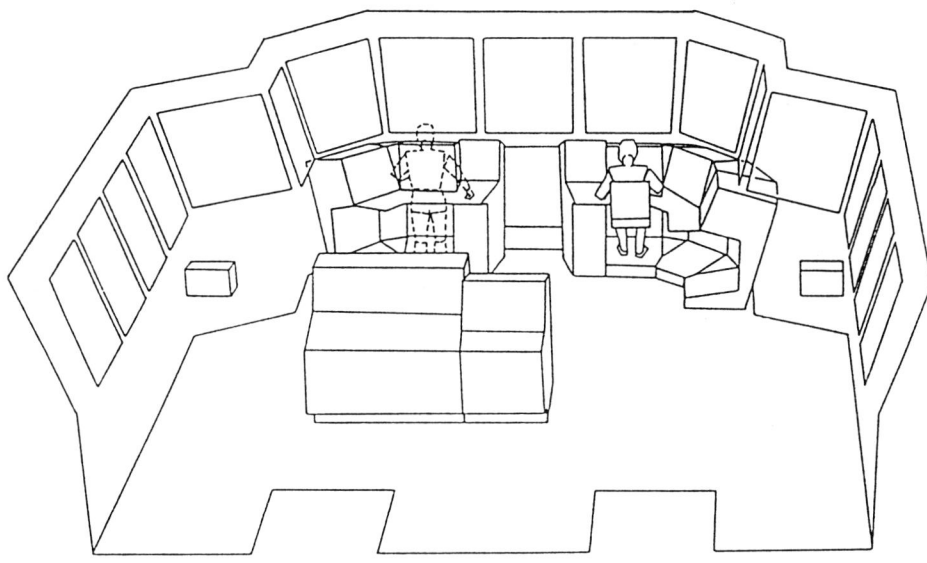

Figure 3. Beamer Bridge 2000

The bridge of a BEAMER 2000 has an integrated bridge system which is safer, more user-friendly and efficient than the present bridge.

Design requirements which were to be fulfilled were with respect to hardware;

-     ergonomic layout of equipment
-     logical display of information

to software;

-     automation
-     interfacing

to workload;

-     reduction of over- and underload
-     improved vision lines on decks and traffic situation
-     winch integrated with navigation workstation, communication with fishing deck.

The bridge of a BEAMER 2000 differs from a conventional bridge:

-     bridge is raised for improved vision
-     glass windows set back at front for vision on decks
-     navigation equipment mounted close to the windows
-     prevention of disturbing daylight reflection by angled windows

- on port and starboard set back of bridge front for vision on side decks
- split console on front with two workstations, containing 19-inch screens, presenting integrated navigation data
- new administration workstation next to the chart table
- navigation data presented in the skippers cabin
- reduction of winch control handles by combined functions.

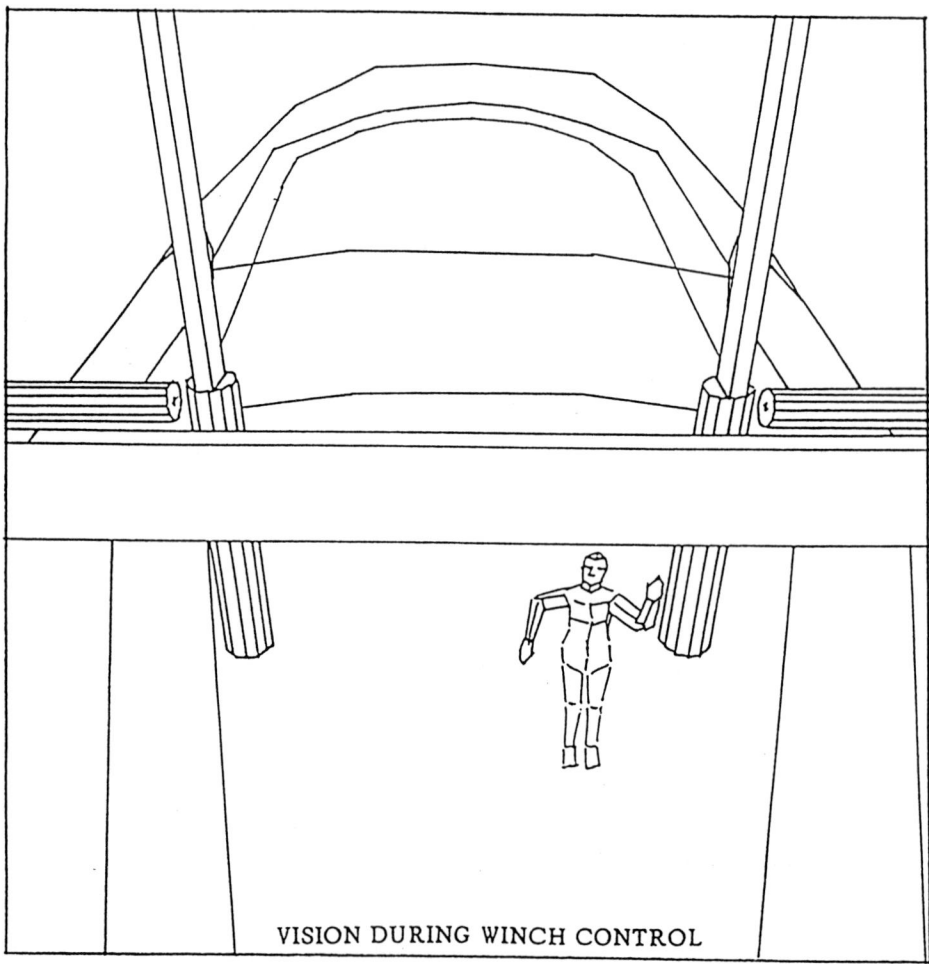

VISION DURING WINCH CONTROL

Figure 4. Vision during winch control

THE REDUCTION OF DRIVER'S VISUAL LOAD USING NEW CONTROL TECHNOLOGIES

Brigitte FAERBER[1], Berthold FAERBER[1] & Helmut SCHWEIKER[2]

University of the Federal Armed Forces Munich, Human Faktors Institute, LRT 11, Werner-Heisenberg-Weg 39, 8014 Neubiberg, FRG[1]

University of Tuebingen, Psychological Institute, Friedrichstr. 21, 7400 Tuebingen, FRG[2]

Abstract
Three different controls, softkeys, cursor positioning and combination of hardkeys and cursor are evaluated. Form functionalities; radio, climate, route guidance and trip computer were tested in a driving simulator. The dependent measures; glance time, handling time, correct actions and acceptance prove the softkey solution as the best new control technology.

1. INTRODUCTION

The technological development of cars leads to an increasing number of sensors and subsystems providing the driver with additional, more or less helpful information. Many ergonomic attempts have been made to reduce or manage the related display problems (see Faerber, 1990; Michon, 1992).Even if the display problems should not be underestimated, the control problems of these new devices are still more difficult. As well as conventional control technology two solutions are currently discussed: the use of a keyboard and speech input. For various reasons both realisations are by no means optimal! Speaker independent and user friendly speech input systems will not be available in the near future.

Keyboards (even if they have only a reduced set of buttoms) need to much space in most passenger cars. Furthermore they distract the driver from his main task, safe driving. As a consequence they can only be used while the car is standing still. This restricts the application range and the acceptance of such control devices.

2. RESEARCH QUESTION

The main question of the research reported is, whether a central mounted multi-functional control can solve some of the design problems. Central mounted means that it is positioned in the optimal reaching area of a right handed person. Multi-functional means that different

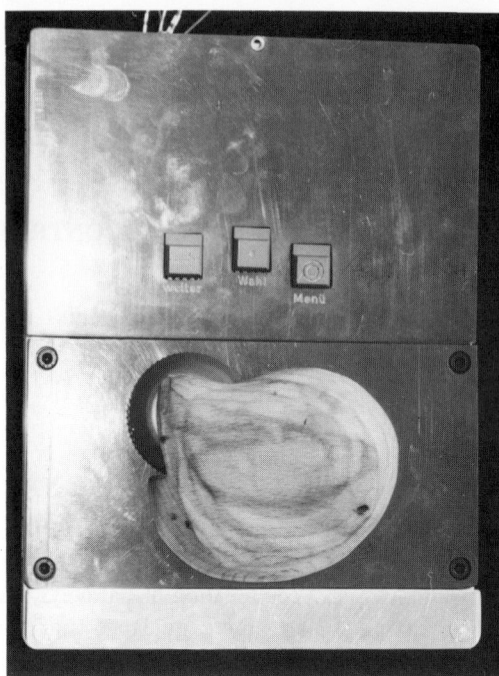

Figure 1a.
Cursor positioning

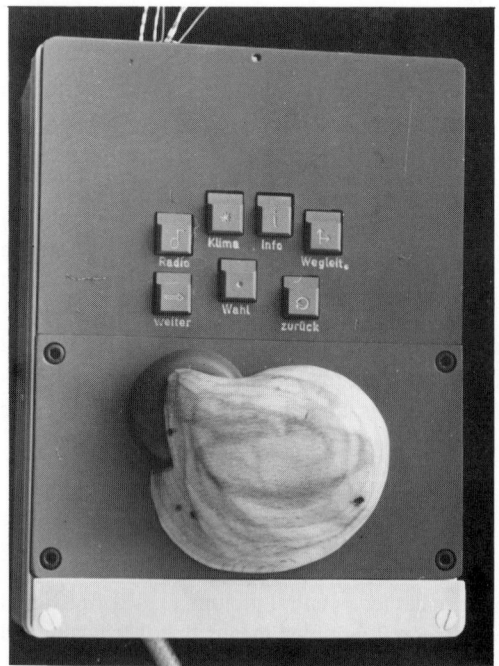

Figure 1b.
Softkeys

Figure 1c.
Hardkeys combined with cursor positioning

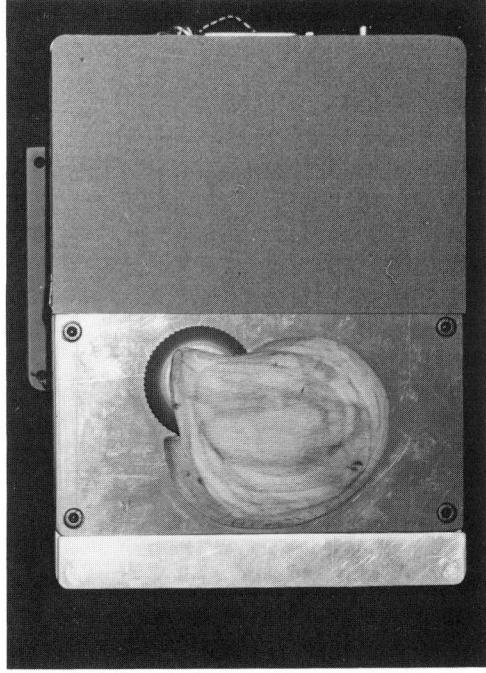

Figure 1d.
Analog device for all continuous functions

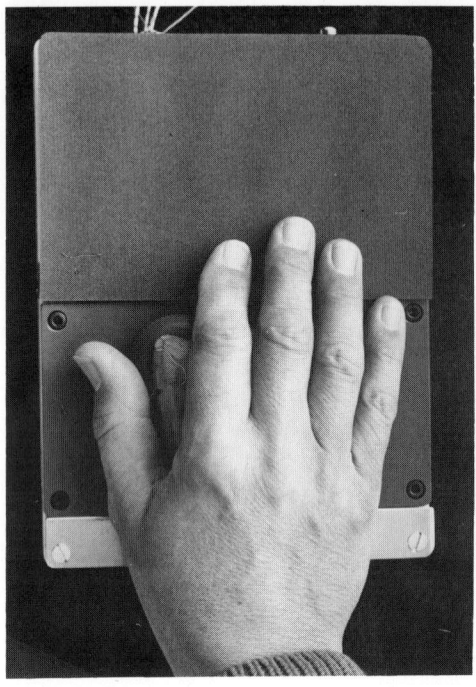

Figure 1e.
Control (analog device only) for the speech input condition

systems, such as; car radio, air conditioning, route guidance and trip computer can be manipulated by one single device. These functionalities were chosen to test the applicability of the control device for conventional (radio, air conditioning) and advanced (route guidance, trip computer) systems. The comparison covered three different kinds of controls (see fig. 1a-c):

- cursor positioning (see fig. 1a)
- softkeys (see fig. 1b)
- hardkeys combined with cursor positioning (see fig. 1c)

These control modes differ with respect to at least three parameters: the number of controls, the possibility of direct manipulation and their reliability.

2.1 Number of controls

Besides others, the reduction of the number of keys is one rational design criterion. While for cursor positioning only three controls are necessary, namely 'step forward', 'select' and 'return', the softkey realisation needs six, and the combination of hardkeys and cursor seven keys (see fig. 1 a - c). The cursor realisation is therefore the most pure one with respect to this criterion.

2.2 Direct manipulation

For the 'direct manipulation' criterion things change. Here the combination of hardkeys and cursor provide the possibility of a more direct manipulation. The items of the main menu 'radio', 'climate', 'route guidance' and 'trip computer' can be directly activated, irrespectable of the actual menu status. If, for example, a user checks his momentary fuel consumption (menu: trip computer) and wants to change the volume of the radio in order to understand the traffic information, he can directly select the radio menu with one key - the hardkey 'radio'. Furthermore, in the default version the system enables him to change the volume of the radio without selecting another item of the radio menu. So, what can be expected from the combination of hardkeys and cursor is a faster manipulation of the different menu functions. The price for this acceleration is an increased number of controls.

2.3 Reliability

The reliability criterion can be best explained by a comparison of softkeys and hardkeys. Hardkeys on the one hand are totally reliable, because they control by each pressing the same single function (e.g. the horn). Softkeys change their meaning in accordance with the selected menu. An example: with the first actuation a softkey selects the climate menu. Within the menu the second actuation of the same key can switch the heating of the rear window to 'on'. The difference between the cursor and hardkey is the specific, but changing meaning of the keys. It should be clear that this kind of manipulation is comparably direct, but has the disadvantage of a loss of reliability. From the above it is easy to recognize that the softkey solution and the hardkey/cursor realisation are quite similar with respect to the number of keys, but they differ with respect to reliability.

The actual meaning of a control for the softkey realisation, or the actual position of the cursor is displayed at a specific part of the dashboard (see fig. 2).

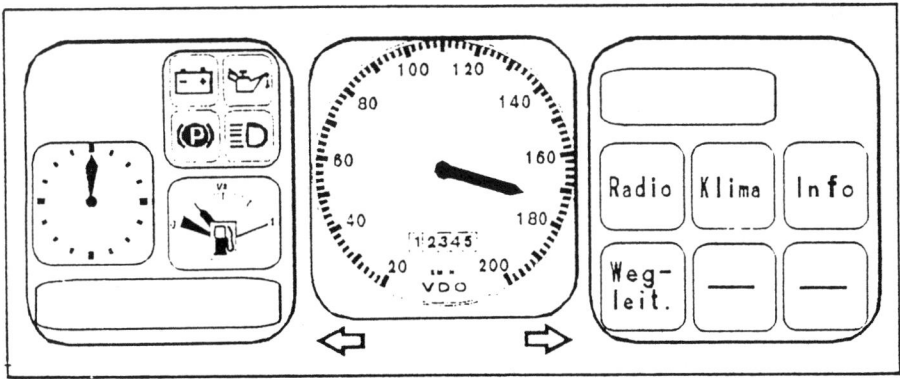

Fig. 2: Dashboard including the display of the actual status of controls.

This separation of display and controls is preferable compared to an integrated solution because the optimal reaching area and the optimal looking area are not identical (Schmidtke, 1981). Summarizing the design problems of this new control technology it should be made clear that all three aspects, namely number of controls, direct manipulation and reliability cannot be optimized independently. The manipulation of one aspect has more or less negative impacts on others.

The experimental evaluation included a further variable: the use of a single analog device for all continuous functions (see fig. 1d). With the help of this analog control all 'up/down' 'more/less' etc. functions can be controlled (e.g. change volume or pitch of the radio; influence heating, fan, air distribution). Depending on the actual menu selection all analog functions like up/down, more/less etc. can be controlled. As a kind of baseline a speech input system was also included in the experimental evaluation. Speech input was combined with the analog device in the way that the menu selection was conducted by voice, while the analog changes (e.g. air distribution 'up') were done manually (see fig. 1e).

3. EXPERIMENTS

The experimental comparison of the different devices was performed in a driving simulator. Subjects had to follow a leading car and execute specific control functions on request. As dependant variables driving performance (steering behavior, reaction time to braking manoeuvres of the leading car), correct actions and glance times to the display were measured. Glance times were recorded by EOG (Electro-Oculogram).

4. RESULTS

From Figures 3a and 3b the results of the control behavior can be seen. The number of correct actions (fig. 3a) are slightly different, the least correct actions occurring at the cursor realisation. However, these differences are not significant. The controlling times show a totally different pattern. Speech input is of course the most direct manipulation. A remarkable result is the difference between softkey and hardkey+cursor on the one side, and the nearly identical action times for cursor and hardkey + cursor. The direct manipulation with the hardkey/cursor combination had no advantage compared to the pure cursor solution. A further data inspection gives the explanation. The switch between the two different control modes (hardkey and cursor) in one control act was a relatively time consuming process equalizing the theoretical advantage of the combined realisation. The significantly shorter action times of the softkey solution compared to the two cursor realisations make clear that subjects are able to cope with an abstract user interface, if a direct manipulation is guaranteed.

The results for the glance times as measure for distraction from traffic are consistent with the action times (fig. 4a and b). Again, speech input is best, followed by softkey, cursor and then hardkey and cursor.

5. CONCLUSIONS

Cursor positioning, which is widely used for man-computer interaction, should not be applied in cars. If the designer does not want to increase the number of conventional controls for new functionalities like trip computer or route guidance systems (which is strongly recommended), speech input or softkey control are considered best. As long as

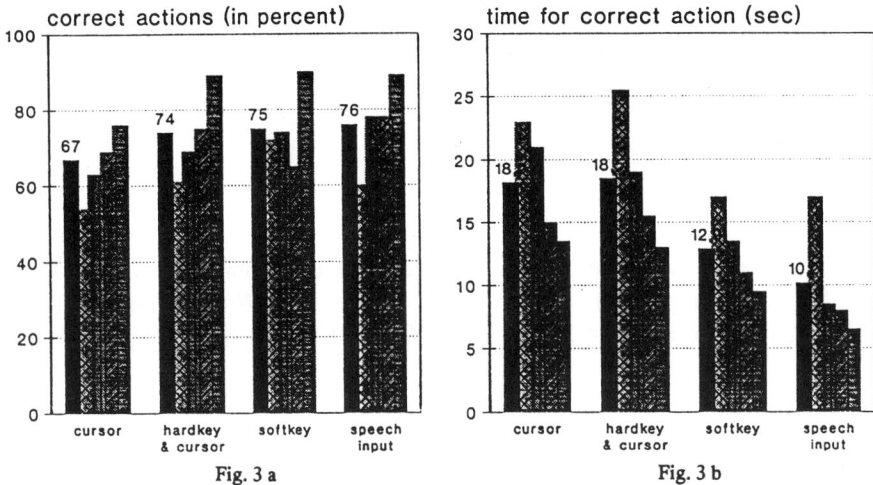

Fig. 3

a: Correct actions of the subjects (%)
b: Time for correct actions (in sec)

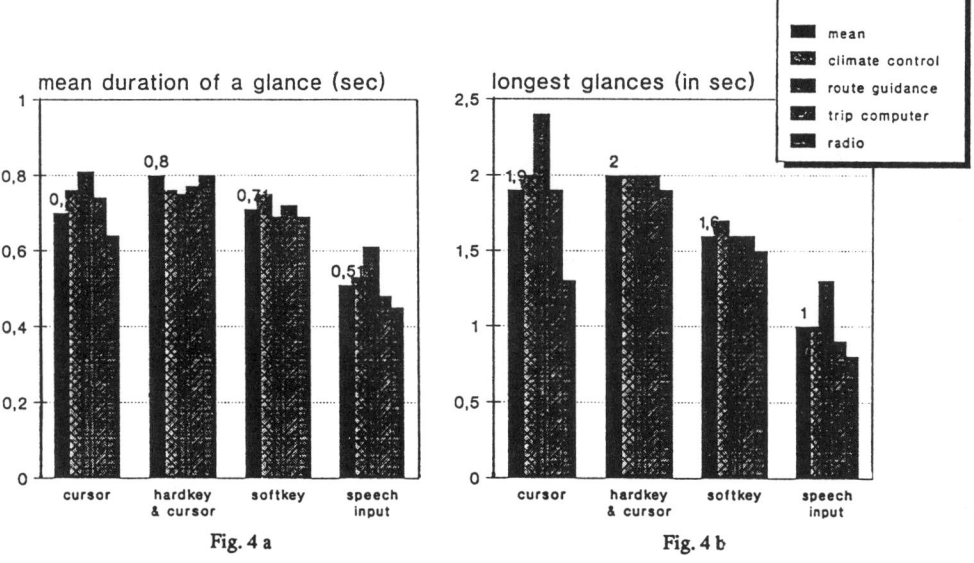

Fig. 4

a: Mean duration of a glance (in sec)
b: Longest glances (in sec)

speech input technology is not reliable and acceptable, softkey control should be applied. The use of a single analog control for many continuous functions proved to be very promising and provides a real potential for reducing controls. However, basic and time critical functions like indicator, horn etc. should not be changed in future cars.

6. REFERENCES

Faerber, B. & Faerber, B.A. (1988). Sicherheitsorientierte Bewertung von Anzeige- und Bedienelementen in Kraftfahrzeugen. FAT-Schriftenreihe Nr. 74. Frankfurt/M.

Faerber, B. (1990). More instruments, more safety? VDI-Berichte Nr. 819. Duesseldorf: VDI.

Michon, J.A. (1992). Generic Intelligent Driver Support. London: Taylor & Francis (in press).

Schmidtke, H. (1981). Lehrbuch der Ergonomie. Mⁿnchen: Hanser.

VISION IN VEHICLES – IV
A.G. Gale et al. (Editors)
© 1993 Elsevier Science Publishers B.V. All rights reserved.

WORKSHOP: ASSESSING THE VISUAL PARAMETERS OF SAFE MONITORING AND PROVIDING A FAIR INTERNATIONAL STANDARD FOR DRIVERS

P.A. Smith

Association of Optometrists, London, U.K.

Report

The outcome of Workshop sessions at previous Vision in Vehicle (VIV) conferences and subsequent progress towards the above objective, were provided by the author. The responses from UK Universities with an interest in vision and driving to a request for research proposals put by the VIV working group (which was set up at VIV2) were presented and a study by the UK Home Office into drivers' vision briefly mentioned before opening the workshop for discussion.

As at previous meetings the need for any proposals to be a compromise and not be punitive were expressed. While there was universal agreement amongst those present that visual acquisition of information was fundamental to the driving situation, it was reiterated that static clinical tests may not be the most suitable way of assessing likely "danger" on the road. On the one hand, there was the desire for a simple test but on the other hand, it was essential that any proposed 'standard' or method of assessment must be effective.

It was suggested that multiple testing and score weighting may provide a more reliable picture of the likely performance of a driver than a single test. A possible technique for presenting such data could be in the form of a star diagram with grading from the centre to the circumference of a circle and parameters as the radius. The need for suitable statistical design and analysis of any data taken was emphasized and the requirements to define the characteristics of a 'normal' driver before attempting to define a 'visually impaired' driver expressed.

After further general discussion, it was accepted that if any progress were to be made in this area data were needed. A pilot study, as has already been proposed in the past, should be undertaken before attempting to obtain support for a European study, but the eventual aim would be to gain support for such a European study.

It was also agreed that any individuals with access to clinical data on drivers, particularly when it related to drivers involved in accidents, should be encouraged to send the information to the office of the AOP in the UK where the information would be collated.

It was expected that data on accidents and driver visual function may be available for the next VIV conference in 1993 . These data would be collated from studies at present underway in the UK.

AUTHOR INDEX

SUBJECT INDEX